edited by KIM-CHONG CHONG &
YULI LIU

CONCEPTIONS OF VIRTUE
East and West

ASIAN AND COMPARATIVE PHILOSOPHY SERIES

Marshall Cavendish Academic

Published 2006 by Marshall Cavendish Academic
An imprint of Marshall Cavendish International (Singapore) Private Limited
A member of Times Publishing Limited

Times Centre, 1 New Industrial Road,
Singapore 536196
Tel: (65) 6213 9300
Fax: (65) 6285 4871
E-mail: mca@sg.marshallcavendish.com
Website: http://www.marshallcavendish.com/academic

ISBN-13: 978-981-210-303-1
ISBN-10: 981-210-303-1

A CIP catalogue record for this book is available from the National Library Board of Singapore.

Printed by Times Graphics Pte Ltd, Singapore
on non-acidic paper

London • New York • Beijing • Bangkok • Kuala Lumpur • Singapore

Marshall Cavendish Academic

ASIAN AND COMPARATIVE PHILOSOPHY SERIES

This series serves as a forum for the exposition and development of different philosophical perspectives on issues central to human life, much of which have received little detailed and systematic exploration from both Asian and comparative perspectives, still less from scholars well-versed in both Asian and Western traditions of philosophical inquiry. The series will be of interest not just to academics and students but also to general readers of philosophy.

Titles in the series

- The Unity of Rule and Virtue: A Critique of a Supposed Parallel between Confucian Ethics and Virtue Ethics
  by Liu Yuli
- Conceptions of Virtue: East and West
  edited by Kim-chong Chong and Yuli Liu
- Self and Others: Some Chinese and Comparative Perspectives
  edited by A. T. Nuyen

Contents

Introduction

KIM-CHONG CHONG

This collection of essays is based on the assumption that there is no sharp East-West divide when it comes to the understanding of central philosophical and ethical questions about the virtues. Thus, the essays are not grouped according to whether they describe conceptions of virtue from the East—represented here by the Chinese and Indian traditions—or from the West. Instead, they are grouped thematically: the relation between virtue and rightness; the unity of the virtues and the way in which certain fundamental virtues hold the virtuous life together; and how some cross-cultural perceptions of the nature of the virtues can be mistaken or need modification. Discussions of virtue and virtue ethics in recent Western philosophical literature have concentrated mainly on the nature of virtue ethics as an ethical theory vis-à-vis its rivals, Kantianism and consequentialism. While this too is discussed by some of the essays in this volume through a consideration of the link between virtue on the one hand, and rightness and goodness on the other, a further dimension is added through the integration of these Western concerns with the perspectives of Chinese and Indian traditions of thought. A particularly interesting feature that emerges in several of the essays dealing with these Eastern traditions is the belief in an integrated and unified life, through upholding what are regarded as fundamental virtues, for example, freedom from illusion, steadiness of mind, and purity (in different senses of the term). The essays are grouped into three parts. In what follows, I shall first describe in general terms the issues in each part before proceeding with a summary of each of the essays.

PART I
VIRTUE AND RIGHTNESS

What determines rightness, and in relation to particular situations, what is the right thing to do? These two questions are by no means the same. The first asks for theoretical understanding and/or guidance, while the second is more likely to be asked by someone who faces a decision, or even a dilemma. The interesting philosophical question here is what is the relation between the two? How does theory guide us, and in turn, what theoretical understanding can we gain from a reflection on our actions? These can lead to further questions, such as, who are the "we" and the "us" that are referred to in the above questions? In other words, can the nature of the group and/or the individual determine "rightness" and what it is right to do in a particular situation? Drawing from Eastern and Western philosophical traditions, and focusing on the virtues, the essays in this section directly and indirectly address the above questions. Together, they spell out the complexities and deny neat theoretical understandings.

In recent decades, virtue ethics has emerged as a rival to other forms of ethics such as Kantianism and consequentialism. Broadly speaking, virtue ethics focuses on the character and attitudes of individual moral agents, while Kantianism and consequentialism focus on universal decision-procedures governing right action. Given the increased concern with applied and professional ethics, however, virtue ethics would seem to be inadequate, since it apparently provides no specific conception of right action. In "Virtue Ethics, Role Ethics, and Right Action," Christine Swanton meets this challenge head-on, by describing how virtue ethics, as she conceives it, has the resources for helping to make specific role-based decisions. Accounts of virtue ethics usually focus on "prototype" virtues, that is, on vaguely general concepts such as "generosity" or "benevolence." Instead of such prototype virtues, Swanton provides an account of "role-differentiated" virtues. This enables her to argue for a target-centered account of rightness: "Rightness is not derivative from agency but from targets, but the targets are set by the aims of virtues." Hitting the target of a virtue means responding successfully to items in its field according to the aim or aims of the virtue. Virtues are constellations of various modes of moral response to items in their fields—modes such as respect, love, creativity, appreciation, promotion (of good). Each of these modes possesses different criteria of success and is itself complex. Thus, consequences are not the only morally relevant feature determining rightness or success. The targets of virtues are role sensitive, and the precise targeting of the virtues is what Swanton refers to as a process of "precisification." This target-centered virtue ethical account of rightness preserves the intuition that success in the external world is the hallmark of right acts as opposed to character or motives. Though expressing fine motives may be the target of some virtues whose aims are concerned solely with quality of inner states, most virtues have at least as a large part of their target some form of successful interaction with the external world.

Gregory Velazco y Trianosky's essay, "Where Do Virtues Get Their Goodness? The Case of Kindness," is a critique of "the pure ethics of duty"—the claim that virtues depend for their goodness entirely on their relations to right action. In other words, the moral goodness of kindness is claimed to be wholly derivative from the prior and independently conceived, rightness of action. But a phenomenological investigation of the concept of kindness reveals the following. Kindness is expressed through the act of letting someone know you care. It also figures centrally in the explanation of why someone might be disposed so to act. That is, an act of kindness is the sort of thing a kind person would do to express concern—to let the other know that he/she cares. Any description of kindness-expressing acts therefore requires reference to the trait of kindness itself. The rightness of an expression of kind concern can of course be described in terms of certain benefits, independently of the moral worth of the kindness. But another part of what makes such an expressive act right is simply that it is what it is, namely, an expression of positive concern or *noticing*. In the kind person, this forms the core of the disposition to promote another's well-being and has a special moral worth independently of the utility it confers. The posture of noticing is the foundation of any bond between persons that is built around mutual acknowledgment and concern, and in this regard, it is the central constitutive element in the human goods of friendship, community, and love.

In "Virtue and Rightness—A Comparative Account," Kim-chong Chong describes the decision of Dorothea in *Middlemarch*, to promise her husband Casaubon that she will complete his scholarly work after his death. This decision is consistent with one that can be derived from agent-neutral principles. However, her decision is a result of her care for and commitment to Casaubon, given the personal history of a trusting relationship. The (purportedly) agent-neutral principles constitute another perspective, and there are different motives and dispositions involved in the agent-neutral and in Dorothea's perspectives. There is a morally qualitative difference here, despite the fact that the decision in each case would be the same. We may gather from this example what virtue ethics is concerned to stress, namely, that "in some central areas of moral life, rightness cannot be understood independently of an individual perspective expressed in terms of certain virtuous motives and dispositions." Chong goes on to compare and to illustrate this in terms of the concept of *yi* in Chinese philosophy, with reference to Confucius and Mencius. This concept has been translated as "right" or "duty," and some accounts have implied that this constitutes an independent deontological standard by which the rightness of actions is judged. Chong argues that for both Confucius and Mencius, there is no such standard independent of the expression of various virtuous motives, attitudes and dispositions. Instead of a blueprint for action, *yi* constitutes what Antonio Cua has referred to as an "ideal theme," one that provides a conception of a quality and style of life which serves as an inspiration and a point of orientation for the virtuous person.

Amber Carpenter, "Questioning Kṛṣṇa's Kantianism," discusses an example from the *Bhagavadgītā* and disputes a deontological characterization of Kṛṣṇa, when he persuades Arjuna to enter into battle against his half-brothers and teachers. Examining the notion of *svadharma* (one's own duty, personal duty), Carpenter notes that there is a notion of duty here that is irreconcilable with Kantian duty. Notions of station, reputation and skill, family, and so on, ground the duty or duties binding upon Arjuna. The social order and place into which he was born, the endowments with which he came to it, and even his personal history, wrote a "law" just for him. It is in virtue of these that he has a destiny which is appropriate to him. However, the grounds which generate obligations, and determine virtues, should not be restricted to roles. Arjuna's *kṣatriya* persona is only one aspect of the situation determining that he has a duty to fight. Implicit in Kṛṣṇa's motivations for urging Arjuna to fight, and slightly more explicit in the reasons he gives Arjuna, is a recognition of the central role of integrity in ethical thinking. Without integrity as a fundamental virtue, any moral code, and any world based on such a code, will fall apart. It may even be more correct to regard integrity as a precondition of any virtue. Full integrity requires in this case a thorough-going commitment to the virtues and values of the heroic code of the warrior.

PART II
VIRTUE AND UNITY

Chong's reference to a quality and style of life for the virtuous person, and Carpenter's reference to integrity as a preconditional and fundamental virtue already hint at the idea that the virtuous life is, in some sense, a unified one. The essays in this section take this further, in mainly two ways. Firstly, through an investigation of the Aristotelian idea of the unity of the virtues, that the possession of any particular virtue means the possession of all the virtues; and secondly, through the idea that there is some fundamental virtue or virtues guiding the virtuous person. One question that the perceptive reader will ask is whether the two ideas are equivalent. The first idea gives one the sense of moral perfection, but this is not necessarily the case with the second idea of a fundamental virtue that helps to unify or structure one's life. The essays that deal with this second idea provide examples of character flaws; they describe the difficulties of living up to ideals of virtue, including the incongruence between having virtuous capacities and failing to act; they provide different lists of what is fundamental, and even where something is said to be fundamental, for example, "purity," there will be different characterizations of what this amounts to.

A. D. M Walker, "Conceptions of Virtue and the Unity of the Virtues," examines the idea that possessing any one virtue involves possessing all the virtues. This doctrine of the unity of the virtues is classically expressed in Aristotle's *Nicomachean Ethics*, and endorsed by some contemporary philosophers. The possession of a virtue is connected to right or appropriate action. But its exercise also involves acting in the right spirit, from the right motive and appropriate feelings and attitudes. Aristotle believes that an understanding and appreciation of what is valuable is impossible if we do not have the right desires and emotions and have not become habituated to acting in the right way. All these require practical wisdom. However, the doctrine of the unity of the virtues conceives of all the virtues similarly and takes practical wisdom to be involved in the same way in each of them. Walker argues that this is unacceptable because it assumes that there is really only one virtue—the names of the virtues being merely different ways of referring to this single virtue. It requires that the possessor of a virtue acts effectively and intelligently, i.e., successfully, within the sphere of operation of the virtues. But on this view, each of the virtues involves far more than we should be prepared to accept as a part of any virtue. Furthermore, there is the requirement that the actions of the fully virtuous person issue from, and be informed by, his own practical wisdom. If so, how far will such a person be willing to listen to, and accept, advice?

Manyul Im, "Wielding Virtue in the *Mengzi* (Mencius)" brings in another difficulty from the perspective of moral agency, and in the context of the classically revered Chinese philosopher, Mencius. If individuals are said to possess capacities for recognizing moral reasons, and if they are culpable for ignoring or not acting upon those reasons when available, then there is a difficulty for a normative moral view that assigns such culpability.

Either the agent is aware of such reasons or not. If aware, then it is unclear why she ignores those reasons. Until that is clear, the blameworthiness of the choice is indeterminate. On the other hand, if she is unaware of the reasons, she cannot be blamed for the choice in question. Choosing to be virtuous in an informed way requires the ability to recognize its goodness and to choose it because of that fact. But that kind of deliberative ability seems to exemplify the *prior* possession of virtue. Manyul Im raises this paradoxical difficulty through discussing the ideas of Mencius. For Mencius, there is a built-in scheme of moral categories through which humans experience the world. The sensibilities associated with natural human experience are necessary psychological tools for moral deliberation. There is also a form of "inner" control that the agent must exercise in order to *engage* those tools and hence complete the exercise of agency. Explicating this idea of inner control allows attributing to Mencius a moral psychology expressible through the metaphor of "wielding" virtue. The expression and exercise of moral capacities are dependent largely on the will exerted through the individual's choices. These include whether one's own moral capacities are to be effective or overridden. For Mencius, the goodness of human nature makes people *good* but their virtue lies in the effective wielding of their own goodness. Through inner determination, one may allow one's moral resources to operate or not. Mencius speaks, in this regard, of the "greater" and "lesser" parts of a person. But what would prompt a person to choose his greater part rather than the lesser? This would have to involve an evaluation of the heart-mind, wherein the moral resources are said to reside. It would not be possible for the person to see the value in following the heart-mind, unless the person was *already* following the heart-mind. And this brings in its train, the problems mentioned above, for Mencius.

The next three essays show how the unity of a virtuous life can be differently conceived: as the absence of illusion and the "steadiness of mind," as metaphysical detachment from a concerned self, and in terms of a conception of "purity." The description of this last conception though, is itself a recognition of the different ways in which "purity" can be conceived.

Jonardon Ganeri, "A Cloak of Clever Words: The Deconstruction of Deceit in the *Mahābhārata*," explores the virtues of trust and truthfulness, and the shame involved in their violation. The individual characters in the epic tale embody different attitudes toward deception. Ultimately, however, the epic battle between two families is about combating illusion in all its manifold forms. The most pernicious form of illusion is the concealment of the self from itself. The *Mahābhārata* is thus a sustained moral reflection on the value of truth and truthfulness. The steady mind is the one that will be objective and impartial, unbiased by its own needs. In this context, the practice of truth is strongly associated with the cultivation of a mind free from directive passions. In this regard, when might it be consistent with the practice of truth to conceal one's beliefs from others? When the disclosure would threaten the very stability of mind upon which the practice of truth rests. However, if this provides occasional justification for lies of concealment, it offers no justification for the manipulative lie. For, to deceive someone by manipulation is to distort one's relationship with the world, and that will always threaten to undermine the calmness and steadiness of mind upon which one's retention of the practice of truth depends.

A more austere, metaphysical form of unity is the theme of Bijoy Boruah's "Virtue-Metaphysics and Consciousness." He discusses the nature of the consciousness that characterizes and sustains the virtuous life of the person who attains the goal of *nirvāṇa* or *Mokṣa*. The classical Indian view of human enlightenment is predicated on the assumption of perpetual suffering, and the possibility of overcoming this through radical detachment. This involves a movement away from an encumbered consciousness marked by *Ahaṁkāra* or an immutable sense of I-ness. The ultimate goodness of a person in the classical Indian tradition is measured by the extent to which the substantive development of a life-history preserves the innocuousness of the structurally first-personal point of view. Once *Ahaṁkāra* shapes the first-personal orientation of consciousness, life is no longer valuationally innocent or innocuous. Borrowing from the work of Ramchandra Gandhi, Boruah focuses on a description of a metaphysical innocuous first-person point of view. Just as there is a non-predicative or attributeless way of regarding another, one can also adopt a non-predicative stance toward oneself in such a way that one's substantive ego-subjectivity would be dissolved. In words that are reminiscent of Wittgenstein, Boruah says, "My (pronominal) attitude towards you is an attitude towards a soul."

Although less metaphysically inclined, there is also a notion of unity involved in an aspect of Chinese Philosophy, as described by Shun Kwong-loi in his essay "'Purity' in Confucian Thought—Zhu Xi on *Xu*, *Jing* and *Wu*." According to Shun, "In the history of Chinese thought, a number of key terms are used to describe an ideal state of existence involving the absence of certain deviant elements that can adversely affect one's response to the world." Shun conveniently refers to this as a state of "purity" involving the heart/mind, and looks at a cluster of terms describing this: *xu* (vacuous, empty), *jing* (still, inactive), and *wu* (not have, nothing). At the same time, other terms describe the operation of things in the world (*ziran* or self-so, *li* or principle, pattern) and how the self should ideally relate or adapt to those things. In this regard, there is a conception of going astray, for instance, in the contrast between humans and *tian* (Heaven, Nature), and how one should respond towards *tian*. Shun focuses on how the cluster of terms surrounding purity and related concepts evolve and come together in the thought of the Song dynasty thinker Zhu Xi (1130-1200 C.E.). The phenomenon of purity can be differently construed, depending on how one conceives of a proper response to the natural order. Interestingly, for Zhu Xi, "purity" does not involve freedom from social engagement or the absence of human thoughts, desires or emotions as such, but the absence of those thoughts, desires or emotions that are *si*, understood as an unbalanced perspective due to certain self preoccupations or projections.

PART III
VIRTUE, SELF, AND GENDER

The third group of essays deals with (what are perceived to be) misrepresentations of the West from the East and vice versa. The first of the essays in this group questions what seems to be a prevalent idea that Confucian ethics is straightforwardly and paradigmatically a "virtue ethics." The second takes issue with the perception that the Chinese/Confucianist would stress social virtues while the Westerner would emphasize personal virtues. The third argues that there is a need to modify the popular conception that the Confucian view of the virtues is highly sexist and discriminatory against women, and that the virtuous role allowed to women in Confucianism is highly limited in this way.

Yuli Liu, "The Unity of Rule and Virtue in Confucianism," denies the general conception that Confucian ethics is a virtue ethics in a strict sense. Here, she is referring to the "reductionist view" of virtue ethics—that deontic concepts such as rightness and obligation are derived from aretaic concepts. The value of Confucian ethics to the development of contemporary ethics does not consist in its being a virtue ethics, but in its distinctive way of understanding morality. Confucian ethics is better conceived of as a unique kind of ethics, in which rule and virtue are united. To this end, she investigates the meaning of *dao* and *de* (in modern Chinese *daode* is the equivalent of "morality"). The *dao* is a universal Way originating from Heaven and Earth, the source of the meaning and value of human life. It is an objective existence independent of the contingent particulars which it informs. In this respect it is similar to Kant's moral law. *De* is the inherent power or tendency of a given thing and in particular its natural effect on other people and things. A person who has found the *dao* in himself is a person of *de*. Thus, both are unified in the heart of a sage, and to follow the *dao* is to do what one desires and what is virtuously required. The heart/mind has the capacity to understand the *dao*. In this regard, humans have the capacity to obtain a harmonious oneness with Heaven. This is *daode*, the metaphysical basis of the unity of virtue and rule in Confucian ethics. For the Confucians, there is no way of obtaining understanding of *dao* through conceptual reasoning, but through a course of the cultivation of *de* in daily life. In her denial of Confucian ethics as a virtue ethics, Liu's essay disagrees with Chong's. At the same time, it should be noted that the aim of attaining a unity with Heaven once again brings out what seems to be a pervasive theme in the Eastern virtue tradition, as described above.

In "The Self and Its Virtues: Is there a Chinese-Western Contrast?" A. T. Nuyen perceptively notes the link between conceptions of the self and of the virtues: how an agent deliberates and acts depends on the agent's psychological dispositions, personal understanding of preferences and priorities, relationships with others and the environment, etc. In short, how the virtues are conceived and acted upon depend on the agent's psychological and epistemic make-up, or what we generally call the "self." Thus, the conception of the self can be said to determine or form the basis for the conception of the virtues, and differences about the latter can be attributed to differences about the former. Nuyen's aim in this essay is to question a certain popular contrast between Chinese and Western conceptions of the virtue. This contrast is based upon another contrast regarding conceptions of the self: the Chinese (or at least the Confucians) take the self to be embedded in the society, or network of social relationships; the Westerner takes the self to be an independent being, standing over and against the society. Nuyen argues that this is mistaken, not so much because of what it says about Confucianism (although here too there could the danger of misrepresentation), but largely because it misconstrues the position of the West. More specifically, this view mistakenly treats one particular strand in Western thinking to be the position of the West.

Sor-hoon Tan, "Women's Virtues and the *Analects*," questions the popular conception that women are inferior creatures in Confucianism. Tan shows that the Chinese tradition has not been monolithically sexist. Some Song and Ming dynasty Confucians were among advocates of sexist womanly virtues (especially chastity), but this was a late development. Early Confucian texts such as the *Analects* hold no theory of gendered virtue. Tan considers the notorious passage: "In one's household, it is the women and the small men that are difficult to deal with ..." After considering various interpretations, Tan concludes that women were "difficult to deal with" because of lack of opportunities for personal cultivation, and if they were difficult to educate, it was because of their position in the social hierarchy. The Confucian ideas of the rectification of names, of standing in a proper relation to one's role, the willingness for ethical change, etc., do not inherently exclude women from the Confucian virtues. The restructuring of gender relations is a fundamental characteristic of modernity, and nothing excludes women from a Confucian meritocracy. If positions are not assigned by birth but gained through qualifications, especially virtues, then women are as entitled to any position as men. This does not mean taking wholesale a virtue ethics that has been articulated in an almost exclusively male context. Our understanding of Confucian virtues must change as we acknowledge and explore women's practices that embody them.

PART I

Virtue and Rightness

CHAPTER 1

Virtue Ethics, Role Ethics, and Right Action

CHRISTINE SWANTON

I. RIGHTNESS: VIRTUE-CENTERED, BUT NOT AGENT-CENTERED

It is by now a well-known criticism of virtue ethics that it is inadequate in the field of applied and professional ethics. The criticism may be directed at inadequacies in a virtue ethical conception of right action, or at epistemological concerns. This paper addresses the former target. A stumbling block to meeting the criticism is the lack of attention by virtue ethicists (and indeed normative ethical theorists in particular) to the field of role ethics. First, virtue ethics needs to supply a conception of right action that is suited to role ethics. I offer an account in section (I) which, though virtue-centered, is not agent-centered. In particular, it does not rely on features of motivation and character which are thought not to be central to acting rightly in a role. Second, the account is applied to role ethics via an account of role-differentiated virtue (section (II)). Such virtues are distinguished from prototype virtues, which, when viewed on their own, may provide ammunition for the objection that virtue ethics is inapplicable. For prototype virtues, qua prototype virtues, are (and are meant to be) vague. However the problem dissipates when an adequate account of role-differentiated virtues is given.

We turn now to the presentation of a conception of right action that is virtue-centered without being agent-centered.

It is defining of a virtue ethical conception of rightness that it be virtue-centered as opposed to, for example, consequence-centered or derived from duties not themselves based on virtues. It is quite standardly thought that virtue ethical conceptions of rightness are thereby also agent-centered. For example Julia Annas claims that rightness must either be derivative from virtuous agency or be independent of it, in which case the account could not be virtue ethical (1993). However I will show in my target-centered account that this presents a false dichotomy. Rightness is not derivative from agency but from targets, but the targets are set by the aims of virtues. That is, I shall deny that a virtue ethical conception of rightness need make essential reference to personal qualities of the agent—in particular, her motives, or character. It will be my contention then, that a virtue-centered conception of rightness need not be agent-centered, and that, indeed, virtue ethical agent-centered conceptions are flawed. I shall offer instead a non agent-centered conception which is better suited to the demands of applied and professional ethics.

The claim that virtue ethics itself is agent-centered is correct. It is a claim that ethics, at its heart, concerns the character of the individual agent, for no society can function well by a system of rules with sanctions and incentives alone. People of bad character will find ways to subvert those rules, interpret them badly, misapply them, or formulate them badly. Furthermore, good character is not just a matter of a tendency to perform right actions: good character consists in an integrated disposition of goodness in reasoning, motives, discernment, emotions, feelings. It is part of good character that an agent of good character acts from a state of virtue, but this is neither necessary nor sufficient for right action. Virtuous agents tend to perform right actions since they are both wise and well-motivated, but wise, well-motivated action does not on my view entail right action.

As Hursthouse points out (1999), "right" is an honorific term. It is important to note however that a term may be an honorific, but in a limited respect. On my view, the respect in which "right" is an honorific is that it signals correctness. A strong intuition, most notably embraced by consequentialists, is that rightness (as opposed to goodness) is conceptually tied to correctness rather than, for example, reasonableness, or moral worth. Rightness is to correctness (as opposed to excellence of character or motivation) as truth is to correctness (as opposed to justified belief based on good reasons).

It should be noted here that there are a number of ways in which an action might be correct: admirable or splendid but not required; admirable or splendid but required (though an agent need not be blameworthy for failure to perform the required action, on account of such factors as inexperience, immaturity, or extreme demandingness). Actions may also be required but not admirable or splendid, and they may be permitted but not required. (The range of permitted but not required actions may range from the highly desirable to the trivial).

A connection between rightness and correctness is particularly important in role ethics. It is often claimed that virtue ethics, with its emphasis on the individual qualities of the agent, is poorly placed to offer guidance in this area. Role ethics is concerned with success in meeting the point and function of the role, and this involves success in, e.g., following proper procedures, success in improving the bottom line or meeting the budget, helping students learn. Quality of motivation, or even of character, is neither necessary nor sufficient for correctly discharging the functions required by role duties. It is not necessary, because we are more concerned that a doctor, for example, gets his or her diagnosis right during a consultation, than in the quality of her character; we are interested in getting the correct advice rather than well-meaning advice when seeking legal opinion. It is not sufficient, because fine motives and fine character are no guarantee of accuracy of advice, or treatment, or diagnosis.

If thoroughly agent-centered accounts of rightness such as "A right action is an action that expresses virtuous character," or "A right action is an action that expresses virtuous or admirable motivation (or at least does not express deplorable or vicious motivation)" (Slote, 2001) are rejected, we may be inclined to adopt an agent-centered account in the following, weaker, sense. Though it is not a necessary condition of an action being right that it expresses a virtuous or admirable state of the agent performing the action, it is a necessary condition of an action being right that it would be performed or chosen by an agent having a certain quality. Such conceptions of rightness I have elsewhere called "qualified agent" accounts (2003). Perhaps the best known of such accounts is that of Rosalind Hursthouse:

> An action is right iff it is what a virtuous agent would characteristically do in the circumstances.
> A virtuous agent is one who has, and exercises, certain character traits, namely the virtues.[1]

Could not such an account satisfy our demand that a right action be a *correct* action? Is it not the case that it is a virtuous agent's determination of the rightness of an action that *constitutes* its rightness? This is not merely an epistemological claim: it is not merely being said here that a virtuous agent is in the best position to know what is right. Rather, on a qualified agent account, her choices (providing she is acting in character) are criterially determinative of rightness.

The qualified agent account assumes that there is no way in principle of understanding rightness or success except via the perceptions or determinations of a virtuous agent. However, in role ethics, this seems implausible. Even the best and wisest doctor can get things wrong, as determined by, for example, facts about the patient, facts which are or can be transparent to the virtuous and non-virtuous alike, or transparent to neither.

A subscriber to the qualified agent account, if an Aristotelian, may make the following reply. It could be claimed that excellence of character entails possession of *wisdom*, and that the rule and the measure of the right is the judgement of the virtuous and thereby the wise person. Hence, it could be argued, the judgement of the virtuous is guaranteed correct. However, not even the most virtuous agent can transcend the limitations of human cognition: the facts of selective perception emphasized by such thinkers on human cognition as Andy Clark (1997), distributed cognition, limited species knowledge, limited expertise, (necessarily) narrow perspectives.

The fact that rightness as correctness may transcend the cognitive powers of even a virtuous agent can be accommodated by a virtue ethical account of rightness which I have called a target-centered account. The account may be schematically described as follows.

(1) An action is virtuous in respect V (e.g., just, generous) if and only if it hits the target of (realizes or attains the end of) virtue V (e.g., justice, generosity).
(2) An action is right if and only if it is overall virtuous.[2]

Two notions need to be explained—the idea of the target of a virtue and that of overall virtuousness.

To hit the target of a virtue is to respond successfully to items in its field according to the aim or aims of the virtue. The field of a virtue is the domain of its concern: the field of friendship, for example, is friends or potential friends, the field of environmental concern is the natural world, the field of charity or benevolence is strangers, people in general, or sentient beings. Different virtues have different aims in relation to their fields. Substantive accounts of these aims may be complex, and indeed controversial. For example, one may argue that the aim of friendship is to express affection, share intimacies, promote the good of friends, spend time with friends, including quality time. Accounts may differ about the contextual salience, importance, or necessity of these aims in the virtue.

The targets of virtues are complex because their aims reflect the different modes of moral response appropriate to the virtue. As I have argued elsewhere (2003), virtues are constellations of various modes of moral response or acknowledgement to items in their fields—modes such as respect, love, creativity, appreciation, promotion (of good). Each of these modes possesses different criteria of success and is itself complex. Since hitting the target of a virtue is a form or forms of success in the modes of moral response or acknowledgement which comprise the virtue, the aims of virtues are complex though integrated. For example, the promotion of good which is an aim of benevolence must be integrated with respect and appreciation.

The target-centered account assumes that there is a non agent-centered way of understanding rightness that is nonetheless virtue-centered, because we can understand virtues as having targets or aims, the reaching or attaining of which may lie outside the existing competence of a virtuous agent. Or even if she is both competent, and acting in character, various circumstances, such as lack of time or standard human limitations, may cause her to make a mistake, where the notion of "mistake" is understood in terms of missing the target of relevant virtues.

It is a crucial aspect of the account that the target of many or most virtues involves some kind of success in the external world. Hence the target-centered conception satisfies the demands of a role ethics mentioned above, that such success is necessary for an action being right. If rightness as correctness can transcend the cognitive powers of even a virtuous agent, how can a virtue-centered account accommodate this fact? It is easy to see how it is accommodated by orthodox consequentialism. Where rightness is defined in terms of actual consequences (as opposed to say, expected or foreseeable consequences), even the most reasonable and knowledgeable human agents may perform wrong acts. Standard virtue ethics however is non-consequentialist. Even if the correct account of the aim or target of one virtue, benevolence, is that its aim is simply to promote good consequences, or enhance agents' good (an account which I think is simplistic) benevolence is but one virtue amongst many.

Since consequences are not the only morally relevant feature determining rightness, according to standard virtue ethics, standard virtue ethics is non-consequentialist.

However, if my account of the target of the virtues is not consequentialist, how can it be that at least a considerable part of success or correctness in action relates to success in the external world as opposed to excellence in inner states? Three important aspects of external success are not consequentialist. I will outline each in turn.

1. Love, including self love, and respect, are important modes of moral response which comprise the virtues. However such modes are not aggregative in their nature. Let us assume that one aspect of success in love, is success in promoting the welfare of relevant individuals in some respect which is contextually determined. Such is the target of role-differentiated virtues of benevolence whose nature arguably involves both relevant forms of love and respect. But the relevant individuals are those with whom the agent has a particularized bond, whether the bonds are, for example, parental, those of friendship, collegial, a nurse-patient relationship, or a therapist-patient relationship.
2. The distinguishing features of some modes of moral response demand success in the external realm. But the criterion of success in those modes is not promoting good consequences. Let me illustrate with respect and creativity. Respect is a mode of moral response which is not concerned with promoting good states of affairs but with treating people in accordance with their status. Hence demeanor cannot be invasive or otherwise inappropriate. Although virtuous creativity is aimed at producing things of value, success in creativity is measured by quality indicators as determined by the internal goals of the relevant activities. These may come apart from consequentialist criteria of success.
3. An important external criterion of success in meeting the targets of virtues has to do with the behavior or manner of the *agent*, as opposed to the effects on others. Behavior or manner may be flawed, even where motivation is impeccable. For example, caring as a virtue has as an important part of its target success in the manner of caring. A doctor may have excellent motivations but be socially inept in his "bedside manner." He may frown or look anxious, have an abrupt

> or excessively sugary manner, talk too much or too little. He may be insufficiently reassuring in dwelling on potential risks or possible (terrifying) diagnoses. Such failure may be a mark of motivational defect such as sadism, but it may also be a result of a culture where informed consent and giving information have assumed excessive salience by comparison with other desiderata.

How do we understand the idea of "overall virtuous"? First we need to understand that the targets of different virtues impose moral constraints on the performance of actions. Let me give an example. In role ethics, we may consider efficiency or effectiveness as a virtue whose target is the successful attainment of the goal or goals of the institution in which the role is embedded. For example, in business that goal is meeting the budget, and the pursuit of profits. Business people with the virtue of efficiency or effectiveness have as part of that virtue emotional and ratiocinative dispositions which constitute focus, tendencies not to procrastinate, resoluteness, decisiveness, organizational skills, courage, and a host of other traits well-suited to serving that goal. However, within a business, the general business goal is distributed according to specific roles within that institution. For example, line managers' goals include making staff happy so as to achieve budgetary targets within their unit. A C.E.O. has a more complex role. Efficiency in her role is more directed toward satisfying large clients, getting more business, dealing with the board, and looking for new opportunities. Adding to this complexity is the fact that attaining the target of efficiency is constrained by attaining the targets of other virtues, for example, benevolence (to the wider community), environmental soundness, honest dealings as understood in appropriate role contexts. As I argue elsewhere however,[3] these constraints must not be so severe as to lose sight of the fact that attaining the *distinctive* goals of (worthwhile) institutions is itself an ethical requirement—an ethical requirement of acting in a role.

The determination of what is *overall* virtuous, therefore, requires that we set the constraints proper to one virtue alongside those set by others in the concrete context of action. Call all these constraints the constraint structure. Determining what is overall virtuous is a process of integrating constraints by narrowing the constraint structure (Robinson 1993, Swanton 2003). What this involves is more fully explained in the next section.

I have claimed in this section that though "rightness" is an honorific term it connotes a limited aspect of excellence in action. One may say that from a virtue ethical perspective an action is excellent *tout court* if and only if it

(a) is right/correct, and
(b) expresses a state of virtue.

An action may be right, on this account, but fail in other ways: ways which warrant withholding the accolade "excellent." Actions may satisfy (a) without (b), and (b) without (a). Actions which fail to be excellent in the first way but are excellent in the second, are for example, right actions which are continent (self-controlled). Such actions may be done for the right reason and hit the target of a relevant virtue such as temperance, but fail to be excellent *tout court* because they fail to express the correct appetitive state and thereby fail to express (full) virtue. For example, someone may desist from having her fair share of chocolate éclairs for the right reason (she wishes to leave enough for her friends from a sense of fairness and out of friendship, (as opposed to wishing not to have her friends think ill of her)). But her action may be less than excellent because she has to fight temptations of greed. In certain circumstances we may also claim that an action is correct (hits the target of relevant virtues) even if done for a bad reason.

Actions which fail to be excellent in the second way but are excellent in the first are wrong actions, which, though wise, are performed from non-culpable ignorance, and may thereby fail to hit the targets of relevant virtues. For example, we may fail to call an action benevolent (or perhaps beneficent) and thereby right, if it misfires and causes harm (or sufficient harm), even though such unintended effects should not be deemed the fault of the agent.

II. THE TARGETS OF ROLE VIRTUES

How do we understand and determine the targets of the virtues in a role context? Recall that the targets of virtues can be understood as imposing moral constraints on the performance of actions, and that determining what is overall virtuous requires that these constraints be integrated. The process of integration is a process of narrowing the constraint structure so that we can understand in the concrete context of action, the targets of relevant virtues. For the purposes of this paper, the context involves the occupation of roles. So for the purposes of this paper the targets of virtues are understood as role sensitive.

Let us now explain the process of integrating constraints by narrowing the constraint structure so that we can understand the idea of role sensitive targets of virtues. The first step in this understanding is to distinguish what I have elsewhere called prototype virtues[4] from role-differentiated virtues. A prototype virtue is a virtue specified at a high level of generality and abstraction, so that the targets of such virtues are themselves vague and underspecified. Until such a virtue is contoured by contextual features, including role features and relevant cultural features, we cannot form an accurate conception of the target of a virtue as applied to a role.

The precisification of the target of a prototype virtue as applied to a role is achieved by narrowing the constraint structure. This process allows one to understand the target of a virtue by moving from the abstract to the concrete by progressively specifying and respecifying constraints as we move from the relatively abstract specification of the requirements of prototype virtues to the concrete particularities of the case. These constraints may be completely transformed as further contextualisation takes place. For example, the prototype virtue generosity is specified in an abstract way: the requirement to be helpful to others, to promote others' good, and to have emotional dispositions relevant to this end. However generosity as a business person does not require that one help one's competitors or promote their good. For that would be to misunderstand the nature of business in a capitalist society as competitive, and as concerned with one's own bottom line. This does not entail that there is no place for generosity as a business person. Rather, the constraints that the virtue imposes must be contextualized in the light of the business purpose. Again, the prototype virtue friendship suggests a number of constraints on action: sharing intimacies, sharing interest and time together, expressing mutual affection. However, as has been argued, these features are not components of friendship as a role virtue qua university teacher or lawyer. This indeed, has led to difficulties in applying and extending prototype virtues such as friendship to roles (Fried 1976).

The first step in the narrowing of the constraint structure, therefore, is to recognize that a prototype virtue such as generosity, is constrained in a role context by role requirements. These are determined by understanding the point or function of the institution in which the role is embedded, and the point or function of that role within the institution. Once the prototype virtue is role-differentiated to become a role virtue, further contextual features need to be evaluated in the constraint structure. These features, such as lack of time and the particularities of orders from superiors also provide constraints which need to be integrated, so that the target of the role virtue, in a context, can be determined.

Consider the following example, which illustrates the process of integrating constraints in a role context. The example illustrates the process of progressive modification of constraints so that we descend from relatively abstract formulations to the concrete particularities of the case.

The constraint which presents the most concern in business ethics can be broadly described as social responsibility. To understand the constraints imposed by this virtue (or constellation of virtues) we need to understand the point of the constraints of social responsibility in the business context. This requires an understanding of social responsibility not as a prototype virtue, concerned with the amelioration of the human condition generally, but of how it is shaped or contoured by the business purpose. This understanding drives the first phase of the process of narrowing the constraint structure. Sensitivity to the business purpose, then, is the first step in the process of modifying constraints in this context. The constraints of social responsibility as applied to business become the constraints of social responsibility sensitive to the business purpose. Of course, this first step in the process of modifying constraints is itself subject to constraints, which further drive the re-specification of the constraint structure.

Consider a C.E.O who is responsible to a boss in another country who argues that a certain charitable expenditure is not in line with the desires of the overall Head of the international organization to whom he himself is responsible, and who takes himself to reflect the desires of shareholders. The charitable expenditure favored by the C.E.O. is vetoed. Such a constraint may reflect a strict Friedmanesque interpretation of the business purpose but notice that this interpretation is not assumed to be correct. Rather the constraint derives from the C.E.O.'s lack of autonomy, a lack which may be alterable in the future, and may not apply to other contexts.

Other important constraints on social responsibility sensitized to business purpose concern local expertise, modes and spheres of operations, and synergies. As a result, it is not part of the target of virtues of social responsibility as applied to role-occupiers within business that they aim to ameliorate social conditions that are outside their field of competence, or in many standard situations, outside their field of operations.

Exemplifying the above points, let us give an illustration of social responsibility functioning as a constraint in a business context. First it should be noted that "social responsibility" is a catch-all phrase for a large range of virtues, including environmental friendliness, compassion, justice, generosity. In our example, we focus on social responsibility as generosity, manifested in a charitable donation.

Constraint

Display social responsibility as generosity.

Modified Constraint

Offer charitable donation or sponsorship sensitized to business purpose.

Constraints

Views of overseas bosses limiting C.E.O's autonomy. C.E.O's limited time, energy, for persuasive dialogue with bosses.

Modified Constraint

Charity sensitized to business purpose as interpreted by boss(es), such that certain options are ruled out.

Constraints

Need for synergy so that business purpose is enhanced. Need for profile so that business purpose is enhanced.

Modified Constraints

Charity connected to high-profile television events such as (in New Zealand) the prevention of youth suicide (very high in New Zealand), or alternatively sports sponsorship such as the America's Cup Defence.

Constraint

Budgetary Provision formulated by C.E.O., ratified by overseas bosses.

Action

Donation of X dollars to the prevention of youth suicide, where donation is advertised on television, in the context of the "Yellow Ribbon" charity program on television.

Notice that in the progressive specification and re-specification of the constraint structure, the space of possible solutions is progressively narrowed by descent from relatively abstract formulation of constraints to their embeddedness in a concrete context. Notice too the contextual variability of constraints. In the case outlined, limited time and energy for persuasive dialogue with bosses was considered an important constraint since the bosses' restrictions did not require unethical donations, and some room for maneuver remained. If bosses' instructions did require unethical donations, then a completely different constraint structure would have to be put in place.

III. DILEMMAS

The question arises: Does the process of integrating constraints (assuming it is done in an excellent way),[5] necessarily terminate in a single best action that is overall virtuous? The question divides into two. First, does such a process of integration necessarily terminate in a single best action? My answer is: not necessarily. The process of narrowing the constraint structure may yield a number of actions, none of which more closely meets the targets of relevant virtues than another. A number of best actions may exist. Even if there is a best action, it is not necessarily the case that alternatives are able to be defeated by reasons accessible to a virtuous agent. The best action is however the right one assuming it is overall virtuous (see below), though an agent is not necessarily to be blamed for failure to perform it.

The second question is: if there is a best action, is it necessarily the case that it is right? Could it be best, without being overall virtuous? For an action to be overall virtuous one might think, it should hit the target of at least one virtue in the relevant context to which it applies. But might there be moral dilemmas in which there is no such action? It may be possible that one of two terrible alternatives is the least bad, and thereby best, but that surely is not sufficient to call it overall virtuous.

Consider, for example, *Sophie's Choice* in which Sophie has a coerced choice offered by a Nazi guard to save one of her two children from the gas chamber (Styron 1979). We may focus on the role virtue of maternal virtue, and find it hard to describe an act open to her which is overall virtuous. Well, we might reply, she could avoid clear maternal vice: she will not say "I don't care which one goes to the gas chamber," she will react with extreme anguish, she will find it virtually impossible to choose. But would we be prepared to say that she hits the target of maternal virtue if she intentionally chooses, though coerced, one of her children to be sent to death? We have two options. We could say that it is impossible for Sophie to hit the target of maternal virtue, or, alternatively, that in the circumstances she does hit the target by avoiding the kind of non-virtuous behavior mentioned above. If the second option is taken, we could say, unproblematically on my view, that Sophie's action was right (permitted) because correct, even though terrible.

The first option presents more of a problem for my view. For it looks as if, were that option to be taken, whatever Sophie does is wrong. Yet given the connection between rightness and correctness on my view, I would be forced into the uncomfortable position of claiming that an action could both be wrong (because missing the targets of relevant virtues in the relevant context) and yet correct. It is correct because it is the best, or one of the best actions she could have performed in the circumstances.

However, am I forced into this position on the assumption that Sophie cannot hit the target of maternal virtue? The answer is "No." There are other virtues in play, such as courage. On my account, an action is right if and only if it is overall virtuous, and if it is impossible for Sophie to hit the target of maternal virtue, she can still hit the target of courage, or strength, or calmness (assuming that some sort of calmness is a virtue that should be in play here).

Though resolutions of even tragic dilemmas can be right because overall virtuous, they cannot be excellent. Constraints have been integrated to produce an action that is overall virtuous in the circumstances, but an excellent act is beyond the realm of possibility for an agent afflicted with such moral ill luck.

The virtue ethical account of rightness which I have called target-centered preserves the intuition that success in the external world is the hallmark of right acts as opposed to fine character or motives. Though expressing fine motives may be the target of some virtues whose aims are concerned solely with quality of inner states, most virtues have at least as a large part of their target some form of successful interaction with the external world. Furthermore, though qualified agent accounts of rightness get closer to preserving this intuition, virtuous agents, even acting in character, have inherent limitations which might cause them to miss the targets of virtues. Functioning rightly in a role certainly demands successful interaction with the external world. A target-centered view of rightness within virtue ethics overcomes the objection to virtue ethics that it is too agent-centered to be of much use in professional and applied ethics.

NOTES

1 *On Virtue Ethics* (Oxford: Oxford University Press, 1999), pp. 28–9.

2 See further Christine Swanton, *Virtue Ethics: A Pluralistic View* (Oxford: Oxford University Press, 2003), Chapter 11.

3 In "Virtue Ethics, Role Ethics and Business Ethics" in R. Walker and P. J. Ivanhoe, eds., *Working Virtue: Virtue Ethics and Contemporary Moral Problems*, Oxford: Oxford University Press, forthcoming.

4 For further elaboration of the idea of a prototype virtue see Christine Swanton, "Virtue Ethics, Role Ethics and Business Ethics" in R. Walker and P. J. Ivanhoe, eds., *Working Virtue*.

5 The process of integrating constraints is done in an excellent way if and only if it expresses what I have called virtues of practice (such as the dialogic virtues). Discussing the nature of the process and these virtues is beyond the scope of this paper which is concerned only with rightness. Suffice to say here that, exercising virtues of practice need not terminate in a right act, though acts expressing virtues of practice will be reasonable. Furthermore, right acts may be performed without these virtues being expressed. See further *Virtue Ethics*, Chapter 12.

CHAPTER 2

Where Do Virtues Get Their Goodness? The Case of Kindness[1]

GREGORY VELAZCO y TRIANOSKY

Where do virtues get their goodness? The question of what makes right acts right has been a familiar one at least since W. D. Ross first put it this way in 1930. Ross' question has been at the center of the great twentieth-century disputes between utilitarianism and deontology; and almost every possible normative-ethical theory of the right has been canvassed. Yet contemporary discussion of the analogous question about virtue has been sporadic, and few normative-ethical theories of virtue have been reviewed and evaluated systematically.[2]

In this paper I will take the first steps in such an investigation by considering what common-sense morality has to say about one extreme, largely hypothetical theory, the pure ethics of duty.[3] According to this theory, virtues depend for their goodness entirely on their relations to right action. I will argue that, as an account of our common-sense moral experience, at least, the pure ethics of duty fails because it is profoundly at odds with our everyday experience of the virtue of kindness.

I begin our investigation with a consideration of common-sense morality for two reasons. The first is its ubiquity. No matter what our theoretical predilections may be, our everyday lives are almost unavoidably entangled with the practices, expectations, judgments, and explanations that constitute common-sense morality. I suspect that even many of us whose philosophical views are at odds with some of the norms of common sense may find ourselves, like Hume, largely returning to them in practice, when we quit our studies and are drawn back into the rush of unreflective quotidian life. To try to understand the logic and the norms of common-sense morality, therefore, is to try to understand much of what in fact structures our actions, our sensibilities, and our understandings of ourselves and others. It is of course true that there are significant variations among common-sense moralities, and that sometimes these have a direct bearing on the sort of investigation I propose to undertake. In the case of supererogation, for example, not only intuitions but the very logical structure of moral judgments may vary significantly between those raised in the Catholic tradition and those raised in anti-supererogationist Protestant traditions.[4] It is equally and notoriously true that common-sense moralities can be narrow, blind, or flat-out mistaken. In the current case, however, I hope that the precepts and ideas of common-sense morality that anchor the discussion will be platitudes—if not always "easy and obvious" ones—uncontroversial and central to our understanding of altruism, personal relationships, and the relation between what we are and what we do. My project is only to draw out their implications in order to reveal the presuppositions, the logical structure, and the values implicit in our everyday thinking about the virtues.[5]

Second, to suggest that an investigation of common-sense morality is an appropriate starting point in normative theorizing is certainly not to suggest that the work of normative ethics is done once this investigation is finished. Nonetheless, we are far more likely to develop a sophisticated and pluralistic understanding of some of the possibilities in normative ethics if we begin with the richness and subtlety of everyday moral experience than if we begin with the fairly simple, unsophisticated structures and distinctions of traditional moral theorizing. Given such a sophisticated understanding, in turn, we will have far more, and far more interesting, options to work with in the construction of our normative theories.[6]

It is useful to begin our consideration of the relation between common-sense morality and the question of where virtues get their goodness with the pure ethics of beauty because its failure is an instructive one. Indeed, the critique of this extreme view will allow us to define a distinct, autonomous field on which normative-ethical theorizing about the virtues may move forward with very little assistance at all from any pre-established theory of the right.

I.

To speak more precisely, the ethics of duty in its pure form makes two normative-ethical claims, one about virtue and one about the right.[7] First, it holds that the moral goodness or virtuousness of a trait must be *wholly derivative* from the antecedent rightness of actions to which that trait is suitably related. So for instance an ethics of duty theorist might claim that honesty is a virtue because and only because the honest person *aims at* telling the truth, and telling the truth is in point of fact the right sort of thing to do; or that courage is a virtue insofar and only insofar as it *increases the probability of* the agent's doing what is antecedently judged to be right; or that what makes the love of justice a virtue is that its *intentional object is* right and just conduct as such. In each of these claims, the "virtue-making" feature of the trait in question is said to be some suitable relation to what is antecedently right. As these examples should suggest, views about what is to count as a suitable relation to the right may vary depending on what version of the ethics of duty one endorses. But even if an ethics of duty theorist combines a variety of claims such as these, ultimately his or her theory still offers a monistic view about where virtues get their goodness.

The second claim a pure ethics of duty makes is that the rightness of at least some actions is wholly prior to any relations they may display to virtuous traits, and is thus entirely underivative from the virtuousness of any such trait.[8] In Bentham's act-utilitarian version of the ethics of duty, for example, it is ultimately the utility of their consequences for sentient creatures that grounds the rightness of actions. It is not, say, the moral worth of the standing motives expressed in one's utile behavior. Similarly, on the textbook ethics-of-duty interpretation of Kant, what makes a right act right is the fact that its maxim can be universalized without contradiction. It is not the virtuousness of any disposition of the agent who performs it.[9]

In short, the ethics of duty in its pure form offers both an answer to our question about virtue, and at least a partial answer to Ross' original question about the right as well. It holds that ultimately the only good-making feature of a trait is some suitable relation to right action; but it also holds that the rightness of at least some actions can be established in turn prior to any connections those actions may have to morally good traits.[10]

The pure ethics of duty so defined is an extreme view. It might even be a view that no one has ever held. Nonetheless, as I have suggested, an investigation of how it fails to account for our common-sense moral experience of the virtue of kindness reveals a great deal about where virtues get their goodness.

II.

Kindness exhibits a great number of distinct though overlapping relations to action. The best way to appreciate why the pure ethics of duty fails to explain where kindness gets its goodness will be to systematize our understanding of these relations, and of their various contributions to the moral worth of traits like kindness. Let us begin with a brief characterization of the phenomenology of kindness itself.

II.A. The Phenomenology of Kindness

Kindness is a form of benevolence. It is a personal form of benevolence, in contrast to impersonal forms like philanthropy or that love of mankind displayed by Bertrand Russell, of whom it was said, "he loved mankind, not men." At the core of the virtue of kindness is a standing concern for, or a disposition to act for the sake of, the well-being, not of some large and indeterminately-defined group, still less of mankind in general, but of particular persons.

Perhaps the best way to understand our common-sense notion of kindness is to consider a range of cases. In paradigm cases, kindness seems to involve a disposition to an immediate and personal response to a direct confrontation with the needs of particular individuals. So, for example, I "do someone a kindness," as we say, when I see that person drop an armload of packages while waiting in the post-office line, and I help to pick them up.

In this respect kindness differs from generosity. I can exhibit generosity in giving a great deal of money to feed the hungry when a special collection is taken up in church; but I show my kindness only—or at least paradigmatically—when I am face to face with the homeless person who is hungry and needs money to buy food. Kindness also differs from generosity in that it does not necessarily require that one give of oneself or one's resources to a significant degree. As the post office example should suggest, a kindness may sometimes be a small thing, requiring little expenditure of effort, time, or money—certainly too small an expenditure properly to be called "generous."[11]

Kindness is also different from some other personal forms of altruism in that it is a disposition to respond to needs that cannot, at least in the circumstances, easily be met by the recipient's own action. This is one way it differs from thoughtfulness, for example. If I happen to see that the latest issue of your favorite magazine is out and I buy it for you, I have not done you a kindness, unless I know, say, that you are confined to your sickbed and unable to get it for yourself. Otherwise I have acted thoughtfully rather than kindly. But even if I get the magazine for you when you are too ill to get it yourself, it seems a stretch to call my purchase an act of kindness, unless the periodical is not merely something you desire but something you actually need. (Suppose, for example, that you needed it for your work.) It would be a kindness to look in on you, perhaps, or to cook a meal for you; but to buy you a magazine or a small trinket is properly a type of gift-giving (as thoughtful acts often are), and the giving of gifts *as such* is not part of the core disposition to act characteristic of a kind person.[12] In contrast, when I help you pick up your packages in the post office, the situation is a little more urgent, and the fact that you need some help (assuming you are unable in the circumstances to gather all the packages up yourself with ease and efficiency) renders my assistance eligible as an act of kindness. If you could just as easily pick them all up yourself, and my assistance were therefore superfluous, then helping you would seem not to be kind but, thoughtful, helpful, or perhaps courteous.

Our notion of kindness appears to be influenced to some degree by the etymology of "kin" and cognate terms. The *Oxford English Dictionary* lends some support to the conjecture that "kindness" in its relevant adjectival form might originally have been a class-dependent term, and that acts of kindness were originally conceived as acts of largesse bestowed on social inferiors by their superiors. In any event, the more democratized conception of kindness with which we operate today is certainly not class-dependent in this way; but the contrast between kindness on the one hand and some other personal forms of benevolence like thoughtfulness still draws our attention to the inequality inherent in the moment of kind action: the recipient needs help, and they cannot easily and efficiently provide it for themselves. The donor is able to help, and can in many cases do so without great cost or effort.[13]

In paradigmatic instances kindness also differs from some other personal forms of altruism because it is a face-to-face virtue. Suppose for example that, upon my return from a happenstance visit as a tourist to a particularly poor village in El Salvador, I decide to contribute funds to that village's hometown association here in Los Angeles, so that monies can be sent back in order to improve the schools or help needy children in the village. My action may well be entirely altruistic, but it seems out of place to call it kind. I have responded at once remove from the situation, seeing it more abstractly as a problem of "helping the children," perhaps, rather than as the challenge of responding here and now to the suffering of the particular children I see before me during my visit. This does not make my action less noble, to be sure; but it does make it more impersonal, and so less properly a case of kindness than of generosity, or perhaps philanthropy.[14]

There are also cases that are more difficult to place with respect to the paradigm. For instance, in his youth the original St. Nicholas, Bishop of Myra in the fourth century C.E., stealthily left gold coins at the homes of the poor and needy. Should we call his acts kind? On the one hand, he was responding to the needs of particular people, as seen in his daily experiences of them. On the other hand, his response comes later, and more indirectly, than it would if he had simply given them money on the spot. Instead of being an immediate response to perceived need, his acts are mediated, perhaps by distrust of his immediate impulses, or perhaps by considerations about the risks of falling victim to the vice of pride in the face of public adulation, or the awkwardness of offering charity to those who are poor but independent, etc. It is not that he has "one thought too many," to use Bernard Williams' famous phrase. St. Nick's altruism is not in question, and *a fortiori* it is not impeached by the reflection that clearly precedes his actions. But our hesitation about calling his acts kind suggests that paradigmatically, kindness involves a disposition to a sort of spontaneous or unmediated response to the situation as it is experienced. On the other hand, St. Nicholas' actions are certainly much more like the paradigm cases of acts of kindness than those of the contributor to the Salvadoran village association. In general, perhaps we should say that, while strictly speaking there may not be a set of necessary and sufficient conditions for kindness, there are dispositions whose exercise is more or less like the paradigm instances of kindness in action. As one's benevolent acts become less and less like the paradigm, at some point we begin to see them as constituting the exercise of a different form of altruism. Precisely at what point we begin to replace attributions of kindness with the use of some other honorific probably depends on the context of judgment, and particularly on which aspects of action or character we wish to emphasize.[15]

Similarly, we may sometimes call an action "compassionate" rather than kind, if we wish to draw attention to the fact that the agent's behavior was informed by an emotional response to suffering that involves seeing the other as a person in need, rather than merely as a potential danger or an inconvenient intrusion into one's quotidian projects.[16] Thus, e.g., the King James Bible says of the Good Samaritan, "... but a certain Samaritan, as he journeyed, came where [the victim of robbers] was [lying by the side of the road]: and when he saw him, he had compassion on him, and went to him, and bound up his wounds" (KJV Luke 10: 33–34).[17] Or we may call an action "helpful" rather than kind if, as in the post office example, the assistance rendered is comparatively minor, and we wish to emphasize that the action exhibited the agent's understanding of the other's distress, perhaps in a situation where other bystanders did not see it, or saw it but were not sufficiently moved to help.[18]

We may conclude this brief account of the phenomenology of kindness by noting that to say kindness is a virtue does not imply that it is always appropriate or right to be kind. There are times when respect takes precedence over kindness, as for example when we allow someone to struggle with the limitations imposed by a disability, knowing how important it is sometimes that people accomplish things for themselves rather than through the assistance of others. Nor is it to say that all forms of concern for the well-being of particular people are virtuous.[19] One may be "too kind," for instance, when one's concern for others causes one to overlook the importance of autonomous choice, or when one's concern for others is intrusive or misplaced. Nor, finally, is it to deny that there are various simulacra of kindness that, so far from being virtuous, are in fact vices. As my conjectural etymology might suggest, one may present the outward face of kindness, and yet seek only to control or subjugate those less-powerful individuals who are the objects of one's concern. Or, one may speak politely, uttering expressions of concern, and yet feel nothing when one turns away from the person in need. In short, to say that kindness is a virtue is neither to exalt it above all other virtues, nor to license all its consequences, nor to praise its imitators.[20]

II.B. Relations Between Kindness and Descriptively-Independent Action

Let us turn now to a more systematic characterization of the relation of kindness to action. As I suggested above, kindness is like many skills and habits in that it is essentially a "potentiality" whose "actuality" is some form of action. More specifically, as I have indicated, it is a trait that involves a core disposition to *act for the sake of a certain end*, namely, the well-being of particular people.[21] It follows that any adequate characterization of that trait must include the description of a certain single, more or less determinate act-type, namely, that which the agent *qua* kind intends to perform: *promoting the well-being of particular people*. This is the activity in which the end of kindness is actualized, or, one might say, in which one's kindness is brought to fruition.[22]

This is not to say that kindness is constituted by nothing more than this core disposition. Like many character traits, virtuous or otherwise, kindness typically presents itself as a constellation of dispositions. Some of these are actional, or dispositions to choose, like the core disposition I have described. Others are not. For example, kind people typically display certain affective dispositions, like the tendency to feel distress and concern at the suffering of others. They also are typically inclined to make and express certain evaluations, like admiration and approval for others who share their core commitment to human well-being. Kind people also characteristically display certain sensibilities, or tendencies to be more aware than many of what others need, and how their needs might be met in the circumstances. Finally, I will argue below in section III.B that, paradigmatically, the kind person will have a certain attitude or posture of concern toward people in need that sustains and informs all the other kindness-constituting dispositions that he possesses.[23]

As I suggested above in section II.A, it is probably unhelpful to try to define a particular arrangement of dispositions whose possession is necessary and sufficient for kindness. If we think instead in terms of paradigms and distance from the paradigms, then we can think of all of the characteristic dispositions I have enumerated, and perhaps others as well, as being at work in the paradigm cases. And, in the absence of a sufficiently large number of these dispositions—or perhaps in the absence of one or two that have key locations in the constellation, so to speak—the trait loses enough of its characteristic shape so that little is gained by insisting that what remains should still count as kindness.

Acting for the sake of the well-being of particular people entails taking oneself to be promoting their well-being. Thus the relation we have been discussing between this type of action and the trait kindness is an *intentional* one. That is to say, it is a relation between a certain trait and what one takes oneself to be doing. For this reason, "promoting the well-being of particular people" is not necessarily an accurate description of what a kind person actually succeeds in doing. The kind person may take herself to be helping you, and yet succeed only in causing you further discomfort or pain.[24] But it is not the kindness of a well-intentioned bumbler like Peter Sellers' Inspector Clouseau that is impugned by his honest mistakes. It is his judgment, his skills, or perhaps his luck.[25]

On the other hand, it is a truism that a kind person usually does in fact do a great deal of good for others. Our world is such that, over a range of familiar circumstances, at least, kindness typically operates to produce pretty much the sorts of results that the kind person intends. Thus we may say that kindness also stands in a fairly regular and general *causal* relation to action: it tends to produce actions that do in fact promote the well-being of particular individuals.

Kindness therefore stands in a sort of double relation to the same act-type, "promoting the well-being of particular people." It not only takes that type as its intentional object, but also tends to cause actions of that same type. Even though the act-type is the same, however, the two relations are distinct. It is part of the intentional structure of kindness that it involves aiming to promote the well-being of particular individuals. In contrast, the relation between kindness and what the agent in fact tends to do is a relation in which kindness stands in virtue of its causal powers, and not (or not as a matter of logic) in virtue of its intentional structure. This distinction remains even if one holds that kindness would not be the trait it is, unless it did in fact tend to produce actions that promote well-being. For even on this supposition, while it will be true that, necessarily, each exercise of the trait must involve aiming to promote well-being, it will still be false that, necessarily, each exercise of the trait must cause one to do what will in actual fact promote well-being.[26]

Though these two relations between kindness and action are distinct, the one intentional, the other causal, they have one very important feature in common. In each case the related act-type can be described *independently of any essential reference to the trait itself.*[27]

There is a vast and heterogeneous class of relations between trait and action that share this important feature, and kindness itself stands in a number of other relations to various independently-describable act-types. Some of these relations are causal and some are intentional; some contribute to the moral worth of kindness and some do not. To take one such relation, kindness can operate to *strengthen* various capacities and dispositions to act that are distinct from kindness itself. Thus it is a familiar fact that kind people are often more understanding, if not easier to take advantage of, than those who are not particularly kind. They are usually more tolerant of the foibles of others, willing to credit their excuses or discount their shortcomings. Similarly, kind people are typically more generous than others. Though I have argued in section II.A above that the two traits are distinct, it should come as no surprise that kind people are often more willing to give time or money to those who ask it of them, whether the recipient is especially needy or not. Again, kind people are usually more considerate, or careful not to hurt the feelings of others, than people who are not kind. Or, because they are committed to helping others, they may be able to respond more patiently to the frustrations and difficulties of trying to help those who may at first resist help even when it is badly needed. In each of these examples kindness stands in a sort of "strengthening-relation," as it were, to the disposition to perform some behavior describable independently of any reference to kindness itself: understanding or tolerant behavior, generous behavior, considerate behavior, patient behavior. None of these dispositions are characteristic parts of kindness itself, however, even though, to the extent that kindness really does strengthen them, the behaviors in which they are actualized may overlap with kindness-actualizing behavior.[28]

To take another causal relation in the class of relations to independently-describable action, kindness also *enables* a person actually to do various things better or more easily. Here it is not the strength of a disposition to independently-describable action that is influenced by kindness, but rather one's skill or effectiveness in performing some such action. For instance, because he or she is more sensitive to the needs of others, the kind person may be able to judge more wisely what the right thing is to do when the needs of others are at stake. Or, because the kind person typically operates as a force for good in the world, he or she may be more effective in inspiring others to do likewise. Wise moral judgment or inspirational action are not paradigmatically kind; but the kind person may be better at them in virtue of being kind.[29]

Now if we focus only on such relations to independently-describable act-types, the pure ethics of duty account of where kindness gets its goodness may seem quite plausible. To take the examples at hand, it seems undeniable that kindness derives at least some of its moral worth from the rightness of that independently-describable act-type, "promoting the well-being of particular individuals," in which it is actualized and which it tends to produce. After all, promoting well-being is right, at least *prima facie*. In many cases it is morally required, and in numerous others it is, if not required, then at least morally desirable.[30] Moreover, intuitively it is the intrinsic value of human well-being itself, and not the moral worth of the disposition to promote it, or for that matter the moral worth of any other standing disposition, that grounds the rightness of so acting. Similar points can be made with respect to the relations between kindness and understanding, generous, or considerate behavior, insofar as these types of action are right. In each of these cases, the conclusion seems entirely reasonable that kindness displays a moral worth that is to some extent derivative from the antecedent rightness of the related act-type. Hence if relations like these (relations to independently-describable act-types) are the whole story, it may well seem that the moral goodness of kindness is *wholly* derivative from the prior rightness of action.[31]

III.

So where does the pure ethics of duty go wrong? Our discussion to date suggests that we are not likely to find the answer so long as we have in view only the relations between kindness and independently-describable action. Perhaps we should turn our attention instead to an entirely different class of relations in which a trait like kindness may stand to action. This is the class of relations to various act-types whose description is always *dependent*, requiring some essential reference to the trait itself.[32]

III.A. Kindness and Descriptively-Dependent Action

There are a number of relations, both causal and intentional, that hold between kindness and various descriptively dependent act-types. Consider, for example, the causal relation between kindness and those actions that count as criterial evidence for its presence. Now of course, unintentional emotional outbursts, involuntary exclamations, facial expressions, and so on can often count as very powerful forms of criterial evidence for the presence of a trait like kindness.[33] But we also say that someone's admiring utterances regarding Mother Teresa indicate that he is a kind person; or that one's sincerely-stated willingness to help reveals one's kindness, or that the hard work someone puts into helping a neighbor shows how kind she is. The notion of a criterion should be a familiar one, loose as it is; and so it should come as no surprise that there is no single feature that all and only the particular act-tokens constituting criterial evidence for the presence of kindness have in common, except that they are just the sort of things a kind person would characteristically do or say.[34]

There are other relations between kindness and action that are *intentional* rather than causal, but in which the description of the related act-type still requires essential reference to that trait. For instance, there is an indefinite variety of actions that may count as deliberate expressions of one's kind concern.[35]

Deliberately to express one's kindness is to act at least in part with the intention of letting the other know of one's concern for him or her as an individual. The aim of this expressive action as such is simply to *make the other aware* that someone values their particular concerns, and is willing to help if they can. Thus asking after another's health can be a way of deliberately expressing kindness, as can offering to help others even when one knows they are quite able to help themselves. Simply being present at "the great event" in order to show one's support can also be a deliberate expression of kindness. Thus it is kindness that is expressed through the act of "letting someone know you care," and so it is kindness that figures centrally in the explanation of why someone might be disposed so to act. The sole feature held in common by all and only expressive acts like these, however, is that they are the sorts of things a kind person would do deliberately to express their kind concern—to let the other know that he or she cares. Hence any description of the set of all and only kindness-expressing acts must be a dependent one, requiring ineliminable reference to the trait of kindness itself. Let us call this type of action, "expressive action" for short.

Naturally, expressive actions may sometimes also be intended actually to help the other. But even when the set of act-tokens in which kindness is deliberately *expressed* overlaps in this way with the set of act-tokens in which kindness is *actualized*, the two relations themselves remain distinct.[36] The relation under discussion is a relation between kindness and a descriptively-*dependent* act-type. The relation between kindness and actions that promote well-being, in contrast, is a relation between the trait and a descriptively *independent* act-type.

What does our discussion of the relations between trait and action imply for the pure ethics of duty? It is useful to explore this question indirectly, by shifting our attention away from the theory of virtue and back toward more familiar ground in the theory of the right. For it is in working toward an adequate explanation of what makes deliberate expressions of kindness *right* that we can uncover the failure of the pure ethics of duty to explain what makes kindness itself morally *good*.

III.B. What Makes Expressive Acts Right?

To begin with, there are certainly many occasions on which deliberately expressing one's kindness is the right thing to do, even if not everyone can do it. Suppose for instance that you are a teacher. There is a certain graduate student of whom you are quite fond. You find out to your dismay that he very often mistakes your withdrawn behavior for indifference. He himself has a personal stake in his relationship with you, his mentor; so even though he knows you think well of his work, he is both distressed and discouraged by this seeming personal indifference. Yet perhaps it would take only a few words or an occasional question to "let him know you care." If you do indeed care for him, and if you could help him so easily at virtually no cost to yourself, wouldn't it be the decent thing to do? Indeed, some might even think you had an obligation, within the limits imposed by professional propriety, so to express your kind concern.

It is natural to think here, as earlier in our analysis of descriptively-independent action, that the rightness of such an action contributes to the moral worth of the trait, kindness, that gives rise to it. Yet here the story is more complex. No doubt letting someone know you care may generate benefits for them. Your protégé may do better work, for instance, or find his self-confidence strengthened. To this extent your particular expressive action may also constitute a promotion of his well-being. To the extent that it is a token of this latter type, of course, its rightness can reasonably be held to be independent of whatever moral worth your kindness may itself possess, and indeed to contribute to it. But this is not the whole story, as any recipient of a kindness knows. Another part of what makes such an expressive act right is simply that it is what it is, namely a deliberate expression of a posture of positive concern or *noticing*. It is because kindness itself involves a positive form of noticing ("noticing" for short), that shy or self-conscious people, who do not want to be noticed, are often embarrassed by a kindness.

To speak more precisely, in the kind person this posture of noticing is the *base* of the core disposition to promote the well-being of particular people. Every disposition has some base, which is the property whose presence suffices to explain the persistence of the disposition. In the case of a disposition to act for the sake of some end, the base is typically some standing attitude, goal, or value.[37] To notice someone is to mirror their needs and concerns in one's own, to take their needs "to heart," as we say. More prosaically, to notice someone is to be moved by their needs and concerns, and to count them in the way that (if not necessarily to the degree that) one counts one's own.[38] Because noticing is in this way a sort of "feeling with," one might call it a species of compassion. But this does not imply that whenever the posture of noticing is operative the individual must be experiencing some felt urge or sensation, any more than the operation of a disposition to choose must be experienced in this way. If noticing is an emotion, it is in this way like admiration or respect. It may have its signature affective phenomena, but these are signs of its presence and probably not essential aspects of the presence of the emotion itself. Perhaps it would be more accurate to call noticing an attitude, as indeed my term "posture" should suggest, so long as we are willing to think of at least some species of compassion as attitudes.

I claim that the posture of noticing has a special moral worth independently of the appropriateness and/or utility of any benefit conferred, or intended, through the act that expresses it. This is because the posture of noticing as I have characterized it is the foundation of any bond between persons that is built around mutual acknowledgment and concern. It is for this reason the central constitutive element in the great human goods of friendship, community, and love. It is the central place of noticing in these goods—its non-moral or human value, if you will—that confers much of its special moral worth on that posture.[39]

These briefly-sketched facts about the human value of kindness are reflected in the characteristic responses of both recipient and observer to "a kindness." It is these facts that explain why we are touched by a gift that shows thought and sensitivity much more than by an equally-useful but impersonally-selected one. These facts also explain why your student, in the above example, can be distressed by the apparent absence of this posture of personal concern on your part, independently of whatever benefits he thinks your kind concern would produce for him were it present. Our pleasure at *being* noticed is the pleasure of being acknowledged, brought into contact with other members of the human race. Correspondingly, our pleasure at *seeing* a kindness done is pleasure at the creation, however fleeting and fragile, of that highly-valued bond of commonality that includes us or those with whom we identify, if only for a moment. So far from constituting the ground of the non-moral value of kindness, our pleasurable reactions reveal, or perhaps in part constitute, our judgment of the tremendous human value of kindness itself.[40,41]

In short, to appropriate Hume's terminology, though not his theory of the good, kindness is not only a trait "useful to others," but also one "immediately agreeable" to them. It is this "agreeableness" that is expressed in the way we appreciate the thoughtful gift as compared with the equally-useful but impersonal one. After all, the kind person aims at the well-being of others to no greater an extent than does the coldest and most unfeeling philanthropist. Nor need kindness tend to produce greater benefits than impartial benevolence. Neither its intentional nor its causal relations to antecedently-right or utile action differ sharply enough from those displayed by thoroughly impartial and removed forms of altruism to explain the special sort of moral worth that kindness seems to display in comparison to the latter. The significant thing that does set kindness apart is the nature of the attitude that is its base. Kindness is based on a personal form of noticing; impartial benevolence is not.[42] It is the human value of this posture of noticing that explains the special moral worth that kindness possesses.

We can now return to the starting-point of section III.B. It is for the reasons I have just adumbrated that expressive actions like letting your student know you care are not, as such, right prior to the value of the posture of concern that they express. Instead, it is only because an expressive action involves showing the other that you hold him or her in your heart that it has human value; and it is only because expressive action has such value that it is right. Thus a satisfactory account of the rightness of expressive acts as such requires acknowledging the antecedent, human value of the posture of concern that constitutes the base of the core disposition of the virtue of kindness, and which is characteristically shared with the other in deliberate expressions of kindness.

III.C. Expressive Acts and the Ethics Of Duty

To what extent is this account of where expressive action gets its rightness incompatible with the claims of the pure ethics of duty? And where exactly does the incompatibility lie? Notice that, first, strictly speaking our account does not say that the rightness of expressive action is borrowed from the *virtuousness* of kindness itself. Rather, what makes expressive action right is in large measure the *human value* of the kindness expressed in it. Both the rightness of expressive actions *per se* and the special moral worth of kindness supervene on that same human value.[43] Thus far our account of expressive action is compatible with the pure ethics of duty's insistence that the rightness of action must at least sometimes be independent of the *virtuousness* of traits.[44]

Second, even if our account of expressive action did imply that the rightness of such action was borrowed from the prior moral worth of kindness itself, this implication would still be compatible with the tenets of the pure ethics of duty. This is because the pure ethics of duty's insistence on the independence of the right is a qualified one. That view claims only that there are at least *some* types of action whose rightness is entirely underivative from the moral worth of any related trait. The pure ethics of duty thus allows for the possibility that there are other types of action whose rightness is derivative from the virtuousness of a trait like kindness; and, thus far, it could be only that expressive action was among these.

The pure ethics of duty runs aground on a third point, however. Recall that this view insists that ultimately there must be at least some types of action whose rightness is in a certain respect foundational. The rightness of these foundational act-types must be prior to whatever moral worth any related virtue happens to have, and it is the rightness of these act-types that constitutes the sole ultimate ground of moral worth that can be acknowledged by the pure ethics of duty. Here is where the incompatibility between the ethics of duty and our account of the rightness of expressive action is located. Our discussion of the right uncovered a crucial fact about our common-sense moral experience of virtue: in that experience, kindness presents itself as having irreducibly plural sources of moral worth. On the one hand, its moral worth is partially derivative from the antecedent rightness of "promoting the well-being of particular people," the act-type in which it is actualized, and which it tends to produce. On the other hand, its moral worth is also to some extent not derivative from any antecedent rightness that related actions may possess, because it is in part grounded on the fact that the trait itself is a humanly-valuable form of concern or noticing. It is this pluralism about where the virtue of kindness gets its moral goodness that is incompatible with the monistic view of the ultimate ground of virtue to which a pure ethics of duty is committed. It follows that, if our common-sense moral experience of expressive action is taken seriously, the pure ethics of duty is mistaken.[45]

IV.

It might be objected that I have misdiagnosed the source of the special value of kindness. Expressive action, it might be said, is not valuable as an expression of some distinct, independently identifiable inner state called "noticing." Instead it is that very action which is a valued form of noticing. After all, what the recipient of a kindness sees is expressive action, and not kind concern *per se*. Unexpressed kindness is of no value, and is appreciated by no one. But if this is correct, the objection continues, then my argument about the non-moral value of noticing shows only that expressive action itself is a constituent of the human good, and not that the trait of kindness is. Hence, the objection concludes, our discussion of expressive action does not demonstrate that kindness itself has some non-moral value that grounds its moral worth prior to any relation to right action. Indeed, it might be claimed that we have simply uncovered another sort of case in which kindness borrows moral worth from the prior rightness of some action to which it gives rise, in this instance expressive action.[46] If this objection is correct, therefore, the strategy of turning to the study of descriptively-dependent act-types has come to naught, and the ethics of duty remains unimpeached by our investigation of kindness.[47]

IV.A. Priority In the Order of Description and Priority In the Order of Importance

This objection, or rather this cluster of objections, brings out some of the complexity of the relations between kindness and descriptively-dependent action in our common-sense moral experience. On the one hand, as I have argued, neither the act-tokens that serve as criterial evidence for kindness nor the act-tokens in which it is deliberately expressed can be described as a set without essential reference to the trait of kindness itself. One might say that in both these cases kindness is first in *the order of description* with respect to the corresponding act-types. On the other hand, it does seem as though these descriptively-dependent act-types have a certain epistemic if not ontological priority over the trait of kindness. Our knowledge of another's kindness surely requires our prior awareness of the actions that, wittingly or unwittingly, reveal their kindness; and one wonders whether a given trait would even count as kindness at all rather than something else if it were not such as to dispose the agent to perform actions like these.

Our primary question, however, does not concern epistemic or ontological priority, but normative priority. The question is, in our common-sense moral experience, does descriptively-dependent action borrow whatever rightness it has from the prior human value of kindness itself, or is it rather that kindness borrows whatever moral worth it has here from the prior rightness of descriptively-dependent actions? By definition, the trait kindness is first in the *order of description* with respect to such act-types. But which is first, so to speak, in the *order of importance*?

We may begin to answer this question by considering the matter of epistemic priority. There is no doubt that we do value actions and events that are criterial evidence for the presence of kind concern. Just as we may prize evidence indicating that someone of whom we think very well also admires us, we might attach great weight to the behavior, involuntary responses, and emotional reactions that indicate the presence of kindness. But it seems clear that what we prize here is literally the *significance* of this criterial evidence. We value these indicators as signs of something that we value.[48] Despite the epistemic or perhaps even ontological priority of criterial evidence over that to which it points, it is the latter that retains normative priority. To value the signs for themselves, and not to value what they signify, is simply the moral equivalent of fetishism.[49]

IV.B. The Human Value of Expressive Acts

The case of actions that constitute deliberate expressions of kindness is somewhat more complex. For one thing, deliberate expressions of kindness will also count as criterial evidence for the presence of kindness, as do any of the actions or other responses to which a kind person is characteristically disposed. But the value we place on expressive action as such is not simply the value we place on any act that signifies the presence of kind concern. If it were, then you would always value having some reliable third party report to you that the other cared, for example, or discovering from a purloined psychological evaluation that the other had sincerely professed great concern for you in counseling, or even just inferring that he cared from some involuntary exclamation or emotional response of his, just as much as you would value having him tell you directly that he cared.

But this is not what our common-sense moral experience shows us. To let someone know you care is not just to do what that which happens to reveal your concern. It is not even just to do such a thing knowingly.

Instead, it is deliberately to take some action with the aim of rendering your care visible in the social world. It is a sort of public opening of one's heart to the gaze of the other to show him what you hold there. As such it is in its own right one of the most powerful and central elements in the goods of friendship, community, and love. This public statement has human value in part just because of the sort of public act it is, and not only because of what it expresses. Nonetheless, what we value is not just this deliberate and public unfolding of the heart, but what is revealed when it is unfolded as well. This is the lesson of our brief discussion of the significance of the criterial evidence for kindness. This is why kindness itself may still be seen and valued by its "recipient" as a form of noticing, even if it is never deliberately expressed. We may still wish to be cared for, or be glad that we are cared for, even when we know that we will never be told this directly, perhaps because the one who cares is shy, or has a rather old-fashioned sense of propriety. We prize being represented in the attention and interests of another. We prize being as it were carried in their hearts. The valuing of expressive action is therefore the valuing of a deliberate expression of something valued. It follows that the rightness of expressive action is grounded to some extent in its own non-moral value as a constitutive element of the human good, and also to some extent in the prior value of the trait kindness as a more fundamental element of that good.[50]

Our original account of the non-moral or human value of caring can now be reformulated. Noticing or caring attitudes are indeed a central constitutive element of the goods of sociality; but deliberately expressing such attitudes is also a distinct element of those goods; and realizing that someone else cares is a third, equally distinct element. The role of any one of these three elements in the human goods of sociality is not reducible to the roles of the other two; and all three must be present in order for any form of sociality like friendship, community, or love to obtain. Indeed, perhaps the forms of sociality are largely if not entirely constituted by the interplay of these three elements: forms of noticing, actions that express these, and recipients' responses to the first two.

Finally, does it follow from this reformulated account of the human value of caring that expressive acts as such are simply a subset of those in which kindness is actualized? Must they always aim to promote the well-being of others? There is a way in which this is so. But here "the well-being of others" cannot be construed as some further thing whose identity and value may both be established without essential reference to kindness itself. Kindness-expressing acts are motivated by kindness, but because they are as an act-type descriptively dependent, they contain in themselves a reference to this very motivation. They may be undertaken for their own sake, as expressive of this motivation; or they may be undertaken for the sake of the response they create in the recipient upon his or her recognition of that motivation, or both. In either case it is true that they are undertaken for the sake of an element of human well-being, and therefore for the sake of a goal that is as such non-morally valuable. However, the non-moral value here lies in the very act qua deliberate expression of kindness, and the recipient's awareness of it as such; and, as I have argued, one can account for the human value of these two elements only by referring to the prior non-moral or human value of kindness itself, the state that is expressed and appreciated.

We may now answer the question with which section IV began. Our investigation to date suggests that, in the theory of virtue, the order of importance follows the order of description. Actions may have epistemic priority (or even ontological priority in some cases) over traits; but if they nonetheless derive their description from a given character trait, it appears that they will to some extent derive their rightness from it as well.

V.

I conclude that kindness does have irreducibly plural sources of moral worth. Moreover, the case of kindness is not a unique one. For one thing, it seems very likely that a similar case can be made for ultimately pluralistic accounts of the worth of other intimate altruistic virtues like compassion, personal loyalty, supportiveness, and a certain willingness to share oneself and one's belongings with others.[51] Indeed, even in the case of a more abstract and impersonal benevolence, part of its moral worth seems to stem from the expression of community it involves. A deliberate expression of one's impersonal concern constitutes a recognition of the needy as sisters and brothers, members of a common moral fraternity. Here the attitude expressed is not exactly a form of what I have called "noticing," but rather a form of acknowledging of the moral significance of others.[52]

The case of impersonal benevolence suggests in turn that our conclusions about kindness may lead even farther afield, to poaching on areas generally regarded as the exclusive provenance of the ethics of duty. Consider for example that form of acknowledgement or recognition called, "respect for persons." On the one hand, you typically show your respect by giving due consideration to the interests of another. For this reason, however it is analyzed, the virtue of respect, if we may so call it, will certainly derive at least a part of its moral worth from various causal and intentional relations to actions like, "giving due consideration," or, "respecting rights." Such actions will be descriptively independent and (we would expect) antecedently right as well. Here as before, when we concentrate on descriptively independent actions, a pure ethics of duty seems to give an adequate account of where the virtue of respect gets its goodness, at least if we have in mind versions of the ethics of duty that acknowledge a plurality of virtue-making relations between respect and action. Yet here again, this is not the whole story, as people who have experienced a lack of respect from those who hold power over them can attest. One's actions can also constitute—or fail to constitute—deliberate expressions of respect. The act-type, "respect-expressing actions," is of course a descriptively dependent one for the same reasons that the act-type, "kindness-expressing actions," is descriptively dependent. But here the explanation of why respect-expressing acts are right may lead to even more radical conclusions than the parallel explanation in the case of kindness. Perhaps we value respect-expressing actions insofar as, and only insofar as, the moral attitude they serve to express is itself of prior and independent moral worth. Indeed, perhaps contrary to appearances, right action in general derives its rightness entirely from the fact that it expresses (or is suited to express) this antecedently virtuous attitude of respect. This is Kant's view, on one recent interpretation. On this interpretation Kant is transformed from the stereotypical defender of the ethics of duty into a proponent of a view that is equally extreme but radically opposed, namely, the pure ethics of virtue.[53]

VI.

The pure ethics of duty fails to accommodate our common-sense moral experience of kindness, and probably of a number of other virtues as well. The ethics of duty is of course an extreme and perhaps entirely fanciful view. However, as I suggested at the outset, what makes these conclusions particularly significant is that a variety of more moderate and more familiar views on where virtues get their goodness are also implicated in its failure.

I have been arguing for the ultimately pluralistic view that part of what gives kindness its moral worth is the human value it has in virtue of being a central constitutive element in goods like friendship, community, and love. One natural response to this argument would be to hybridize the pure ethics of duty by allowing that virtues may get their moral worth either from the right or from what is non-morally good. Thus W. D. Ross himself holds, for example, that some traits (e.g., honesty) are virtues because to have them involves taking as one's end the performance of some antecedently right action. However, he says, there are other traits (e.g., benevolence) that are virtues because to have them involves taking as one's end a non-morally, indeed intrinsically, valuable state of affairs like human well-being. Thus traits like benevolence are virtues, Ross appears to hold, independently of the (unquestioned) rightness of promoting such valuable ends.[54]

VI.A. Rossian Pluralism and the Autonomy of Virtue

Unlike a pure ethics of duty this Rossian view is obviously pluralistic with respect to the ultimate sources of virtue. It allows that causal or intentional relations to non-moral value may be virtue-making in their own right. Nonetheless, even leaving aside the question of whether value must be intrinsic in order to be virtue-making, this hybrid view does not go far enough to accommodate our common-sense moral experience of kindness. Ross' view would still make the moral worth of a virtuous trait wholly derivative from either the rightness or the goodness of some entirely distinct item, action or state of affairs, to which the trait is suitably related. But I have argued that in point of fact our common-sense moral experience reveals that it is the human value of the trait kindness itself that is one of its central virtue-making characteristics. There is to this extent no distinct thing, whether a non-morally-valuable state of affairs or an antecedently-right act-type, from which kindness borrows this portion of its moral worth. To this extent, the moral worth of kindness is *autonomous*, or underived from the goodness or rightness of any other thing. To be sure, the human value of kindness as I have described it is a function of the relation that trait bears to the goods of sociality. But its relation to these traits is not a causal or an intentional one, but a constitutive one. Kindness is not another thing, distinct from friendship, community, and love that either aims at them, or somehow contributes causally to their realization, and in these ways derives its moral worth from their non-moral value. Instead, the moral worth of kindness is derivative from *its own* human value as a central, constitutive element of the human goods of sociality. It appears, therefore, that only a normative theory that allows for what I have called the autonomous worth of the virtues can do justice to our common-sense experience of traits like kindness. Only such a theory is compatible with the claim that the very trait which is a bearer of moral worth may itself be one source of its own moral worth.

On the other hand, it should be clear that these remarks about Ross' hybrid view do not imply that the moral worth of kindness is entirely underivative from any other form of value. It should thus be clear that I explicitly reject the virtue-theoretic analogue of H. A. Prichard's notorious position with respect to the theory of the right. We might say that he held the rightness of actions to be *radically* autonomous. No action ever got its rightness from its relations to any form of value, he claimed, whether that value be the moral worth of some related trait or motive, the non-moral or even intrinsic value of some further intended or realized state of affairs, or even the intrinsic value of the action itself.[55] In contrast, our investigation suggests that in the normative theory of virtue, at any rate, the moral worth of traits like kindness seems always to be a function of some other form of "value" (where the term is construed very broadly to include rightness), whether its own or that of some suitably-related thing.

VI.B. The Primacy of Duty

Can anything be salvaged from the failure of the pure ethics of duty? A brief consideration of this question in closing may help to delineate more precisely the newly-drawn boundaries within which any normative theory of virtue that takes our common-sense moral experience of kindness seriously must operate.

The intuitive motivation for views like the pure ethics of duty is a familiar and characteristically-modern one. It is the thought that the question of what it is right to do is the fundamental one in normative ethics. Our question about where virtues get their goodness is by implication a secondary one, to be answered only after a theory of the right has defined the field.[56] Let us call this thought about the relative priority of the right and the virtuous, the idea of *the primacy of duty*. The current literature suggests a variety of reinterpretations of this idea that may still be defensible even in light of our conclusions about kindness.

First, one might hold that a trait counts as a virtue only insofar as it *does not* stand in any significant causal relation to antecedently wrong action. This interpretation is suggested by Philippa Foot's claim that the courage of a murderer does not "operate as a virtue" in him, on the grounds that it enables him better to do what is wrong.[57]

Another possible reinterpretation of the idea of the primacy of duty is suggested by some of Rawls' remarks, not about virtue but about natural assets and the well-ordered society. This reinterpretation would focus not directly on the relations between some virtue and right conduct, but rather on the psychological compatibility or incompatibility of a given character trait and the sense of duty. On this reinterpretation, a trait could be a virtue only insofar as it could be displayed in a well-ordered society. A well-ordered society, in turn, would be defined in part as one whose "members have a strong and normally effective desire to act" as the principles of the right require.[58]

Though both of these reinterpretations of the idea of the primacy of duty are compatible with our conclusions about kindness, they are comparatively weak. Rawls' own views on the virtues provide a third and much stronger reinterpretation of that idea. The virtues, he says, "are sentiments and habitual attitudes leading us to act on certain principles of the right. We can distinguish the virtues from each other by means of their corresponding principles."[59] In the last hundred years, a surprising number of influential philosophers, including Sidgwick and Moore, have agreed with Rawls in actually defining virtue by reference to some prior notion of the right.[60] Even this stronger reinterpretation, however, is strictly speaking compatible with our conclusions about kindness, for it does not entail the sort of reductionist claims made by the pure ethics of duty about the sources of moral worth. Instead it effectively imposes a restriction, not on where virtues get their goodness, but on what types of traits can be virtues.[61]

These three reinterpretations of the idea of the primacy of duty are members of a family of views on the relation between virtue and the right. The defining feature of this family is that each member view, even the last of the three described above, entails nothing stronger about where virtues get their goodness than the following claim:

> For every virtuous trait, some appeal to principles or concepts of the right is presupposed in the justification or the analysis of the claim that it is a virtue, but the converse does not hold.

From the fact that one must begin either in the analysis or the justification of claims about virtue with principles or concepts of the right, however, it does not follow that the moral worth of traits is borrowed entirely from their relations to the right. Thus members of this family of interpretations of the primacy of duty make a claim that is plainly weaker than the one made by the pure ethics of duty, and one that is entirely compatible with our conclusions about the case of kindness.

Clearly this compatibility is purchased at the price of a fairly strict neutrality for the question we have asked, namely, where virtues get their goodness.[62] Nonetheless such interpretations of the primacy of duty still offer a partial answer to a more general question in normative ethics, namely, whether a normative theory of virtue can be defended that does not at least presuppose in one way or another a prior and independent conception of the right and/or the good. The primacy of duty, interpreted as maintaining the claim formulated above, would answer this question in the negative. However, this is a question about the autonomy of virtue construed much more broadly; and to answer it here would require us to venture too far beyond the facts about our common-sense moral experience of the virtue of kindness.

NOTES

1 I would like to thank the many people whose helpful comments and criticisms have contributed to this paper, including: David Copp, Jacob Hale, Andrew Moore, Graham Oddie, Gerald Postema, Geoffrey Sayre McCord, Douglas Portmore, William Shaw, David Shoemaker, Michael Smith, Christine Swanton, and Michael Wedin. I would also like to thank audiences at the various universities and colleges where earlier versions of this paper have been read.

2 Michael Slote's work stands as the most notable effort to discuss the place of virtue in common-sense morality. See his (1995) and more recently his (2001). Among the most systematic recent discussions of particular normative theories of the virtues are Rosalind Hursthouse (1999) and Christine Swanton (2003).

3 The locus classicus for contemporary discussions of the contrast between the ethics of duty and the ethics of virtue is the work of William K. Frankena. See his (1988), as well as his (1973).

4 For a brief account of the theological and philosophical dispute, see my (1999). For one anti-supererogationist discussion that is explicitly grounded in Reformation thinking, see Gregory Mellema (1991).

5 To this extent the distinction between descriptive ethics and normative ethics is a misleading one. If many of us do in fact embrace much of common-sense morality in our moral evaluations and decisions, a systematic investigation of common sense is to a significant extent an investigation of the morality

that many of us, the investigators, do in fact take as normative.

6 My thanks to Jacob Hale, Douglas Portmore, and David Shoemaker for insightful discussion on the idea of investigating common-sense morality. The notion of centering such an investigation around the platitudes of common sense was suggested to me by Shoemaker.

7 Unless otherwise noted, phrases like "an ethic of duty," or "the ethics of duty," refer throughout to the pure ethics of duty. I also use interchangeably the terms, "moral goodness", "moral worth," "virtuousness," and, where context allows, "goodness." I will reserve the term "value" and its cognates to denote "non-moral value."

8 Except when otherwise noted, I restrict my discussion throughout to questions about the goodness of traits. Strictly speaking, however, the two claims made by the pure ethics of duty should be broadened to cover not only the virtuousness of traits but that of persons and of occurrent psychological states (such as particular desires or motives) as well. I omit this complication in the text as it will not materially affect our discussion. On the relations between judgments of traits and judgments of persons, see my (1991).

9 The preceding two paragraphs are taken from my (1990). The distinction between the ethics of duty and its contrary, the ethics of virtue, reveals only one part of what is at stake in the debates between virtue theorists and duty theorists, as the cited article indicates.

10 Notice that the second clause of this definition of the pure ethics of duty does not entail the first, unless one assumes that all normative-ethical theories must be foundationalist in structure.

11 The point is not that generous acts can never be kind, or vice versa, but that the two traits are distinct. See section II.B for some further remarks on the relations between generosity and kindness.

12 Perhaps this is because we typically make a distinction between what contributes to someone's well-being and what merely pleases them. The giving of small gifts seems as such to aim at the latter, not at the former. This does not mean, however, that there is no relationship at all between kindness and thoughtful acts. See below note 35.

13 If we think that in paradigm cases the cost of a kindness is generally small, that might explain why it seems out of place to call great acts of self-sacrifice kind rather than, say, noble, loving, or generous. Perhaps kindness is a "small virtue," not in the manner of Hobbes' "small morals" (etiquette), but rather in being a part of the "moralities of everyday life," to use Sabini and Silver's wonderful phrase (1990). The moralities of everyday life cover situations in which no substantial departures from conventional behavior are called for, but in which genuine moral issues are nonetheless at stake. Typically these issues involve affirming, sustaining, disrupting, or rejecting relationships between people, whether casual or enduring.

14 My thanks to Jacob Hale for suggesting this sort of example. See also below note 17. Notice that it may nonetheless be my kindness that first motivates me to see that something needs to be done, and that therefore contributes ultimately, not to my acting kindly in the situation, but to my returning home and thinking more carefully about what the best thing to do would be. In general, kindness may operate to encourage or sustain a variety of

other altruistic dispositions, as it does here, or as it does, e.g., when one's kindness leads one to respond generously to a request for money from a homeless person. See section II.B on some of the various types of causal relations in which kindness can stand to action.

15 My thanks to Frank McGuinness for pressing the issue about cases like these.

16 The Good Samaritan passage can be taken to suggest that, unlike the Samaritan, the Levite and the priest who passed the victim by saw him in one of the other less flattering ways I mention in the text. All this is not to say that compassion is simply another name for kindness; but compare section III.B on "noticing" as the base of the core disposition to act for the sake of helping particular persons.

17 The story also suggests that the range of compassionate actions may be far greater than the range of kind acts, if we are willing to read it as implying that not only the Samaritan's initial response, but also his subsequent giving of money to the innkeeper and his returning at a later date to check on the progress of the victim, were also acts of compassion. If this suggestion is right, then there is another way to understand the case of the philanthropic supporter of the Salvadoran village association: it is his compassion that moves him throughout, and kindness as it is paradigmatically understood may play no role at all in explaining what he does.

18 Here again, this does not imply that "helpfulness" and "kindness" are the same thing, or even that they are two different names for the same trait. One may act helpfully out of kindness or out of any one of a number of other noble motives; and one may be helpful in a variety of situations in which kindness is not what is called for, as e.g., when I hand you the item you are looking for but cannot seem to find at the moment.

19 I use this locution because we sometimes wish to withhold the honorific, "kind," from forms of this concern that we do not believe to be virtuous.

20 David Shoemaker and others have helped me to appreciate the importance of some of these points.

21 I do not mean to imply that having a trait like kindness must involve having an articulated sense of the rightness or goodness of what one aims at. See my (1991).

22 Notice that the end for which the kind person characteristically acts is a further state of affairs. It is conceptually independent both of the actions undertaken for its sake and of that disposition to promote it which constitutes the core of kindness itself. I will return to this point in section IV.

23 For a more detailed discussion of the various components of character traits like kindness, see Richard B. Brandt (1970).

24 Compare Christine Swanton's argument against Hursthouse in her (2001: 34–36).

25 One might think that a certain degree of judgment and good sense were constitutive elements of kindness. Indeed, we do sometimes appear to mark off people like Inspector Clouseau by calling them kind-hearted rather than kind, full stop. Even if this is conceded, however, it still cannot be the case that any and all false beliefs or misunderstandings of the situation that

prevent someone's action from in fact promoting the well-being of others necessarily impugn his or her kindness. Thus the distinction drawn in the text would remain.

26 Needless to say, this distinction between a causal relation and an intentional one also remains even if it is the intentional structure of kindness that explains the causal power it has to produce actions beneficial to particular individuals. I am indebted to Gerald Postema for helpful discussion on the distinction between causal and intentional relations.

27 More precisely, in each case the related act-type can be described simply as the set of all and only those act-tokens that constitute promotions of the well-being of particular people.

28 Here the relation between kindness and independently-describable action may seem more indirect, since kindness appears to exert its causal influence on the disposition to perform the action, rather than directly on the action itself. Whether this is correct will depend in part on one's views about the ontology of causal relations in which the relata are dispositions to act.

29 With respect to some of these act-types, some readers may find it difficult to say whether we should think of the dispositions to perform them, or the agent's effectiveness in performing them, as constituting qualities altogether distinct from the trait of kindness, or whether we should think of them instead as qualities that, when present, count as part of the constellation of characteristics that actually constitute kindness. In the text I have presented them as the former. If one thinks that in some of the instances I have cited they are better conceived as the latter, then my examples would need to be revised. The point of principle I am making would remain the same, however, so long as there are some dispositions to act that can be described independently of reference to kindness and that are strengthened by it, or some types of independently-describable action whose performance is enabled or enhanced by it.

30 To the extent that our notion of "the right" includes supererogatory action, as I think it should, phrases like "the ethics of duty" and "the primacy of duty," though well-suited to the contemporary literature, are misleading.

31 Thus a certain pluralism regarding the sources of the moral worth of kindness seems to be part of common-sense morality; but, thus far, that pluralism is entirely compatible with the ethics of duty's monistic view about the ultimate ground of virtue.

32 More precisely, for each dependently-describable act-type, there will be no description of all and only the act-tokens that instantiate it that does not involve essential reference to the corresponding trait.

33 In many cases this is perhaps because they betoken the presence of one of the ancillary affective dispositions that are part of the constellation of dispositions that make up kindness.

34 Moreover, because of the looseness of the criterial-evidence relation, there is of course no necessary connection between any one of these act-tokens and the presence of kindness. See Carl Wellman (1962).

35 At this point a little more can be said about the relationship between thoughtfulness and kindness, discussed briefly in section II.A above. There

I argued that the core disposition of kindness is not actualized in thoughtful behavior because such behavior does not show direct attention to a person's needs. If this is correct then it appears to follow that thoughtful behaviors cannot constitute deliberate expressions of kindness either. This may seem counterintuitive at first, but it may be helpful to see that it does not entail that there is no relationship whatsoever between thoughtful action and kindness. Thoughtful acts may certainly constitute criterial evidence for—or indeed deliberate expressions of—love or friendship; and if, as I argue below in section III.B, kindness is a central constitutive element of love, friendship, and community, then important but indirect relations emerge between thoughtfulness and kindness after all.

36 This is because, even if there happen to be particular tokens of expressive action that can be described without reference to kindness itself, it remains true that there is no description of all and only such kindness-expressing tokens that does not require essential reference to that trait.

37 When the disposition in question is a disposition to act for the sake of some end, the base property normally explains its persistence by rationalizing it, i.e., by showing how it makes sense for the agent to have the disposition in light of his or her more foundational concerns, attitudes, values, etc. Because these in turn can often be understood dispositionally, the resulting structure of explanation may take the form of an appeal to a nested series of dispositions. For a further discussion of the notions of disposition and base as applied to character, see my (2004).

38 E.g., a rational agent characteristically does not regard himself as having reason to meet his own needs or promote his own concerns on a given occasion only if he has a felt urge to do so on that occasion. The kind agent will therefore take a similar view of the conditions under which he has reason to meet the needs or promote the concerns of others.

39 I will return to the topic of the human value of noticing below in section IV. I use the phrase, "human value" to draw attention to the value that kindness has as a constitutive element of friendship, love, and community, on the supposition that these things are themselves "human goods," i.e., necessary components of human well-being. One could hold that, given the argument in the text, what I have in fact established is the claim that kindness is itself intrinsically valuable, since what I have shown is that it is valuable not as a means but as an essential element of these human goods. I am sympathetic to this claim, though I do not think it follows strictly from what is argued in the text. If one agrees that friendship, love, and community have a certain value that is dependent on their being central components of—rather than means to—well-being, and if one agrees that well-being is intrinsically valuable, then I think it is plausible to argue that the value these human goods display as components of well-being is itself a form of intrinsic value. If this argument is accepted, then I think the further conclusion in turn that kindness itself is intrinsically valuable as an essential element of these intrinsically-valuable human goods is also plausible. However, this argument requires that one embrace a conception of well-being on which it is, not some further (dominant) end, distinct from things like friendship, love, and community, but rather an inclusive end, or, a certain arrangement of intrinsically-valuable goods like these. Cf. John M. Cooper's account of

Aristotelian eudaimonia as an inclusive end in his (1975). For the distinction between the value something has as an end rather than a means, and the value something has in isolation, see Christine Korsgaard (1983). Thanks to Douglas Portmore for very useful discussions of these issues about intrinsic value.

40 One might hold that the satisfaction of desire, or perhaps of characteristically human desire, was intrinsically valuable, and that the non-moral value of kindness was purely instrumental, derivative from its causal role in satisfying desire. However, like the hedonistic account of the non-moral value of kindness mentioned in the text above, this argument does not take the phenomenology of common-sense moral experience seriously. I believe there probably is a characteristically and deeply human desire to be noticed. However, this desire itself has an evaluative structure that reveals our judgment of the human value of kindness, just as the characteristically human pleasure at being noticed does. Cf. below note 49 and text, supra.

41 Let us suppose for the sake of illustration that the argument in note 40 is sound, and that we have established that kindness is intrinsically valuable. Is this claim incompatible with desire-satisfaction theories of intrinsic value? It depends on how those theories are formulated. Obviously a theory of intrinsic value which holds that the only intrinsically-valuable thing in the world is the satisfaction of desire is incompatible with the proposition that kindness is intrinsically valuable. But not all desire-satisfaction theories of intrinsic value need be formulated this way. Suppose we accept the familiar distinction, made by R. B. Perry (1954) and others, between claims about what features of the world are (intrinsically) good-making, and claims about what sorts of things in the world are intrinsically good (i.e., actually possess these features). One can then understand a theory of intrinsic value as the conjunction of a general claim of the first sort, regarding the good-making features of the world, and a general claim of the second sort, regarding which items in the world are intrinsically good in virtue of possessing these features. One could then formulate a desire-satisfaction theory of value which held that any intrinsically-valuable thing is so in virtue of possessing the feature, "being the object of some desire." This is a claim of the first sort. But this claim is entirely compatible with holding that many things, including perhaps kindness, or indeed friendship, love, and community are themselves intrinsically valuable, since this is a claim of the second sort. Moreover, on such a theory, the latter claim will be true, provided only that these things are in fact the objects of some desire. The same points can be made, mutatis mutandis, about the compatibility of the claim that kindness is intrinsically valuable with more sophisticated versions of such a desire-satisfaction theory; and about its compatibility with hedonistic theories of the good as well.

42 Here as in section II, the point is not that kindness has greater moral worth than impartial forms of benevolence, but that it has a particular type of moral worth that they lack.

43 For this reason our discussion does not lend support to the claim made by a pure ethics of virtue, if we conceive of that view as claiming that the rightness of action is always derivative from the antecedent virtuousness of some related trait. Indeed, our conclusions are incompatible with that claim,

unless one simply defines virtuousness as the human (or perhaps intrinsic) value of a trait or motive. Anything weaker than such a definitional claim will not resolve the incompatibility, since any weaker claim will not entail that the rightness of expressive action is derived from the virtuousness of kindness. See also note 44.

44 There are a number of philosophers who have held the view that, in general, the rightness of action is some function of the non-moral value of a related trait. See, for example, Richard B. Brandt (1969). Brandt take the relation between valuable trait and right action to be a causal one, agreeing that right actions are those produced by utile traits. (Compare Robert Adams' (1976) discussion of motive-utilitarianism.) As might be suggested by my comments in the text above, however, one could hold instead that the relation between valuable trait and right action was an intentional one, and that the rightness of actions was a function of the non-moral value of the standing motivations those traits expressed. These views are both instances of what I would call a teleological ethics of duty, either in its causal or its intentional form; and both of them entail that the rightness of action is independent of the virtuousness of any related trait. See my (1990).

45 The same conclusion would follow if one were able to establish the proposition that the moral worth of kindness was entirely borrowed from the prior non-moral value of certain related actions. The pure ethics of duty founders provided only that the lines along which value is transmitted, so to speak, do not run through the rightness of any action before they reach the virtuousness of some trait. For a critique of one consequentialist version of this proposition, which he calls "the act-adequacy premise," see Bernard Williams (1973). See section IV for a more general critique.

46 For purposes of this objection I allow the elision from "expressive action is humanly valuable" to "expressive action is right"; but see note 43.

47 In fact, if this line of argument were correct, one might hold that deliberate expressions of kindness were merely a special instance of acting in order to promote the well-being of particular individuals. What would be distinctive about such expressive actions would be only the fact that, because it is the action itself that is a constituent of well-being and not some further state of affairs brought about by it, the agent must intend to benefit simply by a deliberate revelation of the intention to benefit.

48 A putative counterexample to the general claim implicit here: the deliberate sharing of something of no value can itself still be non-morally valuable. This is true, but it is no counterexample. In such a case two "things" are shared, namely, the item itself and the concern to share it. To say "it's the thought that counts" is to recognize the value that such a concern to share possesses independently of the non-moral value of what is shared, and independently of the non-moral value of the act of sharing the item in question. Indeed, the human good of intimacy is constituted in part by the disposition to share as such, in a way parallel to the way that friendship, love, and community are partly constituted by the disposition to express one's kind concern, as I argue in the succeeding paragraphs. Consequently, if the deliberate sharing of something of no value itself has non-moral value, this is true only because the motivation to share itself has a prior and independent value, e.g., as a constitutive element of the human good of intimacy.

49 The claim here is not the desire-satisfaction theorist's claim that what makes these criterial behaviors valuable is that their "recipient" values them. Rather the claim is that our common-sense moral experience reveals that both recipient and observer value what is expressed independently of (also) valuing its expression.

50 Thus I have not been arguing for the claim that the rightness of kindness-expressing action is wholly derivative from the prior moral worth of the trait, kindness. I am claiming only that the rightness of expressive action is to some extent derivative from that source, and further that expressive acts would not be right at all per se were they not expressions of an antecedently- and non-morally-valuable trait.

51 Cf. Lawrence Blum (1980: chapter 7). Compare Sidgwick's discussion of the value of the emotion expressed in benevolent action in (1966: 222–3).

52 Perhaps both acknowledgement and noticing may be conceived as falling under some broader category like recognition.

53 This interpretation is suggested by Onora O'Neill (1983: 395–6).

54 W. D. Ross (1930: 160–2).

55 H. A. Prichard (1968).

56 Cf. Sidgwick's remarks on the contrast between Greek ethics and modern ethics (1966: 105–6), and in his (1960: 6–7).

57 Philippa Foot (1978: 14–18).

58 John Rawls (1971: 436–7). The quoted discussion of the notion of a well-ordered society is at Rawls (1971: 454). (I have substituted the phrase "the right" for Rawls' more limited term, "justice.") Cf. Alasdair MacIntyre's remarks on the morality of law and its relation to the morality of virtue in (1981: 141–3, 186–7).

59 John Rawls (1971: 437; cf. 192).

60 Henry Sidgwick (1966: 217–27); G.E. Moore (1968: 71–173).

61 Cf. Frankena (1973) and (1988). I do not find this restriction plausible, as I think that not only the sources of virtue but also the types of traits that can be virtues are irreducibly plural. But that is a story for another occasion.

62 On the other hand, if one accepts the above claim of the primacy of duty, it does seem at the very least implausible to hold that the moral worth of traits is not borrowed to any extent at all from the (admittedly) prior rightness of related actions.

CHAPTER 3

Virtue and Rightness: A Comparative Account

KIM-CHONG CHONG

INTRODUCTION

One central issue that virtue ethics addresses is the relation between the virtues and rightness. However, it is unclear from the outset why this should be an issue. It would seem that "rightness" is a—if not the—central feature of any ethical system, since it is precisely the function of ethics to adjudicate between rightness and wrongness. And rightness and wrongness would seem more appropriately to be features of actions than they are of the virtues and character. Thus, it would appear odd to talk of the "rightness" of a particular virtue rather than of an action. If it is not odd, then what we are referring to must be some aspect of the virtue such that it has consequences for the rightness of action. Even if the proper term for some virtue is that it is a "good" virtue to have, this goodness must ultimately translate into the rightness of an action or actions. Otherwise, talk of goodness or virtues would appear to be empty.

Generally, the above would seem unexceptionable. But differences arise when we ask what determines "rightness." For the consequentialist, the right action is that which leads to the best consequences for all concerned. For the Kantian deontologist, rightness would depend upon whether the action falls within the injunction of the categorical imperative, "Act only on that maxim through which you can at the same time will that it should become a universal law." On one standard interpretation, this is a test of an action to see if it is morally right or permissible. On another, more recent interpretation, the categorical imperative is regarded as a test of maxims or the subjective principles of individual agents. In this respect, the categorical imperative is not (directly) a test of action, but of the principle or principles under which a proposed action would fall.

The undertaking of such a test would lead the agent to question her own motives.[1] In effect, the Kantian would seem to be engaged in the same project as the virtue ethicist, in highlighting the importance of dispositions, motives, and character in determining the rightness of actions. But it could be argued that the formulation of Kantian ethics just proposed is still not distinctively a virtue ethics, since rightness is still conceived independently of the virtues, in accordance with duty and universal moral law.

While much has been said in the literature about the debate between the three different forms of ethics in the Western tradition, little has been said about how specific forms of ethics in the East figure in the debate. But first, it has to be said that there is no reason why any Eastern ethics should be seen and measured against the framework provided by the consequentialist/deontologist/virtue distinctions. To the ordinary person (Western or Eastern) "uncorrupted" by such a framework, there is bound to be something artificial about these categorizations. Thus, it might be held that from the ordinary person's standpoint, sometimes, principles are important, while at others, the manner in which a person acts is paramount in deciding whether he or she has done the right thing or not. Nevertheless, for the sake of the discussion to follow, it would be necessary first, to lay out what seems to be distinctive about virtue ethics in relation to its rivals.

The Eastern form of ethics I shall be discussing in this essay is the ethics of Confucius and Mencius. In particular, I shall discuss their conception of *yi*, or what has sometimes been translated as "right" or "rightness." I shall show that this conception of rightness stresses character and motivation, and can help to illuminate the concerns of virtue ethics in the Western tradition. However, I shall not make any straightforward claim that both Confucius' and Mencius' ethics constitute a "virtue ethics." This is because, virtue ethics, at least as understood in the recent literature, is developed against the consequentialist and deontological accounts. Neither Confucius nor Mencius has anything to do with such a debate, or hold any such philosophical baggage. Confucius emphasizes the importance of a certain moral orientation in one's life, and the assessment of one's actions is based on how well one lives up to or expresses the virtues and attitudes that describe this orientation. At the same time, he is a conservative sociopolitical thinker who emphasizes upholding the ritual rules, for the maintenance of social harmony. Mencius argues for the internality of *yi* as a predisposition toward rightness and differentiates this from the appetitive and sensory desires. He is concerned to combat a certain view of human nature, as consisting only of the biological desires. There are indications in the *Mencius*, however, that point toward the necessity of external standards for moral judgement, and I shall remark briefly on these at the end of the paper. These indications also point to the development of Confucian ethics in another thinker, Xunzi.

CHARACTERIZING VIRTUE ETHICS

For my purpose, it would be convenient to take a recent characterization of virtue ethics in order to see what is distinctive about it. This characterization is provided by Michael Slote,[2] who initially describes virtue ethics as "agent-focused." That is, the focus is on "the virtuous individual and on those inner traits, dispositions, and motives that qualify her as being virtuous (*TME* 177)." This contrasts with "act-focused" forms of ethics that are based upon moral laws, rules, and principles. The latter emphasize the rightness or wrongness of actions, or ask whether certain actions are morally permissible or obligatory, according to suitably prescribed rules and principles. The important concepts here are "deontic," having to do with duty, right and obligation. Virtue ethics on the other hand emphasizes the "morally good," "admirable," and "virtuous." These are "aretaic" concepts centering on the character of the agent (*TME* 177). The primary opposition for Slote is between act- and agent-focused conceptions of ethics. The term "deontic" would include consequentialism, and cuts across the usual opposition between the deontological ethics of Kantianism, and the teleological ethics of consequentialism.[3]

The point of contention between virtue ethics and other forms of ethics—primarily Kantian and consequentialist—is whether the aretaic is derivative of the deontic, or vice versa. In this regard, some agent-focused forms of virtue ethics ultimately fail to distinguish themselves from the theories that emphasize deontic terms and is in this sense still act-focused. Slote mentions Aristotle's ethics as an example:

> For Aristotle, the excellence or rightness of an action doesn't essentially depend on the motives or habits that gave rise to it, or on the character of the person who did it. Rather, the virtuous individual is someone who, without relying on rules, is sensitive and intelligent enough to perceive what is noble or right as it varies from circumstance to circumstance, but this metaphor of perception seems to indicate that being virtuous involves being keyed in to facts independent of one's virtuousness about what acts are admirable or called for.

> A more radical kind of virtue ethics would say that the ethical character of actions is not thus independent of how and why and by whom the actions are done. Rather, what is independent and fundamental is our understanding and evaluation of human motives and habits, and the evaluation of actions is entirely derivative from and dependent on what we have to say ethically about (the inner life of) the agents who perform those actions. The more radical kind of virtue ethics is thus *agent-based*, not merely, like Aristotle's views (on one common interpretation), agent-focused (*TME* 178).

There are two sets of distinctions here. One is the distinction between act- and agent-focused. Another is the distinction between act-focused and agent-based. According to Slote, in an agent-focused ethics like Aristotle's, the virtues merely gear us toward a clearer perception of facts that are independent of the virtues. The cultivation of virtuous motives would enable one to perceive the right action, but on an act-focused conception of right that is independent of motives. An ethics that is agent-based, on the other hand, moves radically away from an act-focused conception of rightness. According to an agent-based ethics, whether some action is right depends on the motives and habits that give rise to that action. One example of an agent-based ethics is Plato's theory of the health of the soul where actions are evaluated according to how well they preserve the harmonious interaction between the soul, the spirit, and the desires. Slote refers to this as a kind of morality of inner strength, and recognizes that it can be accused of being egoistic (*TME* 218). But there are other forms of agent-based virtue ethics that are based upon the motives of benevolence or care, and perhaps the best example he gives in this regard is in response to the following question about the effectiveness of agent-based virtue ethics: how is an examination of motives rather than facts about people and the world relevant to solving practical moral problems?

The example concerns a woman whose aged mother is hospitalized and who may require "heroic measures" to keep her alive (*TME* 230–231). How would this woman's benevolent motives help her decide what to do? According to Slote, the woman's benevolence offers her an answer because it directs her to find out more about her mother's condition and prospects: the quality and duration of life, future suffering and incapacity, etc. If the woman does not do so but decides on the basis of ignorance, this would demonstrate callousness toward her mother. In effect, it is "morality as benevolence" that enables her to make the judgment that she ought to find out more before deciding on the course of action to take. If it emerges that the facts point to horrendous pain and debilitating prospects for the mother, then "the woman's decision is once again plausibly derivable from morality as benevolence. At that point, it would be callous of her to insist on heroic measures and benevolent not to do so and the proper moral decision can thus be reached by agent-based considerations (*TME* 231)."

Against Slote, it could be argued that the example of the benevolent woman still does not help us see what is radically distinctive about virtue ethics in the agent-based sense. The problem with Slote's clarification of agent-based virtue ethics in terms of the example is that it could still be interpreted in the Aristotelian way mentioned: her benevolence may help her to perceive the right action, but surely, whether she acted rightly is an evaluation that can be (and perhaps has to) be made independently of her benevolence. After all, benevolence does not guarantee doing the right thing. We need therefore to get clearer about the significant difference—if any—that virtuous dispositions and motives may make to the rightness of ethical decisions.

For this purpose, it would be useful to bring in a related distinction between agent-relativity and agent-neutrality.[4] One of the tenets that virtue ethics reacts against is the following: "Basic moral judgments are universal in form. They contain no essential reference to particular persons or particular relationships in which the agent may stand."[5] This is universality or agent-neutrality, a tenet that is common to both Kantian and consequentialist ethics. Although it is unclear that a virtue ethics must necessarily oppose acting upon agent-neutral reasons in all cases, it is opposed to the above tenet. Thus, virtue ethics would emphasize the importance of agent-relative reasons in at least some central areas of moral life. These reasons have to do with who I am, how I am related to someone in a certain situation, the history of this relationship, etc. We can conceive of cases where both agent-neutral and agent-relative reasons can lead to the same conclusion about what it is morally right to do. The interesting question in such cases is whether there is a sense in which what is "morally right" can still be conceived differently. If there is such a difference, this must be due to some perspective of the agent, since the conclusion reached by both agent-neutral and agent-relative reasons are manifestly the same. It is such a perspective, I would contend, that virtue ethics is trying to capture.

To illustrate, consider an example from George Eliot's *Middlemarch*.[6] The pedantic scholar Casaubon has been compiling a book on the *Key to all Mythologies*. Seriously ill, he asks his wife Dorothea to promise to complete it after his death. Dorothea knows that the work is worthless, and it would be an enormous burden if she promises. If she says no, it could upset him and precipitate a heart attack. On the other hand, she has been helping him all along with his work, he has implicit trust in her, and if he were to go on living she would surely continue to help him. She resolves to promise. Although he dies before she can make her promise, it would seem "obvious" to anyone who is faced with this problem that even if Dorothea—or anyone—had actually promised, she should not be expected to carry it through. In other words, she should promise but break it after Casaubon dies.

We can say that there are two agent-neutral principles behind this proposed moral solution: (1) One should not do anything to worsen the health of another, and (2) No one is obliged to carry on a worthless task of another's after his/her death. Principle (1) overrides principle (2) since there is the risk of someone dying should one refuse to promise. All things considered, one should promise. Nonetheless, principle (2) sanctions the thought that one can subsequently break the promise. The thinking behind the decision to promise therefore is that Dorothea is not morally obliged to promise in the first place, but because of the overriding consideration of Casaubon's health, she ought to do so, with the implicit understanding that she is not obliged to keep the promise.

Compare this with the basis of Dorothea's own decision to promise. This is illustrated by how the obligation to keep her promise becomes questionable after Casaubon's death. She discovers he had added a clause to his will stating that she shall lose her inheritance of his property if she were to marry his nephew. To Dorothea, this cheapens and perverts the relation of trust and dispels the feeling of duty that she had towards him. This shows her decision to promise was based on a commitment to a trusting relationship.

We note the following points. Both the relevant agent-neutral and agent-relative reasons lead to the same decision to promise. However, the basis of the decision is different in each case. In the agent-neutral case, the decision is based on principles that purport to be applicable to anyone in such a situation—including Dorothea. In Dorothea's (agent-relative) case, however, the decision is based upon the personal history of a relationship of commitment and trust. Her subsequent decision to break the promise is based upon the feeling that her trust was betrayed. The agent-neutral perspective is therefore not Dorothea's perspective, and it would be arbitrary to assume that the principles behind the agent-neutral perspective should guide her actions.

Although the decision is the same in both cases, i.e., to promise, there is an important sense in which what the decision amounts to in each case is not independent of the motives and dispositions that lead up to it. Dorothea's decision to promise involves her care for and commitment to Casaubon. The agent-neutral decision to promise involves avoiding the infliction of potentially life-endangering pain on someone, and where doing so obliges one to go through the motions of making a promise. The different motives and dispositions result in a morally qualitative difference in the two decisions. In mentioning Dorothea's motives and dispositions, we note something about her virtuous character: despite her knowledge of Casaubon's intellectual inadequacies—contrary to the earlier expectations that had led her to marry him—she remains committed to him. This commitment is also motivated by the belief that there was mutual trust. The decision to break her promise involves the belief that this had been betrayed. In other words, for Dorothea, the significant moral facts are not independent of these motivational beliefs, and what is right for her in this context cannot be meaningfully conceived, independently of these beliefs. Another way to put this is to say that it would be out of place to contend that she did the wrong thing by (sincerely) promising, since this judgment is based on criteria that are independent of her dispositions, motives and character. This, then, is perhaps what virtue ethics is concerned to stress: that in some central areas of moral life, rightness cannot be understood independently of an individual perspective expressed in terms of certain virtuous motives and dispositions. In what follows, we shall see that both Confucius and Mencius too emphasize the expression of qualitatively virtuous perspectives in their conceptions of rightness. But their claims will have to be understood against a different contextual background.

CONFUCIUS AND MENCIUS ON *YI* OR "RIGHTNESS"

In the "Introduction" to his well-known translation of the *Analects*, D. C. Lau discusses the status of the concept of *yi* in Confucius' ethics.[7] According to Lau, *yi* may refer to either the action or the character of an agent. In the former case, *yi* refers to an act as being "right" or as commanding a "duty." In the latter case, *yi* describes the agent as "righteous" or "dutiful."

Lau holds, however, that the description of someone as being righteous or dutiful is derivative of her consistently right actions. In this regard, *yi* contrasts with *ren* or "benevolence":

> As a character of moral agents, benevolence has more to do with disposition and motive than objective circumstances. The reverse is true of rightness. Rightness is basically a character of acts and its application to agents is derivative. A man is righteous only in so far as he consistently does what is right. The rightness of acts depends on their being morally fitting in the circumstances and has little to do with the disposition or motive of the agent. .... no moral system can be solely based on moral virtues, and Confucius' system is no exception. .... Although Confucius does not state it explicitly, one cannot help getting the impression that he realizes that in the last resort *yi* is the standard by which all acts must be judged while there is no further standard by which *yi* itself can be judged. After all, even benevolence does not carry its own moral guarantee.[8]

The above characterizes what Lau refers to as an "act-ethics," as opposed to an "agent-ethics." Lau is claiming the priority of deontic concepts such as "duty" and "rightness" for any moral system, over aretaic concepts specifying aspects of a virtuous character, including dispositions and motives. Although the concept of *yi* can also refer to a virtue of character, it is held to refer more basically to the rightness of actions according to some standard. *Yi* or rightness is the ultimate standard by which all acts must be judged. This includes actions based upon the rules of ritual or *li*. This standard apparently also judges the virtues, dispositions and motives for as Lau puts it (above), "benevolence does not carry its own moral guarantee."

In stressing the rightness of actions according to some standard, Lau refers to the rules of ritual. But it is well-known that for Confucius, these rules are not to be mechanically applied, and there is much stress on the appropriate feelings, attitudes and emotions that go with the point of the ritual, for example, grief and respect. At the same time, however, rituals underscore a certain conservative orientation, and Confucius is well-known for having stressed the importance of tradition in providing for a stable and harmonious sociopolitical environment. The rituals provide a certain cultural and normative form, and Confucius complains that the society of his day is in chaos because people have ignored these forms. It would be artificial therefore, to impose the ethical framework provided by the distinctions of deontology and virtue onto Confucius' ethics, forgetting the sociohistorical context of his times and his concern to bring about social order amidst chaos. Having made these qualifications, however, we cannot but be struck by the fact that for Confucius, the notion of *yi* or "rightness" is not, philosophically speaking, something determinate. Thus Confucius says that "In his dealings with the world the gentleman is not invariably for or against anything. He is on the side of what is *yi* (4.10)." This is linked to another statement, "I have no preconceptions about the permissible and the impermissible (18.8)." Thus, instead of being a determinate principle of rightness, *yi* seems to constitute a basic moral orientation: "The gentleman has *yi* as his basic stuff (*zhi*) and by observing the rites puts it into practice, by being modest gives it expression, and by being trustworthy in word brings it to completion (15.18)."

As the "basic stuff" of a person, *yi* incorporates the following attitudes: not having a mean frame of mind that is merely concerned with profit (4.16); being able to enjoy the simple material conditions of life, and at the same time, indifferent to wealth and rank especially when they can only be obtained through improper means (7.16); and having moral courage (17.23). A deeper understanding of why these attitudes are morally important requires placing them within the ideal of *ren*. Although this can refer to a specific virtue of benevolence, it is also an ideal of moral excellence, or what Antonio Cua has referred to as an "ideal theme, as opposed to an ideal norm." The difference lies in the fact that where a norm provides a programmatic blueprint for action, a theme provides a conception of a quality and style of life which serves both as an inspiration and a point of orientation.[9] The perspective of *yi* that we have described is a part of this theme of life. In Confucius' ethics, one's actions are evaluated according to how well one exemplifies this theme.

Mencius takes the concept of *yi* further in moral psychological terms. He deepens the moral sense of *yi* by distinguishing it from the desires. Every human being is said to possess the sense of *yi* such that it is possible for people to be morally motivated, independently of desires and sometimes against the desires. In this regard, Mencius can be said to have an "internalist" thesis that is compatible with the Kantian, insofar as he holds that moral considerations can themselves be motivating, independently of the desires and emotions. However, Mencius does not pair this conception of moral motivation with the definition of morality in agent-neutral or impartialist terms. Neither is there any discussion of a rational will that discovers the moral law. Instead, the sense of *yi* is based upon a direct dispositional response to certain events. This response is placed within an account of human nature.

The account has a certain background or context. Mencius is anxious to combat the idea (promulgated by some thinkers during his time) that *yi* as rightness, or *ren yi* as morality are entirely human constructions with no basis in human nature. He is worried that if rightness and morality are conceived as entirely human constructs, this means that one is free to take more than one attitude toward them. In this regard, Mencius would not accept the following description of what it is to be virtuous that Slote gives in his interpretation of Aristotle: "being virtuous involves being keyed in to facts independent of one's virtuousness about what acts are admirable or called for." What would such facts be, or how may we describe them? One possibility is this. Taking Confucius' ethics as a framework, it is possible that someone does not live up to the emotions and attitudes that make up the spirit of the rites. In other words, she sees them as formal or mechanical rules to be followed, and as a matter of convention goes along with them, or at least tries not to transgress them. In this sense, the ritual rules are external to her. This notion of "external" provides one way of understanding what could be meant by "being keyed in to facts independent of one's virtuousness." In other words, various social, moral and political rules constitute independent moral facts that have to be taken into account or negotiated in one's actions. The virtues in this regard could incorporate prudence, sagacity, and the formation of habitual frames of mind that would enable one to be keyed in to or geared towards certain social and political facts, as well as facts about one's ultimate happiness.[10]

Mencius would reject this way of looking at the virtues. For him, they have a deeper relation to human psychology. The dispositions that form beginnings of virtue are not conventional norms, but an essential part of human nature. Mencius' conception of *yi* can be seen within the context of his debate on human nature with his philosophical opponent Gaozi (Kao Tzu). The latter holds that the categories of "good" (*shan*) and "not good" do not belong to human nature (*Mencius* 6A:6).[11] He believes that *ren yi* (translated by Lau as "morality") is something that is externally imposed on human nature. To Mencius, this is potentially morally subversive. As he says to Gaozi, it would bring "disaster upon morality (6A:1)." In the debate (6A:1–6A:5), Mencius questions Gaozi's usage of "internal" and "external." Gaozi understands "internal" in both a sociobiological sense as well in terms of the desires. That is, Gaozi understands *ren* in terms of the example of having an affection for a member of one's own family as against a non-member, and makes no distinction between such affection and the desires for food and sex. For Gaozi, *yi* is something that can be explained in terms of conventional norms. He takes the evincing of respect or reverence for someone as an instantiation of *yi* behavior. To him, respect is no different from say, a quality like "whiteness": the respect is the same, irrespective of whether it is for an elder from within my own family, or outside of it (just as the whiteness of different things remains white, 6A:4). Moreover, the respect accorded to someone can vary according to the circumstances. For example, although an elder may be given precedence on a certain occasion, he may have to give way to a younger person due to the higher status accorded to the latter, in another ceremonial context. This shows that *yi* is external (6A:5).

Mencius shows up the confusion in Gaozi's position. The fact that there is no difference in respect for an elder from my own family and an elder from outside my own family does not establish the "externality" of *yi*. For by the same logic, since there is no difference between enjoying my own roast or another's, one could also argue that (absurdly) my enjoyment of roast is "external" (6A:4). Similarly, although respect may vary according to the ceremonial context, this does not establish that respect is external. For by the same token, one may take a hot drink in winter but a cold drink in summer, but this does not establish that my desire to drink is "external" (6A:5).

The confusion in Gaozi's usage of "internal" and "external" throws doubt upon his thesis that *yi* is external. For it is uncertain what it means to say that *yi* is external given that (after Mencius' interrogation) one no longer has confidence in the suitability of Gaozi's usage of "internal/external." From Mencius' perspective, the so-called internality of the desires could just as well be external since the acquisition of what is desired is subject to various contingencies.[12] In this regard, to make no distinction between *ren* on the one hand, and the desires on the other, is to misunderstand the nature of *ren*. Similarly, to understand *yi* as "external" on Gaozi's construal of "internal/external" is a mistake. For Mencius, both mistakes show a lack of understanding of the full potentialities of human nature and what it is to be a human being.

According to Mencius' theory of the original goodness of human nature, all human beings possess the heart/mind (*xin*) of compassion; shame and loathing; respect; right and wrong (2A:6, 6A:6). These are referred to as "sprouts" that are originally present in human nature. There are difficulties with the evidence for this account. For instance, it can be questioned to what extent the well-known example of the child on the verge of falling into a well (2A:6) can be taken as evidence for the heart/mind of compassion. But we may evaluate what Mencius says not so much as an account of "original" human nature but of human moral psychology. From this perspective, what he says is not unreasonable, although by contemporary standards, a tough-minded philosopher could point out that the theoretical apparatus supporting his views are thin. In effect, according to Mencius, human beings are such that they have a sense of what it is to be related to others in certain ways, as well as conceptions of what limits there are on action. This includes both not doing or accepting certain things that are humanly unworthy, and not willingly accepting certain treatment of oneself (e.g., even a starving beggar may not pick up food thrown at him). A description of these attitudes brings out what Mencius means by the internality of *yi*.

Relevant to our discussion is the sprout of *xiu wu* or shame and loathing. This is the sprout or the beginning (*duan*) of *yi*. The examples that he discusses in 6A:10 are illustrations of *yi* (translated by Lau here as "dutifulness"): given a choice between life and (doing what is) *yi*, he (Mencius) would choose *yi* because "though life is what I want, there is something I want more than life." And even though I loathe (*wu*) death, "there is something I loathe more than death," and "there are ways of remaining alive and ways of avoiding death to which a man will not resort." Kwong-loi Shun has noted that the term *xiu* is closely linked to another, *chi*. The latter is "more like the attitude of regarding something as contemptible or as below oneself than like the emotion of shame." And "while *chi* is focused more on the thing that taints oneself, *xiu* is focused more on the way the self is tainted by that thing." *Yi* is linked to these attitudes, and as such it is a self-directed term: "it involves a concern to distance oneself from situations that are below oneself, as measured by certain standards to which one is committed. In fact, the character for righteousness (*yi*) was initially either a near relative of or derived from the character for "I" (*wo*), and it had the earlier meaning of a proper regard for oneself or a sense of honor."[13]

Confucius' distinction between *li** (considerations of profit) and *yi* is taken up by Mencius. In fact, the distinction is stressed in the *Mencius* right from the beginning (1A:1). Mencius peremptorily dismisses King Hui of Liang's attempt to talk of how he can profit his state. Instead, Mencius wishes to discuss *ren* and *yi*, and points to the dire consequences that can follow if everyone thinks in terms of how they can profit themselves, their families and their states. "No benevolent man ever abandons his parents, and no (*yi*) man ever puts his prince last." Benevolence, for Mencius, is not a desire like the desire for food and sex, but involves feelings like affection for parents as the basis of filial piety, compassion in the sense of being unable to bear the suffering of others, and a general concern for others. In this regard, benevolence and *yi* are internal to human psychology and involve feelings and values that are not equivalent to mere desires.

Mencius elaborates upon the connection between *yi* and courage. In 2A:2, he provides lively examples of different forms of courage. First, there is the brutish courage of the person who never showed "submission on his face" or let anyone "outstare him." For this person, "to yield the tiniest bit was as humiliating," and he would "no more accept an insult from a prince ... than from a common fellow coarsely clad. He would as soon run a sword through the prince as through the common fellow. He had no respect for persons, and always returned whatever harsh tones came his way." Second, we have a description of the person who looks "upon defeat as victory," and regards someone who calculates the chances of victory before weighing in to be "simply showing cowardice in face of superior numbers." Although Mencius thinks that the second person "had a firm grasp of the essential" compared to the first, there is yet a third and even more superior form of courage. Here he quotes the disciple of Confucius, Zengzi (Tseng Tzu) who recounts what he had heard from the Master about supreme courage: "If, on looking within, one finds oneself to be in the wrong, then even though one's adversary be only a common fellow coarsely clad one is bound to tremble with fear. But if one finds oneself in the right, one goes forward even against men in the thousands." Mencius goes on to talk of the relation between the will and *qi* and what he calls *hao ran zhi qi* (Lau: "flood-like *qi*"). This is something that requires more extensive investigation and cannot be undertaken here.[14] But to quote Mencius:

> This is a *qi* which is, in the highest degree, vast and unyielding. Nourish it with integrity and place no obstacle in its path and it will fill the space between Heaven and Earth. It is a *qi* which unites *yi* and the Way. Deprive it of these and it will collapse. It is born of accumulated *yi* and cannot be appropriated by anyone through a sporadic show of *yi*. Whenever one acts in a way that falls below the standard set in one's heart, it will collapse. Hence I said Kao Tzu [Gaozi] never

> understood rightness (*yi*) because he looked upon it as external. You must work at it and never let it out of your mind. At the same time, while you must never let it out of your mind, you must not forcibly help it grow either (2A:2).

Presumably, the development of *yi* is such that it requires a patient nurturing of one's sprout of shame and loathing, giving one a kind of courage that is contrasted with the other forms of courage described earlier. There is a motivational power to moral courage that makes it superior to these other forms of courage, and perhaps *hao ran zhi qi* refers to the vital energy that makes this possible. Mencius is therefore illustrating the internality of *yi*, as we may gather from his reference to Gaozi not having understood *yi* because he regarded it as external.[15]

EXTERNAL STANDARDS

We have discussed the sense in which *yi* is a moral orientation for Confucius and an internal disposition for Mencius. Some writers have noted that there is a presumption in the *Mencius* that *yi* enables us to judge the appropriateness of *li* (the rites, ritual principles) in some sense that is independent of the appeal to *li* itself.[16] This could be interpreted in two ways. First, this could mean that *yi* is still internal, involving the dispositions, motives and attitudes that are involved in the spirit of *li*. Second, this could point instead to some external standard, in terms of what it is reasonable or rational to do. For besides the sprouts mentioned, the heart/mind seems also to have the ability to make reasoned judgments, suggesting the ability to discern reasonable standards. This possibility arises in 6A:7, where Mencius refers to the fact that "reason (*li***) and rightness (*yi*)" are common (*tong ran*) to all heart/minds. This could be interpreted as the fact that the heart/mind has the ability to make reasonable judgments, and also that the heart-mind has ideal objects which it commonly approves, just as the sensory organs do. In the earlier sentences of 6A:7, reference is made to certain sages who are said to have discovered certain objects of taste, hearing and sight, etc. Similarly, reason and rightness are also things that the heart/mind approves of.[17]

Despite this possibility, the concept of *li*** or reason is mentioned in conjunction with *yi* in 6A:7 without explanation. Its only other reference in the *Mencius* is in 5B:1 where it occurs as *tiao li* or a kind of pattern/order in the context of the orderly progression of music, and analogously, the beginning and end of wisdom and sageness. Undoubtedly, Mencius had a clear idea of what is reasonable. This is shown in 4A:17 where the ritual taboo of touching one's sister-in-law's hand is overruled when she is drowning. This is an application of *quan* or "weighing" the situation. Despite the fact that Mencius is reasonable, this should not entitle us to conclude that Mencius understood *yi* in terms of external standards. The earlier discussion points more to an understanding of *yi* as an internal disposition.

But in case it should be thought that this is the end of the story for Confucianism, it must be pointed out that for another Confucian, Xunzi (who comes after Mencius), *li*** or reason becomes prominent. For Xunzi, morality and the laws are possible because they have a (external) rationale that can be known and practiced. Xunzi is of the opinion that everyone has the cognitive capacity to learn this rationale, as well as the instrumental capacity to carry out what one has learned. However, one may not, for various reasons, be able to learn fully or to carry out what one has learned, despite having the capacity.[18] It might appear that there is room here for the suggestion of moral principles or standards that are independent of the virtues, with the implication that the virtues are only means towards the discovery or perception of these principles or standards. But the picture is more complicated, and in his discussion of the relation between *yi* and *li*, A. S. Cua notes that *yi* is an ethical notion that can be explicated in deontic, aretaic, epistemic and psychological terms. In this regard, it is a "plurisign adaptable to a range of meaning or significance in the various contexts of discourse."[19] Although he gives some prominence to the "epistemic" function of *yi* that focuses on reasoned judgment, involving explanation and justification of ethical judgments, Cua is careful to note that "the question of priority regarding *li* and *i* [*yi*] cannot be answered in an absolute or abstract statement of priority. It is a contextual question to be answered in dealing with the normal and changing circumstances of life."[20] In the final analysis, Cua reverts to the interdependence of the basic Confucian virtues (*ren*, *li*, and *yi*) as "constitutive rather than mere instrumental means to the fulfillment of *tao* [*dao*]."[21] In effect, this brings us back to his idea of an "ideal theme" or the orientation of a form of life mentioned earlier.

CONCLUSION

Earlier, we discussed Slote's example of the benevolent woman who has to decide whether to take "heroic measures" to save her mother. Her care for her mother is what disposes her to find out more about the facts of the situation and in this sense directs her actions. The objection to this is that benevolence and care are not sufficient for right action. Someone who is benevolent and caring can still do the wrong thing. In order to clarify the nature and significance of virtue ethics, we brought in the example of Dorothea, where I would contend that the notion of her acting wrongly is out of place, if this is based on criteria that are independent of her dispositions, motives and character. Her decision to promise Casaubon to complete his work after his death is based on personal commitment and trust. Thus, although one could come to the "same" decision based on agent-neutral considerations, the sense of her action is different. What it is right to do is governed by her commitment and trust, and the disposition of her character.

Both Confucius and Mencius have a conception of rightness which is not independent of character, and both emphasize emotions, attitudes and feelings as expressive of right action. This sits well with recent arguments by Western virtue ethicists that it is not necessarily the case that the right thing to do is to maximize certain ends. Instead, it could be that in certain central cases of the moral life, what is important is that certain values be expressed or instantiated.[22] In this regard, we may say that for the virtue ethicist, the virtues exemplifying the goodness of a conception of life are not instrumental means to the good, but instead constitutive of the good. The virtue concept of *yi*, together with the ideal of *ren* make up the early Confucian perspective of good, or more broadly (as Antonio Cua puts it) an "ideal theme" of life.

Mencius, as we have seen, stresses the internality of *yi* or rightness. This conception of rightness is in turn rooted in a conception of what it is to be a human being, with the capacity to relate to others compassionately, with feelings of shame and loathing, with a sense of modesty and courtesy, and with a sense of rightness. This is a reminder, if you like (since there will be objections to its adequacy as a "theory"), of what it is to be a human being. In other words, human beings are not simply biological agents with various uncontrollable appetitive and sensory desires. And the motivational reasons for moral action are not like the desires. Instead, they are independent of the desires and can judge or limit the desires.

This is similar to Kant's view of moral motivation, but with the important difference that the motivation comes from the heart, and is not a function of pure reason.

The notion of what is reasonable or rational is certainly present in both Confucius and Mencius, but not in a way that can be explicated very much beyond the virtues. In Xunzi, the notion of *li***, variously translated as "pattern," "reason," "rationale," "principles of rationality," etc., is taken much further. But as we have seen, this is not unqualified, and it should not be automatically concluded that Xunzi must be interpreted in either deontological or consequentialist terms. It could be that for Xunzi, the virtues are better instantiated through the establishment of certain institutional structures, instead of being left to individual virtuous effort. But this would be a topic for further exploration.

NOTES

1 Marcia Baron, "Kantian Ethics," in Marcia W. Baron, Philip Pettit, and Michael Slote, *Three Methods of Ethics* (Oxford: Blackwell, 1997), pp. 35–38. Hereafter abbreviated as *TME*.

2 Michael Slote, "Virtue Ethics," in *TME*. Although I shall only be referring to *TME*, Slote's views can also be found in his paper "Agent-Based Virtue Ethics," Roger Crisp and Michael Slote (ed.), *Virtue Ethics* (Oxford: Oxford University Press, 1997) and in his book *Moral Motives* (Oxford: Oxford University Press, 2001).

3 It might be pointed out that consequentialism does not fall under the category of being deontic because of its teleological focus on the good and the derivative nature of the right as maximizing the good. But Slote is concerned to contrast virtue ethics with "ethics of rules" that "characterize acts as morally right or wrong, morally permissible or obligatory, depending on how they accord with appropriate rules." Slote refers to these "moral epithets" as "deontic." (Slote, *TME* 177). I thank A. T. Nuyen for pointing out the need for some clarification here.

4 "Agent-neutral" and "agent-relative" are terms made popular by Thomas Nagel, *The View from Nowhere* (Oxford: Oxford University Press, 1986). See p. 152: "If a reason can be given a general form which does not include an essential reference to the person who has it, it is an *agent-neutral* reason ... If on the other hand the general form of a reason does include an essential reference to the person who has it, it is an *agent-relative* reason."

5 Gregory Trianosky, "What is Virtue Ethics All About?" *American Philosophical Quarterly* 27:4 (1990), p. 335.

6 George Eliot, *Middlemarch* (Harmondsworth: Penguin, 1976). The example concerns events in chapters 48–50 of the novel. I have discussed this example in more detail elsewhere, but in the context of theories of rationality. See Kim-chong Chong, *Moral Agoraphobia: The Challenge of Egoism* (New York: Peter Lang, 1996), pp. 70–73. Interestingly, Greg Pence, "Virtue Theory,"

in Peter Singer (ed.) *A Companion to Ethics* (Oxford: Blackwell, 1991), begins his discussion of virtue ethics by mentioning Dorothea's problem: "For most of the novel, Dorothea struggles with herself and agonizes over questions like, 'What kind of person would I be if I leave him (Casaubon)? If I stay?'" Pence comments, "It is just such questions of how one ought to live in shaping one's own character that have recently engaged moral philosophy." See Singer (ed.), p. 249.

7 D. C. Lau (trans.), *Confucius: The Analects* (Harmondsworth: Penguin, 1979), pp. 26–27. Translations and passage numbers follow this text. Lau translates *yi* variously as the moral quality of an act: "right," "duty"; an obligatory act: "righteous," "dutiful"; descriptive of an agent: "righteous," "dutiful." I have discussed Lau's views on *yi* in more detail in "The Aesthetic Moral Personality: *Li, Yi, Wen* and *Chih* in the *Analects*," *Monumenta Serica* 46 (1998). (Another version of this paper was published without permission as "Confucius' Virtue Ethics: *Li, Yi, Wen* and *Chih* in the *Analects*," *Journal of Chinese Philosophy* 25 [1998]).

8 Lau, p. 27.

9 A. S. Cua, "Confucian Vision and Experience of the World," in his *Moral Vision and Tradition*, (Washington D.C.: Catholic University of America Press, 1998), p. 30.

10 I take it that this is one way in which Aristotle's ethics can be characterized, with the goal of *eudaimonia* broadly construed as a form of happiness.

11 Translations and passage numbers follow D. C. Lau (trans.), *Mencius* (Hong Kong: Chinese University Press, 1984), 2 Volumes.

12 See, for example, 7A:3 where Mencius says: "Seek and you will get it; let go and you will lose it. If this is the case, then seeking is of use to getting and what is sought is within yourself. But if there is a proper way to seek it and whether you get it or not depends on Destiny, then seeking is of no use to getting and what is sought lies outside yourself."

13 Kwong-loi Shun, "Self and Self-Cultivation in Early Confucian Thought," in Bo Mou (ed.), *Two Roads to Wisdom? Chinese and Analytic Philosophical Traditions* (Chicago and La Salle, Illinois: Open Court, 2001), p. 236. The following passages in the *Mencius* should also be considered. 4B:8, "Only when there are things a man will not do is he capable of doing great things." 5B:7, "A man whose mind is set on high ideals never forgets that he may forfeit his head," said in the context of being summoned improperly. 3B:1, where there is the example of the charioteer who refuses to go along with the underhanded methods of the archer. Here too, we have the mention of *xiu* and what one will not (bring oneself to) do.

14 But see the discussion in Kwong-loi Shun, *Mencius and Early Chinese Thought* (Stanford: Stanford University Press, 1997), pp. 115–119. Also, Jeffrey Riegel, "Reflections on an Unmoved Mind," *Journal of the American Academy of Religion*, Thematic Issue 47:3 (1979): 433–457.

15 Kwong-loi Shun's explanation is as follows: "What Kao Tzu [Gaozi] did was to obtain *yi* from ethical doctrines, impose it on the heart/mind, and then let it guide *ch'i* [*qi*] ... Kao Tzu did not know *yi* because he regarded it as external and was therefore mistaken about its source, and he was not good at nourishing *ch'i* because he was helping *ch'i* grow by imposing a mistaken

conception of *yi* from the outside. The observation that *ch'i* will collapse if it does not unite with *tao* (the Way) and *yi* suggests that Mencius probably thought that Kao Tzu's unmoved heart/mind would not last, since it was not rooted in a correct conception of *yi*." Shun, *Mencius and Early Chinese Thought*, p.119.

16 See Shun, *ibid.*, p. 57. See also A. S. Cua's discussion of the relation between *yi* and *li* in "Basic Conceptions of Confucian Ethics," in his *Moral Vision and Tradition* (Washington D.C.: Catholic University of America Press, 1998).

17 In 6A:15, Mencius also says, "The organs of hearing and sight are unable to think and can be misled by external things. The organ of the heart can think. But it will find the answer only if it does think; otherwise, it will not find the answer." The word for "think" is *si*. This need not be interpreted as some rational cognitive capacity that is extra to the sprouts of the heart/mind. Instead, Mencius is lamenting that some people have lost their original heart/mind and only if they consider what they inherently have will they be able to recover its contents, i.e., the moral sprouts.

18 See John Knoblock, *Xunzi: A Translation and Study of the Complete Works* Vol. 3 (Stanford: Stanford University Press, 1994), passages 23.5a and 23.5b. Knoblock translates *li*** as "rational principles."

19 A. S. Cua, "Basic Concepts of Confucian Ethics," *ibid.*, p. 278.

20 Ibid., p. 283.

21 Ibid., p. 283.

22 Marcia Baron, "Kantian Ethics," in *TME*, p. 23, citing Christine Swanton, "Profiles of the Virtues," *Pacific Philosophical Quarterly* 76 (1995): 47–72.

CHINESE GLOSSARY

ben xin	本 心
chi	恥
dao	道
duan	端
hao ran zhi qi	浩 然 之 氣
li	禮
*li**	利
*li***	理
quan	權
ren	仁
ren yi	仁 義
shan	善
si	思
tiao li	條 理
tong ran	同 然
wo	我
wu	惡
xin	心
xiu wu	羞 惡
yi	義
zhi	質

CHAPTER 4

Questioning Kṛṣṇa's Kantianism

AMBER DANIELLE CARPENTER

It has been claimed that we are best off seeing Kṛṣṇa—at least as he is depicted in his conversation with Arjuna in the *Bhagavadgītā*—as a sort of deontologist, an extreme sort.[1] As the prince Arjuna's confidante and advisor, Kṛṣṇa insists that Arjuna enter into battle with his brothers, against their half-brothers and teachers who have usurped the throne. Like Kant, Kṛṣṇa speaks in terms of duties—duties whose claim on us cannot be over-ridden by any other sort of considerations. I want to dispute this characterisation of Kṛṣṇa, firstly, to contest the interpretation of the *niṣkāma karma* (desireless action) principle on which the charge of deontology rests. But I want to dispute it also, and more importantly, because I think Kṛṣṇa's moral voice is rather more rich and interesting than our classifications of "deontological" and "consequentialist" (even broad consequentialist) allow.

I. *NISKAMĀ KARMA*

The best case to be made in favor of Kṛṣṇa as a deontologist is his support of the view famously articulated in that part of the *Mahābhārata* excised and treated separately as the *Bhagavadgītā*. A considerable portion of the *Gītā* dwells on the principle that one should not act with a view to the fruits of one's labors. "Work alone is your proper business, never the fruits: let not your motive be the fruit of works ..." (II.47).[2] Isolated from its epic context, and developed as an independent view, this principle has indeed acquired, as Sen writes, "great theological importance."[3]

Is this view—*niṣkāma karma*, that perfect action is not done with a view to the fruits—rightly regarded as 'high deontology'? Even where 'deontology' need have nothing in particular to do with Kant's arguments, but has rather to do with a hostility to consequentialist thinking—"doing one's duty irrespective of consequences"[4]—I think the answer is "no". In order to count as deontological, in the strongest sense, the *niṣkāma karma* ideal would have to be interpreted as advising that we act (rightly) when we act without any regard for what *any of* the consequences are. But this is not, in fact, what Kṛṣṇa says.

In fact, Kṛṣṇa says, "... so unattached, should the wise man do, longing to bring about the welfare [and coherence] of the world" (III.25).[5] When acting well, we should after all have an eye on some consequences—on just the sort of impersonally considered, overall, sorts of consequences familiar from classical consequentialism. The injunction to "act, longing to bring bout the welfare of the world" is a strikingly utilitarian attitude. There is some way that it would be good for the world to be, and good action is that which arises out of a desire to make the world better than it is. Kṛṣṇa, however, does not quite say that, that end-state is what I should look to when considering whether an action is right or wrong, good or bad. In fact, as we shall see more closely later on, Kṛṣṇa's view as the *Gītā* develops is disturbingly free from any useful or practical advice for distinguishing right acts from wrong, disturbing especially when what is at stake is whether or not to wage war on one's power-hungry brethren. But however we are to discern right from wrong action, it is at least clear that Kṛṣṇa's endorsement of *niṣkāma karma* does not rest on a rejection of *all* consequences as informing the rightness or wrongness of an act. His point is rather that I must act, if I am to act well, without concern for whether the consequences benefit me. "Hold pleasure and pain, profit and loss, victory and defeat to be the same" (II.38). I must not look to whether I get some profit from the act. I should not, when considering how to act, be looking for *rewards*—"Be without personal aspirations or concern for possessions, and fight unconcernedly" (III.30).

Now this looks deontological inasmuch as Kant, for example, argued vehemently that acting for the sake of reward—for the sake of mere happiness—destroyed the moral worth of an act. Personal gain as a motivation extinguishes whatever was especially "morally" good in the action. One might think this Kantian view of the fragility (and exclusivity) of moral worth implausibly hard. For if I return the wallet in order to get the reward, it still seems something good was done, and I did the right thing, even if it was a less than perfect act; and if that greengrocer prices his goods fairly because he knows that he can only retain customers if he builds their trust, there is something good—even morally, not merely instrumentally good, or pleasant—in his fair pricing policy.

But when Kṛṣṇa advocates acting without a view to rewards, he does not seem to be endorsing something even so strong as the hard-hearted view outlined above, that there is *no* worth in action done for the sake of reward.[6] This will be partly because "worth" is not divided between moral and non-moral: If an action is to retain any worth, it will be also moral worth, or it will be as much distinctively "moral" worth as the fully perfect action. But the *niṣkāma karma* view remains deontological in its emphasis on the importance of motivation. A selfishly motivated act may be a somewhat good one, or the partially right thing to do; but non-selfish motivation invariably issues in better action. "The act as such is far inferior to the application of singleness of purpose to it" (II.49). Right motivation alone always improves the quality of an act; but whether or not a motivation is right is determined in part by *which* sorts of consequences one looks to in deciding what to do.

There might be two reasons one might invoke to support this claim that right motivation always improves the quality of an act. Non-selfish motivation might issue invariably in better action because there is some special, intrinsic goodness to non-selfish motivations.[7] All non-selfishly motivated action includes the fact that there has been some non-selfish motivation going on, and this is good in itself. Or, one might think that non-selfish motivation invariably issues in better action because it is only freedom from interest in reward that helps one to see clearly what is in fact to be done—what one's duties in fact are *and/or* what overall state-of-affairs would be preferred. I think the latter is a preferable way of reading the *niṣkāma karma* doctrine, and shall have more to say about this later. It would put Kṛṣṇa and the principle of *niṣkāma karma* neither in the deontological nor the consequentialist camp. If we are looking for post-Enlightenment bedfellows, the principle of non-selfish action taken on its own bears more similarity to impersonalist doctrines of all sorts than it bears to deontology in particular.[8] In fact, I think this resemblance is also illusory, and perhaps more misleading than helpful, if we are to see what is philosophically engaging in the conversation between Kṛṣṇa and Arjuna, in the early chapters of the *Bhagavadgītā*. But before considering this, we should look at Arjuna's arguments against going into battle.

II. ARJUNA'S NON-CONSEQUENTIALISM

There is something else wrong with the picture of Kṛṣṇa as the arch-deontologist, oblivious to consequences, trying to persuade a consequence-sensitive Arjuna to fight. While it is true that Kṛṣṇa recommends that Arjuna fight because it is his duty, Arjuna's reluctance to fight is equally based on a sense of duty. In fact, he is eager to clarify that it is not consequences that he has in mind when he considers whether the war is right: "I do not long for victory," he says, "nor for the kingdom nor yet for things of pleasure" (I.32), "I do not want to kill them, though they be killers, Madhusūdana, even for the sovereignty of the three worlds, let alone earth!" (I.35)—all of these being the best possible consequences that could come from war, from Arjuna's point of view. He is duty-bound—in fact, everyone is duty-bound—not to wage war on their teachers, elders, and brethren. "For, Kṛṣṇa, were we to lay low our own folk, how could we be happy? And even if, bereft of sense by greed, they cannot see that to ruin a family is wickedness and to break one's word a crime, how should we not be wise enough to shun this evil thing, for we clearly see that to ruin a family is wickedness" (I.37–39). Arjuna is not just expressing a preference, reluctant to face up to a rather unpleasant but (morally) necessary task—giving an honest opinion of an elderly aunt's hideous hat, or telling the axe-wielding psychopath at the door where to find the kids. Arjuna counters Kṛṣṇa's claim that it is his duty to fight with the counter-claim that it is equally, or more, his duty *not* to fight. "We have *no right* to kill the sons of Dhṛtarāṣṭra and their kin" (I.37).[9] Arjuna appeals to very general—universalisable—claims about what is to be done and not to be done.[10] It is not his duty in particular, but *everyone's* duty to refrain from waging war on one's family and teachers. Waging war on one's family is not to be done—ever, by anyone. The point is cast in quite impersonal terms at I.40*ff.*, concluding with Arjuna's dismay that "we have resolved to commit a great crime as we stand ready to kill family out of greed for kingship and pleasures" (I.45). And a few lines later, Arjuna says, "Better were it here on Earth to eat a beggar's food than to slay [our] teachers" (II.5).[11] Finally, in an argument typically invoked against consequentialists, Arjuna adds, "Besides, we do not know which is for us the better part, whether that we should win the victory or that they should conquer us" (II.6). Since both the actual consequences, and the relative value of various consequences is not something we can judge in advance (or perhaps at all), we must, in deciding what to do, stick to certain principles.

If we still thought Kṛṣṇa was a deontologist, it might look now as if we've got *two* arch-Kantians on our hands, locked in dispute over just which maxim, in this particular instance, can in fact be willed universally without contradiction. Such disputes can certainly arise, even in the Kantian moral world in which only the possible can be morally necessary; Kant's description—or rather, re-description of moral dilemmas as the conflict between a "ground" for action (Ross's "prima facia duties") and an actual reason (determining a moral duty) would make such a dispute, in certain circumstances, likely.[12] Sometimes, some thing has all the look of a moral duty, but it is not one. And it is natural to suppose that disputes would in such cases arise—what else could be the point of exercising public reason?

Yet if we consider further the progression of the discussion between Arjuna and Kṛṣṇa, we have reason to doubt whether this is a battle between two deontologists over what is morally required, reasons that go beyond our interpretation of the *niṣkāma karma* principle.

III. DIVINE COMMAND—A CAVEAT, AND RESTATEMENT OF THE PUZZLE

In describing "Kṛṣṇa's view" in the *Mahābhārata*, and particularly in the *Bhagavadgītā*, I shall be considering primarily the first few chapters of the discussion between Kṛṣṇa and Arjuna—I shall be considering, that is, those chapters in which there is something resembling a discussion. In so doing, I will be setting aside several chapters in which something with perhaps more right to be called "Kṛṣṇa's view" is developed. In order to explain why, I shall summarize the remainder of the *Gītā*, as it relates to the pressing question: Should Arjuna do battle against his wicked kin?

Kṛṣṇa's first attempt to give Arjuna a reason to fight relies on the immortality and unparalleled value of the soul. The soul is eternal, and it alone has value—therefore, we should not fear killing someone, since after all we do his immortal soul no harm. "The wise are not sorry for either the living or the dead. Never was there a time when I did not exist, or you, or these kings, nor shall any of us cease to exist hereafter" (II.11–12). Arjuna is rightly dissatisfied with this response to the problem. For even if it makes it the case that killing one's kin, or anyone else, does not annihilate them, neither is it a strong argument in favor of such a course of action. Arjuna notes that if the soul generally is supremely valuable, then far from giving reason to fight, Kṛṣṇa has given Arjuna reason to devote *himself* to the life of the mind. "If you think that the soul is loftier than the acts," he asks, "then why do you command me to do a cruel deed?" (III.1)

Kṛṣṇa responds by introducing the principle of *niṣkāma karma*. And he grounds the value of detached action (at least in part) in the fact that this is the sort of action God engages in. "In the three worlds there is nothing that I need do," says Kṛṣṇa, "nor anything unattained that I need to gain, yet action [is the element] in which I move" (III.22). And further, Kṛṣṇa argues that while He has done the work of establishing the order of the universe (especially the social order), "I am the doer, [the agent]" and yet "[I am] the Changeless One who does not do [or act]. Actions never affect Me. I have no yearning for their fruits... Knowing this the ancients too did act, though seeking release: so do you act as the ancients did in the days of old" (IV.13–15). The argument seems to put together two common ideas: (1) God is self-sufficient, and not in want of anything;[13] and (2) to make ourselves as like God as possible is to make ourselves as good as possible.[14] In Kṛṣṇa's view, since God acts without wanting to get anything out of it, so too should human beings act. This desireless acting is presented by Kṛṣṇa as a devotional act. The appropriate attitude to take into deciding how to act is a devotional rather than an acquisitive one. Thus action is taken in the spirit of a sacrifice (IV.24–33).

But this, so far, is a purely procedural consideration—it indicates a rule for *how* to do what we do, not for what to do. Again, Arjuna notices that this does not adequately address the question; it gives him no more reason to fight than not to fight. Thus in Chapter VIII, he is still asking, "What is that which appertains to self? What, O best of men, are the works? What is that called which appertains to contingent beings? What is that which appertains to the divine?" (VIII.1). Kṛṣṇa's advice seems to be, "Whatever you do, do it out of devotion to God, and not for personal profit." But as far as that goes, it seems perfectly compatible with Arjuna dropping his weapons, and walking away from the fight—not in order to save his own life, nor in order to avoid killing his kin, but simply in the spirit of devotion. We might say, for example, that Arjuna is renouncing the battle-field glory, sacrificing it to Brahman, and thus his action—walking away from the battle—is a pure and good one. Procedural constraints alone, where these are explained in terms of maintaining a certain mind-set, cannot decide which of two actions ought to be done (devotionally).

I do not mean to dismiss the claim that devotion as a virtue should have on us. But it does not answer Arjuna's question, and at least for a spell, Arjuna realises this, and presses the point. We still need to know what works or deeds it is that God requires or recommends we do out of devotion to Him—unless He is equally happy with whatever we do, so long as we do it disinterestedly (in which case Arjuna would have no reason in particular to fight).

This line of thought is precisely the one that Kṛṣṇa follows in the *Bhagavadgītā*. For ultimately, the reason he gives Arjuna to fight is that He, Kṛṣṇa, is God—and He says, "Fight." This, of course, does give Arjuna a good reason to fight. When God truly shows Himself, and says, "Do X," then we are rightly overwhelmed as Arjuna is, by awe and humility and devotion (XI.14, 34), and see incontrovertibly that X is to be done—for that is what God commands. "Here I stand with no more doubts. I shall do as you say" (XVIII.73). Such a reason needs no further explanation, for a genuine divine command is pretty much the best reason there can be for an action, given the nature of God.[15]

But taking Kṛṣṇa as a character within a dialogue trying to determine what is right, and why, we are still left with a mystery on our hands. For divine command merely tells us what Arjuna ought to do, and why *he* is motivated to do it. But we still do not have an argument for *why* Arjuna should fight. Why, we still wonder, is Kṛṣṇa so determined that Arjuna should fight? Kṛṣṇa presumably knows that, whatever the outcome of the battle, it will involve near-universal devastation on all sides. After all, Arjuna's suggestion is not the cowardly one that he alone should skive off, save his own skin but leave the others to the dirty business of killing and dying. He wants rather that his side of the war as a whole should give up their just claim to the kingdom, thereby averting mass destruction of many innocent and worthy lives (I.31–39). Is Kṛṣṇa's rejection of this suggestion simply wilful and wanton—He wants to see a good fight, and a good fight He will see?—or beyond our understanding? Perhaps it has not given us to peer into the mind of God, or to *understand* what makes something good and right, or bad and wrong.

While this may ultimately be the best interpretation of the *Gītā* available to us, Kṛṣṇa does, at first, try to give Arjuna *arguments*, and *reasons*. And, in fact, even after Arjuna has seen and accepted Kṛṣṇa's divinity, his dissatisfaction merely returns in a different form: Granted that we are to do what is commanded by God, how, Arjuna asks, do we reliably distinguish what is divine, or divinely commanded, from what is not? Thus after seeing Kṛṣṇa's divine form, but before agreeing that his duty is to fight, Arjuna asks, "How may I know you, yogin, in my constant meditations? In what various modes of being may I meditate on you, my lord?" (X.17). Looking at the many reasons Kṛṣṇa tries to give for pressing Arjuna to battle, we find a less capricious sort of explanation for why it is good and right that Arjuna lead his brothers into battle. For Arjuna, this will play itself out in the various ways in which "meditation on the self" can inform one of the right course of action.

IV. KṚṢṆA'S PARTICULARISM—*SVADHARMA*

For all that certain modes of expression sound superficially like an impersonal universalism, both Arjuna and Kṛṣṇa acknowledge as morally relevant aspects of the situation that could only have extremely narrow application. Thus the reasons given will sometimes be reasons personal to Arjuna. Thus if we look at the terms in which Kṛṣṇa casts his appeal to duty (*dharma*), they are not usually of the "Kantian", universalisable kind, nor are all of them even loosely deontological (universal), or general principles or obligations. On the contrary, in *svadharma* ("one's own duty", or "one's personal duty") there is a notion of duty at work irreconcilable with a Kantian sort of duty.

Kṛṣṇa levels a whole battery of arguments against Arjuna's unwillingness to fight. Some of these can be implied from the name-calling that is supposed to humiliate Arjuna into going into battle. For example, "Do not act like a eunuch, Pārtha, it does not become you! Rid yourself of this vulgar weakness of heart, stand up, enemy-burner!" (II.3) It is not *fitting* for Arjuna to act "unmanly"; perhaps it would be suitable for someone who was genuinely weak, ill-prepared, or accustomed to other sorts of tasks to back out of the battle. But none of these is true of Arjuna. Hesitation now, in the final hour, is specifically a "cowardice unseemly *to the noble*" (II.2).[16] The final name Kṛṣṇa applies to Arjuna evokes the sort of quality that is properly his—'enemy-burner.' Naturally, in the context of epic verse, it is common for persons to be addressed by a multitude of names, many of them descriptive. But the choice of that description here emphasizes that it is of Arjuna's character not to leave his enemies standing; and that it is unseemly for such a person as Arjuna is to walk away from the battle. In Arjuna's case, to walk away now would be to *play* the eunuch—to act the role of someone he is not.

Recalling Arjuna to himself, as grounds for entering into the fray, does not just take the form of appealing to his particular personality, however. While Kṛṣṇa argues that killing is irrelevant, for the killed are not destroyed, he directs his argument specifically to Arjuna as having a certain place in society. Arjuna is the generic "strong-armed prince" (II.26). Twice, he is appealed to specifically as the "son of Kuntī" ("Kaunteya",

II.15, II.38), and twice as Pārtha, the son of Pṛthā (another of Kuntī's names,[17] II.21, II.42). As Kṛṣṇa moves from this argument into the *niṣkāma karma* doctrine, via an argument about the importance of "singleness of purpose" (II.41), Arjuna becomes the "scion of Kuru" (II.42), or literally "bull of the Kuru (clan/family/race)."[18] Again, the claim is not that it is somehow extraordinary that Kṛṣṇa should call Arjuna by his patronymic, or in this case metronymic; rather that just these epithets are used here in order to recall to Arjuna his social situatedness—he has certain relations within a particular family, he is a son of just this woman and no other. This place he holds within a certain family, and particularly as the son of just this woman, has a claim on him. It is *as* the son of Kuntī that Arjuna should "rise up, resolved upon battle" (II.37). It is as the great hope for the honour of the Kuru race, as the bull of the Kurus, that he should be unhesitatingly resolved to act. In the same 35 couplets, before the "desireless action" doctrine is introduced (II.11–46), Kṛṣṇa three times addresses Arjuna as "Bhārata", identifying him as a descendant of the universal monarch who gave his name to the people arrayed on both sides of the battle lines, thus calling attention to another aspect of Arjuna's social identity (II.15, II.18, II.28), and perhaps recalling to him the expectations and mores peculiar to his people.

These epithets are finally accompanied by an explicit appeal to the values of his station. For Arjuna is a prince of the warrior class. And for *him*, it would be a great evil to live in shame, although it may not be a great evil for another sort of person: "for one who has been honored, dishonor is worse than death," says Kṛṣṇa (II.34). "There is nothing more salutary for a *kṣatriya* than a lawful war. It is an open door to heaven" (II.31–32). It is appropriate to recall that Arjuna's objection to fighting was that it *must* be unlawful to kill one's kin, even if they have wronged you, humiliated you, dispossessed and tried to assassinate you. By insisting that the battle now with the offending kinsmen is a lawful one, Kṛṣṇa implicitly recalls their offences. In arguing for war, Kṛṣṇa is arguing also that these offences committed against Arjuna and his brothers require punishment by Arjuna.

Especially humiliating to Arjuna is the thought that, if he turns away from the battle now, people will not only say that he is a coward: his "ill-wishers will spread many unspeakable tales about [him], condemning [his] skill—and what is more miserable than that?" (II.36) Arjuna is the star pupil of the foremost archer of his time; his bow, Gāṇḍīva, is a gift from the Gods in honor to Arjuna's skill. From such renown and accomplishment, to be reduced to cowardly *and* incompetent in the mouths of men is insufferable. Moreover, in bringing these thoughts forward, Kṛṣṇa asserts that it is not wrong to take such "personal" considerations into account. It would mean something for *Arjuna* to turn away from battle, that it would not mean for an ordinary foot-soldier to do the same. And this difference in meaning must be taken into account as one of the real factors determining the rightness of a course of action. Thus one of the reasons why Arjuna should fight is that he has, through no choice of his own, the stature to act as an example to others. "For it was by acting alone that Janaka and others achieved success, so you too must act while only looking to what holds together the world. People do whatever the superior man does: people follow what he sets up as the standard" (III.20–21).

These questions of station, of reputation and skill, of family, amount to "one's own law"—*svadharma*. They ground the duty or duties binding upon Arjuna in particular. He is not the exclusive author of his own law; the social order into which he was born, the place he was born into, the endowments with which he came to it, and even his personal history (where this refers only very partially to his own choices), wrote a "law" just for him. It is in virtue of these that he has a fate, or destiny, which is appropriate to him, and not merely the workings of a capricious but inexorable necessity.[19] It is to his own, his proper, duty or law (*svadharma*) that Arjuna ought to look (II.31), and it is *svadharma* which he betrays in refusing to fight (II.33).[20] It may be that to act contrary to duty involves an irremediable loss of self, of integrity or dignity. Or it may be that it is just plain wrong. It is not entirely clear from the arguments Kṛṣṇa gives; he suggests the latter rather than the former when he says of action motivated by self-interest: "From this interest grows desire, from desire anger; from anger rises delusion, from delusion loss of memory, from loss of memory the death of the spirit, and from the death of the spirit one perishes" (II.62–62).

I do not think it an accident that these frequent reminders of Arjuna's social, and particular familial relations should so immediately precede the introduction of the argument for desireless action, nor that the resolution of the dilemma should lead directly into the considerations of the nature of the self for which the *Bhagavadgītā* is best known. I had suggested earlier (sec. I, p. 3) that there are two different ways we might understand the "improving" power of right motivation. Right motivation might just be a good in itself; or it might be something through which, and in virtue of which, we are able to properly assess our overall situation, and discern which relations, obligations, and potential consequences ought to weigh with us, and to what extent. Naturally, right motivation could be improving for both reasons, and the emphasis Kṛṣṇa puts on the devotional quality of action without a view to reward suggests the former rather more than the latter. But the appeal to family and position immediately preceding the introduction of desireless action returns explicitly, when it is realized that acting with a certain motivation, or quality of heart, cannot on its own determine *which* course of action one should (devotionally) embark upon.

Thus after the explication of desireless action, and of the ultimate immortality of all beings, Arjuna still wonders what words and deeds are right. "What does one whose insight is firm say? How does he sit? How does he walk?" (II.54). Even was he to master the principle of acting devotionally, rather than for one's own happiness, Arjuna still would need to know whether he should kill his kin "desirelessly" or walk, without desire, away from the battlefield. Proper motivation, as thus far understood, is not enough. In Kṛṣṇa's own words: The wise man "has no reason at all to do anything or not to do anything" (III.18?). If, however, we couple the principle of acting without desire for reward with the injunction to attend to the self, Arjuna begins to get an answer to his question (III.1: "Why urge me to this fearful action?"). For although ultimately, the self which he should recognize is the eternal self which can be a part of the divine, for practical purposes, the immortal self of Arjuna is embodied and embedded in social life in a particular way. And it is looking to this complex self, or the self as it is implicated here and now, that Arjuna should consider the question of whether to enter the battle. "Even the man of knowledge," as contrasted with the man of action (III.3), "behaves according to his nature" (III.33). While the life of the mind may lead to correct insight and action, so too may the *vita activa*; and, although Kṛṣṇa does not say this explicitly, presumably what Arjuna is supposed to know about himself, when he comes to consider the question, is that he was born and bred for the active life. All of Kṛṣṇa's epithets and arguments up to this point have been reminding Arjuna of this. Active engagement with worldly concerns belongs to him properly, while other types of worthwhile life do not. And it is for this reason that he would be doing wrong to walk away from the battle in meditative absorption. Kṛṣṇa again appeals to Arjuna's particular obligations: "It is more salutary to carry out your own law poorly than another's law well; it is better to die in your own law than to prosper in another's" (III.35).

It is appreciation of a situation as a whole, with judgement unclouded by desire for profit (III.37–43), which provides one with the ability to discern what is the required action, here and now, from less worthy alternatives. Regarding a situation without concern for personal gain will allow one to see it clearly, and will resolve doubt (V.25). "The knower of *brahman* who stands upon *brahman* is steady of spirit and harbors no delusions" (V.20). This perspective is attained by those who "have tamed their thinking and know themselves" (V.26). And while knowing oneself will of course involve knowing oneself as related to God, it will also involve knowing oneself as related to one's fellows, and as related to the whole order of creation (XI.1).

V. DESTINY AND INTEGRITY

A closer consideration of the reasons Kṛṣṇa gives in the first part of the *Gītā* thus suggests that it is because Arjuna is just the person he is, with just the particular family, social status and history that he has, that it has become *Arjuna's* duty to fight. To be sure, Kṛṣṇa is not arguing in terms of what will please Arjuna or make him, or anyone else, happy—in this sense, his argument is no more consequentialist than it is Kantian. Rather, Kṛṣṇa seems to think that duties are generated in idiosyncratic ways, depending upon the particular relations in which individuals stand to one another, and depending upon the irreducibly particular past which shapes a person and a situation into the individual he, she or it is. When Kṛṣṇa enjoins Arjuna to "look to your own law (*svadharma*)" (II.31), he resembles nothing so much as a moral particularist.

This is in keeping with what B. K. Matilal has said in defense of Kṛṣṇa's "deviousness" throughout the *Mahābhārata*.[21] Kṛṣṇa is not unprincipled, if by that one means unscrupulous or wanton. He has a keenly developed sense of what is to be done—it is uncompromising, he feels himself bound by it, and difficult though it may be to articulate in advance, the constraints on what is and is not to be done are fully captured neither in consequentialist, nor in deontological terms. Justice must be done, and that means that oaths must be kept and the greedy punished; honest Yudhistira must lie, thus betraying himself in order to save his brothers and kingdom, just as he had betrayed his brothers and wife through gambling them and their kingdom away. And Arjuna, foremost archer, bearer of Gandiva, embracer of battle and of role,[22] must fight.

Thus the sort of particularism I attribute to Kṛṣṇa—and to Arjuna insofar as he is responsive to the *arguments* Kṛṣṇa gives, rather than merely to the fact that it is god giving them—is as distinct from "hard case" particularism as it is from "Sartrean particularism". On the one hand, one might make the weak claim that there are *some* cases of moral judgement for which there is, and can be, no universal rule.[23] There are hard cases, and these hard cases show us that morality is not always a matter of universally applicable principles, but is sometimes one of personal judgement. As I have been describing it, *all* judgements about what is to be done should, according to Kṛṣṇa, be made with a view to "one's own law."

But this should not be confused with the view that morality is merely a matter of personal judgement—with heavy weight on the word "personal." The extreme of this line of thought is frequently taken to be Sartre, who seems to claim that decisions generally are at once constructive of and expressive of who we are as persons—and that is pretty much all there is to be said on the matter of rightness and wrongness.[24] The only standards of success and failure applicable are those used for evaluating the degree to which we "stand behind" our decision, fully and sincerely endorse what we do and therefore who we are, without self-deceit.

This is not quite the kind of personhood that Kṛṣṇa's particularism implies or is interested in. The person who is the locus of individually tailored obligations is not primarily something one constructs through one's actions, but something constructed socially, historically, and to a certain extent "objectively." One is born a prince, or one is not, and certain things follow or not accordingly. One's elder brother is a scrupulously honest compulsive gambler (not an ideal combination) or not, and one's teacher has or has not attempted to assassinate and defraud one of one's kingdom. Finally, this prince of a great kingdom has seen his wife publicly humiliated by one's cousins, or he has not. But if he has, and if his exile has been endorsed by the archery teacher of whom he was the star pupil, and if he twice followed his brother in an attempt to regain the throne, if he learned avidly and excelled all others in the skills appropriate to a warrior, ... and so on, then certain things are his duty that a deontologist could never have imagined in advance. Out of the immense weight of the detail of who one is, a destiny arises—the obligation to respond to and enact the future fitting for such a past, the behavior and characteristics integral to and befitting who one has become. This might resemble, if anything, the Stoic view of individual duty being determined by our four *personae*—our rational nature, our natural endowments, the careers we have chosen, and the positions we occupy by chance.[25] But it should be clear that the grounds which generate obligations, and determine virtues, should not be restricted to "roles"; Arjuna's *kạtriya* persona is only one aspect of the situation which determines that his path lies in the battle ahead, and it is an aspect still not sufficiently well-described to be fully determining. This, I suggest, is how we should understand the force of Kṛṣṇa's appeal to *svadharma*, as opposed to, say *kuladharma* (duty peculiar to the family) or *varṇāśramadharma* (duty peculiar to class). The fact that Arjuna has consistently taken on, or embodied in a specific way, what it means to be a warrior, through his own choices and actions, figures in making it meaningful that Arjuna fight this battle, in a way it is not necessarily meaningful for the "generic" *kṣatriya*. Moreover, the way Arjuna has been treated (what has been done to him) and the expectations others have of him also play a role in determining whether it is his duty to fight here and now.

Thus, when hermit Utaṇka criticises Kṛṣṇa for failing to avert the war, Kṛṣṇa explains that it was out of his hands. "It is impossible," he says, "to transgress destiny (*diṣṭam*) by either intelligence or might" (*MBh.* 14.LII.16).[26] Utaṇka is beside himself with outrage at this excuse: "Since, though able, Kṛṣṇa, you did not rescue those foremost ones of Kuru's race ... I shall, without doubt, curse you! Since you did not forcibly compel them to forebear ... I shall, filled with wrath, denounce a curse on you" (*MBh.* 14.LII.20–21). Before revealing his divine identity, and that it would be therefore very imprudent for Utaṇka to lay a curse on him, Kṛṣṇa *apologizes* for having been unable to avert the war (*MBh.* 14.LII.23). Since we see Kṛṣṇa in the *Gītā* bending over backwards to persuade Arjuna to enter the fray, we might be tempted to see Kṛṣṇa's appeal to fate and his apologies after the fact as disingenuous. But if destiny is something constructed socially, through the combination of one's actions and characteristic with the values and social system, as well as the character and acts of others (Yudhiṣṭira's gambling; Duryodhana's mercilessness; Droṇa's disrespect for moral teaching), then *once the characters have declared themselves*, within the context in which their actions take one very specific significance, the die is cast. As Kṛṣṇa explains it, "When I live in the order of the Nāgas, I then act as a Nāga, and when I live in the order of the Yakshas or that of Rākshasas, I act after the manner of that order. Born now in the order of humanity, I must act as a human being. I begged them (the Kauravas) piteously. But stupefied as they were and deprived of their senses, they refused to accept my words. I frightened them, filled with wrath, referring to some great danger. But once more I showed them my usual (human) form. Possessed as they were of unrighteousness, and enveloped by their proper time,[27] all of them have been righteously slain in battle, and have without doubt gone to Heaven" (*MBh.* 14.LIII.18–21). There are modes and manners appropriate to each form of life, and persons within that form of life are constrained by these. They draw the most general circle around what can and ought to be done. Here, Kṛṣṇa specifically attributes the inevitability of the war to the obstinancy of the Kauravas. There must be many such reasons, culminating indirectly in the duty of Arjuna to fight. Even Kṛṣṇa cannot make the meaning of the lives of each of the persons involved something other than what all the characters and social elements of all jointly combine to make it.

Although the obligations falling to Arjuna are specific to him, they are none the less obligations for that. And although they are his duty in virtue of his past, his circumstances, his station and relations to others, including his skilfulness in arms, they are not in any way necessarily his personal wishes. What it becomes his duty to do in virtue of who he is, is not at all what he would choose to be his duty, and not at all what he would want to do, or can even fully comprehend as right and justified, so long as he thinks in absolute terms, without reference to things that are true of him in particular and no one else. It is his objectively constructed identity, including his current circumstances, together with his past choices (e.g., to try in the first place to regain for his elder brother the throne that was rightfully his) which compels certain things to be his duties, and ultimately his destiny. And thus he needs persuading to begin the war that marks the beginning of the end of the *Mahābhārata*; and thus when Kṛṣṇa persuades him, he does so by reference to "duties" and "law"—not to ends, but also not to impersonal principles, or maxims.

Kṛṣṇa's argument relies on an appeal to *who Arjuna is*. His insistence is that Arjuna act according to his character, as well as with understanding of how he fits into an overall structure of a well-ordered universe. It is, in a sense, an appeal to Arjuna's integrity. But it is in maintaining his integrity that Arjuna will participate in a war of ghastly destruction. Should we say then that the lesson of the *Mahābhārata*, and of the *Bhagavadgītā* in particular, is that sometimes one ought to act out of character? Perhaps integrity is not so important after all, and Kṛṣṇa is positively *wicked* in his exhortation of Arjuna to act according to his values, and according to the expectations that are on him (III.29).[28]

But integrity will not be so easily dismissed, and I think to focus on the rightness or wrongness of Kṛṣṇa's action here distracts from this larger point to be got from the *Gītā*; and similarly to focus merely on whether Arjuna should in fact (in some impersonal sense) fight, distracts from at least one lesson we might take from his relation to the action of the *Mahābhārata*. Implicit in Kṛṣṇa's motivations for urging Arjuna to fight, and slightly more explicit in the reasons he gives Arjuna, is a recognition of the central role of integrity in ethical thinking. Without integrity as a virtue—a fundamental virtue—any moral code, and any world based on such a moral code, will fall apart. For this reason, it may even be more correct to regard integrity as the precondition of any virtue, rather than as a virtue in its own right to be fitted in among others. Full integrity requires in this case a thorough-going commitment to the virtues and values of the heroic code of the warrior. Unless Arjuna and his brothers, and his kin on the opposing side, follow through completely in their endorsement of, and adherence to, this heroic code, we will not get a critique of that code, and we will be tempted to mis-locate the problem. If Arjuna had walked away from the battle, more people would have survived—some of them wicked, some of them innocent, and some of them heroic according to the values and expectations embedded in the social world of the *Mahābhārata*. And had he walked away, we might criticize his act as weak or cowardly; we might praise the act as wise and self-sacrificing. The act of Arjuna walking away would be the focus of a debate of whether what he did was ignoble or a noble foregoing of his own glory. But we would not be forced to question whether the glory itself is a *good* that Arjuna sacrificed; we would not be forced to question whether the whole code that demands, or would demand, wholesale slaughter in order to be fully lived, is itself the culprit. In apportioning praise and blame within the *Mahābhārata*, and within the schema of values it represents, each side of the bloody war comes off as well—and as badly—as the other. But only because of this, and because the extreme bloodiness of the battle is a *necessary consequence of* the heroic code, a battle that becomes *necessary* within the values according to which each of the characters has conducted his life, and within the moral—social climate which prevails—only because the devastation is the inevitable consequence of the demands of *dharma* as understood by all concerned, can the story as a whole operate as a critique of the whole system of values. Because Arjuna lives, and so many die, adhering to the demands implied by a certain moral climate and order can his story itself stand as a critique of that moral climate.

NOTES

1 Amartya Sen, in his "Consequential Evaluation and Practical Reason", describes Kṛṣṇa's view as "high deontology" (*Journal of Philosophy*, vol. XCVII, no. 7. July 2000), p. 481. See also Arindam Charkrabarti, "The End of Life: A Nyāya-*Kantian* Approach to the Bhagavadgītā" (*Journal of Indian Philosophy*, vol. 16, no. 4 (1988) 327-334.

2 Bhagavadgītā, translated by J. A. B. van Buitenen (Chicago: University of Chicago Press, 1981). All subsequent quotations from the Gītā will be from this edition, with occasional modifications according to the rendering of R. C. Zaehner (Oxford: Oxford University Press, 1973).

3 Sen, op. cit., p. 481

4 Sen, ibid.

5 See also III.20. It is not, then, so surprising that Gandhi should have found the principle an inspiring one (cf. Sen, ibid., p. 481). The view that it is in terms of the best overall course of the world that we should discover what we ought to do is a highly idealistic one.

6 Compare Arjuna's question to Kṛṣṇa at VI.37, and Kṛṣṇa's response: "Still, Kṛṣṇa, a non-ascetic who, while having faith, allows his mind to stray from this yoga before he achieves the ultimate success of yoga—what becomes of him? Does he not, like a shredded cloud, fade away, a failure either way ...?" (VI.37–38). "No, Pārtha, neither here nor hereafter is he lost, for no one who does good can go wrong, my friend. He goes to the worlds which are gained by merit, and when he has dwelled there for years without end, this 'failed yogin' is born high in the house of pure and prosperous folk, or in the family of wise yogins" (VI.40–42).

7 This is usually considered distinctive of a deontological ethical framework, although according to Sen (*op. cit.*, pp. 487–492) a broad consequentialism could also endorse such a claim.

8 This is especially so if we follow B. G. Tilak in taking the force of Kṛṣṇa's argument to be that "a man should not entertain the proud or desireful thought that 'I shall bring about lokasaṃgraha...'"(quoted by Simon Brodbeck, in his excellent 'Calling Kṛṣṇa's Bluff' (*Journal of Indian Philosophy* 32 [2004] 81–103). A rejection of the pride associated with taking credit for an action as one's own may be precisely the move the impersonalist moral philosopher should make, in order to make a virtue out of a defect. For it is the special value of an action's belonging to me rather than you that gets equally lost on all sorts of impersonal theories of morality, whether deontological or consequentialist (see B. A. O. Williams, "Persons, Character, and Morality" in *Moral Luck: Philosophical Papers 1973–1980*. Cambridge University Press, 1981).

9 Following Zaehner's translation here, but the emphasis is mine.

10 Since there is some debate about whether injunctions such as "Thou shalt honour thy mother and thy father" are to be considered universal, in the

strictest sense —since they license partiality towards certain individuals—I will settle for Arjuna's claim being a "general" one, and concede that not all would be happy with considering such a claim consistent with deontological ethics. (For some discussion, see Lawrence Blum, "Against Deriving Particularity" in *Moral Particulalism*, Brad Hooker, ed. Oxford: Oxford University Press, 2000, p. 208; and Alan Gewirth, "Ethical Univeralism and Particularity" in *Journal of Philosophy* 85 (June 1988), 283–302). My own view is that such a principle is consistent with deontology, in spite of its superficially restricted scope ("one's kin"); for it may be that sound family relations are the basis of the trust that makes society possible. In fact, this seems to be the thrust of Arjuna's argument at I.40 *ff.* If one is liable to attack, rather than protection, from the family, then the constant fear and insecurity would undermine all possibility of personal relations. "Waging war on one's kin" is thus impossible to universalise without contradiction.

11 Again, following Zaehner here.

12 Kant. *Metaphysics of Morals.* pp. 217–225.

13 See, for example, *Euthyphro* 13a-15c.

14 A popular view later in the European tradition, often taken to be initiated by *Theaetetus* 176b-e: "That is why a man should make all haste to escape from earth to heaven; and escape means becoming as like God as possible."

15 This straighforward take on the authority of divine command is defended by Paul Rooney in his *Divine Command Morality* (Aldershot: Avebury, Ashgate Publishing, 1996); but even the more cautious defenses of God's authority, resting on His power (P. T. Geach, *God and the Soul.* London, 1969), or on His benevolence, His creative and sustaining role (e.g., R. G. Swinburn, *The Coherence of Theism*. Oxford: Clarendon. Oxford, 1993; esp. Ch. 11, pp. 212–213) would be adequate to explain Arjuna's compliance with Kṛṣṇa's command. A fine discussion of this issue can also be found in Robert Adams' *Finite and Infinite Goods* (Oxford: Oxford University Press, 2000), pp. 249–291.

16 Emphasis mine.

17 According to Apte, while this epithet can apply to any of the Pāṇḍava princes, it is generally applied only to Arjuna (Prin. Vaman Shivaram Apte, *The Practical Sanskrit-English Dictionary*, revised and enlarged edition. Kyoto: Rinsen Book Company, 1998).

18 It is interesting to note about this transitional passage (II.37–II.47) that Kṛṣṇa's first argument that Arjuna should disregard his own happiness—"holding alike happiness and unhappiness, gain and loss, victory and defeat, yoke yourself to the battle" (II.38)—is grounded in an appeal to Arjuna's happiness. He should act without considering how the battle turns out, because however it turns out, it will be *good for Arjuna*: "Either you are killed and will then attain to heaven or you triumph and will enjoy the earth" (II.37). Given Arjuna's vehement rejection of any good won by killing his kin, we should expect this argument to carry very little force for him.

19 More will be said about this in section V.

20 Looking to later chapters if the Gītā, Brodbeck (*op. cit.*) explains the sort of agency recommended by Kṛṣṇa through a metaphysical particularism that

closely parallels, and may ground, the moral particularism I am arguing for here. "The notion of svabhāva used here must logically be specific to individual people rather than to individual varṇas," he argues (p. 90), "We would even want to go further and describe svabhāva as variable within one lifetime." Brodbeck does not make this connection himself; while he reverts to the less nuanced claim, "There is no getting around it: ... Arjuna is a *kṣyatriya* and so must— and will—fight", he also does emphasize the particularist nature of moral reasoning (p. 98).

21 "In Defence of a Devious Divinity" in *Epics and Ethics* (Jonardon Ganeri, ed., Delhi: Oxford University Press, 2002), pp. 89–107.

22 Van Buitenen refers us to *Mahābhārata* V.151.20 *ff*., where Arjuna replies flatly to Yudhiṣṭira's hesitations, "It is not right to retreat now without fighting."

23 Peter Winch offers what to my mind is one of the better defenses of moral particularism in his paper "Ethical Integrity." But the moral particularism (if it is that) that he sets out there may not be "global particularlism," but rather the weaker sort. In his example from *Billy Budd*, when Captain Vere decides to try, and finally execute Billy, he makes a decision that is certainly a *moral* decision, but which neither sets nor is beholden to a standard which could be used to judge anyone else in the same (or "relevantly similar") situation. But Winch's example gives us no reason to suppose that all, or even most, moral thinking is of this tough kind.

24 Jean-Paul Sartre's *Existentialism and Humanism* has the oft-cited example of the youth who must choose between caring for his mother and joining the French *Résistance*.

25 See Cicero's *de Officius* I.107–125 for the primary formulation of this view. In his "Personhood and Personality: The Four-*personae* Theory in Cicero *De Officius* I" (*Oxford Studies in Ancient Philosophy* 6 (1988), pp. 169–199), Christopher Gill disputes the coherence of the view; yet it remains intuitively compelling—see, for example, Richard Sorabji's interesting discussion in *Emotion and Peace of Mind* (Oxford: Oxford University Press, 2000), pp. 249–50, and Brad Inwood's "Rules and Reasoning in Stoic Ethics" (*Topics in Stoic Philosophy*, Katerina Ierodiakonou, ed., Oxford: Oxford University Press. Oxford, 1999), pp. 95–127.

26 The *Āśwamedhikaparvan* of thc *Mahābhārata*. Critical edition of Raghunath Damodar Karmarkar. Bhandarkar Oriental Research Institute. Poona, 1960), p. 203. Translations mostly following that of Pratāpa Chandra Ray, C. I. E. Bhārata Press. Calcutta, 1894, Book 14.LIII and LIV.

27 Does *parītāh kāladharmaṇā* mean "enveloped by what their time demanded", or "meeting their appointed hour"? If the former, then this again would point to demands of a semi-particular sort on the Kauravas—demands upon them in virtue of the time (of life, of the circumstances). Even the latter suggests fate's hand, although without suggesting that a fate belongs non-arbitrarily to a person.

28 "Because they are confused about these forces of nature, people identify with the actions of these forces, and he who knows it all has no reason to upset the slow-witted who do not."

PART II
Virtue and Unity

CHAPTER 5

Conceptions of Virtue and the Unity of the Virtues

A. D. M. WALKER

The thesis that possession of any one virtue involves possession of all the virtues—for the sake of convenience let us call this the thesis of the unity of the virtues (UV)—can be elaborated in many different ways and supported by many different lines of argument. One popular line of argument appeals to the part which practical wisdom is said to play in the full possession of a virtue. The argument, which has its origins in Socratic thought about the virtues, is stated in canonical form in Aristotle's *Nicomachean Ethics* and has been endorsed, albeit with qualifications, by a number of contemporary philosophers.[1] In view of its distinguished ancestry let us call this argument the "classical argument" (CA) for the unity of the virtues. My concern in this paper will be exclusively with CA and, more particularly, with the conception of the virtues which provides the foundation of the argument, a conception which has received less attention than it should have done from contemporary neo-Aristotelians.[2] In Part I of the paper I shall outline Aristotle's statement of CA and in Part II sketch some contemporary versions of the argument; in Part III, I shall bring into focus the conception of the virtues which is presupposed by CA, and in the remainder of the paper (Parts IV–VI) raise some doubts about the acceptability of this conception.

I.

Aristotle presents CA in the course of his discussion of practical wisdom (*phronesis*) in *Nicomachean Ethics* VI. Having remarked that one cannot be good in the full and proper sense without practical wisdom and that it is impossible to be practically wise without virtue, he adds, almost as an afterthought, that these points serve to undermine the claim that the virtues can be possessed independently of one another. This claim, he continues, is plausible "in relation to the natural virtues, but not in relation to the virtues that make a person good without qualification; since if practical wisdom, which is one, is present, they will all be present along with it" (1144b35–1145a2). Clearly, as it stands, this statement of CA is too succinct to be easily understood: it needs to be set out in a little more detail.

First of all, CA presupposes a distinction between the different ways in which a virtue may be possessed—the contrast between "natural virtue" and "virtue proper." Aristotle has explained earlier in the discussion in VI 13 (1144b1–17) that children may possess natural virtue: they may be naturally disposed towards certain virtues, being by nature, e.g., fearless or gentle in their treatment of others. He also mentions elsewhere in the *Nicomachean Ethics* (1095b4–9, 1151a17–19), though curiously there is no reference to it in VI 13, that in the course of their upbringing children may learn, and internalize, certain precepts (e.g., about the circumstances in which it is appropriate to take a risk and act courageously), their natural dispositions being disciplined and shaped by these precepts: they may come to possess "habituated virtue." Natural virtue and habituated virtue provide the basis for, but fall short of, full virtue. What distinguishes full virtue or virtue proper[3] from the lesser forms is, Aristotle says, precisely the possession of practical wisdom: "it is not possible to be good in the full and proper sense without practical wisdom" (1144b31).

Aristotle has two reasons for insisting that practical wisdom is necessary for the possession of a full virtue. First, he assumes a connection between possession of a virtue and right or appropriate action so that, e.g., the person with the virtue of courage is led by his courage to act rightly in dangerous situations. Since a central part of practical wisdom is an understanding of what is valuable and what is worthless, practical wisdom is clearly necessary for possession of a virtue proper: a natural virtue, however well habituated, cannot reliably secure appropriate action when its possessor finds himself in unfamiliar situations or situations in which different values conflict. As Aristotle puts it, "one may be led astray [by one's natural dispositions], as a strong body which moves without sight may stumble badly because of its lack of sight" (1144b8–14). Aristotle's second reason for regarding practical wisdom as indispensable for possession of a virtue proper is linked to his insistence that the exercise of a virtue involves not just doing the right actions, but doing them in the right spirit, i.e., from the right motive and with the appropriate feelings and attitudes. Thus even if the possessor of natural or habituated courage somehow always managed to do the right action in dangerous situations, he could not, without practical wisdom, possess the full virtue of courage because he could not act in the right spirit, i.e., he would not have a proper appreciation of all the relevant considerations and so would not act with, and out of, a genuine understanding that this was in the circumstances the best action to take.

The final stage of CA—i.e., the claim that possession of practical wisdom is sufficient for possession of all the virtues—depends on Aristotle's belief that an understanding and appreciation of what is valuable and what is worthless is impossible if we do not have the right desires and emotions and have not become habituated to acting in the right way: the person with perverse desires and wayward emotions and the person who has been brought up in bad habits cannot genuinely understand and appreciate what is valuable and what is worthless. Hence without the natural virtues—or, we may add, without the habituated virtues—one cannot acquire practical wisdom. But, against this background, may we not reasonably conclude, as Aristotle does, that once the possessor of all the natural virtues acquires practical wisdom, this acquisition will transform his natural virtues into virtues proper?

It is clearly crucial to CA that, as Aristotle stresses in his brief statement of it, practical wisdom itself should have a unitary nature. If practical wisdom were itself divisible into parts, with a different part completing each natural virtue, the argument would collapse. But one reason why Aristotle can justifiably assume the unity of practical wisdom is apparent from what has been said in the penultimate paragraph. The practical wisdom necessary for the possession of a virtue proper must reach decisions about the best course of action when the demands of different virtues conflict, when the values associated with the different virtues favor different and incompatible courses of action. It must therefore be capable of understanding and appreciating these different values and of determining the relative weight to be accorded to them in particular circumstances. It must have the capacity to take a "global" or "synoptic" view[4] and so cannot be divided into discrete parts and portioned out between the different virtues.

II.

CA continues to play a part in philosophical thought about the relationships between the virtues, and in recent decades versions of the argument have been offered to justify at least limited support for UV. It is significant, for example, that in Rosalind Hursthouse's recent excellent book *On Virtue Ethics*, which seeks to provide an authoritative exposition of the views of contemporary neo-Aristotelians, she both endorses UV, albeit with qualifications, and defends it with a version of CA, appealing to the indispensability of practical wisdom for the possession of any genuine virtue. As she acknowledges (Hursthouse: 154, n. 10), her rather brief discussion reflects the influence of very capable papers by Gary Watson and Neera Badhwar; and since both Watson's and Badhwar's papers well illustrate, in different ways, the extent to which CA retains an attraction for contemporary neo-Aristotelians, it will be helpful to outline the relevant parts of their papers.

Although Watson does not use the expression "practical wisdom," the core of his argument, on which I shall concentrate, in effect spells out part of CA, maintaining that the practical wisdom which is necessary for the possession of any virtue is sufficient for possession of all the others "to some degree" (Watson: 60). He begins by drawing a distinction which is not identical with, but analogous to, the distinction presupposed by Aristotle's argument. He does not contrast two forms of virtue, natural virtue and virtue proper, i.e., two stages in the acquisition of virtue, but two conceptions of virtue, i.e., two different ways of "thinking about virtues" (ibid: 57): the "straight view" of the virtues (SV) and the "due concern view" (DCV) (ibid: 58–59). Common to both views is the assumption that a virtue is a tendency to "feel, desire, deliberate, choose, and act" in certain ways. The difference between them is that according to SV the stronger the relevant tendency, the greater the degree to which one possesses the virtue (so that, e.g., the stronger one's tendency to give to others, the more generous one is), whereas according to DCV a virtue is to be identified with the possession of the relevant tendency *to the right degree* (so that one has the virtue of generosity when one's tendency to give to others is neither too weak nor too strong). According to DCV, then, each of the virtues is essentially a "due and proper concern" with a particular set of considerations, the courageous person having a "due and proper concern" for his own safety, the truthful person a "due and proper concern" that others be told the truth, and so on. For reasons with which we are already familiar, Watson champions DCV at the expense of SV. The former view, unlike the latter, takes appropriate account of the fact that a virtue is an "excellence of character," i.e., "a characteristic readiness to feel, desire, deliberate, choose, and act *well* in certain respects" (ibid: 58–59, my italics), and hence "cannot lead one seriously astray" (ibid: 58).

On the basis of DCV, Watson seeks to establish UV in two stages, arguing in the first stage that the full possession of any virtue involves possession of all the others *to some extent*, and in the second stage moving from this "weak version" of UV to the "strong version," viz., that the full possession of any virtue involves the full possession of all the others.

Watson's argument in the first stage is that if a person is to possess a particular virtue, i.e., have a due and proper concern for a certain set of considerations, he must have, at least in the context of the exercise of this virtue, a due and proper concern for the considerations associated with all the other virtues, since without this latter concern his concern for the considerations associated with the first virtue cannot be "due and proper."[5] For example, the person with the virtue of truthfulness has a due and proper concern that others be told the truth, and can be relied on to act rightly and well, whenever truth-telling is an issue. No doubt he will usually tell the truth—but not always. Sometimes it is wrong to tell the truth—when, e.g., this would involve a serious breach of confidence, or put an innocent person's life at risk, or hurt someone's feelings unnecessarily, or merely satisfy the questioner's prurient curiosity—and in these circumstances, and no doubt in many others, the person with the virtue of truthfulness will not tell the truth. But, clearly, in order to act rightly in all these different circumstances he needs to have a due and proper concern for the considerations which are the particular concern of trustworthiness, kindness, humanity, justice, etc.,—indeed for the considerations associated with *all* the other virtues, since he can be relied on to act rightly whenever truth-telling is an issue, and no one can know in advance in what circumstances the issue of truth-telling will arise for him.

Clearly this line of argument can be generalized: if it is persuasive in relation to the virtue of truthfulness, it should be no less persuasive in relation to all the other virtues. Equally clearly, however, what has been shown so far is only that the full possession of one virtue involves possession of all the others "to some degree" (ibid: 60). It has been shown, e.g., that in circumstances in which truth-telling is an issue the person with the virtue of truthfulness must have a due and proper concern for the considerations associated with all the other virtues, but this is not to say that he has a due and proper concern for these considerations *in all circumstances, whether truth-telling is an issue or not*, i.e., that he *fully* possesses all the other virtues. In other words what we have so far is an argument for the "weak version" of UV.

The transition from the "weak" to the "strong version" of UV is effected in the second stage of Watson's argument, which I need summarize only very briefly. In effect Watson asks: "Would it not be strange if, e.g., the person with the virtue of truthfulness were entirely kind, trustworthy, fair-minded, etc., in circumstances in which truth-telling is an issue, but not entirely kind, trustworthy, fair-minded, etc., in circumstances in which truth-telling is not an issue?" He recognizes that an affirmative answer to this question depends on substantial assumptions about human psychology—assumptions about the consistency of our responses, the stability of our understanding and motivation, across the entire range of circumstances in which we may find ourselves—and acknowledges that these assumptions are open to empirical confirmation or disconfirmation. Nonetheless he considers them "plausible enough" (ibid: 62), and hence concludes that he has presented a *prima facie* persuasive case for the "strong version" of UV.

It is, of course, this second stage of Watson's argument that is most obviously fragile. It seems to be a fact that our responses—both in terms of understanding and in terms of motivation—are *not* always uniform across the whole range of circumstances in which we may find ourselves: a person may, e.g., understand the need not to cause others pain or to hurt their feelings, and respond appropriately, in some types of situation but not in others. This is, surely, the lesson to be learnt from Milgram's obedience experiments[6] and from the way in which prejudice can create "blind spots" in the responses of otherwise decent and kind-hearted individuals.

This criticism would certainly meet with the approval of Neera Badhwar, whose paper challenges Aristotle's assumption about the unity of practical wisdom, arguing that it is possible to possess and display, practical wisdom in some areas of one's life but not in others. There is, she argues, no good reason to believe that "the goodness of a human life consists of a variety of goods, ... all of which [are] interrelated in such a way that fully understanding one requires fully understanding all" (Badhwar: 313). Practical wisdom, according to Badhwar, is not a unity: a person may be practically wise in one domain or area of his life, but not in others, e.g., in his career but not in his family life, or as a friend but not in the way he manages his financial affairs (ibid: 315–320).

Despite her rejection of the unity of practical wisdom, however, Badhwar accepts the other elements in Aristotle's argument for UV, and herself offers a version of CA in support of what she calls the thesis of the limited unity of the virtues (LUV): the virtues, she maintains, "are disunited across different domains (areas of practical concern), but united within domains" (ibid: 307). There are two aspects to her position. First of all, our lives can be compartmentalized into distinct domains only to a limited extent. Some practical concerns, such as "the concern to lead a good life and be a good person ... cannot for conceptual reasons" (ibid: 316) be confined to certain domains and excluded from others. And, besides, practical wisdom is "potentially general" (ibid: 320): aspects of practical wisdom involve an understanding of principles that apply outside any particular domain. Hence, Badhwar believes, once we have achieved practical wisdom in one area, it will tend to "spill over" and affect our attitudes and understanding in other areas; and so "it cannot be that an individual who is wise and virtuous in one domain might be fundamentally ignorant of the good in most other domains" (ibid: 320).

Secondly, and more relevantly to my concerns in this paper, Badhwar takes UV to be true within any one domain, holding that the person who possesses one virtue in, e.g., his professional life must possess all the other virtues in his professional life. This aspect of her position she defends, at least in part, by means of a version of CA which resembles Watson's argument for the "weak version" of UV. Since the person who possesses, e.g., the virtue of courage within a domain can be relied on to act rightly and well within the domain whenever considerations about his personal safety are relevant, and since this is impossible without a proper concern for the considerations associated with the other virtues in the domain, the possession of courage within the domain requires the possession of the other virtues in the domain. Further, since Badhwar also believes that "every human activity capable of showing [practical] wisdom is complex enough to involve psychological and normative considerations relevant to *all* the virtues" (ibid: 322, my italics), she is in a position to agree with Aristotle that possession of one virtue involves possession of *all* the virtues, with the proviso that this thesis is applied not globally, but only within domains.

Rosalind Hursthouse concludes her own discussion of UV, in which, as I have said, the notion of practical wisdom plays a large part, by endorsing a position similar to Watson's "weak version" of UV and Badhwar's thesis of the limited unity of the virtues: "anyone who possesses one virtue," she says, "will have all the others to some degree, albeit, in some cases, a pretty limited one" (Hursthouse: 156).

III.

UV, then, still finds defenders among contemporary neo-Aristotelians, and for these philosophers CA seems to be their preferred way of arguing for whatever version of UV they wish to defend.[7] Nor is the appeal of CA to be wondered at. The argument undeniably has a certain elegance: it is a simple argument which reaches a very remarkable conclusion, yielding a considerable return for a relatively small investment. The extent to which its elegant economy contributes to the attractiveness of CA should not be underestimated. The argument appeals to a feature of the virtues which is taken to belong equally to all of them, and hence is in a position to conclude of each, without exception, that its possession involves possession of all the others. We do not need to look individually and in detail at each of the virtues, or concern ourselves with the particularities of the different virtues: we know in advance, if CA is successful, that possession of *any* virtue involves possession of all the others.

CA has, over the years, been the target of many objections, but these have tended to fall into one or other of two categories. Philosophers sympathetic to the Aristotelian tradition, leaving unchallenged the conception of the virtues which provides its foundation, have tended to concentrate on the subsequent steps in the argument: they have doubted, for example, whether practical wisdom, to the extent that it is necessary for the possession of any one virtue, is unattainable without all the other virtues.[8] By contrast, philosophers hostile to the Aristotelian tradition, rejecting out of hand the conception of the virtues which underlies the argument, dismiss CA on the ground that it begins from a position too remote from any they could be expected to accept.[9] It is a consequence of this that the distinctively Aristotelian conception of the virtues on which CA is built—the conception of a virtue as an excellence of character, i.e., a personal quality which ensures that its possessor acts rightly and well within the sphere of operation of the virtue—has gone relatively unscrutinized by philosophers within the Aristotelian tradition: they have not asked themselves whether, even from their own point of view, this conception—for the sake of a name let us call it the "orthodox conception" (OC)—embodies an entirely acceptable way of thinking about the virtues. It is this issue which I wish to explore in the remainder of this paper, examining the "orthodox conception" from a position sympathetic to the Aristotelian tradition and in the context of CA.

IV.

I shall begin with two questions which concern not so much the orthodox conception itself as the fact that in the context of CA it is taken to capture equally well the nature of *all* the virtues. CA, it is clear, conceives of all the virtues in the same way and, connectedly, takes practical wisdom to be involved in the same way in each of them. This feature of CA is merely the obverse of its elegant economy: it is because it assumes that all the virtues are in certain fundamental respects similar to one another that it can speedily reach its conclusion about the truth of UV. This assumption about the essential homogeneity of the virtues is perhaps most evident in Watson's version of CA, which begins by defining each of the virtues as a "due and proper concern," benevolence being such a concern "for the well-being of others," temperance such a concern for "the natural pleasures of life," and so on (Watson: 58). The point is less explicit in Badhwar and Hursthouse, but insofar as they are proponents of CA, they are also committed to the view that all the virtues are fundamentally similar to one another, practical wisdom being involved in each in much the same way.

But, first of all, how plausible is this assumption about the essential homogeneity of the virtues? If we ask whether, e.g., Watson's "due concern" view applies equally well to all the virtues, the only answer is that, to an unprejudiced eye, it does much better with some virtues than with others. Temperance does indeed seem to consist in "a due and proper concern for the natural pleasures of life": the temperate person accords appropriate weight to the natural pleasures of life in his deliberations, and has desires and attachments which reflect the weight he places on these pleasures. What is more, this due and proper concern seems to depend on practical wisdom in precisely the way which CA assumes to be true of all the virtues: it involves a survey of the various goods which are to be found in human life and a reflective judgment about the appropriate place of the natural pleasures amongst this array of goods. Temperance, it seems, necessarily requires a proper view of the part which the natural pleasures should play in human life. However, this synoptic aspect of practical wisdom is, at the very least, not centrally involved in such forms of benevolence as kindness, compassion, and generosity. It is not that a person's kindness cannot be criticized as lacking in practical wisdom, but rather that the practical wisdom the lack of which typically constitutes a defect in kindness seems to relate to success in achieving the object of that virtue. Thus my kindness may be marred by insensitivity, tactlessness, or lack of imagination—qualities which militate against my achieving what, as a kind person, I wish to achieve: I mean well and have others' good at heart, but fail to appreciate what they really want or, rather differently, appreciate what they want, but fail through tactlessness or poor judgment to promote it effectively. The aspect of practical wisdom which I thereby lack is not the synoptic aspect central, e.g., to temperance, but an aspect more specific to kindness. The naturalness of this way of thinking about practical wisdom in relation to kindness is borne out by such facts as that when I act wrongly out of kindness, e.g., helping someone by an act of dishonesty, this is accounted as a defect not in my kindness but in my honesty, and that when I fail to help someone whom I should help because I am too afraid, this is attributed not to a lack of kindness on my part but to a lack of courage.

But, secondly, what specifically are the virtues which come within the scope of UV and hence are assumed by CA to conform to the orthodox conception? We might begin to compile a list: kindness, sympathy, courage, honesty, scrupulousness, truthfulness, considerateness, fortitude, fair-mindedness, decency, tact, gratitude, generosity, etc. Does UV apply to literally *all* these virtues?

Some philosophers have responded to this question by reducing the multiplicity of particular virtues to a small number of general virtues, treating, e.g., kindness, generosity, and sympathy as in effect sub-virtues within the general virtue of benevolence, truthfulness and honesty as sub-virtues within the general virtue of justice, and so on; and then defending UV by means of CA at the level of the general, not the particular virtues. The most distinguished exponent of this approach is Aquinas, who regards each of the particular virtues as "annexed" to one or other of the four cardinal virtues—courage, justice, temperance, and prudence (practical wisdom)—and explicitly defends UV (in part by means of CA) as a thesis which holds at the level of the cardinal virtues.[10]

Contemporary defenders of UV tend not to follow Aquinas in this respect: Hursthouse, Watson, and Badhwar, e.g., recognize a great many particular virtues without ever suggesting that they can be regimented in the style of Aquinas, with each assigned as a sub-virtue to one or other of the cardinal virtues.[11] They are closer to Aristotle, who does not appeal to a doctrine of the cardinal virtues and whose list of virtues in the *Nicomachean Ethics* runs well into double figures. Notoriously, though, Aristotle's list raises a difficulty for his defence of UV: it distinguishes magnificence (*megaloprepeia*), which is displayed in the appropriate expenditure of great wealth on public projects, from generosity (*eleutheriotes*), which is concerned with the appropriate expenditure of wealth on a smaller scale (IV 2, especially 1122a18–29), and similarly distinguishes magnanimity (*megalopsuchia*), which concerns the appropriate attitude to great honors, from a (nameless) virtue which concerns the appropriate attitude to minor honors (IV 3–4, especially 1125b1–8). Aristotle says that while in each case possession of the "large-scale" virtue implies possession of the "small-scale" virtue, the converse is not true: a person may possess the virtue of generosity and the nameless virtue concerned with the right attitudes towards minor honors, but not possess magnificence or magnanimity: lacking great wealth and high social status he may not be in a position to possess these virtues. Aristotle, it seems, does not in fact endorse UV without qualification: he appears to believe that one may fully possess all the other virtues without possessing magnificence or magnanimity.

My concern in all this, however, is not with the details of Aristotle's position—whether, e.g., he can somehow rebut a charge of inconsistency[12]—but with the need which it illustrates for careful thought about the way in which the virtues which are the subject of UV should be individuated. Are they to be individuated in a coarse-grained way (as they are by Aquinas when he uses CA to defend the unity of the cardinal virtues) or in a fine-grained way (as they are by Aristotle when he distinguishes magnificence from generosity)? If the virtues are individuated in a fine-grained way, it is easier to form an idea of the content of each virtue, and the full possession of the virtue seems a (more) realistic possibility. But at the same time it becomes increasingly difficult to accept that one and the same person can possess *all* the virtues: there will be particular virtues (like Aristotle's magnificence) which can be exercised only in circumstances in which very few individuals can ever find themselves; and, more seriously, there will be pairs of virtues which are by definition mutually exclusive, i.e., cannot by definition both be possessed by one and the same person—such as the virtue of monastic poverty and the Aristotelian virtue of magnificence, or the virtue of virginity and the virtue of conjugal chastity, to give the examples cited by the fourteenth-century Franciscan Gerard of Odo (who follows Aquinas in defending UV by means of CA only with respect to the cardinal virtues).[13] This problem does not, of course, arise if the virtues are individuated in a coarse-grained way (so that, e.g., the single virtue of benevolence embraces kindness, sympathy, considerateness, etc.): there is no reason to believe that each of us cannot possess, e.g., all the cardinal virtues. But now there is a different problem: what does the full possession of a virtue individuated in the coarse-grained way (e.g., a cardinal virtue) involve? If, as CA assumes, a virtue ensures that its possessor acts rightly and well within its distinctive sphere of operation, it seems that a person who fully possesses a virtue individuated in the coarse-grained way, must possess all the forms of the virtue, i.e., all the sub-virtues which fall under the virtue. But if, e.g., the person who fully possesses the virtue of courage and can be relied on to act rightly and well whatever the dangerous circumstances in which he might find himself, must possess all the different forms of courage—physical courage, moral courage, military courage, etc., and, within military courage, all its different forms: the courage of the infantryman, of the cavalryman, of the fighter-pilot, of the bomber-pilot, etc.—he becomes a mere chimaera, a fantastical figure whose existence is no more possible than is the idea of a triangle which is, to use Berkeley's words, "neither oblique nor rectangle, equilateral, equicrural, nor scalenon, but all and none of these at once."[14] The full possession of a virtue, individuated in the coarse-grained way, does not seem any more feasible than does possession of *all* the virtues when they are individuated in a fine-grained way.

Perhaps defenders of UV can somehow negotiate the horns of this dilemma, steering a course between the Scylla which threatens a fine-grained individuation of the virtues and the Charybdis which threatens a coarse-grained individuation of them. Badhwar, in particular, with her recognition that a person may possess a virtue in one domain but not in another, and her cautious commitment only to the limited unity of the virtues, may be thought to be in an especially good position to respond to the dilemma. I am not sure about this, but I shall not pursue the point. What has been said so far is not intended to do more than raise some preliminary doubts about CA's assumption that OC adequately captures the nature of all the virtues. For all that has been said so far, it may be that these doubts can be dispelled by the strength of the case which proponents of CA do, or could, present in support of the orthodox conception. This is the issue I shall address in the next part of the paper.

V.

It is a conspicuous feature of recent versions of CA that their exponents leave significantly underdefended the conception of the virtues on which the argument is built. It is not that they spend no time on the defense of the orthodox conception, but that their defense is at best perfunctory: they commend OC by comparing its merits only with the demerits of manifestly unsatisfactory conceptions of the virtues. Thus Watson plays off the due concern view against the straight view; Badhwar, like Watson, favorably compares OC with the "common view [which implies] that the virtues are straightforward propensities to feel and act in certain ways, regardless of our goals and motives" (Badhwar: 311); and Hursthouse invokes as foils to OC conceptions of the virtues "as no more than mere tendencies to act in certain ways, perhaps in accordance with a rule" (Hursthouse: 11) or as "discrete, isolable ('independent') character traits" (ibid: 154) such as "the Humean form of benevolence," i.e., "simply ... a tendency to feel concern for others and be prompted to action by that concern" (ibid: 154). These defenses of OC have the form of arguments by elimination. But it scarcely needs to be said that the probative force of such arguments depends on the *completeness* of the range of alternatives from which all but the preferred alternative are eliminated, and that the arguments of Watson, Badhwar, and Hursthouse do not meet this condition. Watson's two alternatives, for example, seem to stand at opposed ends of a spectrum of possibilities, and hence rejection of the one (SV) clearly does not justify acceptance of the other (DCV): we might reasonably favor one of the intermediate possibilities.[15]

If contemporary exponents of CA say little by way of defending the orthodox conception, this may be because they believe that OC represents, uniquely, the Aristotelian view of the virtues, that, more accurately than any other, it captures the way in which Aristotle thinks about the virtues in the *Nicomachean Ethics*. Does Aristotle not take it to be the mark of virtue to feel and act "at the right times, in reference to the right objects, towards the right people, with the right motive, and in the right way" (1106b16–28), and does he not say that "the courageous person will face [what is fearful, but not beyond human strength] in the right way, as prescribed by reason, for the sake of what is fine" (1115b10–24)? Now if the point is simply that the orthodox conception is to be found in the text of the *Nicomachean Ethics*, it may be conceded; but the support which this gives to OC is surely minimal. Are we expected to agree that OC is the most acceptable conception of the virtues merely because "Aristotle hath said it"? If, however, the point is that OC is the conception which coheres best, or uniquely, with the main elements of Aristotle's moral philosophy so that neo-Aristotelians are committed by their general approach to the adoption of the orthodox conception, it is easily shown to be without substance.

Let us accept, as Rosalind Hursthouse suggests,[16] that for those who favor an Aristotelian approach to moral philosophy the good person is the "rule and measure" (1113a31–33) of acting rightly and well, i.e., that the criteria for acting rightly and well are supplied by the fully virtuous person. Aristotelians are therefore committed to holding that the person who fully possesses all the virtues can be relied on to act rightly and well whatever the circumstances. But it is vital to recognize that this places relatively little constraint on what is involved in the possession of any particular virtue, and hence that exponents of CA, in characterizing the particular virtues in accordance with OC, go beyond what is required by their commitment to an Aristotelian approach. The orthodox conception—to clarify—distinguishes the different virtues by assigning to each its own sphere of operation, understood as the range of circumstances to which the considerations distinctive of the virtue are relevant, and stipulating that within its sphere of operation each virtue is sufficient to ensure that its possessor acts rightly and well *all things considered*. In other words, OC requires of each virtue within its sphere what is true of the virtues collectively without restriction to any particular sphere. It is clearly this feature of the virtues, viz., that each ensures that its possessor will act rightly and well *all things considered*, that justifies the link between each of them and the global or synoptic aspects of practical wisdom, and thus enables CA to proceed. But it is entirely possible within an Aristotelian approach to conceive of the virtues rather differently, e.g., to stipulate less demandingly that what each virtue ensures within its particular sphere of operation is not that its possessor acts rightly and well *all things considered*, but that he acts rightly and well *relative to a certain range of considerations*, viz., the considerations which are the distinctive concern of the virtue. On this alternative way of distinguishing between the virtues, according to which each secures action which is good in a certain respect, it will still be the case, as Aristotelians must insist, that the person with *all* the virtues can be relied on to act rightly and well all things considered, but CA will not be able to proceed because the full possession of a virtue, so conceived, will not require the global or synoptic aspects of practical wisdom.

Defenders of the orthodox conception may concede that theirs is not the only possible "Aristotelian" conception of the virtues, but maintain nonetheless that it is to be preferred to its rivals for another reason. Appealing to the common-sense thought that the virtues are praiseworthy or admirable qualities—the thought that, as Plato's *Protagoras* put it, the virtues are "the finest of all things," "as fine as anything can be" (*Protagoras* 349e)—they may argue in favor of OC on the grounds that, on this conception, the virtues emerge as better, finer, or more admirable characteristics than they do on any of the rival conceptions. How, they may ask, could a person not prefer to possess a characteristic which ensured that he acted rightly *all things considered* within a particular range of circumstances rather than a characteristic which ensured only that he acted rightly *in certain respects* within the same range of circumstances? Whatever its initial plausibility, however, this argument is not cogent. The rhetorical question it asks is confused and misconceived. We are in effect invited to consider whether, *if we could have only one virtue* but not any of the others, we would prefer to have the virtue in the form which corresponds to OC or in the form which corresponds to the alternative conception. But if, as CA maintains, possession of any one virtue in the form which corresponds to OC involves possession of all the virtues, the answer urged on us by the rhetorical question undermines that question's presuppositions. Besides, is this really the right question to ask? Should we attach weight to the answer to this question rather than to the answer to a different question, viz.: Would the person who possessed all the virtues and could be relied on to act rightly and well all things considered whatever the circumstances prefer to possess his virtues in the form which corresponds to OC or in the form which corresponds to the alternative conception? This question, so far as I can see, does not elicit an answer which favors either conception of the virtues over the other.

In any case, even if it was true that on the orthodox conception the virtues emerged as finer or more admirable qualities than on any rival conception, this would not conclusively establish the superiority of OC. That the virtues should be qualities as fine and admirable as can be is only one among a range of different types of considerations we must take into account before we can decide for or against the acceptability of a particular conception of the virtues. We cannot, e.g., ignore facts of human psychology, since we can hardly endorse a conception of the virtues which makes their possession by human beings a psychological impossibility. We must also give some weight to our ordinary ways of thinking and speaking about the virtues: no satisfactory conception of the virtues, it might be argued, can diverge too far from our "commonsense" conception. And no doubt many other types of consideration are relevant. Clearly whether OC is an acceptable conception of the virtues is a very large issue which I cannot hope to resolve in this paper. What, more modestly, I should like to do by way of concluding the paper is to outline three considerations which, I believe, count heavily against the acceptability of OC.

VI.

One reason for doubting the acceptability of OC is that it seems, on closer investigation, to lead to an uncomfortably strong version of UV, not (as CA would have it) to the thesis that there are many virtues related to one another in such a way that the person who possesses one must possess all the others, but to the thesis, which Socrates defended, that there is really only one virtue, the names of the different virtues being merely so many ways of referring to this single virtue.[17] What OC commits us to, in other words, is not the Aristotelian thesis of the reciprocity of the virtues, but the Socratic thesis of their identity.

According to OC a virtue proper ensures that its possessor acts rightly and well within the sphere of operation of the virtue. Thus the virtue of courage proper is sufficient for acting rightly and well in dangerous circumstances and must therefore include whatever is necessary if its possessor is to be relied on, in dangerous circumstances, to feel and act "at the right times, about the right things, towards the right people, for the right end, and in the right way" (*Nicomachean Ethics*: 1106b21–22). As CA has insisted, it seems that practical wisdom must be a part of courage proper—as indeed of all the other virtues—if its possessor is to be in a position to meet the exceptionally demanding condition which OC lays down for the full possession of a virtue. But do we not need to go further? Can *any element of any other virtue* be excluded from courage proper? As Watson reminds us, it cannot be known in advance what considerations will bear on acting rightly and well in dangerous circumstances, i.e., what considerations the courageous person will find in conflict with, and hence need to weigh up against, his personal safety. But, by the same token, it cannot be known in advance what other features or elements of the other virtues may be called for if he is to act rightly and well *in all respects* in dangerous situations: sometimes his courageous action may need to be informed by the kindly or sympathetic feelings characteristic of certain forms of benevolence, sometimes (e.g., if he acts in response to the violation of others' rights) he may need to act out of a sense of indignation or outrage (which seem to be emotions associated with the virtue of justice); and so on. Since courage, as conceived of by OC, must be sufficient by itself to secure that its possessor acts rightly and well in all respects in dangerous circumstances, it seems to include not only practical wisdom but all the virtues. Courage must be identified with all the virtues. And since this argument can be applied equally to each of the virtues, it seems that we are committed to the Socratic thesis of the *identity* of the virtues—or, if we prefer Badhwar's version of UV, to the identity of the virtues within a domain.

This conclusion is reinforced if we reflect on situations in which (as we should ordinarily put it) two virtues are brought into play, e.g., situations in which acting rightly and well calls for both kindness and courage, as when in the pre-integrationist American South a white person who befriended a colored person might have needed not only kindness to help but courage to face social disapproval and possible ostracism by his fellow whites. Since, by OC, a virtue is sufficient for acting rightly and well within its sphere of operation, it seems that we can say that the agent's possessing the virtue of courage is sufficient for his acting rightly and well in this situation; but we can equally well say that his possessing the virtue of kindness is sufficient. It seems both that the agent's possession of courage will ensure that he acts appropriately whether or not he possesses the virtue of kindness, and that his possession of kindness will ensure this whether or not he possesses the virtue of courage. The obvious way to defuse this paradox is to hold that "courage" and "kindness" are names for the same thing, the perfect virtue which ensures that its possessor will act rightly and well whatever the circumstances. This virtue, it may be added, is called, according to the circumstances, sometimes justice, sometimes truthfulness, sometimes generosity, sometimes honesty, etc., and in the circumstances of our example may be called, indifferently, either courage or kindness, or both.

The second ground of objection, like the first, begins from the fact that, according to OC, each virtue is sufficient to ensure that its possessor acts rightly and well within the sphere of operation of the virtue, but it emphasizes a different aspect of this conception to reach the conclusion that, on OC, each of the virtues involves far more than we should be prepared to accept as a part of any virtue. As has already been said, OC requires that the possessor of a virtue acts effectively and intelligently, i.e., successfully, within the sphere of operation of the virtue. As Rosalind Hursthouse puts it, "each of the virtues involves getting things right" (Hursthouse: 12). Thus in a situation in which kindness requires that the victim of some misfortune be comforted, the person with the virtue of kindness will not merely be moved to offer comfort to the distressed person, but will succeed in comforting him: he will not, by inept timing or inappropriate choice of words, make matters worse, but will have the tact, sensitivity, and understanding which allows him to achieve his objective.

It is vital to appreciate, and not underestimate, what this "success condition" demands of the possessor of a virtue. If what was ruled out, as incompatible with the full possession of a virtue, was merely the kind of silliness, incompetence, stupidity, or foolishness which any reasonable or sensible person could be expected to avoid, we might not feel uneasy. But OC seems to demand rather more than this—as Irwin clearly brings out in his discussion of the reasons which may have led Aristotle to recognize magnificence as a virtue distinct from generosity. The generous person who comes into a fortune and wishes to spend some of it on a large-scale project for the public good, may fail to act rightly and well not through lack of commitment, lack of good will, or even lack of good sense, but through, e.g., lack of experience: he "may well have little idea of what the public good requires ... he may easily be deceived by bad advice; he may not know how to cooperate with other people on projects for the public good and he may not see the necessity for cooperation." (Irwin, 1988a: 63) Badhwar makes the same point when she says that the kind person who "lacks experience with children" may often fail to act rightly and well with regard to them: "his general knowledge that children need physical, intellectual, and emotional sustenance, and his genuine desire to provide these, will not suffice to tell him what such care specifically consists in, or how to interpret children's behavior and motives ... his actions and emotional reactions will often be wrong, for example, harsh instead of fair, indulgently permissive instead of kind." (Badhwar: 315)

If the "success condition" implicit in OC is interpreted in line with Irwin's and Badhwar's remarks, possession of a virtue proper involves possession of a good deal of factual information and a wide range of skills. Thus it will be part of the virtue of kindness that one understands the nature and needs of those with whom one comes into contact, that one is familiar with the conventions of the society in which one finds oneself, and that one has the social and interpersonal skills necessary for the achievement of one's benevolent objectives. Perhaps Irwin exaggerates when he says that this way of thinking about the virtues "would make it reasonable for a completely virtuous person to be a doctor or a plumber or to acquire all sorts of other empirical knowledge that might come in handy on some occasion" (Irwin, 1988a: 75) and that "Aristotle seems to have no escape from an *encyclopaedic conception* of virtue and wisdom." (ibid: 75, my italics) But it certainly seems hard to resist the thought that, according to OC, the person who would be really kind, who wishes to acquire the full virtue of kindness, should, no doubt among many other things, apply himself to textbooks of psychology and social anthropology and enroll for courses of instruction in, e.g., the techniques which form part of the repertoire of professional counselors. In this respect OC clearly stands at some considerable distance from our everyday conception of the virtues. While, as I have already said, we do think that ignorance of certain very obvious facts and lack of certain very basic skills can detract from a person's possession of a virtue, we do not think that when, e.g., it is a matter of being kind to children, the person who acts rightly and well because he has had long experience of children or has mastered a technique, e.g., for dealing with temper tantrums is *ceteris paribus* thereby more kind than the person who fails to act rightly and well through inexperience or unfamiliarity with the technique. According to our ordinary way of thinking, as Philippa Foot says, "there belongs to wisdom only that part of knowledge which is within the reach of any adult human being: knowledge that can be acquired only by someone who is clever or has access to special training is not counted as part of wisdom." (Foot, 1978: 6)[18]

A third reason for doubting the acceptability of OC relates to its requirement that the actions of the fully virtuous person issue from, and be informed by, *his own* practical wisdom. In *Nicomachean Ethics* VI 12, 1143b30–33 Aristotle raises the question whether those who wish to act rightly and well need to be practically wise themselves: why, he asks, could they not manage perfectly well by consulting, and following the advice of, another person who was practically wise, much as those who wish to be healthy consult, and follow the advice of, a doctor? Aristotle has good reasons for insisting that the fully virtuous person must be practically wise himself, and we may agree with him that, even if it were possible, the person who always acted rightly and well but only on the advice or instruction of another could not be the possessor of virtue proper. Aristotle does not go into detail about the relationship between the virtuous actions and the practical wisdom of the fully virtuous person, but it is reasonable to interpret him as holding that the virtuous person's every virtuous action issues from, and is informed by, *his own* practical wisdom *exclusively*—and, as we shall see, this interpretation is presupposed by CA.

But, if this is so, how far will the fully virtuous person be willing to listen to, and accept, *advice*? It would seem absurd—though, as we have already seen, not utterly indisputable—to suggest that he would not sometimes need, and accept, straightforwardly factual information from others or advice on technical matters from appropriate experts. But at the same time it is clear that when it is a matter of the "sorts of things [that] conduce to the good life in general" (*Nicomachean Ethics*: 1140a28), when, e.g., the fully virtuous person reflects on the way in which he should bring up his children, or the desirability of a change of career, his acting rightly and well must be informed exclusively by his own practical wisdom, and thus he cannot accept, and be guided by, others' advice. Whatever the precise scope of practical wisdom, the greater the part which a proper understanding of evaluative truths plays in acting rightly and well, the less open the fully virtuous person will be to advice.[19]

All this, I take it, presents the fully virtuous person in an unattractive light. We applaud open-mindedness and the willingness to take others' views seriously, and condemn the arrogance of those who think they have nothing to learn from others. It may be urged in defense of Aristotle's fully virtuous person that he does not *need* advice: he does not merely *think* he knows, but *does* know, what is best, and so really does have nothing to learn from others. But even if it is true that he has no need of others' advice, the fact remains that in not needing, and never seeking, advice he loses any opportunity to exercise, and therefore to possess, certain virtues, such as the openness of mind, reasonableness, and humility involved in seeking advice and taking it seriously, and the good judgment involved in the selection of advisers. Aristotelian defenders of OC may suggest that these qualities are not genuine virtues precisely because the fully virtuous person has no need of them—it is, after all, partly for this reason that Aristotle himself refuses to recognize shame (*aidos*) as a virtue without qualification (IV 9, especially 1128b29–34)—but this suggestion, I feel, bespeaks the desperation of those anxious to uphold a thesis at all costs. In any case, and rather differently, may we not question *how well* the fully virtuous person, as described, can advise others? While he will have had experience of seeking advice in the days of his childhood and youth when he was the possessor of natural or habituated virtue, he will have had no recent experience as an adult of seeking advice from other adults; and we cannot but wonder whether, having no need of, and never seeking, advice himself, he can advise others in the right way, whether, e.g., his manner or attitude may not alienate them. Whatever Aristotle may have wished to say about this picture of the fully virtuous person, it remains, for us, an unattractive picture.

Clearly there is another way of interpreting the requirement that the fully virtuous person's every action issue from, and be informed by, *his own* practical wisdom. On this, more relaxed—and more realistic—interpretation of the requirement the fully virtuous person has greater need of, and is more open to, others' advice: he is sometimes unsure what will be best and takes advice. His practical wisdom reveals itself in these circumstances not only, socratically, in his recognition of his limitations but in his wise choice of those with whom to consult, in his ability to discriminate good advice from bad, and in his proper grasp of the considerations and proposals which others bring to his attention. In these circumstances it is still the case that the virtuous person's action issues from, and is informed by, *his own* practical wisdom: he does not act in the way in which the possessor of merely natural or habituated virtue would act, but with a proper appreciation of all the relevant considerations, and with, and out of, a genuine understanding that this is in the circumstances the best action to take—an appreciation and understanding, however, that he has achieved, on this occasion, only by drawing on the practical wisdom of others.

However, while this interpretation presents the fully virtuous person as an altogether more attractive figure, it is an interpretation which exponents of CA have reason to reject, inasmuch as it threatens to undermine their argument. We may concede that, even on this interpretation, that aspect of practical wisdom which consists in a synoptic appreciation of what is valuable and what is worthless is necessary for possession of a virtue proper, but it seems that a sketchier, more impressionistic, and less detailed grasp of these matters will now suffice; and insofar as this is so, it is correspondingly less plausible to claim that the possession of practical wisdom, to the extent that this is necessary for the full possession of one virtue, requires possession of all the others.

In conclusion, I must emphasize that, although, in my view, there is little to be said in favor of OC and much to be said against it, I am far from claiming to have said the last word on the issue. And so far as concerns the soundness of CA and the truth of UV, this is, of course, even more obviously the case. Perhaps it would be possible to devise a version of

CA which rests on a less extravagant conception of the virtues than OC but which nonetheless reaches a conclusion not too far removed from UV—perhaps, but I have my doubts. But even if CA cannot be salvaged, it does not follow that UV is false. Clearly there are connections between particular pairs of virtues, no doubt different kinds of connection in the case of different pairs; and it may be that in the end this intricate network of heterogeneous connections between the virtues may require us to believe that full possession of one involves possession of all the others. It may be that UV is true; but if so, I think we do better to establish its truth by this slower, more detailed, and piecemeal style of argument than by the elegant economy of CA.[20]

NOTES

1 Versions of the argument are to be found in Hursthouse, 153–157; Watson; Badhwar; McDowell; Dent, 158–159; and Annas, 73–78. A measure of support for UV, on various grounds, is to be found in Foot (1978), 14–17; Broadie, 258–260; and Ackrill, 136–138.

2 Some critical reflection on the conception is to be found in Irwin (1988a), 72–76, and Watson, 66–70 (though Watson's doubts, as he makes clear, still leave him with a conception of the virtues which can yield a version of UV by means of CA).

3 I shall use the expressions "full virtue" and "virtue proper" interchangeably as translations for Aristotle's *kuria arete*.

4 Irwin (1988a: 69) says: "only [practical] wisdom takes the global point of view"; Badhwar (325) speaks of "the synoptic nature of practical wisdom."

5 As Watson (59) acknowledges, McDowell takes this argument by itself to establish the "strong" version of UV.

6 For a brief account and helpful discussion of Milgram's obedience experiments see, e.g., Goldie, 160–166.

7 For contemporary defenses of UV which do *not* appeal to CA see, e.g., Ackrill, 136–138, and Broadie, 258–260.

8 See, e.g., Telfer.

9 Irwin (1988a: 67) lists some of the conceptions of the virtues which clearly cannot provide a foundation for CA.

10 Aquinas defends UV by means of two arguments, the second of which is a version of CA. See *Summa Theologiae Ia IIae*, q. 65, a. 1.

11 Badhwar (307) speaks of "the major Aristotelian virtues—justice, courage, temperance, generosity, and kindness" and says "her discussion of UV ... will be confined to these major Aristotelian virtues and their cognates." But it is hard to know what to make of this remark—partly because kindness is not a virtue recognized by Aristotle in the *Nicomachean Ethics*, and partly because Badhwar immediately goes on to add to her list autonomy and integrity, which she acknowledges are not "explicitly identified in Aristotle" (Badhwar: 307).

12 For a good discussion of this issue see Irwin (1988a), Kraut, and Irwin (1988b).

13 See Gerard of Odo, *Expositio in Aristotelis Ethicam* Book VI, q. 17, and the useful summary in Walsh, 458–459.

14 Berkeley (1710), Introduction para. XIII.

15 In Walker (357–358) I outline what I call the "intermediate view" of the virtues, a view which remedies the obvious defects in the straight view but does not demand as much of a virtue as the due concern view does. According to the intermediate view, the virtue of generosity, e.g., is the tendency to give to others, and the stronger the tendency, the more generous one is, provided (a) the tendency does not lead to violations of the *minimal requirements* of the other virtues, i.e., does not lead one to act in a way which instantiates a *vice*, and (b) can be relied on to lead to effective and intelligent action, i.e., never leads one to act in a way which is foolish or pointless. According to the intermediate view a virtue does not ensure that its possessor will always act rightly and well within the sphere of operation of the virtue, but does ensure that he does not go far astray, that he does not go wrong in certain ways. The intermediate view, I believe, has claims to superiority over both the straight view and the due concern view. At the very least it is a more credible rival to the orthodox conception than are the straight view and the other conceptions with which Watson, Badhwar, and Hursthouse have contrasted the orthodox conception.

16 See her characterization of virtue ethics in Hursthouse, ch. 1.

17 Socrates' views are to be found in Plato, *Protagoras*, especially 329c–d, 349b, and 361b, and *Laches* 198a–199e. On the interpretation of the Socratic version of UV see Penner.

18 But, interestingly, she has said earlier (Foot, 1978: 4): "Charity requires that we take care to find out how to render assistance when we are likely to be called on to do so, and thus, for example, it is contrary to charity to fail to find out about elementary first aid."

19 Aristotle's view that the person who needs advice is inferior to the person who does not is revealed in his approving quotation at *Nicomachean Ethics* I 4, 1095b10–13 from Hesiod's *Works and Days*: "Best of all the person who himself sees all that concerns him; good too the person who listens to others' good counsel ... ."

20 I should like to thank Angela Walker for her helpful comments on an earlier draft of this paper.

CHAPTER 6

Wielding Virtue in the *Mengzi*

MANYUL IM

INTRODUCTION

In this paper I want to consider the nature of responsibility that one has for one's own moral character at various levels of development, based on the way that the foundational Confucian figure Mengzi (Latinized "Mencius") conceives of it. I will argue that for Mengzi, there are two quite separable aspects to moral character. First, there is the set of capacities for making correct moral judgments and for having correct motivations or proper emotional responses. We may refer to these as the Mengzian conception of moral *capacities*. Second, there are the agent's episodes of choosing from among available courses of action, often through the further, somewhat indirect process of choosing to engage one's available types of feeling and motivation. We may refer to this as the Mengzian conception of moral *agency*.

I argue that the main focus of concern for Mengzi is the responsible exercise of agency in the latter sense, i.e., in the employment and expression of the aforementioned moral capacities. Hence, I take the understanding of such ideas about agency to be the primary challenge for interpretations of Mengzi. The development and cultivation of moral capacities is, by contrast, of relatively minor concern. In arguing for this, I go against some prominent recent interpretations of Mengzi's ethics.[1] In addition, taking larger philosophical aim, I will consider whether it is coherent, ultimately, to conceive of a person's agency as distinct from her moral capacities. There are interesting and somewhat compelling reasons for trying to distinguish them—reasons that emerge from considering Mengzi's theoretical motivations. However, I will suggest ways in which the resulting picture of moral agency may be problematic.

My arguments will proceed along the following general lines. Moral capacities and agency involve two very different aspects of human development for Mengzi. However discussions of the two are often inter-linked in passages of the *Mengzi* so that some care is required to see their important differences. For Mengzi, moral capacities constitute innate human nature, *ren xing*, and as such are fairly potent in all humans as a matter of course. Their proper *expression* might be captive to other abilities—for example, speech and other modes of voluntary control over one's body—which may require development or cultivation. But Mengzi does not have an overriding concern with the development of moral capacities *per se*. There is no effort required for developing them to morally effective levels, though he makes clear that their development is vulnerable to certain types of interference.

On the other hand, the exercise of virtuous moral *agency* for Mengzi seems dependent on possession of two psychological components. The first component, the ability to deliberate well morally, involves the exercise of many of the innate moral capacities. That ability comprises both cognitive and affective sensitivities for Mengzi, including what I argue elsewhere[2] is a "built-in" scheme of moral categories through which he believes humans experience the world. Part of what that means is that for Mengzi, human experience is by nature morally tinted. The sensitivities or sensibilities associated with natural human experience are necessary psychological tools for moral deliberation. In addition, however, there is also a form of "inner" control that the agent must exercise in order to *engage* those tools and hence complete the exercise of agency. This second component is in my view the most difficult aspect of Mengzi to understand. However, we need to make some sense of it since the text makes it clear that it constitutes an essential aspect of moral agency distinct from the other capacities that are involved. That such control is distinct from those capacities is clear from Mengzi's ideas about the agent's own, controlling role in preventing "self-interference" with either the development or expression of one's moral capacities.

It is from explicating this idea of inner control that we can attribute to Mengzi a moral psychology expressible through the metaphor of "wielding" virtue. The expression and exercise of an individual's moral capacities, and even the relative constancy of their development, are dependent largely on the will exerted through that individual's choices. Surprisingly, those choices include choices of whether one's own moral capacities—including, presumably, one's powers to deliberate morally—are to be effective or overridden. Such "inner" choices, as model episodes of agency in Mengzi, are his key to putting into effect the virtuous capacities that are already potent and awaiting deployment. Hence, the virtue of an individual turns on the wielding, or correct *use*, of his good nature. We might say that for Mengzi, the goodness of human nature makes people *good* but their virtue—or perhaps better, their *virtuosity*—lies in the effective wielding of their own goodness.

LOCATING AGENCY IN THE *MENGZI*

There are some preliminary things to say about how we are to understand the idea of "agency" in the *Mengzi*, given that it is a text historically and culturally distant from contemporary philosophical contexts in which the concept is discussed. It is of course possible that a particular, historical framework of character traits and moral virtues may not be able to support a recognizable notion of agency. In very broad terms, I assume that such a notion must contain conceptual apparatus for generating a consistent account of the difference between someone's acting—that is, being an *agent*—versus having something happen to her. This assumption is basic because it is an essential part of the philosophical concept that an agent is capable of being an "actor" or "doer" and not only something that has things done to it. Furthermore there may be a more or less specified, narrower idea of moral or rational agency within the broader notion of the ability to act on other things. Within a view about character traits, virtues and vices in particular, such distinctions are important if that view is to give attention to assignment of praise or blame onto the agent. For even if there are things that have *happened* to an agent for which she may be praised or blamed on a moral account, there should have been something she did—and did for reasons—that ultimately caused such a thing to happen, otherwise praise or blame seems misplaced. That much, it seems to me, is implied conceptually by a recognizable practice of praise and blame which in turn, seems to be a necessary part of moral agency.

Turn now to the *Mengzi*. Mengzi is portrayed in the text as the erstwhile gadfly to various rulers of the Warring States, each of whom seeks to expand his own power and unify the perceived civilized world. Mengzi seems intent on making the most of the audiences he is given—he is at once critical, didactic, and encouraging. It is in such moments that we glimpse outlines of Mengzi's ideas concerning moral responsibility and, by implication, agency. In particular, Mengzi tends to discourse on the responsibilities that someone in the ruler's position has toward his people and to the set of ritual, ceremonial, and interpersonal norms that constitute *ren* ("benevolence"), *li* ("ritual"), and *yi* ("rectitude"). These terms generally refer to the categories of action that seem most nearly to map onto the concepts of morality and ethics, broadly construed, in the West. Implied by Mengzi's praise, chastisements, and urgings of the rulers is a somewhat hidden view about moral agency. But the latter is only obscured by the fact that Mengzi's lengthy discourses lack any single term that could be translated as "agency." However, if we understand "moral agency" to refer broadly to the ability to initiate actions that are subject to moral assessments, it is clear that a notion of agency underwrites Mengzi's interactions with the rulers.

Once his views about agency are brought into relief and we move on to questions about the *appropriateness* of Mengzi's praise or criticism of rulers and others, it becomes necessary to look carefully at the nature of the actions he criticizes. In particular, the criticisms and ensuing advice that Mengzi sometimes gives when a ruler has failed to live up to the ideals of benevolence, ritual, or rectitude suggest that there is a complexity to his assumptions about the nature of such failures. We see that for Mengzi there are two different types of moral "failure," each of which poses interpretive difficulties because of their theoretical implications for Mengzi's overall view.

On the one hand, there are instances in which Mengzi is critical of people for lack of moral responses to situations (i.e., not benevolent, ritually insensitive, or not in accordance with rectitude), because they have somehow become incapable of those responses. We can call this Mengzi's criticism of *insufficient development*. On the other hand, he is critical of some people for a lack of moral response that he blames simply on their refusal even though they are fully capable of choosing and acting morally. We can call this his criticism of *improper choice*. It is important to distinguish these types of criticism, for they pose different interpretive and theoretical questions. For example, if Mengzi is critical of insufficient development in a person, then questions arise about how Mengzi supposes such lack of development was caused. Some ways that a person can fail to develop morally will certainly not seem to be that person's own fault though other ways may seem in some sense to be. However, if the criticism is of improper choice, questions arise about how Mengzi conceives of that choice being made so that it is an improper choice made knowingly and hence with blameworthy responsibility.

NATURAL DEVELOPMENT OF MORAL CAPACITIES AND THE NATURE OF INTERFERENCE

For tackling the issue of morally culpable failure to develop sufficiently, we need to clarify Mengzi's views about the development and possible cultivation of human moral capacities. Recent commentators have thought and tried to argue that one of the most interesting things about Mengzi is that he is concerned with moral cultivation.[3] He is, with regard to ethics, the ancient Chinese counterpart, as it were, to Aristotle, interested in moral character and committed to cultivation of virtuous feelings and choices through learning and habituation. Often cited as evidence of this are agricultural and other vegetative growth images employed throughout the *Mengzi*. However, the Aristotelian "cultivation-of-virtue" model is not quite right for interpreting these images. There is significant dissonance between Aristotelian ideas of cultivation and the commitments regarding moral agency and responsibility that Mengzi displays in certain prominent passages.

The key concept in Mengzi's views about moral development is the "nature," *xing*, of humans. Mengzi thinks human nature is good. I follow A. C. Graham in taking the concept of a thing's nature to have been more or less established, by the time of Mengzi, in the following way. The concept of *xing*, according to Graham:

> ... begins as the course of a human life, and comes to be translatable by "nature" when its scope is extended to all things ... and to all that characterizes them when they are developing or have developed along the courses proper to them. (1990: 11)

Graham offers further that the concept of a thing's proper course of life involves the idea of "how [it] develops when free of interference" (14). We should note here that Graham's analysis of *xing* does not aim to provide any clear noncircular *account* of *xing*'s normativity, only the argument that it is a normative concept. The idea of a "proper" course of development or of development "free of interference" does not explain why or how something good, right, or desirable for an organism can come apart from its *actual* course of development and/or its *actual* inclinations. "Interference" and "proper course" are too conceptually intimate for one to be very helpful in explaining the other. However, Graham's analysis does provide some analytic clarity for thinking about the implications of statements about human *xing*.[4] In brief then I take Mengzi's claim that human nature is good to mean that if people develop, in some way "free of interference," then they will have correct and praiseworthy inclinations and responses, to each other and to events in the world. I take this to resonate with a general view which we may attribute to Mengzi and some other thinkers of his time: that what Heaven produces and brings to fruition—what is *natural* in a non-empircist sense—is normative, not descriptive. This is familiar (though not always clear) conceptual territory in the early to late history of Western philosophy as well. What is natural is not merely whatever happens to be brought about, but what ideally would be brought about if certain events and actions didn't somehow get in the way of it.

We may begin to clarify such ideas by asking what kinds of things for Mengzi count as interference to natural development. The relevance of this issue to the interpretation of agricultural and vegetative growth analogies for human moral development is direct. What counts as helping plants achieve their natural developmental potential? On the other hand, what counts as interfering with their natural development? At least two passages show that Mengzi had some clear ideas about the nature of interference in the cases of natural *plant* growth, though it is difficult in either passage to make out his intended analogy to human growth.

In one passage where Mengzi talks about how one nourishes one's "great, flowing *qi*," he applies an agricultural analogy:

> … Do not forget it but do not help it to grow either. Do not do as the man of Song did: The man of Song was unhappy that his sprouts were not growing, so he pulled at them. [At day's end] he returned home wearily and said to his household, "I don't feel well today; I've been helping the sprouts to grow." His son ran back to the field to look and found the sprouts withered. (2A: 2)

The warning on the *plant*-half of the analogy seems clear enough: that *helping* a plant to grow by trying forcefully to accelerate its natural progress is a form of interference that is detrimental to the plant. The larger context of this passage deals with nourishment of *qi*, but it is difficult, as Mengzi himself states, to explain how the nourishing of one's *qi* is related to moral virtue. However, there are some things that can be gleaned from the discussion.[5] In 2A: 2 Mengzi explains to his interlocutor Gongsun Chou the relationship between *qi* and *yi*, "rectitude." *Qi* is intimately associated in Warring States texts with "biological life and vitality," hence it may be thought of as "vital energy" or "vital breath."[6] It is the energy that "fills" (*chong*) the human organism as Mengzi tells us earlier in the passage. He clearly links various states of that energy to states of relative tranquility or of agitation, indicating that emotional states depend on the dynamic between *qi* and the heart-mind. He tries to explain how the commitment to rectitude is essential to keeping one's *qi* not only minimally effective but also highly potent. Mengzi glosses this highly potent *qi* as "great flowing *qi*" (*hao ran zhi qi*). It is here that the most difficult passages emerge, including a very quick reference again to the rival philosopher Gaozi:

> Gongsun Chou: May I ask how far you have advanced?
>
> Mengzi: I understand words/speech (*yan*) and I am good at nourishing my great flowing *qi*.
>
> Gongsun Chou: May I ask about what you mean by "great flowing *qi*"?
>
> Mengzi: It is a difficult set of words/speech. To bring about such *qi*, vast and unyielding to the utmost, use correct nourishment without injuring it; then it will fill the space between Heaven and Earth. To bring about such *qi*, mate (*pei*) rectitude with the Way. Without this, it will decompose (*nei*). This is a process of giving birth (*sheng*) through gathering (*ji*) rectitude. It is not something procured (*qu*) by rectitude under cloaks (*xi*). Attempt (*xing*) it with things that don't satisfy the heart-mind and it will decompose. Because of this, I say that Gaozi never understood rectitude by regarding it as external.

If we read the main discourse by Mengzi to be fixated on a "mating" (*pei*) and "giving birth" (*sheng*) metaphor, it brings into relief two emphases. First, there is a double-aspect to rectitude: it is not only a moral and psychological principle but also a physiological one. That is necessary for making sense of its influence on *qi*, for *qi*, as we have seen is significantly physiological. However, it is clear from the point of his discourse here that *qi* also has a moral, social aspect to it. The point of filling the space between Heaven and Earth in this context must be to exert moral and political influence. Second, Mengzi means to emphasize a careful and arduous process of producing (*sheng*, "giving birth to") that kind of *qi* and hence its moral influence, in contrast with the idea of simply procuring (*qu*, "picking up") such influence. We should note that, significantly, this sort of long process is not that of giving birth to rectitude: the practice of rectitude is required *antecedently* as a means to producing such *qi*.

The end-goal of the process is that of giving birth to worldwide moral influence: "great flowing *qi*" is a reference to an arduously acquired *effect* of rectitude—rectitude's "offspring" as it were.[7]

What this makes clearer about the agricultural analogy in 2A: 2 is that the farmer of Song is depicted as trying to produce the effects of a long process without the patience to let it unfold. Hence, the relevance of the analogy to Mengzi's discussion here is most likely to his point that exerting a great moral influence on the world takes patience. A person in Mengzi's position who is trying to make a legitimate king, *wang*, from one of the overlords who aspire to the task cannot take short cuts. A legitimate king will only be produced through the gradual and patient practice of rectitude. Moving away from rectitude is what amounts to attempting to take a short cut. If our reading is on track, the point of the agricultural analogy in 2A: 2 doesn't have much to do with general human moral development. Instead, it is an analogy about persevering steadfastly with right action in the face of sometimes very gradual change. Stronger, the effective exertion of steadfast and patient moral influence has a fully developed ability for right action as a *prerequisite*.

We see another analogy with natural plant growth in 6A: 8 that emphasizes not only how tender, growing plants can have their natural growth interrupted, but also how fully grown plants can have their already mature natural growth decimated:

> The trees on Ox Mountain were once beautiful ... then they were chopped up with axes. How could they remain beautiful? However, they got some rest day to day and waterings from rains, and they were not without buds and shoots. But then the cattle and sheep came to graze on them. This is why the mountain seems so bare and why when people see how bare it is, they think it must never have had trees on it. But how could that be the mountain's nature? (6A: 8)

The analogy of this passage seems to concern the interruption of moral growth more clearly than the last passage. For in this instance Mengzi explicitly compares the mountain to the morally depraved human heart-mind, which *naturally* would have its benevolent and righteous inclinations, were it not for the effects of interfering forces. Half of the analogy is easy enough to understand: chopping at trees with axes and grazing on buds and shoots are forms of interference with the natural growth of trees. However the other half of the analogy, namely, what constitutes interference with human moral development is worth examining more closely. In his explanatory remarks, Mengzi seems to suggest that the interference to a person's development comes at the person's own hands:

> Now consider what resides in a person—could he really be without the heart-mind of benevolence and rectitude? A person's casting aside his inborn heart-mind (*qi suo yi fang qi liang xin zhe*) is like taking the axes to the trees.

The analogy of the mountain can be misleading if we're not careful to note Mengzi's explanation. It is easy to think that interference might come from something "external" to the mountain and its nature—the woodsmen come to interfere with tree growth. More difficult is the idea that a person himself interferes with his own nature. If the person has a nature that guides or directs his growth, what would cause him to stray from it? It is important to see that Mengzi does not explain such straying in terms of further external interference beyond the person's *own* act of interference.

Of course, Mengzi recognizes instances of moral depravation in which the bad influence on a person is due to external interference that is not constituted by the person himself.[8] But that is a separate and less interesting point for our purposes, for it should be clear that Mengzi is genuinely concerned with cases in which he believes a person has become his own stumbling block. In particular, a person can be his own worst enemy with regard to moral *development*; he may prevent himself somehow from developing in a naturally good direction.

RESPONSIBILITY FOR CHOOSING ONE'S MORAL MOTIVATION

Issues about development and cultivation aside, it also appears that a person can end up interfering with the exercise of his already fully developed moral capacities. This has to do with morally culpable failure to choose correctly. The choices for Mengzi concern responses and desires that are available to the person with which to motivate herself. He seems to believe that through a person's own inner determination, she may allow such responses and desires their effectiveness or prevent them from motivating her. Relevant to such self-determination are two views that Mengzi seems to have about responsibility for one's own moral responses and actions. On the one hand, he seems to think a good person characteristically has some rather strong and, in an important way, *uncontrollable* inclinations—inclinations that nevertheless have moral worth. On the other hand, Mengzi also seems to have a general expectation that people are quite capable of not only doing what is right, but also *feeling* what is right. Mengzi is in general quite willing to criticize and hold responsible those rulers who, by his reckoning, are simply *refusing* to do and feel what is right.

It is possible to glimpse both these aspects of Mengzi quickly in a single passage. In *Mengzi* 1A: 7, Mengzi has an audience with King Xuan, who asks Mengzi about what it takes to be a king.[9] Mengzi replies that one should protect or preserve his subjects. When King Xuan wonders whether he is capable of this, Mengzi replies that Xuan is. The reason Mengzi believes this is because he heard that when the king saw an ox being taken to sacrifice, he couldn't bear the terror the animal was feeling and so commanded that it be spared. Xuan spares it but rather than forsaking the sacrifice, he commands that the ox be replaced with a lamb—which, significantly, Xuan will not see. Some people thought the king was being miserly in replacing the ox with a smaller beast, but Mengzi states that he himself takes the king to have acted from a better motivation, compassion.

Mengzi here makes an important comment: "That is the attitude of a gentleman towards animals: once having seen them alive, he cannot bear to see them die, and once having heard their cry, he cannot bear to eat their flesh. That is why the gentleman keeps his distance from the kitchen." Mengzi says the gentleman stays away from the kitchen because he thinks the gentleman cannot help feeling compassion for animals about to be slaughtered—if he sees them. The point of the gentleman keeping distance from the kitchen is to avoid feeling compassion for certain animals, since their slaughter is required for sacrificial ceremonies. It is quite clear that Mengzi implicitly endorses this behavior, since he nearly always trots out "the gentleman" as a moral exemplar.

Not only in the case of animals, but also in the case of other people, either underlings or superiors, the Mengzian gentleman is like this: certain emotional responses which *suit* him for virtuous action in many instances are in some circumstances rather bad for the gentleman to engage. Two quick examples: 4A: 18, which says that the gentleman avoids personally giving his own son instruction, because he is rather likely to become harmfully angry with his own son—though, importantly, not with the sons of others; and 5A: 1–3, in which tales of the sage-king Shun show how a gentleman's unflagging devotion and loyalty to his rather unvirtuous parents and brother can prove dangerous for himself and his kingdom in some circumstances.

What is interesting is that the lesson of the Mengzian gentleman is not that there is something wrong or deficient with a person whose character is such as to be excessive in his or her responses to certain circumstances. It is rather that *that* is just how the morally good person is: the kinds of responses to the world and to each other that enable humans to be good are not easily controlled. The gentleman or sage king figures out ways to control them, however, for the sake of utility perhaps by removing himself from circumstances in which such strong responses may prove problematic.

The second important facet of self-control, and hence of moral responsibility in the *Mengzi* also makes an appearance in the "ox-sparing" passage of 1A: 7. Since it is clear that the king can have compassion for an ox, Mengzi informs Xuan that he is quite capable of ruling. Xuan merely has to extend such compassion to his people. The king's failure so far to have done this hasn't been due to his inability, Mengzi says, but rather due to his not having done what he was quite capable of doing. In response to Xuan's doubts, Mengzi asks the following rhetorical question:

> Should someone say to you, "I am strong enough to lift a hundred jun [about 700 kg] but not a feather; I have eyes that can see the tip of a fine hair but not a cartload of firewood," would you accept the truth of such a statement?

The compassion that the king feels is sufficient to reach to the sacrificial beasts yet he doesn't feel compassion for his human subjects. Mengzi criticizes the king, saying:

> That the feather is not lifted is an instance of not using (*bu yong*) one's strength; and that the cartload is not seen is an instance of not using one's sight; that one's subjects aren't taken care of is an instance of not using one's compassion. The reason that you are not a good king is that you won't (*bu wei)* be one not that you can't (*bu neng*) be one.

A similar diagnosis of moral unwillingness is expressed by Mengzi in a conversation with Cao Jiao in 6B: 2, though the concern there is with what would seem to us and to Cao Jiao to be the quite difficult attainment of sagehood. Mengzi is asked by Cao Jiao whether all men are capable of being a Yao or a Shun, two legendary sages. Mengzi replies that this is so.

Cao Jiao asks how this is possible. Mengzi replies: "Just do it, that's all" (*wei zhi er yi yi*). Then he goes on to explain:

> Here is someone who cannot lift a chicken. This is, indeed, a weak person. Now if one were to lift a ton, then one would indeed be a strong person. In other words, whoever can lift the same weight as Wu Huo is also a Wu Huo. The trouble with a person is surely not lack of sufficient strength, but the refusal to do it . One who walks slowly, keeping behind his elder brothers, is considered a well-mannered younger brother. ... Walking slowly is surely not beyond the ability of anyone. It is simply a matter of not doing it.

What is striking about Mengzi is the extent to which he takes seriously his teaching that "The sage and I are the same kind" (6A: 7). Ordinary people, on Mengzi's view, can be held to the same expectations as the sage. That is due apparently to the moral motivational power people have naturally in virtue of being human. Someone like King Xuan, who only seems *accidentally* to have shown morally admirable compassion—and at the wrong kind of object, at that—is very clearly thought by Mengzi to be capable of being a virtuous king, and not merely of *becoming* virtuous eventually, but just as capable as a very strong person is of picking up a feather. A viable account of Mengzian moral agency must square with this facet of his thought.

CHOOSING ONE'S BETTER PART

Elsewhere in the text, Mengzi seems to offer an explanation of why people such as the rulers of his day were *not* actually compassionate despite being naturally and strongly disposed to be. In his explanation, the idea of the inner control an individual has is given more analysis. Mengzi engages in an analysis that parses the individual into better and worse elements, in 6A: 15:

> Gongduzi asked: We are all people equally, but some become great men (*da ren*) and some become petty men (*xiao ren*). Why is this?
>
> Mengzi replied: Following the greater part of oneself (*da ti*) makes one a great person; following the lesser part (*xiao ti*) makes one a petty person.
>
> Gongduzi asked: But if we are all people equally, why is it that some follow the greater part of themselves and some follow the lesser?

> Mengzi replied: The organs of the ears and eyes do not think (*si*) and are surrounded by things (*wu*). When there is interaction with things, [those organs] are only led around. The organ of the heart-mind thinks and because it thinks, it can attain (*de*) things; if it does not think, it cannot attain things. This is what is given to us by Heaven. First, take a stand (*li hu*) on—establish—the greater; then the lesser is unable to take over. That is all there is to being a great person.[10]

One question regarding this passage has to do with the notion of *si*, "to think." What exactly this is, and in particular, whether "thinking" captures the meaning of the Classical Chinese word, is something that needs exploration. But first, I want to point out some things we can say with relative confidence about this passage.

First, the "lesser" part of a person is meant to refer here not only to the senses mentioned—the eyes and ears—but also to other lesser parts; I'll say why in a moment. And clearly the "greater" part of a person refers to the heart-mind. In fact Mengzi refers to these parts of a person as sources of specific kinds of desire. This we can gather from part of another discussion in passage 7B: 24 of the text:

> Mengzi said: The mouth being drawn to flavors, the eyes to colors, the ears to sounds, the nose to fragrances, and the four limbs to rest and ease—these are all natural. ... Benevolence being appropriate between father and son, propriety between ruler and minister, ritual between guest and host, and wisdom being appropriate to sagacity ... these are the will of Heaven.[11]

It is noteworthy that the limbs are included in a list of what are otherwise sense organs. This emphasizes, I think, that the primary organizing principle here is taxonomy of *desire*, which does not necessarily have to do with perceptual capacity. That allows us to expand the scope of the first passage, 6A: 15, which only talks about the eyes and ears. Also, that the heart-mind is the topic of the latter half of 7B: 24 is clear from numerous other passages in the *Mengzi* which locate the desires and other attitudes specific to benevolence, propriety, ritual, and wisdom in the heart-mind.[12]

So, in summary, there are these two kinds of desires: the lesser kind, which seems comprised largely of desires for sensual pleasures but also of desires for bodily needs—i.e., appetites; and the greater kind of desire, which includes those desires involved in benevolence, propriety, and so on. We might call the lesser desires, "sensual-desires" and the greater, "desires of the heart-mind" for convenience.[13]

Most importantly, for seeing what these passages from Mengzi have to do with our previous discussion of the parts-analysis of individuals, it seems clear that Mengzi is not only concerned with these greater and lesser parts of a person. There is a third thing of concern, namely, the person who can follow one or the other of those parts. Toward the end of the passage, as we can see, Mengzi speaks of one being able to take a stand on, or establish the greater part of oneself. It is in this relationship between the person and his own parts that we seem to have the notion of a person on the macro-level, somehow being involved with the parts of which that same person is composed. There is, of course, another way of describing the situation, which may initially sound quite normal and unproblematic. If we think about these greater and lesser parts in terms of the kinds of desires that a person can have, we might say that what is described by Mengzi is the relationship between the person and his own desires: what a person becomes depends on what desires he chooses to pursue. That indeed may sound quite fine, but problems emerge for Mengzi when we look more closely at his parts-analysis of an individual—in particular at the expanded role the heart-mind plays in virtue of its so-called "thinking" ability.

Let us refer back again to passage 6A: 15. The heart-mind, on Mengzi's view, is able to think and hence "attain" things. We can begin to understand this by looking at the contrast presented by Mengzi. Recall that the heart-mind has a relative advantage to the other organs because the other organs are surrounded by things and are "led around" by them. The contrast, then, for attaining things is: being led around by them. To make sense of this contrast we need to see first that Mengzi makes a connection between thinking and the heart-mind's evaluative ability. In passage 6A: 10, we get a discussion by Mengzi of the heart-mind's ability to judge the relative values of things:

> Fish is something I desire;[14] bear's paw[15] is also something I desire. If these two are available and I cannot have both, I will forgo the fish and take bear's paw. Life is also something I desire, as also is propriety; if these two are offered but I cannot have both, I will forgo life and take being proper. ... If among the things people desire there were nothing they desired more than life, then what would prevent them from using any means whatsoever to keep their lives? ... But in fact

> there are means that they will not use for the sake of life and there are things they will not do to avoid peril. Hence there are things which they desire more than life and things they avoid more than death. It is not only extraordinary people who have a heart-mind of this kind; all people have it.

Then in passage 6A: 13, Mengzi makes clear that thinking, *si*, is very closely tied to evaluation:

> Anyone who wants to raise the *tong* or the *zi* trees ... knows how to nourish them. But when it comes to themselves (*shen*), they seem not to know how to nourish. Could their concern for themselves really be inferior to the concern they might have for the trees? That would be an extreme lack of thought (*si*).

Now, on Mengzi's view, the ability to think is what enables the heart-mind to avoid being "led around" and instead to "attain things." A desire in general, we might think, aims for something represented as in some respect or other good.[16] But that does not ensure that when a person desires something, she has a considered judgment—or makes a judgment at all—*that* it is a good thing to pursue.

So a person may have some desires for things which either upon reflection she would not desire—because upon reflection she would judge them to be unworthy. Such desires would be uninformed by evaluation. On the other hand, desires may be informed by value—judgment of a thing's value can hook up to the "normal" aim of desiring—the aim of pursuing things or states of affairs which are good in some way. Hence, judging that something is good or not-so-good can rationally affect a person's desire.[17]

The idea of a person's "lesser" organs being led around by things can be understood along these lines. Desires for the sensual pleasures listed in 7B: 24—flavors, colors, sounds, etc.—are not informed, in Mengzi's view, by the value of those pleasures. Hence they are desires which respond to things blindly, being led around, as it were, by whatever objects catch their fancy. In contrast, what it means for the heart-mind to "attain things" rather than being led around is for a person to be led in her desires and actions by her conception and discernment of what is good.

Having put all that together, it might seem possible now to say what Mengzi's explanation is, for why some people become good and others do not. The explanation involves an analysis of a person into component parts. First: the heart-mind, which serves as the source of desires that are informed by judgments of value—judgments which the heart-mind itself makes; and second: the other organs which serve as the sources of uninformed desires. The people who pursue their informed desires are those who are the "great" people, and those who pursue their uninformed desires are those who are the "petty" people.

However, if someone merely *happened* to be a person who pursued her informed desires, it would hardly seem praiseworthy. Or, if the rulers of his day merely *happened* to be the sort to pursue their *un*informed desires, they would hardly seem blameworthy. This is because of two things: first, praise and blame are things that should apply to the person at the macro-level: the whole person *as agent* is the appropriate object of praise or blame. Second, the mere fact that one part of a person dominates other parts is insufficient by itself to make the attribution of blame or praise, at *any* level, appropriate. This is because it may seem necessary to conceive of praise or blameworthy action as something the person *does* and not merely as what *happens* within the person. What is required is to reinsert the person into the explanation as agent, as the chooser, of the "greater" part over the "lesser" parts. This, as we see, Mengzi implies by attributing the cause of greatness or pettiness to the person's agent-role in "taking a stand" on either his greater or lesser parts.

But here, things turn problematic. For what would prompt a person to choose his greater part rather than the lesser part? That would have to involve some kind of evaluation that such a choice was the better thing to do. But such evaluations can only take place in the heart-mind. That is to say, the heart-mind is *the* part of the person which performs the role of evaluation. So it would not be possible for the person to see the value in following the heart-mind, unless the person were already following the heart-mind. This is, in the philosophy of Mengzi, a version of what David Nivison has called, "the paradox of virtue," a problem that Nivison thinks plagues "Chinese moral philosophy."[18] It seems that one cannot, on Mengzi's analysis, choose to follow one's greater part with good reason; that seems to be because one cannot yet choose with good reason unless one is already following one's greater part. Hence, the choice to follow one's greater part would have to be uninformed by the *value* of making such a choice. But if that is the case, the appropriateness of praising a person for following the better part of himself would seem jeopardized.

The focal point of this puzzle in Mengzi is the apparent bifurcation between the choice-making ability and the capacities that seem necessary for recognizing the moral reasons that would inform a choice. Because of that separation, the decision either to engage one's morally good capacities or to disregard them cannot be a well-informed one—at least not in the sense of being informed by the weight of morally good reasons to act. But if it is not informed in such a way, there will be a problem with assessing the moral worth of the choice.

What this problem in Mengzi reveals in broader focus is an apparent dilemma for his view or for any normative moral view that assigns culpability to an agent for a choice that disregards the reasons provided to her by her capacities for recognizing moral reasons. Either the agent is aware of such reasons or not. If she is aware, then it is unclear why she ignores those reasons. But until that is clear the blameworthiness of the choice is indeterminate. This horn of the dilemma generates the philosophical puzzle of weakness of will. On the other hand, if she is not aware of the reasons, then it seems to follow that she cannot be blamed for the choice in question—not directly at any rate. We should consider an "ought-implies-can" principle. Justified judgment that one *morally* ought to choose something seems to require that the agent be reasonably capable of making such a choice in an appropriate way. In particular, praise or blame for making or failing to make the choice requires choosing in an informed way. But choosing to be virtuous or to reject virtue in an informed way requires the ability to recognize its goodness and to choose it because of, or reject it in spite of, that fact. But that kind of deliberative ability seems to exemplify the *prior* possession of virtue.[19]

If it somehow made sense for a person to utilize one's own powers for good and hence *be* good according to one's will to be good, requiring only that will, then it should be as simple as Mengzi makes it sound for a person to "wield all under Heaven with one's palm" (*tian xia ke yun yu zhang*).[20] However, being motivated theoretically to retain a strong notion of praise or blameworthy agency and at the same time to provide explanations for moral failures, Mengzi ends up in a tricky, possibly incoherent, position. For he must characterize the virtuous agent or the morally failed one as being in control of capacities, the exercise of which seem necessary antecedently for exactly that kind of control. But such a theoretical balancing-act appears too difficult for Mengzi, or for anyone, to maintain.

NOTES

1 See for example Tu (1979) ch. 4, Yearley (1990) ch. 3.II, and Ivanhoe (1990) especially, pp. 34–79.

2 Im (2004).

3 Ibid. See also Graham (1990), Nivison (1996), Shun (1997), and Van Norden (1992).

4 In Im (2004) I argue that Mengzi has a view that can offer an explanation for the normativity of *xing*. His arguments about *xing* imply that human drives, senses, and the heart-mind have essentially normative dictates as part of their functioning within the organism from birth. Hence those dictates can come apart from courses of desire or action that actual developments or inclinations of the person produce.

5 For extended discussion, see Im (2004).

6 Roth, Harold D. (1999), *Original Tao*, New York: Columbia University Press, p. 41. In other Warring States contexts, it refers more simply to breath or vapor.

7 *Pace* Nivison (1996), chapters 7 & 8.

8 For example, in 3B: 6.

9 I discuss the implications of 1A: 7 more fully in Im (1999).

10 A similar discussion of "greater" and "lesser" parts is found in 6A: 14.

11 To avoid distraction, I will refrain from discussing here the particular point of this passage, which is to soften the distinction between something's being "by nature" and something's being "the will of Heaven."

12 For example, 2A: 6 and 6A: 6.

13 It should be noted that this distinction is not reflected in Mengzi's use of the term *yu*, "desire." One may "*yu*" things as diverse as eating fish and acting with propriety, as we shall see later in discussion of *Mengzi* 6A: 10.

14 The term used here and throughout the passage for "desire" is *yu*.

15 A culinary delicacy.

16 This should perhaps be qualified as what a desire aims for in the normal case. It may be that in some mood states (such as depression) or if someone is truly malevolent, there might be desires for things without those things desired as being good in any way whatsoever.

17 I argue for a more sophisticated, epistemological notion of the heart-mind's ability to *si* in Im (2004). There, I argue that the comparison between the heart and the other sources of desire involves a continuum of "naturally good" desire. The heart-mind for Mengzi, alas, is also fallible even though it is better able to correct and justify both its own desires and those from other sources within the person.

18 Nivison (1996), p. 80.

19 There is no quick solution to this. Take the only other criterion that seems available: prudential reasoning. Praise or blame along that criterion is not going to be *moral* praise or blame. Worse, the choice of the moral good might actually end up being prudentially blameworthy if we don't assume a necessary link between a person's good and the moral good.

20 *Mengzi* 1A: 7.

CHAPTER 7

A Cloak of Clever Words: The Deconstruction of Deceit in the *Mahābhārata*

JONARDON GANERI

The mouth that lies shall kill the soul. (Psalms 1:11)

I. FALSE WORDS

False words have but few functions—one is to mask, another to manipulate. To lie is to assert as true what one thinks to be false, and in lying one conceals a central part of oneself, the part made out of belief, intention and will. "There be three degrees, of this Hiding, and Vailing of a Mans Selfe," said Francis Bacon in his essay "Of Simulation"; namely secrecy, "when a man leaveth himselfe without Observation, or without Hold to be taken, what he is"; dissimulation, "when a man lets fall Signs and Arguments, that he is not, that he is"; and simulation, "when a Man industriously, and expressely, faigns, and pretends to be, that he is not".[1] Bacon was not the first to observe that it is sometimes right to conceal oneself from others; not everyone has a "right to the truth" (for instance the inquisitor, or the indoctrinator), and even those who do can forfeit it. "Nakednesse," said Bacon, "is uncomely, as well in Minde, as Body; and it addeth no small Reverence, to Mens Manners, and Actions, if they be not altogether Open." If one cannot maintain an "absurd silence" in the face of the overly inquisitive, the great advantage of the lie is "to reserve to a Mans Selfe, a faire Retreat."

To lie is also—at least if one is believed—to speak falsely as if in fact, and in so doing to corrupt the listener's relationship with the world.

In lying, I make your world a world of my invention. If a statement is in general a gift of truth, the lie is a false gift. To mask and to manipulate, then, are the twin, if separable, uses of a lie (the distinction follows from the fact that an assertion "*p*" communicates two things: that *p*, and that S believes that *p*.) An appraisal of sincerity, truthfulness and trustworthiness will depend on a corresponding analysis of the mask and the manipulation. That it is right, occasionally, to conceal oneself from others is, we have said, a reasonable view; but is it right ever deliberately to distort another person's conceptual scheme, their "view" of the world, to enmesh them within an illusion of one's own making?

The *Mahābhārata* is an epic tale of illusion, deceit, and the manipulation of myth, and nowhere are these themes more visible than in the story of Droṇa in book seven, the *Droṇaparvan*. The morality of deception is investigated simultaneously on four levels, through the respective powers of four myth-makers. There is, first of all and most obviously, Yudhiṣṭhira himself, whose false words induce Droṇa to lay down his weapons. In the figure of Yudhiṣṭhira the story explores the morality of myth-making between individuals, the virtues of trust and truthfulness, and the shame involved in their violation. Kṛṣṇa, Bhīma and Arjuna embody different ethical voices—Kṛṣṇa for a straight deception, Bhīma for a "crooked" deception that pretends not to be one, and Arjuna for no deception at all. Yudhiṣṭhira might have preserved his moral integrity and saved himself from shame, had he followed the counsel of either Kṛṣṇa or Arjuna, but in opting instead for Bhīma's slippery double deceit (hiding both the truth and the fact of deception), he displayed the moral weakness we associate with his name. Myth-making at another level is woven into the fabric of the story, the great battle between Pāṇḍava and Kaurava. The weapons of battle, in fact, really are myths and illusions, summoned up by mantras to envelop the enemy in a cloud of deception. Droṇa is, in this sense, a great myth-maker, but greater still is his son Aśvatthāman at whose invocation the deadly *nārāyaṇa* itself is deployed. In this great battle for truth, the power of the weapon is a measure of the legitimacy of the illusion that sustains it (it is much too simplistic to say that the Kauravas use only illusion, and the Pāṇḍavas only truth). The third myth-maker is our story-teller himself, Vyāsa, who, extraordinarily, has himself enter as a character within his own story. On the road, Vyāsa meets first Aśvatthāman and then Arjuna, and to each one retells the tale of the mighty battle in the form of cosmological allegory. But here we see the story-teller in the very act of practising his craft, giving Aśvatthāman and Arjuna subtly different versions of the story, manufacturing in them different understandings of the moral foundations of what has taken place. More than that—all this is done in front of us, the readers, for he is "showing off" his myth-making skills with the help of the device that has himself enter the plot. He is revealing to us what this story is all about—the clash of illusions, the fight of illusion by illusion, the elusiveness of truth. Nobody emerges unscathed: not Arjuna, who is perhaps the most resilient in his opposition to the use of all forms of illusion; nor Kṛṣṇa, who promotes a tactical morality, who makes illusions self-destruct; nor yet Yudhiṣṭhira, through whom the morality of rules is exposed as a sham. The battle takes on cosmogonic dimensions when, in Vyāsa's retelling, a fourth myth-maker is introduced in the shape of Rudra, the lord of creation, who has the power to determine each individual's relationship with the world "from the outside" as it were—i.e., by creating the world. To one individual alone the creator gives the power to refashion the relationship that has been created, a power, as one might put it, to overpower. This is Nārāyaṇa who is twinned with Nara who is equated with Arjuna, who therefore alone can defeat Aśvatthāman's mighty arsenal of illusion. God has fashioned a correspondence of word and world, but man can refashion it; God has created a moral order, but man has to recreate it. Truth and morals are god-given, but god has also given to man a greater gift, the power to re-work truth and morals when the times require it, to repair god's work,[2] to refine his first approximation. The world-creator, the myth-maker and the story-teller have this in common—they give to their created characters the power to retell the story and so to revise their relationship with the world.

II. DROṆA: THE CHRONICLE OF A DEATH FORETOLD

Droṇa's murder has been foreseen already. Much earlier in the *Mahābhārata*, on the eve of the mighty battle between Pāṇḍava and Gaurava, warring factions of a divided family, Arjuna succumbs to the force of moral scruple. He is unwilling to take up arms against Droṇa, who was the teacher of the Pāṇḍava brothers in the arts of weaponry, if not in the crafts of moral reason:

> "How can I fight back at Bhīṣma with my arrows in battle, or at Droṇa, Madhusūdāna? Both deserve my homage, enemy-slayer! It were better

> that without slaying my gurus I went begging instead for alms in this land than that I by slaying my covetous gurus indulge in the joys that are dipped in their blood. And we do not know what is better for us: that we defeat them or they defeat us; Dhṛtarāṣṭra's men are positioned before us, after killing whom we have nothing to live for. My nature afflicted with the vice of despair, my mind confused over what is the Law (*dharma*), I ask, what is better? Pray tell me for sure, pray guide me, your student who asks for your help! There is nothing I see that might dispel this sorrow that desiccates my senses, if on earth I were to obtain without rivals a kingdom, nay even the reign of the Gods!" Having spoken thus to Hṛṣīkeśa, enemy-burner Guḍākeśa said to Govinda, "I will not fight!" and fell silent. *(Bhagavadgītā* 2.4–9; trans. van Buitenen)

In its entirety, the *Bhagavadgītā* is a prelude to Droṇa's murder, an anticipation of the moral quandary his existence will cause for the Pāṇḍava brothers Yudhiṣṭhira, Arjuna and Bhīma. Kṛṣṇa, the side-kick sūta, gives counsel, and we shall have reason to see that his persuasiveness secures only the acquiescence but not the moral acceptance of Arjuna. When Droṇa is killed, Arjuna will regard himself and the whole Pāṇḍava army as condemned to hell by that act. And is the assessment of the poet Vyāsa very different when, having had Droṇa very conspicuously ascend to heaven, he endows his son Aśvatthāman with a *nārāyaṇa*, the supreme weapon of divine retribution? If, in the end, Vyāsa permits the Pāṇḍava brothers to remain alive, purveying the mass carnage on the battlefield of Kurukṣetra, it seems to be only in order that he has someone there who is able to give voice to the folly of their ways.

The *Droṇaparvan* is the chronicle of a death foretold. It begins with Duryodhana, eldest of 100 brothers, the 100 sons of the blind king Dhṛtarāṣṭra who command the Kaurava army. Duryodhana, fearful of losing the battle, hits upon an ingenious but disingenuous subterfuge. He directs Droṇa to secure the capture of Yudhiṣṭhira, whom he can then command to tell the Pāṇḍavas to surrender. For Yudhiṣṭhira, he reasons, is known for his impeccable truthfulness, and the Pāṇḍavas will certainly believe what he says if by him told. Duryodhana, in other words, connives to exploit Yudhiṣṭhira's virtue, to bend it against him and into his own service. The success of his scheme requires that Droṇa take Yudhiṣṭhira alive, and this Droṇa vows to do. Twice early on Droṇa encounters Yudhiṣṭhira, and twice apparently tries with all his considerable might to kill him, fortunately for his own vow without success. Once Arjuna encounters Droṇa, and Droṇa flees while Arjuna appeals for him to stay awhile and talk. We can only speculate what Arjuna might have said, and whether he might have been able to avert with words and worldly reason what was instead to come. Droṇa flees, but with his expertise in the theory and practice of weaponry, and with the Kaurava army at his command, he begins to overwhelm the Pāṇḍava troops. Fear then enters the hearts of the Pāṇḍavas, and Arjuna, who alone among them possesses the skill to defeat his teacher, still refuses to fight. Kṛṣṇa chooses this moment again to speak to Arjuna, this time with an astonishingly base suggestion:

> He cannot in any way be defeated by force in battle. Casting aside virtue, O Pāṇḍavas, resort to a method fit for victory, so that Droṇa might not kill everyone in battle. I think that he will not fight if [his son] Aśvatthāman were killed. Let some man say that he has been slain in battle. (7.164.67–69)

Although it is not included in the stemma of the critical edition, many manuscripts—indeed all except the Kaśmīrī—insert after 7.164.67ab the line: "With weaponry cast down, he can be killed in battle by mortal men" (see 1305*, p. 953). The ambiguity and moral puzzlement that accompanies Kṛṣṇa's advice is evident even within the manuscript base itself! If we follow the Kaśmīrī recension, as do the editors of the critical edition, then Kṛṣṇa's recommendation is only that Droṇa be disarmed, not that he himself be killed. This is a position which permits Kṛṣṇa a little more moral leeway than any of the other recensions, Northern or Southern, which force Kṛṣṇa to assume full complicity in the murder of Droṇa, casting him as entirely conscious of the mortal consequences of his recommendation.

Be that as it may, the varied response from the three present Pāṇḍava brothers to Kṛṣṇa's devious proposal reveals a great deal about their respective moral voices. Arjuna immediately and unequivocally dissents. Yudhiṣṭhira hesitates and falteringly condones. Bhīma embraces the idea, and with enthusiasm makes it his own. He kills an elephant belonging to the Pāṇḍava army, whose name also happens to be Aśvatthāman, and then announces to Yudhiṣṭhira that Aśvatthāman has been slain. Our narrator Vyāsa tells us that Bhīma, "keeping in his mind the fact that it was an elephant by the name of 'Aśvatthāman' that had been killed, spoke falsely" (7.164.73). Droṇa falters, but is not duped. Indeed, he is provoked into going on a rampage, massacring large parts of the Pāṇḍava force and strewing the earth with their remains. Now, curiously, the noble sages of old are made to enter the field, wherein they entreat Droṇa to desist from his "exceedingly cruel acts," which, they reason, are both unjust and unbecoming of a brāhmin. Droṇa begins seriously to question the rectitude of his behaviour, and to wonder whether it is perhaps true what Bhīma said. He begins to worry, we might say, whether he is rightly avenging a deceit or wrongly perpetrating an atrocity while in denial about the truth concerning his son. In this state of moral perplexity he turns to Yudhiṣṭhira, whom he believes would never tell a lie. It would appear that Kṛṣṇa also thinks the same, for he now inveighs Yudhiṣṭhira as he had previously done Arjuna:

> If Droṇa fights in anger for even half a day, I say truly that your army will meet with destruction. To protect us from Droṇa, a falsehood (*anṛta*) is better than the truth (*satya*). A falsehood uttered for the sake of a life is untouched by falsehood. (7.164.98–99)

Bhīma joins in, telling Yudhiṣṭhira about the dead elephant Aśvatthāman, and Yudhiṣṭhira crumbles:

> Sinking in fear of untruth but addicted to the victory, Yudhiṣṭhira improperly said "the king is dead, or the elephant" (*avaktavyam abravid rājan hataḥ kuñjara ityuta*). (7.164.106cd)

Those improper words[3] of Yudhiṣṭhira do the trick: Droṇa collapses in grief and, laying down his weapons, assumes the posture of a yogī. But in a dramatic metaphor, Vyāsa conveys to us Yudhiṣṭhira's fall from grace. His chariot, which had up until now floated a few inches above the earth's surface, abruptly crashes to the ground! Yudhiṣṭhira will never again be taken at his word. Nor will things go as planned for the Pāṇḍavas. For it will turn out that the real Aśvatthāman's vengeance is mightier than anything the Pāṇḍava conspirators had foreseen. Only Arjuna's last-minute intervention will save them from complete annihilation. And we shall have cause to wonder whether or not it was Kṛṣṇa who created this mess, provoking Aśvatthāman into avenging his father, discrediting Yudhiṣṭhira, and putting Arjuna in an impossible moral position from which he would emerge wishing only for death. In the final analysis, is it not Kṛṣṇa upon whose head falls the moral responsibility for this result?

How, indeed, is Kṛṣṇa's advice here consistent with his own counsel on the eve of the mighty battle, when Arjuna was wracked with doubt about the morality of the war and his own part in it? Do we recognize here the "deontological" Kṛṣṇa, who lectured on the virtues of detached action in the *Bhagavadgītā*? There, he seemed to offer Arjuna quite different advice, albeit still exhorting him to fight. The advice he gave there is that all action motivated by desire for the fruits or results of one's actions leads only to further desires and so, ultimately to the propagation of suffering. For one can never satisfy all one's desires, and the more one acts with the hope of getting rewards, the more one is liable to disappointment and frustration:

> When a man thinks about sense objects, an interest in them develops. From this interest grows desire, from desire anger; from anger rises delusion (*saṃmoha*), from delusion loss of memory, from loss of memory the death of the spirit (*buddhi*), and from the death of the spirit one perishes. (*Gītā* 2. 62–3)

If the doctrine of *karma* is right, then it seemed that those who make morality regulative of their activities will achieve integrated and stable selves, in the sense of having well-coordinated projects, plans and interests. Morality would not undermine our interests, but would rather be the necessary condition for there to be a harmony among them, of the type that pursuit of our overall good requires. But Kṛṣṇa argues that none of this matters; for any goal-directed activity, if motivated by the desire to achieve one's ends, will generate only further discontent and lead eventually to the disintegration of the self as the locus of a unified set of purposes. How then ought one motivate oneself to act, if not from a desire for the results of the action? What Kṛṣṇa claims in the *Bhagavadgītā* is that the only virtuous action is action free from desire for any result (*niṣkāma karma*):

> Your entitlement is only to the action, not ever at all to its fruits. Be not motivated by the fruits of acts, but also do not purposely seek to avoid acting. (*Bhagavadgītā* 2. 47)

If action based on desire for its results leads only to a disintegration of the soul, and "nonaction," way of the ascetic and renouncer, is also ruled out, then what is left? Kṛṣṇa, I think, transforms the older idea that deliberative action is related to self-constitution. For instead of saying that it is the pursuit of a coherent set of projects that leads to an integrated and stable self, Kṛṣṇa says that this is a function achieved by performing the action itself, freed from all consideration of its karmic results. Deliberative action alone is what holds things together, and makes a person "connected" (*yukta*):

> The connected man, renouncing the fruits of his acts, reaches the peace of the ultimate foundation, while the disconnected man, who acts on his desires because he is interested in fruits, is fettered by the consequences (*karma*). (*Bhagavadgītā* 5.12)

And it is by doing the action that is "natural" or "proper" to oneself, that one achieves this:

> Each man attains perfection by devoting himself to his own task: listen how the man who shoulders his task finds this perfection. (*Bhagavadgītā* 18.45)

In summary, the attitude of Kṛṣṇa in the *Bhagavadgītā* seems to be this. We have to act, for action is what holds a person together as an integrated agent. But desire for the results of some plan of action cannot be a motivation for acting, since such motivations actually undermine rather than reinforce the agent's integrity. Kṛṣṇa's advice to Arjuna is that he must act instead according to his particular duties and obligations, but remain detached from any self-interest in the results of his actions. To act in a way that is true to one's self is what it is to act well, and the consequences, as prescribed by the principle of *karma*, can then only be good. But to be motivated to act by those consequences would be to lose sight of who one is and will lead eventually to the fragmentation of oneself as the source of a coherent set of goals and plans.

Can we find any underlying pattern in these two interventions of Kṛṣṇa, one at the very beginning of the battle and the other near to its end? Appearances notwithstanding, there is indeed a consistency in Kṛṣṇa's character. His role in the great epic, it seems, is to oversee the unfolding of a chain of events that is destined to be, and he intervenes whenever human beings threaten to throw things off-course, whether it be because of their moral weakness or indeed their moral strength. The battle was meant to take place, but Arjuna's moral queasiness and willingness simply to surrender put it in jeopardy right at the outset; the battle was also meant to be won by the Pāṇḍavas, and again this "proper" outcome was thrown into doubt by Droṇa's colossal strength of will. If human beings orient themselves in moral space with the compass of duty and rule, Kṛṣṇa represents orientation by the pole-star, seeing to it that the final destination is reached even if the path taken must sometimes meander and backtrack.

III. MORAL VOICES

Let us now complete the story. Seeing Droṇa assume the defenceless pose of a yogī, Dhṛṣṭadyumna, who Bhīma has earlier deputised to protect Yudhiṣṭhira , and who is Bhīma's lieutenant in matters both military and moral, attacks, fights and kills Droṇa. Adding insult to injury, Dhṛṣṭadyumna severs the head of Droṇa and parades it by its locks, much to the disapproval of the Pāṇḍava troops and of Arjuna in particular, who, we are later informed, had cried out to Dhṛṣṭadyumna not to kill Droṇa but to bring him alive. Droṇa ascends to the realm of Brahmā, but his ascent is witnessed only by Sañjaya, Arjuna, Yudhiṣṭhira and Kṛṣṇa (and possibly also Aśvatthāman); nobody else knows. Following Droṇa's murder, indeed, (moral) panic sets in, causing disarray within the Kaurava army. Seeing this, and apparently unaware of his father's death, Aśvatthāman asks Duryodhana why the Kaurava troops are fleeing, and upon hearing the entire story, delivers his own moral assessment of the event:

> I have heard of the ignoble, wicked deed perpetrated by that impersonator of virtue, and I have heard of that very cruel "son of virtue" (*dharmaputra*, i.e., Yudhiṣṭhira). For those engaged in warfare, either victory or defeat is certain—one of these two must occur. There [in warfare], killing will be praised. Such killing of a fighter in battle as is in accordance with the rules is not worthy of grief, for it is thus seen by the sages. No doubt, my father has gone to the world of heroes. Reaching such an end, that best of men ought not be mourned. But the trustworthy and rightfully engaged [Droṇa] was seen by the whole army to have his hair grasped, and that cuts me to the core. From love or hate or contempt or pride or even immaturity, people perform unjust deeds, as again from disrespect.[4] Dṛṣṭadyumna will see its very dreadful consequences; and also, having acted with the greatest ignobility, the false-speaking Pāṇḍava. The earth will today drink the blood of that "lord of virtue" who, by deceit (*chadmanā*), made the teacher surrender his weapons. (7.166.19–27)

Aśvatthāman's moral evaluation is very interesting. Blame does not attach as such to Dhṛṣṭadyumna for killing Droṇa, for there is nothing immoral about killing one's enemies in battle. Blame does attach to Dhṛṣṭadyumna for humiliating Droṇa after death, and it attaches too to Yudhiṣṭhira, for the deceit that made Droṇa's death unfair. Aśvatthāman holds Yudhiṣṭhira morally responsible for the murder. Any attempt to defend Yudhiṣṭhira with the argument that Droṇa's death was an unintended outcome of his actual intention, which was only to make Droṇa desist from battle—an appeal to the "doctrine of double effect"—is categorically rejected here. Precisely because Yudhiṣṭhira resorted to deceit, he is morally responsible for the "double effect" his misdeed produced. Aśvatthāman will not permit Yudhiṣṭhira to shirk responsibility, either through the connivance of the muttered word "elephant" which clothed Yudhiṣṭhira in false virtue, or because someone else did the actual killing. Yudhiṣṭhira is responsible because Droṇa trusted him, and by trusting him, put himself in Yudhiṣṭhira's care (he allowed Yudhiṣṭhira's world to become his own). Yudhiṣṭhira failed in the duty of care his very trustworthiness created. Yudhiṣṭhira did not protect Droṇa, whom he himself had made dependent on Yudhiṣṭhira for his protection.

We will see that Arjuna's moral assessment of the episode is a little different. He is soon to be called upon again, for it is now revealed that Aśvatthāman has in his possession a divine weapon known as the *nārāyaṇa*, a weapon Aśvatthāman received from his father Droṇa, who was himself given it by the lord of all creation, Nārāyaṇa, in return for his piety. The *nārāyaṇa* is a weapon so powerful that it can slay the unslayable, and its chief feature is that it will turn upon its owner if used unfairly, injudiciously, or repeatedly. That too is its symbolic function—it is a weapon that represents the reversal of fortunes, the inversion of fate; as a weapon of illusion, the illusion it stands for is the mirror image. Sure enough, the employment of the *nārāyaṇa* soon results in an inversion of fortunes for the two warring factions: now it is the Pāṇḍava troops who flee from the battle in a state of disarray and defeat, now it is Yudhiṣṭhira who inquires, as Aśvatthāman had done before, as to the cause of his army's (moral) panic. Replying, Arjuna delivers up the sternest of rebukes in a speech that is his definitive moral assessment of the event:

> The teacher was told a deceit (*mitthyā*) by you, your honour, as a means to gaining the kingdom. Done by one who knows what is right (*dharmajña*), this is a very great wrong. "The Pāṇḍava is endowed with all virtues, and he is also my pupil; he will not speak falsely," such was the opinion he formed of you. You told our teacher that "he is dead, the elephant"; this being but a falsehood wearing the truth as an armor-skin (*satyakañcukaṃ nāma praviṣtena tato `nṛtaḥ*). Laying down his weapons, he became dispassionate and insensible ... For even though I cried out mightily as one who loves his teacher, unheeding of his duties, the pupil killed the master. (7.167.33–41)

> Ignobly and with light heart, we performed that act of treachery against the learned teacher in order to gain the kingdom. My teacher believed that for my love of him I would abandon my sons, brothers, father, wife and indeed life itself. But I neglected him even though he was being killed, because of my desire for the kingdom. Therefore, o mighty king, with head hung down I go to hell. For having caused the death of the unarmed, wise and sagely brāhmin teacher, it is better to die than to live. (7.167.47–50)

Arjuna's verdict is clear—a crime has been committed, the murder of an innocent, pious and unarmed man. The motive was base self-interest, the method was underhand, and the opportunity came when Droṇa disarmed himself. This passage stands in curious relationship to the apparent moral of the *Bhagavadgītā*. Is Arjuna saying that he now regrets taking Kṛṣṇa's advice, allowing himself to be drawn into an unworthy fight simply because he is a *kṣatriya* and that's what *kṣatriya* do? Or is he saying something else, that Kṛṣṇa had taught that one should act without regard for the fruits of one's action, and this cardinal principle of moral motivation has been violated? But it was Kṛṣṇa himself who had urged them to deceive Droṇa. Notice too that Arjuna differs from Aśvatthāman in his moral assessment of the event. While Aśvatthāman had identified the deceit but not the killing of Droṇa as the source of moral injustice, Arjuna locates the injustice in the killing itself. Yudhiṣṭhira is certainly held up for criticism, not because of his fall from truthfulness, but because of his complicity in Droṇa's death. Kṛṣṇa had recommended deceit as the only way to make Droṇa desist from his frenzied rampage, but he had not said that Droṇa should be killed (not, at least, in the critical edition—this defence of Kṛṣṇa's moral conduct is unavailable in the less forgiving recensions of the text). The suggestion was a skilful way to bring an end to the carnage without resort to violence. A lie is justified when it non-violently prevents violence—it is a paradigm of non-violent activism. Arjuna shares the commitment to non-violent struggle, but he is more of a pacifist. Like Gandhi, he is willing to die for his beliefs but not kill for them, and unlike Kṛṣṇa he is not willing to cheat with other moral rules even to save himself. If Kṛṣṇa is the Dionysian moral hero of the tale, Arjuna is its Apollonian epic fall-guy.

It is now Bhīma's turn to provide a moral assessment of Droṇa's death, which in his case takes the form of an apologetics. His principal argument is that Droṇa's behaviour was morally culpable, not because he went on a rampage but because in doing so he violated his caste, behaving more like a *kṣatriya* than a brāhmin. The Pāṇḍavas, on the other hand, were just doing what *kṣatriya* do. Yudhiṣṭhira, furthermore, had not actually told a lie; rather, he had fought one illusion by means of another:

> You cut us to the core with these words, o destroyer of foes, that are like acid being poured into the wounds of injured men. You break my heart, which has been pricked by those thorn-words. An ethical man, you profoundly misunderstand the unethical, for you do not praise either yourself or us, though we be praise-worthy. (7.168.14cd–16)

> Departing from his own duty (*svadharma*) and resting in the duty of a warrior (*kṣatradharma*), this doer of evil deeds kills us with weapons not of human origin. Calling himself a brāhmin, he summoned an illusion (*māyā*) of an unendurable kind, and by an illusion (*māyayā*) has he today been killed. Arjuna, what is improper in this? (7.168.24–25)

The fight of illusion with illusion is, indeed, the leitmotif of this book, and Bhīma is correct so to redescribe the event. What remains unclear is whether it is permissible to use any illusion to fight another, or whether there are limits to the morality of deceit. Bhīma's moral voice one of social role and ethical duty, "my station and its duties" in the language of Bradley. If Yudhiṣṭhira embodies one strand in the closely woven ethics of the *Bhagavadgītā*, and Arjuna another, then Bhīma manifests yet a third, the voice of caste, hierarchy and social order.

IV. THE WEAPONRY OF ILLUSION

Confronted by the still more powerful illusion that is the *nārāyaṇa* weapon, the Pāṇḍava troops are in disarray. Yudhiṣṭhira himself surrenders to despair, and having given the order to flee, prepares to lay down his own life for Droṇa's sake, but not without first listing Droṇa's own various misdemeanours (7.170.31–36). His moral voice is hesitant to the last. Once again stepping in to repair the unjust results of Yudhiṣṭhira's weakness of will, Kṛṣṇa instructs the Pāṇḍava troops how to foil the *nārāyaṇa* weapon. If the *nārāyaṇa* is the illusion of reflection, if its violence is always reflected violence, then it is clear what should be done:

> Swiftly set down your weapons and dismount from your modes of transport—this is the method of counteraction prescribed by the great soul. All of you must come down to the ground from your elephants,

> horses and chariots. This weapon cannot kill those who are weaponless on the ground. Wherever soldiers fight against the force of the weapon, the Kauravas become stronger. But the men who dismount their vehicles and throw down their weapons will not be killed in battle by this weapon. Anyone who retaliates even mentally (*manasāpi*) will be killed even if they try to hide underground. (7.170.38–42)

Another symmetry of plot and play—the Pāṇḍavas must now disarm themselves, just as Droṇa had done earlier. And if Droṇa, having surrendered his weapons, was then unlawfully killed by the Pāṇḍavas, is it not ironic that they must now try to save themselves the same way, unsure if, defenceless, the Kauravas will slaughter them? Is this the way for them to ameliorate their sin, by assuming the guise of the victim? Kṛṣṇa's intervention once more takes the form, we must also note, of cunning non-violent activism. He again alerts Pāṇḍavas to a non-violent resource, through which they can resist the might of the weapon of mass delusion, the *nārāyaṇa*. Faced yet again with Arjuna's non-violent pacifism, Bhīma's violent activism, and Yudhiṣṭhira's indecisive vacillation between them (a violent pacifism?), Kṛṣṇa finds the solution in a strategy of non-violent activism. Typically, the method is not to fight one illusion-weapon with another (as Bhīma recommends), nor by turning the power of the illusion-weapon against itself (that is what the *nārāyaṇa* does), but by undercutting the illusion at its roots, depriving it of its power. Droṇa's energy and anger was itself the product of an illusion, in his case that he had forgotten the reason he was fighting, which was that he wanted a better world for his son. If Kṛṣṇa proposed that Droṇa be tricked, the motive was not the self-interested manipulation of another human being, but rather that Droṇa be reminded of his reasons for fighting and thereby freed from the illusion that was driving him. Likewise here: if one's true enemy is one's own violence and anger reflected back, the way to "win" is to pacify oneself (cf. the discussion of self-control in the *Bhagavadgītā*—this, perhaps, is the deep ethical message of the episode).

Does the trick work? Only Bhīma refuses to lay down his weaponry, and has to be dragged by Kṛṣṇa and Arjuna out of the cloak of flames that envelopes and permeates him. Duryodhana calls upon Aśvatthāman to redeploy the *nārāyaṇa*, but Aśvatthāman explains:

> That weapon, o king, will not return (*na āvartate*), nor can it be used a second time. If made to return, it will without doubt kill the one who uses it. (7.171.27)

The *nārāyaṇa* is a weapon of inversion, and the inversion of an inverse returns the original. Instead, in a theatrical scene of mock combat, Aśvatthāman fights Dhṛṣṭadyumna. They pierce each other with hundreds of arrows, without, it would appear, doing any real damage. Aśvatthāman now strikes out at the other Pāṇḍavas, hitting Arjuna with six arrows, Kṛṣṇa with six, Bhīma with five. Now it is the turn of Bhīma and Aśvatthāman to envelop each other in clouds of arrows. Bhīma comes off worse, is rendered unconscious, and gets carried off the field-stage in his chariot. Seeing Bhīma defeated, the Pāṇḍava forces panic and disperse, while Aśvatthāman causes general carnage.

The scene is set for the final battle. Only now does Arjuna, the most accomplished fighter on the Pāṇḍava side, enter the fray. He is angry, and he speaks to Aśvatthāman in provocative and unmeasured terms, the like of which he has not spoken before; terms, the narrator explains, unworthy and unbecoming of him (7.172.1–13). Asvatthåman is infuriated, and invokes another magical weapon, the *āgneya*, an unprecedented weapon of searing heat that sends the very cosmos into a fever and made even the sun turn away. Darkness envelops the world and engulfs the Pāṇḍava forces, and even Arjuna and Kṛṣṇa are thought to be dead. Now, however, Arjuna summons into existence the only antidote to the *āgneya*, and indeed to every other weapon—a weapon called *brahmā*. Aśvatthāman, despondent, as baffled as his weapon, departs the fight. His parting remark reveals the cause of his despair: he says "all this is false!" (*sarvam idaṃ mitthyā*, 7.172.42cd). Just as the power of his weaponry has been exposed as an illusion, so too his belief in the rightness of his actions. It is all a mirage, moral substance as ephemeral as military substance. Nothing one believes to be true and real is incapable of being shown, at the next moment, to be untrue and unreal. Is everything, then, just an illusion? Who better to answer that question than the story's narrator, Vyāsa himself, and with elegant poetic justice, it is none other than Vyāsa whom Aśvatthāman just happens to run into on the road (.172.43). Beholding him he asks:

> "Oh sir! Oh sir! An illusion (*māyā*) or an act of chance—I do not know what this must be. In what way is this weapon false (*mitthyā*)? Where have I transgressed? (7.172.45–6) Why were Kṛṣṇa and Arjuna, both bearing the traits of human beings, not killed? Thus I inquire, dear sir; please answer truthfully (*yathātatham*). (7.172.49)

Vyāsa now lets Aśvatthāman into a most remarkable secret. There was once an ascetic of exceptional prowess called Nārāyaṇa, whose great austerity freed his mind from worldly attachment and led him to behold the creator and guardian of the universe:

> He then beheld Rudra, the master, origin and guardian of the universe, the lord of all the gods, the supreme deity, who is exceedingly hard to see, who is smaller than the smallest and larger than the largest. (7.172.55–57a)

Nārāyaṇa's austerity and devotion is repaid: Rudra grants him a number of boons, the most significant one of which is that:

> You will be stronger than me if ever we were to enter into battle. (7.172.78cd)

Nārāyaṇa's great asceticism has another consequence: a sage called Nara, the equal of Nārāyaṇa himself, is born from it.

Vyāsa now decodes the story of the *Mahābhārata*, dispeling the allegorical illusion. Kṛṣṇa is Nārāyaṇa, "this god who moves about, confusing the world with his illusions (*māyāya*)" (7.172.79cd) Arjuna is Nara, the very equal of Kṛṣṇa (7.172.80) Vyāsa tells Aśvatthāman that he too, in earlier lives, was adored by the gods and was as pious and ascetic as Kṛṣṇa and Arjuna themselves; indeed:

> O noble minded one, spirited and wilful as a result of all your ritual acts and austerities, [you are yourself] born of Rudra. (7.1.72.82)

Aśvatthāman, we are told, now understood; revering Kṛṣṇa, he calls an end to the war. Thus ends five days of immense carnage, and Droṇa repairs to heaven.

Why then did Aśvatthāman's weapon fail? We are not told explicitly, but can easily surmise. In the great homology between battlefield and cosmos, Aśvatthāman is Rudra's stand-in, and is fighting against a weapon he himself has made more powerful than himself. For he has given to Arjuna and Kṛṣṇa, who stand for Nara and Nārāyaṇa, the greatest weapon of all, namely, the power to break illusions. They alone are able to dismantle the framework of false illusions, the lies, the deceits; not indeed because they "always tell the truth," but because they know how to deconstruct deceit from within, undercutting the energy that sustains its violent power. Vyāsa too, entering the story he himself has told, shows us, the readers, how to dismantle it, how to extract ourselves from the illusion he creates. For indeed the whole battle and everything in it is an illusion, a mirror image of the cosmos and an allegory for moral elusiveness in real life. That is how Vyāsa explains the meaning of the battle to Aśvatthāman.

By this time, Vyāsa has strolled over to the other side of the battlefield, and Arjuna confesses to him that he has had the most remarkable vision. In the midst of battle, Arjuna says, he seemed to see before him a person burning like fire, who killed the enemy before Arjuna had time to; indeed:

> The people thought that I had demolished all the enemy, who were [in fact] demolished by him. Following behind, I destroyed again those troops [already] destroyed by him. (7.173.7)

In what has become a familiar trope, Arjuna's apparent killings turn out, after all, to be only illusions, the fact of their being illusions being concealed by still another illusion. The presence of the illusion is itself concealed. Vyāsa explains that the person whom Arjuna saw was none other than the great lord Rudra. Rudra is the soul of the universe, and the doer of all deeds in the universe (7.173.68) Indeed,

> The disciplines dealing with the soul—the branches of the Vedas, the Upaniṣads, the Puranas—that great lord is what is most fully concealed there. (Following 7.173.69 in mss. N [Northern Recension]; see 1466* [p. 1051])

When Vyāsa explains the meaning of the battle to Arjuna, it is through a ritual cosmological homology. Rudra, we are told, fashioned the very cosmos in the shape of a chariot ready for battle

> And Śiva, having made the two mountains, Gandhamādāna and Vindhya, the two bamboo poles; and the earth with her oceans and forests the chariot; and Śeṣa, the lord of snakes, the axle; and that lord of lords having made the sun and moon the two wheels; and his two attendants, Elapatra and Pusṣpadanta, the two linchpins; and the mountain Malaya the yoke, and the architect of the gods, Takṣaka, the bindings; and the valiant Śiva made the four ropes to tie the horses; and having made the four Vedas the four horses; and the auxiliary Vedas the bridle-bits; and the *gayatri* and the *savitri* hymns the reins; and the syllable *om* the whip, and Brahmān the charioteer; and having made the mountain Mandara the bow, and Vasuki, the king of snakes,

> the string; and Visnu the finest arrow-shaft and Agni the arrow-head; and the wind the two tails with feathers, and a bolt of lightning the sword; and mount Meru the standard shaft; he Śiva then rode upon that divine chariot made out of all the gods. (Following 7.173.56ab in mss. N [Northern Recension]; see Appendix I, no. 25 [pp. 1141–2])

If Arjuna's moral stance throughout the epic has been one of non-violent pacifism mixed with a kind of fatalism, this now receives justification in the idea that the whole course of battle is bound into an isomorphism with the evolution of the cosmos. Arjuna and Aśvatthāman are given different explanations by Vyāsa, but in each case the explanation serves to rationalize the battle, to unravel its significance and render intelligible the actions of the individual participants. One thing, by now, should be amply clear. This was no simple battle of good over evil, with god on one side and evil-doers on the other. In the end, it looks much more as if the two sides in the battle were not fighting against each other at all, but rather together battling in different ways against a common enemy. That enemy was illusion in all its manifold forms. The most pernicious form of all being the concealment of the self from itself, for that leads to desire, and desire leads to anger, and a man who acts with anger in his soul is damned in the three worlds, for he is ensnared all the more in an illusion of his own making. The battle itself is a pantomime, with mock fighting, mock words and mock weapons, the deaths are mock deaths, and the lives mock lives too—everything is untrue.

V. ON TRUTH AND LIES IN THE MORAL SENSE

Yudhiṣṭhira deceived Droṇa but did not lie. His infamous muttered utterance of the word "elephant" in apposition with "Aśvatthāman is dead" preserved truth at the expense of trust. In resorting to this linguistic manoeuvre, Yudhiṣṭhira placed himself in the unlikely company of the Catholic casuists of medieval England who, faced with St. Augustine's absolute prohibition on lying in *De Mendacio* and *Contra Mendacium*, but forced to speak under conditions of persecution, and taking their lead from St. Thomas Aquinas' remark that "it is licit to hide the truth prudently by some sort of dissimulation," introduced the new doctrines of equivocation and mental restriction, whereby one made what one said strictly true but intentionally deceptive. Yudhiṣṭhira, however, was a special case—his need to resort to casuistry resulted from his personal reputation for absolute truthfulness rather than any universal prohibition on lying. Indeed, in the Hindu epic and religious literature, a general endorsement of the virtue of truthfulness is balanced against a recognition that there can be circumstances in which it is permissible and even obligatory to lie. Kṛṣṇa's recommendation of a straightforward lie in an exceptional circumstance is, in fact, more squarely within the prevailing moral framework than Yudhiṣṭhira's austere conception of what it is to follow a moral rule.

An acknowledgement that truthfulness is among the principal virtues is already to be found in the *Chāndogya Upaniṣad*:

> When a man is hungry, thirsty, and without pleasures—that is his sacrificial consecration; and when he eats, drinks, and enjoys pleasures—by that he performs the preparatory rites; when he laughs, feasts, and has sex—by that he sings the chants and performs the recitations; austerity (*tapas*), generosity (*dāna*), integrity (a*rjava*), non-injury (*ahiṃsā*), and truthfulness (*satyavacana*)—these are his sacrificial gifts. (Ch 13.7.1–4)

Truthfulness is situated here within a framework of co-dependent virtues, themselves related to a conception of human flourishing through a ritual homology. The passage already raises the question of the relationship between truthfulness and other supporting or commeasurable virtues, and with that the possibility that truthfulness might come into conflict with other virtues of equal centrality. The idea that one only injures oneself by lying is hinted at in the *Praśna Upaniṣad*:

> Then Sukeśa Bharadvaja asked him: "Hiraṇyanābha, a prince of Kosala, once came to me, Lord, and asked this question: 'Do you know the person consisting of sixteen parts?' I told the prince: 'I don't know him. If I had known him, how could I have not told you. Up to his very roots, surely, a man withers when he tells a lie (*anṛta*). That's why I can't tell you a lie.' He got on to his chariot silently and went away. So I ask you: who is that person?" (Praśna 6.1)

In the *Chāndogya*, we were told the story of Satyākama (Ch. 4.4.1–5). Satyākama (lit. "one whose desire is for truth") confesses to his teacher the obscurity of his origins, and the very frankness of his admission permits his teacher to conclude that he is indeed a brāhmin, for only a brāhmin would speak truly without regard to the humiliation. It might seem that Satyākama could have avoided injury to himself (in the form of humiliation) by telling a lie. The morale of the story, though, is that speaking the truth trumps the preservation of oneself from embarrassment or other such forms of emotional harm.

Later thinkers do not regard it as obligatory to tell the truth when there is a question of self-preservation from physical harm, or of doing and preventing harm to others. Manu succinctly brings out the logical relationship in such cases of conflicting obligation:

> A man should tell the truth and speak with kindness (*priya*); he should not tell the truth unkindly nor utter lies out of kindness. This is a constant duty. (Manu 4.138)

If we take "kindness" here to include the virtues other than truthfulness, Manu's clever formula implies that the "constant duty" (*sanātana-dharma*) is to joint satisfaction of all the virtues, there being no categorical obligation to one when it is in conflict with another. One is not obliged to tell the truth regardless, when doing so involves one in an "unkindness," nor is one obliged to lie even when doing so would be "kind." In a situation where the only choice is between speaking truly but unkindly or speaking untruly but kindly, an appeal to the standing virtues will not be able to guide one's action. Yudhiṣṭhira found himself in exactly such a situation, having to choose between a truth that would lose the battle finally for the Pāṇḍavas and a lie that would decisively win it. Arjuna recommended the first course of action, Kṛṣṇa the second, and Bhīma a suspiciously casuistic fudge. The problem with the casuistic resolution is that it is hard to see how there can be any moral difference between deception by assertion and deception by conversational implicature; and if that is right, then, ironically, it is more honest simply to lie.

In the twelfth book of the *Mahābhārata*, the *Sāntiparvan*, Bhīṣma is on his deathbed, and at Yudhiṣṭhira's request enters into a lengthy moral discourse. If Yudhiṣṭhira's deeds and misdeeds in the course of the battle are not explicitly referred to, this is nevertheless the place where a moral assessment of them is attempted. Of particular significance, then, are the sections where Bhīṣma discusses the moral status of truth and truthfulness (12.110, 12.140 and 12.156). Bhīṣma stresses more than once that it is not always immoral to lie, and that one has to use one's reason and intelligence in each particular case to discriminate between the moral and the immoral:

> Therefore, O son-of-Kuntī, one who is wise and self-restrained

> should dwell in this world resorting to his intellect (*buddhi*) in the discrimination of the moral and the immoral (*dharmādharmaniścaya*). (MB 12.139.94)

We have just been told the story of a brāhmin Viśvamitra who chooses to eat dog-meat rather than to starve, the moral being that the preservation of one's own life justifies erstwhile violations of religious duty. Yudhiṣṭhira's response is extremely telling: he says that if an act so detestable that it resembles a lie is permissible, then moral duty (*dharma*) itself is made loose, and there is no act from which one should desist (12.140.1). In raising the spectre of moral chaos, Yudhiṣṭhira reveals the fear that motivates the inflexible rule-follower and displays again his moral cowardice. Unable to trust his moral judgement, he prefers instead a blind allegiance to the moral law. Bhīṣma proceeds to give Yudhiṣṭhira a sharp lesson in the necessity for kings to have sound practical reason! A king should not depend on a morality derived from one faction alone, but must use his intellect (*buddhi*) to draw wisdom from a variety of sources and examples. For the moral sometimes assumes the outward form of the immoral; the sin involved in killing one who ought not to have been killed is on par with the sin of not killing someone who ought to be killed (i.e., one cannot simply follow the rule "do not kill") (12.140.26ab). Yudhiṣṭhira then asks Bhīṣma if there is any rule at all which permits of no exception, to which Bhīṣma responds that the only rule is to worship learned and pious brāhmin as if they are gods. A cruel turn!—Up to this point, Yudhiṣṭhira might have hoped to find some comfort in Bhīṣma's words for his decision to deceive Droṇa, but now it is almost as if Bhīṣma plays a trick on him. The rule-follower's desperate need is for a rule to follow—then let it be "don't kill revered brāhmins" rather than "don't tell lies." Yudhiṣṭhira's rule-following morality leads down a blind alley.

How then ought one's moral reason guide one when what is at stake is whether to tell the truth or tell a lie? More than once in the *Mahābhārata* are inserted verses from the *dharmaśāstra* giving a list of exemptions to the general prohibition on lying (e.g., following 7.164.99 in some mss.; 12.110.18ab). Typically, five exemptions are noted in the *dharma-sūtras*, although there is no great consistency in the list:

> A man may tell a lie at a marriage; during a sexual encounter; when his life is at stake; when there is a risk of losing all his property; and for the sake of a Brāhmin. These five types of lies, they say, do not

> entail loss of caste. (Vasiṣṭa 16.36; trans. Olivelle)
>
> According to some, telling a lie at a marriage, during sex, in jest, or in grief is not a sin. (Gautama 23.29; trans. Olivelle)
>
> When speaking truly would lead to the death of a śūdra, vaiśya, kṣatriya or brāhmin, one should tell a lie, for that is better than the truth. (Manu 8.104)

Apparently, then, it is the generally accepted norm that a lie carries no moral sanction when it falls into one or more of the following categories:

- the protective lie (defence of self or others, esp. kin and brāhmins),
- the dutiful lie (benefiting someone to whom one owes respect, esp. teachers),
- the marital lie,
- the jocose lie,
- the amorous lie.

A "pernicious" lie, by contrast, is a lie that benefits the liar and harms someone else. It is curious indeed that Kṛṣṇa should appeal to the rough-cut norms of conventional morality in his attempt to persuade Yudhiṣṭhira, if indeed his designated role is that of moral innovator. Kṛṣṇa's argument, in effect, is that Yudhiṣṭhira's lie falls into the category of the protective lie. Arjuna dissents from this evaluation: for him, the lie is pernicious, deriving solely from a desire to re-acquire the kingdom.

Kṛṣṇa and Arjuna have differing moral assessments, then, of Yudhiṣṭhira's atypical speech-act. How are we to decide which of them is right? On what grounds can we decide if Yudhiṣṭhira was, after all, displaying a virtuous disposition, the disposition to trustworthiness in speech, where that denotes a reliability to say the "right" thing, the thing the particular circumstance calls to be said? In one section of the *Śāntiparvan*, the book of the *Mahābhārata* where some explicit form of moral assessment of the epic tale is attempted, this question is addressed head on. Yudhiṣṭhira asks Bhīṣma our question, and coming from his lips the question has an unmistakable poignancy:

> Yudhiṣṭhira said—Bhārata, how does one live who desires to reside in morality (*dharma*)? Wise bull of Bhārata, do reply to this inquiry! Concealing the world, truth (*satya*) and falsity (*anṛta*) occur together.

> Of these two, O King, which should one practise who is settled on morality? What is truth? What is falsity? And what is the morality constant for all (*sanātana*)? At which times ought one speak the truth, and at which times ought one to speak falsely? [12.110.1–3]
>
> Bhīṣma said—Speaking the truth is a good (*sādhu*), and there is nothing higher than truth. I will tell you, Bhārata, something that is very difficult in the common world to understand. When the truth would be false, and also when the false would be true, one should not speak truly; one should speak falsely. For this reason, a fool is in a state of confusion when not resting on the truth. Discriminating between truth and falsity, then, is the one who understands morality. (12.110.4–6)
>
> A person might obtain great merit though he be ignoble, stupid and cruel; as for instance Valāka, who slew the blind monster [by mistake—he was simply out to kill]. How extraordinary that a fool, desiring to be moral without understanding morality, might obtain to great sin; [yet another] instance is the owl on the bank of the Gaṇgā. Your question here is similar: it is extremely hard to say what is moral. Although very hard to find a reply, this will be attempted now by means of the use of reason (*tarka*). Morality (*dharma*) has been described as for the sake of the glory or dignity (*prabhāva*) of creatures, from which morality is determined to consist in non-violence (*ahiṃsā*). Morality is, it is said, that which upholds and maintains (*dhāraṇā*), creatures being supported by morality. From that, morality is determined to consist in maintenance. Some people say that morality has its basis in the scriptures, but other people deny this. We do not condemn this, for not all morality is based in scriptural prescription. (12.110.7–12)
>
> One ought never speak with those who, wanting another's money, seek to please. This is certainly the right thing to do. If one is able to get free by remaining silent, one should not make a sound. If one has to speak, or if not to speak would invite distrust, then it is better to speak falsely than the truth—this is the considered opinion. (12.110.13–15ab.)

Bhīṣma displays greater sensitivity to what B. K. Matilal has aptly termed the "elusiveness" and "ambiguity" of *dharma*[5] than is always apparent in *dharmaśāstra* writers like Manu (e.g., Manu 2.83—"truthfulness is better than silence.") Sometimes it is wrong to tell the truth; sometimes, indeed, it is right to lie. When? Bhīṣma's answer is clear—when one conceals the truth from a person who has *no right to the truth*. To give somebody something of value (a truth, a piece of wealth) to which they have no rightful entitlement is not to display any virtue; indeed, it is to fall victim to a vice. A person of sound moral reason is able to discriminate and decide for themselves in each particular case whether the person who makes a demand has a right to what is being demanded, the basis for that judgement involving an assessment of the person's reasons for wanting it. One might indeed incur a great moral wrong in blindly following some such moral precept as "Do not lie," as the example to which Bhīṣma alludes and reveals. This is the case, mentioned in the *Karnaparvan*, of a man who reveals the whereabouts of an innocent fugitive to a would-be assassin. It is a curiosity of comparative ethics that virtually the same example would be used by Kant, and Augustine makes a similar case in giving voice to the same sense of moral puzzlement during his discussion of the rights and wrongs of lying:

> Concerning these persons therefore, whom we have set forth, there is no small question. The one, who knows or thinks he says a false thing, and says it on purpose that he may not deceive: as, if he knows a certain road to be beset by robbers, and fearing lest some person for whose safety he is anxious should go by that road, which person he knows does not trust him, should tell him that that road has no robbers, on purpose that he may not go by it, as he will think there are robbers there precisely because the other has told him there are none, and he is resolved not to believe him, accounting him a liar. The other, who knowing or thinking that to be true which he says, says it on purpose that he may deceive: for instance, if he tells a person who does not believe him, that there are robbers in that road where he really knows them to be, that he to whom he tells it may the rather go by that road and so fall among robbers, because he thinks that to be false, which the other told him. Which then of these lies? The one who has chosen to say a false thing that he may not deceive? Or the other who has chosen to say a true thing that he may deceive? That one, who in saying a false thing aimed that he to whom he spake should follow the truth? Or this one, who in saying a true thing aimed that he to whom he spake should follow a falsehood? Or haply have both lied? The one, because he wished to say a false thing: the other, because he wished to deceive? Or rather, has neither lied? Not the one, because he had the will not to deceive: not the other, because he had the will to speak the truth? For the question is not now which of them sinned, but which of them lied: as indeed it is presently seen that the latter sinned, because by speaking a truth he brought it about that a person should fall among robbers, and that the former has not sinned, or even has done good, because by speaking a false thing he has been the means of a person's avoiding destruction.(*De Mendacio*, §4)

Bhīṣma's argument defends lies of concealment, when the person from whom one is concealing the truth does not have a right to the truth. On the other hand, his argument gives no succor to pernicious lies, lies that manipulate others when they have not asked for the truth, usually for one's own gain.

Now a new subtlety in the Droṇa story begins to unfold. The lie that deceived Droṇa—was it a lie of concealment or a lie of manipulation? Did Droṇa himself request the information, or was he "fed" that information with the intention of contorting his view of the world? We see now a clear difference between the sentence "Aśvatthāman is dead" as uttered by Bhīma and the same sentence as uttered by Yudhiṣṭhira. In the mouth of Bhīma, the sentence is a manipulative lie, intended to produce in Droṇa a false belief he had until then no reason even to suspect. But the seeds of doubt were laid, and by the time Droṇa turns to Yudhiṣṭhira, he is demanding the information from him. Sense can now be made of the puzzling intervention by the great sages of the past, who suddenly appear and inveigh Droṇa to desist. The cumulative effect is to reinforce in Droṇa's mind the necessity of demanding the information from Yudhiṣṭhira. And now the question is no longer whether to manipulate Droṇa by feeding him lies, but rather the issue is whether Droṇa has a right to the truth which he demands. The ethics of concealment have replaced the ethics of manipulation, and we have entered the territory of the honest lie.

Is the attempt to classify Droṇa with the bandit and the inquisitor successful? One reason to think that he does not, after all, have a right to the truth about his son from Yudhiṣṭhira is that he is "trading upon" Yudhiṣṭhira's virtue, exploiting his reputation for truthfulness for his own ends, and surely virtue is not so easily abused. Droṇa, we might say, is trying to be a "free-rider" on Yudhiṣṭhira's goodness. Yudhiṣṭhira simply beats him at his own game (thus 12.110.26—"One who uses illusion (*māyā*) should be met with illusion; one who is good should be answered with goodness."). That is, indeed, one great lesson of the *Droṇaparvan*—the need to fight illusion with illusion, the requirement not to play straight against a crooked opponent. In that sense, Kṛṣṇa is right; but Arjuna is right too in his moral assessment, for when one plays dirty against the dirty, there is no hope of emerging with one's honor, dignity and self-respect intact. Arjuna is right that the Pāṇḍava warriors can feel only regret for what they have done, but wrong to imagine that choosing the beggar's life would be, ethically, better (*Bhagavadgītā* 2.2). If Yudhiṣṭhira was later to feel regret for what he had done, perhaps it was the kind of regret any ethically sensitive person would feel when they have had to deceive another human being for the sake of the greater good, rather than the kind of regret that is mixed with shame, when one regrets doing something one knows one should not have.

Our good poet Vyāsa naturally cannot leave it at that. Yudhiṣṭhira, we are reminded, uttered the words being "desirous of victory," and pathetically muttered "elephant" under his breath. That was no casuistic attempt to outwit the inquisitor, but a feeble concession to vanity. And if it is true that Yudhiṣṭhira's motive was victory, then the lie was simply pernicious. True to form, Vyāsa again muddies the dark waters of moral reflection.

VI. THE VIRTUES OF TRUTH

The *Mahābhārata* is a sustained moral reflection on the value of truth and truthfulness. Is truth an intrinsic good or simply an instrumental one? If intrinsically good, does that imply that there is nothing more to be said in its defense? Or is there some way to explain why something is of intrinsic value without reducing that value to others? Bernard Williams has an extremely insightful discussion of the notion of an intrinsic value, and specifically of the idea that truthfulness is an intrinsic value (Williams 2002). He claims that for something to be an intrinsic good it must be stable under reflection, which requires that "the agent has some materials in terms of which he can understand this value in relation to other values he holds, and this implies, in turn, that the intrinsic good, or rather the agent's relation to it, has an inner structure in terms of which it can be related to other goods" (2002, 92). He continues:

> For us to get clear about trustworthiness as an intrinsic good, we need to answer two kinds of question. First, we have to decide what disposition or set of dispositions trustworthiness is; as we might also say, what it needs to be.... Second, we have to see what those other values may be that surround trustworthiness, values that provide the structure in terms of which it can be reflectively understood ... That [structure] has been differently understood in differing cultural circumstances. Everywhere, trustworthiness and its more particular applications such as that which concerns us, sincerity, have a broadly similar content—we know what we are talking about—and everywhere,

> it has to be related, psychologically, socially, and ethically, to some wider range of values. What those values are, however, varies from time to time and culture to culture, and the various versions cannot be discovered by general reflection ... Sincerity has a history, and it is the deposit of this history that we encounter in thinking about the virtues of truth in our own life. This is why at a certain point philosophy needs to make way for history, or, as I prefer to say, to involve itself in it. (2002, 92–3)

This is a manifesto for the cross-cultural study of value. It is extremely interesting, therefore, to find Yudhiṣṭhira asking precisely the two questions Williams says need to be asked, and to hear Bhīṣma answering by situating the value in question (here truth) within a framework of values and emotions that help to make sense of it as something of worth:

> Yudhiṣṭhira said—When it comes to morality, the gods, the fathers and the sages all commend truth. I want to learn about truth—tell me about it, O Grandfather. What is the indicating mark of truth, O King, and how is it to be secured? What might truth obtain, and how? Tell me this. (12.156.1–2)

> Bhīṣma said—Bhārata, mixing the moral duties of the four castes is not recommended, [yet] the truth is unchanged among all the castes. For the good, truth is always morally right, truth is the morality constant for all (*sanātana*). One ought submit oneself to truth alone, for truth is the highest path. Moral duty is truth, as is austerity (*tapas*) and mental discipline (*yoga*); Brahmā is truth, constant for all. Truth, it is said, is a high ritual. On truth, everything stands. Having spoken thus of the customary forms of truth, I will now describe in sequence its indicating marks. And you must also hear about how truth is secured. Bhārata, among all people, truth is of thirteen kinds. Without doubt, truth is impartiality indeed, as well as self-control; it is freedom-from-envy, toleration, modesty, patience and freedom-from-spite; it is renunciation, contemplation, nobility, steadiness, perpetual calmness and non-violence—these, O King, are the thirteen aspects of truth. Truth is thus indeed imperishable, eternal and unchanging. Not in conflict with any moral duty, it is secured by means of mental discipline (*yoga*) (12.156.3–10). ... These thirteen forms are the several indicating marks of the one truth; they partake of, and they speak of, the truth, Bhārata. One cannot speak enough of the qualities of truth, and that is why the gods, the fathers and the sages commend truth. There is no higher morality than truth, nor a greater sin than falsehood. Truth is the foundation of morality; therefore, one should not suppress truth. From truth comes generosity, rituals with offerings, rituals with fire,

> the Vedas, and indeed everything else determinative of morality. Truth has been held in the balance against a thousand *aśvamedha* horse sacrifices, and truth indeed outweighed them. (12.156.22–26)

We have been accustomed, at least since Kant, to see the value of truth as grounded in a sense of respect for the autonomy of others; to deceive is to manipulate, and that is a way to treat the other as a means to one's own advancement and not as an end in themselves. A more archaic conception situates truth in a framework of ethical emotion: to be true to one's word is a matter of honor, and with dishonor comes public shame and private remorse. Bhīṣma here gives voice to a complex third structure of values and sentiments that ground a sense of the intrinsic value of truth. A different list in the *Bhagavadgītā* situates truthfulness within an even wider matrix of virtues,

> Fearlessness, inner purity, fortitude in the yoking of knowledge, liberality, self-control, sacrifice, vedic study (*svādhyāya*), austerity, uprightness, nonharming (*ahiṃsā*), truthfulness, peacableness, reliinquishment (*tyāga*), serenity, loyalty, compassion for creatures, lack of greed, gentleness, modesty, reliability (*acāpala*), vigor (*tejas*), patience, fortitude, purity, friendliness, and lack of too much pride comprise the divine complement of virtues of him who is born to it, Bhārata. Deceit, pride, too much self-esteem, irascibility, harshness, and ignorance are of him who is born to the demonic complement, Bhārata. (*Gītā* 16. 1–4)

Not all the virtues in this wider matrix are virtues specifically involved in the maintenance of a practice of truth. Bernard Williams has classified the virtues of truth into two general categories—virtues of sincerity and virtues of accuracy. Sincerity is a disposition towards trustworthiness in speech, a reliability to do what one has said one will and say what one believes. Accuracy is a disposition towards honesty in belief, the promotion of forms of conduct that ensure that the beliefs one acquires are consistently correlated with the way things really are. Earlier in this book, I argued that a third virtue of truth needs recognition, which I called the virtue of receptivity (see §2.2). This is the disposition to allow a truth, once believed, to have its full weight within the structure of one's mental space, the disposition to resist the insulation of belief. Receptivity and accuracy are the virtuous counterforms of concealment, sincerity the counterform of manipulation.

Let us consider in more detail how each of the 13 virtues listed by Bhīṣma comes to be a form of a virtue of truth. One outcome of this exercise will be to achieve a clearer assessment of the respective moral strengths and weaknesses of Yudhiṣṭhira, Bhīma and Arjuna, Kṛṣṇa and Aśvatthāman. Helpfully, the text supplies definitions of the truth-related virtues:

(1) Impartiality (*samatā*). Impartiality is sameness as between what is good for oneself and what is bad for one's enemy, and is grounded in the elimination of both desire and aversion, love and hate (12.156.11).

(2) Self-control (*dama*). Self-control is constantly not to envy another, steadiness/fortitude and depth, freedom from fear and anger. It is acquired by knowledge (12.156.12).

(3) Freedom from envy (*amātsarya*). Freedom from envy was called by the wise generosity and dedication to one's duty. One becomes free from envy by constantly remaining with truth (12.156.13).

(4) Toleration (*kṣamā*). In the matter of toleration and intolerance, a good man tolerates entirely the agreeable as well as the disagreeable. It is acquired by a good man, possessing the truth. (12.156.14).

(5) Modesty (*hrī*). Out of modesty, someone whose mind is tranquil does much that is good and does not boast. It is acquired by moral duty (12.156.15).

(6) Patience (*titikṣā*). Patience, also called forbearance (*kṣānti*) is that by which one tolerates for the sake of moral duty. It is acquired by steadiness/fortitude, and has as its purpose the encouragement of ordinary people (12.156.16).

(7) Renunciation (*tyāga*). Renunciation is the renunciation of both love and material possession. For one who has cast off both attraction and aversion is there renunciation, and not for any other (12.156.17).

(8) Nobility (*āryatā*). He who exerts himself to do good deeds for creatures is said to be noble. It consists in freedom from passion, and is without a form [of its own] (12.156.18).

(9) Steadiness (*dhṛti*). Steadiness is that by which one remains unperturbed in pleasure as in pain. The wise man who wishes for his own good fortune should always cultivate it. One should always have toleration and then truth. The clever man who casts off joy and dread and anger acquires steadiness (12.156.19–20).

(10) Calmness (*sthira*) [no definition].

(11) Non-injury (*adroha*). Not injuring in action, thought or speech is a constant duty of a good man (12.156.21).
(12) Kindness or freedom from spite (*anugraha or anasūyatā*). Kindness too is a constant duty of a true and good person (12.156.21).
(13) Generosity (*dāna*) (12.156.21). So to is generosity (but the original list has contemplation (*dhyāna*) instead).

Why is it these virtues that render intelligible the practice of truth within an Indian context? The underlying theme is that of the mind as unsettled by emotions like fear, anger, greed or even attachment and attraction. A mind thus wracked by strong emotion will place the satisfaction of desire above the determination of truth. The practice of truth makes sense only within a framework of virtues that puts great weight on steadiness of mind. The steady mind is the one that will be objective and impartial, unbiased by its own needs. In this Indian context, the practice of truth is strongly associated with the cultivation of a mind free from directive passions. Once more it is receptivity which emerges as the cardinal virtue of truth, ahead of both accuracy and sincerity. When, then, might it be consistent with a practice of truth to conceal one's beliefs from others? When the disclosure would threaten the very stability of mind upon which the practice of truth rests. If this provides occasional justification for lies of concealment, if offers no justification for the manipulative lie. For to deceive someone by manipulation is to distort their relationship with the world, and that will always threaten to undermine the calmness and steadiness of mind upon which their retention of the practice of truth depends. To manipulate another with a lie is, in that sense, to harm their well-being. Concealment is a weapon of resistance, and is consistent with the maxim of not harming ("to reserve to a Mans Selfe, a faire Retreat," as Bacon put it). Manipulation is a weapon of aggression, and is not. Gandhi characterized the relationship between the maxim of not harming (*ahiṃsā*) and the practice of truth (*satyagraha*) as a means-ends relationship, and this captures some of what Williams meant in speaking of an "inner structure"; but we should not think of the relationship in excessively instrumental terms, for what is in question is not how the practice is made, but how it is made sense of, and that is what preserves each of the virtues involved as itself an intrinsic good.

Bhīma, we can clearly see, lacked all the virtues on our list and saw no harm in lying. Arjuna possessed them all, and could not bring himself to lie or to condone the lie. Yudhiṣṭhira's possession of the virtues was present but shaky; his practice of truth was not properly grounded in a solid cultivation of the virtues of truth, but remained at the level of a rule to be followed. He did not really see that in deceiving Droṇa he was not only doing him harm, but was doing him exactly the sort of harm a proper understanding of the value of truth would never permit. By corrupting Droṇa's relationship with the world, he deprived Droṇa of the ability to sustain the very calmness of mind that would have brought the carnage to an end: he deprived Droṇa of the capacity to be human. Had he been Kṛṣṇa, he might have attained of a higher-level understanding of his action, one that sees it in terms of a necessary realignment of Droṇa's attitude, an attitude that has become misshapen. Yudhiṣṭhira, however, does not see Droṇa as someone in the grip of a delusion from which he must be deceitfully freed. Yudhiṣṭhira sees Droṇa as a force that must be stopped, even at the expense of Droṇa's own humanity. He lacked the "reflective understanding" of the practice of truth that would have permitted him either to endorse the lie as Kṛṣṇa did, or to follow Arjuna and reject it. He knew that it was good to be truthful, but he had no insight into the framework of correlative virtues that go to makes sense of truthfulness as a good in itself. Kṛṣṇa managed to impart some of that understanding to Arjuna, but had less success with Yudhiṣṭhira, and none with Bhīma. This inability to comprehend the point of a virtuous practice was the source of Yudhiṣṭhira's great moral failing, and it would in the end cost the Pāṇḍavas dear.

NOTES

1 *Essayes*, "Of Simulation," pp. 18–20.

2 Cf. the discussion of vedism in B. K. Smith, *Reflections on Resemblance, Ritual and Religion* (New York: Oxford University Press, 1989).

3 Taking the clause to be one of direct speech, as is usual in Sanskrit, the name "Aśvatthāman" is not used. Might this then be a rare instance of indirect speech in Sanskrit, the actual words uttered by Yudhiṣṭhira being "Aśvatthāman is dead," adding "the elephant" in murmured apposition? The impropriety of the statement is not necessarily a mattter of its being false; even if true, it is intentionally deceptive.

4 See Manu 8.107.

5 B. K. Matilal, "Elusiveness and ambiguity in dharma-ethics," in his *Epics and Ethics (Delhi: Oxford University Press, 2002).*

CHAPTER 8

Virtue Metaphysics and Consciousness

BIJOY BORUAH

Whether in the West or in the East, the normative intellectual tradition of humanity recognizes virtues as excellences of character. It therefore is a truism to say that a virtuous person possesses or develops a character that excels in certain respects of action and attitude. It is perhaps more pertinent to say that a person develops a virtuous character, because excellence of character is acquired by self-transformative practice and effort. In this developmental sense, a self-transformative life geared to progressive excellence of character can be imagined to attain perfection. It may be perfection in respect either of particular virtues or a combination of particular virtues. But it may also be perfection of character in an overall and radical sense, of attaining the kind of virtuous personality that promises the possibility of enlightenment. In the most special case, the perfectly virtuous person is believed to carry the promise of attaining some metaphysically conceived ultimate goal of life, such as Buddhist *Nirvāṇa* and Hindu *Mokṣa*.

In this paper my intention is to reflect upon the nature of a virtuous person—an *ideally* virtuous person—who is considered to be so because this person believes, and acts on the belief, that attaining *Nirvāṇa* or *Mokṣa* is the ultimate virtue of life. My reflection will be focused on the nature of the consciousness that characterizes and sustains the virtuous life of this person. For it is in the analysis and articulation of consciousness that we are likely to identify the crucial attitude of mind that structures the constitution of a perfectly virtuous person.

The task undertaken here may be described, for two reasons, as an exercise in *virtue-metaphysical* theory. One is that the ideally virtuous person is depicted as one whose life is essentially connected to a metaphysically virtuous end, such as *Nirvāṇa* or *Mokṣa*. The other reason is that the kind of consciousness that generates the attitude appropriate to the metaphysically virtuous end itself has a metaphysical character, i.e., a character that defies a purely empirical grasp.

RADICAL LIBERATION

Why would the attainment of *Nirvāṇa* or *Mokṣa* be regarded as a matter of ultimate virtue? The answer is simple. Both Buddhism and the other schools of classical Indian philosophy are unanimous on what they take to be a fundamental yet deep truth, namely that desire or attachment is the root cause of perpetual human suffering. They also are unanimous on the possibility of overcoming perpetual suffering by engaging in the austere practice of non-attachment and desirelessness. It thus is apparent that the attitude of detachment would be considered a superior virtue if being able to be free from perennial human suffering is recognized as an achievement of utmost worth.

One sense of being virtuous—perhaps a trivial sense—is that of trying to be free from vice. If, for instance, greed, violence, infidelity, tendency to lie, and intemperance are vices of character, then freeing oneself from these vices is engaging in the self-transformative virtuous practice of actualizing self-control, non-violence, fidelity, truthfulness and temperance. Thus, becoming virtuous has a conceptual dependence on becoming free from vicious tendencies. And it is this notion of *freedom* that is central to the virtue-metaphysical theory that I am concerned with here.

Desire and attachment may not appear as vices in the ordinary view of life. They would be considered as vices only if they are excessive, and, consequently, motivation for unwholesome activities. Indeed, the ordinary view of life might regard a life of moderate desire and attachment as a virtuous life. Moderation itself would be deemed a virtue in this sense. Since self-control is a familiar virtue, its exercise in the moderation of our proclivity towards attachment to worldliness would clearly be recognized as an evidence of a virtuous personality. It is partly by virtue of self-control, combined with knowledge that enables self-understanding, that a person secures freedom from the tenacity of desire and attachment. This freedom, which is a prerequisite to a transformation of one-self into a person who is not subdued by apparently irresistible desires and attachments, is surely a virtuous state of mind.

Would anything be wrong with such a conception of freedom as a condition for a virtuous state of mind when viewed from the standpoint of the classical Indian tradition? Yes, what would be wrong is that this conception of freedom *compromises* itself with the human "weakness" of being moved by desire at all. It is not freedom *enough*, as the tradition would say, if one is capable of "taming" desires in accordance with some principle of practical rationality, while fully allowing that the flow of desires and attachments continue unabated in the stream of life. For the painful truth of mundane life is that, so long as we remain desire-driven characters that invariably become attached to the world, unhappiness (and, at worst, suffering) is bound to disturb the rhythm of life. This is true whether a desire (moderate or not) is satisfied or not. Even when a desire is satisfied, the mental state of satisfaction would be immediately succeeded by a state of discontent because of the formation of a new desire, either for the same kind of object but of higher utility, or for an object of a different kind. Happiness becomes totally contingent on securing the object of attachment, even when the desire is a moderate one. And since the chain of desires is never-ending, that contingency of happiness is ineradicable.

The wisdom of the classical Indian tradition therefore conceives of the truly virtuous mind as capable of a freedom *more* radical in nature. It also conceives of the happiness of a truly virtuous person as free from the kind of contingency that characterizes the ordinary view. Hence what is held, descriptively as well as prescriptively, is that our natural proneness to desire and attachment has to be transcended on a permanent basis. The mind has to be absolutely free from the propensity to relate itself to the world, including oneself, with attachment. Thus the classical Indian view of human enlightenment is predicated on a theory of radical detachment.

Detachment is freedom from attachment and therefore desire. Detachment or non-attachment as an attitude that grounds radical liberation is a supreme virtue of life, given of course the soteriological teleology of life aiming at ultimate self-liberation, *Nirvāṇa* or *Mokṣa*.

CONSCIOUSNESS CENTERED AND DECENTERED

What is the crux of the phenomenon of desire and attachment in relation to the self or consciousness of the person? What constitutes the fulcrum of the predicament of a life conditioned to the vagaries of desire and attachment? Alternatively, what would be the attitudinal constitution of a person whose life is not encumbered in this predicament? Both these questions need to be answered in terms of a *metaphysical* account of human consciousness, an account that would also illuminate the supremely virtuous character of a life of detachment.

The issue in question concerns the nature of consciousness that shapes the attitude of a person encumbered in desire and attachment, and how that consciousness relates the person to the world. The truth is that such a person's consciousness is marked by a self-constraining orientation in that it is ego-formative or constructive of an apparently immutable sense of I-ness, described as *Ahaṁkāra*. However, the sense of *Ahaṁkāra* is not just what the formal idea of a "first-person point of view" means, i.e., the sense that an experience or any state of mind is invariably an experience or state of a conscious subject. Rather, it is a much more substantive posture that consciousness assumes towards whatever it is conscious of. *Ahaṁkāra*-consciousness is a subject of experience that essentially embodies an affective-volitional orientation towards the object. In other words, it is not just that I have an experience of the object, but that the experience's being *mine*, or the *my*-ness of the experience, looms large in my consciousness. Consequently, as the my-ness that sticks to the experience "colors" the object experienced, I end up being attached to the object.

The predicament of a life vulnerable to the vagaries of desire and attachment is an ego-centric predicament. *Ahaṁkāra*-consciousness, or consciousness centered on the ego, limits the possibility of the person's happiness in the world to the ego-specific boundary demarcated by this consciousness. The world is so set up by this consciousness that the self of the person becomes the center of the world, or, to say the same thing, the world is centered on the self of the person. The relation of the person with the world is that of ego-specific fixation, geared to a succession of desires and continuity of attachment. Along with this occurs the anxiety of expected satisfaction and, when desires are not fulfilled, the pain of frustration. And the cycle of the predicament continues unabated.

The uncompromising mode of freedom from suffering or unhappiness is to dissolve the predicament by identifying and understanding the nature of the basis of the predicament, and then exercising the power of mind to weed out the very basis from the plane of consciousness. This would be consciousness' radical withdrawal from ego-specific attachment to the world. A theory of detachment would therefore be a theory of radical freedom in the above sense of the phrase.

Consciousness, as we know it from the human case, has a natural tendency to act as a centripetal force in the life of an individual person. The view of the world that consciousness affords is invariably centered in the individual's psyche. This "center" of consciousness constitutes *the* point of view from which the individual's relation with the world is defined *for* the individual. Apparently, this centrality is irreducible as well as irreplaceable as far as the individual's existence in the world and intercourse with others is concerned. Ego-centricity, or what I call ego-specificity, is just another name for this irreplaceable "point of view" of centered consciousness.

The ego-specific point of view of centered consciousness is not just the *perspective-specificity* of perceptual cognition on the part of a particular subject of consciousness. Also, it is not the fact that every conscious state is intrinsically anchored in the conscious subject in which the state arises. Both these facts about the subjective point of view are, of course, facts about ego-specificity, or perspective-specificity, or consciousness as such. Indeed, ordinary consciousness is inherently perspectival, which is what is known as the "first-person perspective" of conscious experience. This, however, is the *formal* notion of ego- or perspective-specificity, a feature of consciousness in the descriptive-structural sense of it.

There is, on the other hand, a *substantive* sense of ego-specificity of consciousness—of consciousness being centered on the subject—that attaches to the first-person perspective an intentionality of a different kind. The intentionality of the first-person perspective in the substantive sense is that of one's being conscious of something with a spontaneous self-regarding concern. In this mode of consciousness of the object, the subject is not just "formally" connected with the object, without viewing the object as having any stake whatsoever in the "life" of the subject. Rather, the subject's first-personally concernful attitude towards the object ineluctably gives rise to an attachment to it. This is precisely what *Ahaṁkāra*-consciousness means.

CONSCIOUSNESS DECENTERED

Radical freedom, as required by the theory of detachment, is predicated on decentering consciousness from its substantively ego-specific locus. It involves reorienting consciousness from its first-personally concernful intentional stance towards *ego-neutrality*. Evidently, the ego-neutralization of consciousness would result in the corresponding neutralization of the propensity for ego-specific attachment to anything in the world. What is most significant here is that a person driven by the forces of ego-neutral consciousness would have a unique mode of being-in-the-world. For such a person it would be a centerless world—a world not centered on any ego-specific substantive concern. Any first-personally concernful terms would not define the character of the world of such a decentered self. To be a conscious subject in a centerless world is to afford a view of the world which is, in the famous phrase of Thomas Nagel, "a view from nowhere."[1]

To view the world from "nowhere" does not, of course, mean the dissolution of first-person subjectivity, or the inherently first-personal character of conscious experience. Any conscious awareness of the world is intrinsically an awareness of something from the point of view of the conscious subject. In point of fact, it is the "point of view" itself that constitutes the subject's being a *subject* of awareness. Being a subject is having a point of view, a perspective on to the world. This fact reiterates the formal sense of ego-specificity of consciousness. It should therefore be free from confusion that Nagel's "view from nowhere" is consistent with accepting that any view of consciousness is a view from the first-person perspective, that is to say, a view from somewhere.

Clear as it is now, the first-person perspective as a formal feature of consciousness is innocuous from the virtue-metaphysical standpoint. Being a matter purely of the structural aspect of consciousness, the ego-specificity of that perspective carries no connotation of *value* and, thus, has no direct bearing on the virtue or otherwise of the person. It therefore is no locus of *Ahaṁkāra*.

But the important question is what relation there is, if any, of the first-person perspective in the formal-structural sense with the first-person perspective in the substantive sense. Is the latter perspective of ego-specificity a distinct form of intentionality that ontologically parallels the intentionality of the former perspective? In other words, is human consciousness generative of two ontologically distinct forms of ego-subjectivity, one formal-structural and another substantive? Are the two stories of ego-subjectivity autonomous of one another to the extent that each story is irrelevant to the other in any crucial respects?

My reflections on this issue incline me to contend that the phenomenon of substantive ego-specificity is not the outcome of a *second* ego, ontologically distinct from the innocuous ego of the formal ego-specific consciousness. Consciousness has the potentiality just for one ego-subjectivity, which is primordially constitutive of the first-person perspective in the formal-structural sense. The fact of the matter, it seems to me, is that formal ego-subjectivity assumes a substantive character as soon as the subject indulges in having what might be described as a "self-gratifying concern" with the world. Substantive ego-subjectivity would thus be a taint on formal ego-subjectivity, and hence the taint can conceivably be removed. Radical liberation consists in the removal of this taint on an otherwise innocuous ego-subjectivity.

Reverting to the idiom of consciousness, it can now be said that consciousness decentered is consciousness emancipated from the attitude of self-gratifying concernfulness towards the world. It would be consciousness without any substantive ego-subjectivity. In such a state of consciousness, the first-person perspective would be accorded no more centrality than that of being a bare subject of consciousness, comparable to a "bare particular." The individuality of the subject that constitutes the first-person perspective would then be a purely *nominal* individuality. And the consciousness of the world being centered in the individual subject would, in point of fact, be a matter of the individual's being just a "nominal center" of consciousness.

What, I hope, has come to light from the foregoing discussion is that the first-person perspective that structurally constitutes a subject of consciousness also constitutes innocuous ego-subjectivity. Now the question is that of the virtue-theoretic import of the concept of the innocuous ego, or nominal individuality. It is, I think, the wisdom of the classical Indian tradition, philosophical as well as soteriological, to have identified such a decentered consciousness as the sole and certain basis of detachment required by a theory of radical liberation. To the extent that this tradition professes a view of the utmost virtuous life that is predicated on attaining what is considered to be the ultimately virtuous condition of existence, it aptly recognizes the necessary precondition for that supremely virtuous attainment *in* the attainment of a state of consciousness entirely marked by innocuous or nominal ego-subjectivity. The possibility of attachment, or what I have called "self-gratifying concernfulness," is ruled out from the life of a person who is governed by decentered consciousness. With that is also ruled out the possibility of suffering.

THE VIRTUOUS SOUL OF COMMUNICATIVE CONSCIOUSNESS

In this section I shall focus on what I consider to be a unique illustration of human consciousness marked by nominal individuality in the phenomenon of inter-personal addressing, i.e., the dialogical scenario of I-You relation. This discussion will be an elaboration and reconstruction of a unique interpretation of the idea of a soul given by a contemporary Indian philosopher, Ramchandra Gandhi.[2] I shall extrapolate on Gandhi's ideas with a view to showing how the core idea of his conception of a soul sits well in the virtue-metaphysical account of decentered consciousness developed here.

It is quite unusual of any philosopher to locate the site of a metaphysical analysis of the idea of a soul in so ordinary a context as that of the act of addressing one another. The communicative link of an "addressive encounter" is evidently pronominal, i.e., it is a communication between You and I. Gandhi's basic point is that these two pronominal expressions represent a communication-establishing thought that can be grasped only in terms of the idea of a soul understood, in Gandhi's own words, as "the idea of that as which we imaginatively see one another in acts of addressing one another" (p. 4).

What exactly is it for two persons to "imaginatively see one another" when they enter into "addressive" relation with one another? Gandhi alludes to imagination here in order to articulate a distinctive mode of viewing one another as persons, namely the "attributeless" mode, that secures and sustains the addressive relation. The addresser views the addressee from a purely non-predicative vantage point, so that the addressee figures in that frame of mind as You *simpliciter*, imaginatively abstracted from whatever *de facto* attributes or sortal predicates are true of the person addressed. I, the addresser, cast you, the addressee, non-attributively, quite simply as you *yourself*, without letting my attention to have any recourse to the factual-descriptive apparatus of sortal and referential identification.

Gandhi remarks: "In addressing me you gain a *special inward access* to me as myself, and not as a creature of a particular kind, but quite simply as myself" (p. 26, emphasis added). The "special inward access" that the addresser is said to have access to is what may be described as the "bare personal core" of the person addressed. It is a very special kind of *communion* between you and me that depends on your reaching out to me in a state of mind unmediated by whatever attributive-predicative characterizations are known to you to be true of me.

It is understandable how Gandhi's idea of a soul as consisting in the non-attributive way of "seeing" a person is consistent with the religious notion of a soul. But Gandhi's construal bypasses the substance-ontological idiom in which the traditional discussion on the idea of a soul is problematically entangled. For, as Gandhi says, "we should speak not of the immateriality of the soul, but of the mode of *non-substantival seeing* of one another which is the seeing of one another *as* souls" (p. 5, emphasis added). The reality of a human soul is grounded in nowhere else but the human attitude of "non-substantival seeing"—i.e., non-attributive viewing—of one another. With this non-predicative attitude one sees the "pure subject" in the other, not in the sense of seeing an ineffable, predicate-less being in the other, but in the sense of inwardly accessing the subject by imaginatively bracketing out the outwardly identifiable set of predicates.

One might say that the idea of a soul can be grasped by bringing it under the "image" of a pure subject in the above sense. One might even add that the degree to which this grasp is successful is proportionate to the extent to which the set of predicates can actually be bracketed out. For the full image of a pure subject becomes manifest in an utmost imaginative abstraction of the subject from the entire gamut of predicates that form the "impure" identity of the subject. In Gandhi's account, therefore, the soul is not a mysterious subject, a distinct ontological remnant purged of all predicative connections. Rather, the intimation of a soul is an acquaintance with a subject of consciousness that figures in the attitudinal space of someone viewing another person non-attributively.

The communicative-dialogical thrust of Gandhi's theory of a soul makes the non-attributive attitude primarily *other*-regarding. But I believe that his theory can be given a *self*-regarding twist without incurring any distortion of meaning of the overall theory. What if one were to adopt the non-predicative stance towards oneself, by imaginatively detaching the set of predicates that constitute one's own *de facto* identity? What if one were to reorient one's own mode of being-in-the-world in terms of the non-substantival mode of self-perception and self-awareness?

The answer, I think, is that one's (what I have earlier called) substantive ego-subjectivity would be dissolved, and one would have had one's consciousness of the world decentered. And for a decentered subject, being-in-the-world would mean being-in-a-centerless-world. This is because the realization of an attributeless self-consciousness would inevitably amount to oneself becoming (what, again, I have earlier called) a *nominally* individual subject of consciousness, characteristic of the first-person perspective in the formal-structural sense. No room would be left for the formation of substantively ego-specific individuality in the space of a consciousness that brackets out the attributive-predicative mode of self-recognition.

If what I have added to Gandhi's theory by way of giving it a self-regarding conceptual twist is indeed on the right track, then I am allowed a significant extrapolation on that theory. Thus, I can further add that the possibility of other-regarding non-attributive attitude presupposes the actual ability to adopt that attitude towards oneself. Unless I personally realize what it is like for me to be myself *simpliciter*, substantively ego-neutral, and merely nominally a particular center of consciousness, I would not succeed in casting you as you *yourself*, without bringing you under any substantive image constructed out of a set of predicates. I must at first neutralize my own substantive ego-specificity, so that my attitude towards you is freed from the propensity to identify you in attributive-predicative terms that are readily available to me given my ego-specific relation with the world.

Put simply, I must cast myself as a pure subject, and (existentially) be the subject I cast myself as, in order that I may, in the "spirit" of that pure subject of consciousness, actually come to regard you as another pure subject of the same kind. The point being made here is, in essence, that the ability to "see" another person as a soul rides on the self-regarding ability to reconceive of the individuality of one's own consciousness as having nothing more than a nominal essence. For it is only when a consciousness is unburdened of any substantive essence or individuality that it liberates itself from the tendency to view another person under this or that attribute.

THE HIDDENNESS OF PRONOMINAL PERSONAL IDENTITY

Suspicion is likely to arise as to whether an act of addressing actually involves the adoption of the non-predicative attitude or the attributeless mode of thinking of the addressee. Ordinarily, one would think, when you address me, you do so with the thought of communicating with someone recognized as so-and-so, and this predicative-recognitional mode of attention upon me is *part* of the act of addressing someone. The pronominal indexical **You**, by using which you pick *me* out, is, as it might be thought, a substitute for me conceived as so-and-so, a particular person of some kind. In this sense, the second-personal singular pronoun is a truncated element of the full expression: "You, so-and-so." The thought of a particular so-and-so is always implicitly and contextually tied up with this pronominal indexical.

Perhaps our ordinary practice of addressing one another is, more often than not, marked by the predicative-recognitional mode of attention towards one another. We actually tend to enter into the **I-You** relation by deploying a predicatively loaded concept of "You." But I think this tendency massively betrays the "spirit" of inter-personal relation that obtains solely in what might be called the "pronominal frame of mind." What is unique about this spirit is that the **I-You** relation is a relation occurring between two persons in their pure "pronominal identity." It is a relation between **You** *as such* and **I** *as such*—between two pure subjects of consciousness.

For me to adopt the **You**-stance towards another person is to pick out that person in his or her pronominal identity. And his or her pronominal identity is constituted merely by what makes the person a conscious subject, the thought of whom can be imaginatively detached from the range of predicates that determine what kind of person he or she actually is. The very point of using the second-personal singular pronoun is to invoke the conscious subject *as such*, i.e., the pronominal identity of the addressee. Of course the pronominal identity of the person does not mean anything like a predicateless identity of the person. It only means that, in so far as the person is to figure as **You** in relation to me, the predicatively secured identity of the person is irrelevant. All that is needed or relevant for the purpose of bringing the person under the **You**-thought is the minimal identity of the person as just a conscious subject—a potential bearer of predicates.

The **You**-thought is not a truncated version of the fuller thought "You, so and so." For me it is one thing to think of the other person as so and so, and quite another to conceive of that person under the **You**-thought. The crucial difference is that I can establish a communicative contact with the other person—with so and so—only if I bring the so-and-so person under the **You**-thought, or adopt the personal "**You**-stance" towards the otherwise impersonal (and grammatically third-personal) other. It is by viewing the other person through the pronominal lens, as it were, and thereby coming to terms with the pronominal identity of the person, that I really gain an inward communicative access to the person in question.

The crucial point that I am laboring to drive home is that a person's pronominal identity is clearly distinguishable from his or her *de facto* predicative identity, and that pronominal personal identity spontaneously comes to the fore when the person is viewed by disregarding, or holding in abeyance, his or her predicative personal identity. Inter-personal communicative worthiness of the person consists in, and depends on, relating with the person through an immediate access to the pronominal identity of the person. Thus, an inter-personal communication between myself and someone else would not get off the ground so long as I did not "lift" the person from the predicative level of being so and so to the non-predicative pronominal level.

THE UNIVERSALITY OF PRONOMINAL PERSONAL IDENTITY

I have argued, in the above discussion, that the second-personal pronominal identity of persons is *sui generis*, and that inter-personal communication depends upon the fact that one's communicative access to another person is achieved through spontaneous non-predicative recognition of the other person's pronominal identity. I would now like to highlight a further feature of the **I-You** communicative scenario that follows directly from the nature of pronominal personal identity.

A question may be raised as to *what* the second-personal singular pronoun, as an indexical expression, is indexed to. It should by now be clear enough that it is not indexed to the addressee identified as a so-and-so. For "You" does not stand for, or mean, "You so and so," even though we utter that expression to refer to a so-and-so person. Strictly speaking, a **You**-thought is not the thought of any so-and-so; it is rather the thought of a conscious subject as such, who is capable of giving an appropriate response to my vocative call. Even though any such conscious subject would invariably be a so-and-so person, it is not *qua* so-and-so that such a subject qualifies for subsumption under **You**-thought. Rather, the **You**-thought subsumes the conscious subject *simpliciter*, with its capacity to be a responsive audience, quite irrespective of whatever factual characteristics it is actually a bearer of.

What follows from the foregoing analysis of the idea of pronominal personal identity has, I claim, a virtue-metaphysical consequence. In so far as I think of another person under the **You**-thought, or view the person through the pronominal frame of mind, the *individuality* of the individual person would, in my addressive-communicative view, be that of *nominal* individuality. I relate myself with the person by having, so to speak, a pronominal regard towards him or her. When I so regard the person, I do not individuate him or her in terms criterial of sortal and referential identification. Instead, I come into contact with an individual **You** whose individuality is, as it were, gratuitous. For once the predicates are bracketed out, or held in abeyance, you are conceived of as a "pure" subject that is constituted by "unqualified" consciousness. And consciousness unqualified is in essence universal consciousness—that is consciousness unaffected by any features that leave the "imprint" of individuality upon it. From my addressive vantage point, you therefore are not an individual subject of consciousness, but a subject of universal consciousness.

There is, thus, an "image of universality" that is attached to second-personal pronominal individuality. The individuality of the person *qua* **You** is truly grasped in terms of this image of universality. The individual subject that you are, in relation with me in my act of addressing you, is essentially a subject that cannot really be individuated. You—the particular **you** upon whom my pronominal mode of attention is focused—are a universal subject, a soul indeed. My (pronominal) attitude towards you is an attitude towards a soul.

What exactly is virtuous about having an attitude towards you which is an attitude towards a soul—understood as an "image" of a universal subject of consciousness—in terms of which the **You**-thought is grasped? I think the virtue of this attitude consists mainly in the *sanctity* of the image of universality that I bring to bear upon my mode of access to you. My pronominal access to another person embodies that attitudinal sanctity in virtue of which the **I-You** relation itself becomes virtuous. What precisely is virtuous in this is that, the pronominal attitude being essentially non-attributive, the addressing *I* discerns a *prima facie* universality in the individual person addressed and conceived as **You**. It is the universality of the fact that you are, first and foremost, a conscious subject as such, whatever attributes or personal particularities, good or bad, you might have actually accumulated in the course of your life.

In identifying you as **You**, I accord (a virtue-metaphysical) priority to your being a conscious subject *at all*. That you are a conscious subject *at all*, potentially responsive to my vocative call, is a *sacrosanct* truth enshrined in the **I-You** relation. It is this sacrosanct truth about you, or about anyone as **You**, which the second-personal pronominal indexical is meant to capture.

The foregoing interpretation would of course indicate that the second-personal pronominal indexical has a certain metaphysical significance that is relevant to a theory of virtue. What is metaphysically significant is the point made about pure individuality in a person, a person conceived as a subject of universal consciousness. Since at the level of pure individuality the subjectivity of the person is determined by universal consciousness, there is a sense in which one particular person so conceived is virtually indiscernible from another particular person. The individuality of the particular person thus becomes nominal, and the image of universality overshadows what physically appears as a distinctly individuated person.

THE PRIMACY OF THE "IMAGE OF UNIVERSALITY"

It might be felt that there is something counterintuitive in the assertion that the universality of pronominal individuality is a virtue. For it might be held that my pronominally viewing the other person under the image of universality would have to ignore the factual question of whether the person leads a life of virtue or vice. My addressive stance, which casts the person as **You**, would have to be indifferent to my knowledge, if I do know, that the person in question is actually, say, a hardcore criminal. When the individuality of the particular person is rendered nominal, the individual identity of the person, predicatively identified as a criminal, would also be rendered irrelevant. The blinding light of universality would, so to speak, keep my eyes off the vicious identity that is otherwise writ large on the person. How, then, could the recognition of a person under the "image" of universal consciousness be a matter of virtue, given that the non-predicative pronominal perspective of universality adopted towards the addressee would inevitably erase or conceal the stamp of vice that the person might actually bear on him or her? It would thus seem that the argument for the alleged sanctity of the **I-You** relation is unsound.

Natural though the above objection is, it can be circumvented by having a closer look at the implications of the so-called "image of universality." What is universal about pronominal individuality is that the person accessed pronominally has the pristine character of pure individual identity, marked by a basic consciousness that has the *potentiality* for the substantive development of a life. Apart from its innocuous ego-subjectivity, i.e., the first-person perspective in the formal-structural sense, this consciousness of pure individuality is substantively ego-neutral or devoid of the sense of *Ahaṁkāra*. It also is sheer freedom in the sense of total freedom from any ego-specific, self-gratifying desire and attachment. It is this universal (i.e., ego-neutral) consciousness that is said to be the core of any individual conscious subject worthy of a vocative call. The second-personal singular pronoun is indexed to *this* universal consciousness that is instantiated or represented by an individual person.

When I address myself to, say, a criminal individual—i.e., I call him or her **You—I** of course mean to pick out the particular person who has actually committed a crime. But, to the extent that I adopt the addressive stance towards the person, my picking out the person under his or her substantive or predicative identity (i.e., as a criminal) is ontologically (if not psychologically) preceded by my reaching out to, or focusing on, his or her pre-substantive pronominal identity. In other words, the addressing-stance on my part would amount to saying, or thinking: "You, who in essence are a representative of substantively ego-neutral, universal consciousness, have developed yourself into a substantively ego-specific (e.g., criminal or vicious) person."

Thus, it is essentially by reference to the sanctity of this pure subjectivity, and hence full freedom, of ego-neutral consciousness, which is the *ground* of potentiality for development into a particular kind of life (vicious in this example), that the actualization of the life of a criminal is to be estimated as a condemnable deviation. The developmental path traversed by the person is reckoned as a betrayal of the possibility of a benign personal development.

Pure, pre-substantive subjectivity can also be profitably connected with the first-person perspective. While the structurally first-personal perspective is innocuous, its innocuousness is, at the same time, a measure of virtue. For the ultimate goodness of a person, at least in the classical Indian tradition, is measured by the extent to which the substantive development of a life-history preserves the innocuousness of the structurally first-personal point of view. What really is innocuous about this point of view is that it (this point of view) is just a brute structural fact of being a conscious subject at all—i.e., a fact intrinsic to conscious subjectivity. It is, in this sense, valuationally innocent, even though this first-personally structured innocuous conscious subject is replete with the possibility of losing all "innocence" in the course of substantive development of the subject's life.

What the above point implies is that the conscious subject is very likely to lead a life that is not just structurally first-personal in orientation. The life would in all probability acquire a substantively first-personal orientation, whereby the development of a life would be shaped by the concurrent development of the sense of substantive my-ness or specificity or *Ahaṁkāra*.

Once *Ahaṁkāra* shapes or conditions the first-personal orientation of consciousness, life is no longer valuationally innocent or innocuous, and the degree of the loss of innocence could be so maximal as to turn a life into one of *evil*. Cold-blooded criminality would be an example of such a maximal loss of innocence. Such a criminal drive or passion would usually reflect an unperturbed hold of the forces of *Ahaṁkāra*. But so would also be certain forms of love as much as hatred. A love for someone or something, despite its benign appearance, would be no less a deviation from that pristine innocence of consciousness, provided the lover is driven by the pull of substantive my-ness.

TWO FACETS OF VIRTUE CONSCIOUSNESS

The metaphysical theory of virtue that has emerged in my account of human consciousness is predicated upon a fact that is in fact virtue-neutral or valuationally innocent. This "neutral" or "innocent" fact is the structurally first-personal orientation of consciousness. It is a fact of consciousness as it is, in its pristine originality. I now want to claim that what I have described above as a theory of consciousness is essentially drawn upon the classical Indian philosophical picture of consciousness. But this claim invites two major questions that need to be addressed. While the first question relates to whether there is a unified theory of consciousness in the classical Indian philosophical tradition, the second question concerns the important issue of whether consciousness, in any of the classical Indian versions of it, is structurally first-personally oriented at all. I shall address myself to these two questions in the order in which they have been stated.

As to the question of a unitary conception of consciousness, the answer is in the negative.[3] While there are major differences within the different schools of the Hindu orthodox systems, the way in which heterodox Buddhism differs from the orthodox Advaita Vedānta truly reflects the gravity of the difference on the nature of consciousness. Consciousness in the Vedāntic view is, very roughly speaking, eternal and constitutive of a substantive reality known as *Ātman*, the individual self, which ultimately is one with the universal, all-pervasive ultimate reality known as *Brahman*. One might say that the Vedāntist has a substantivist conception of consciousness and, therefore, subscribes to the substantivist ontology of selfhood.

In contrast, the Buddhist conception casts consciousness as transient in nature—as a series of ever-perishing or fleeting moments. Wedded to process ontology, the Buddhist view logically amounts to a non-substantivist conception of consciousness. Consequently, no positive theory of selfhood is part of the ontology of consciousness. The flow of consciousness does not add up to a self. One might say that, in relation to the Vedāntic view, the Buddhist position on the nature of consciousness and selfhood is deflationary.

Given these two metaphysically contrasted views of consciousness represented by the two central strands of classical Indian philosophy, how would it be possible to derive a unitary theory of virtue from the mutually conflicting resources of classical metaphysics? Furthermore—and this is to come to terms with the second question stated above—is consciousness, both in the substantivist and deflationary versions, really susceptible of the structurally first-person point of view? What I mean to consider here is whether there can truly be a first-person perspective as an inherent structural feature of consciousness, whether this structure is Vedāntic or Buddhist. These two questions are interrelated and an answer to the one would also lead to an answer to the other. I shall start my discussion with the latter question.

(a) The Inflationary Facet

Consciousness in the Vedāntic view being universal and undifferentiated, the self constituted of that consciousness, namely *Ātman*, is universal and essentially impersonal. Personal individuality, which is what underlines the first-personal point of view, is therefore constitutively ruled out by the very nature of *Ātman*-consciousness. If at all, it is the third-person perspective that is more truly a feature of that consciousness. Strictly speaking, the possibility of a *first person* is extrinsic to *Ātman*-consciousness, and the so-called I-ness (*Ahaṁ*) attributed to *Ātman*-consciousness is not really a first-personal point of view as the phrase is ordinarily understood. *Ātman*-consciousness has universal scope, leaving no room for a second "me" or "my-ness" to represent another individual first-personal point of view. This is precisely the sense in which the idea of "nominal individuality" discussed earlier is supposed to be understood.

How, then, is the fact of a first-person perspective as it really attaches to consciousness in the ordinary course of life to be accounted for? Vedāntic theory explains this fact in terms of the concept of *Jīva* or phenomenal self. Phenomenal consciousness that pertains to the *Jīva* is undifferentiated and universal consciousness rendered differentiated and individualized under the spell of *Avidyā* or cosmic ignorance. Conscious existence in the phenomenal plane is that of the life of a *Jīva*, with its individualized, ego-specific, personal mode of development. The substantively first-personal point of view is a structural feature of *Jīva*-consciousness. *Ahaṁkāra* is just another name for this feature of phenomenal consciousness.

The eschatological view of Vedānta is that ultimate liberation consists in the possibility of an austere transition from the phenomenal life of differentiated and ego-specific consciousness to the state of undifferentiated and universal consciousness. The attainment of ultimate liberation would also be the attainment of ultimate virtue. But if a virtue-theory is to be *ethically* relevant, it has to be primarily related to human existence at the phenomenal level, taking into full consideration the prevalence at that level of the substantively first-personal point of view. The virtue-theoretical contention that I wish to make here is therefore attuned to this requirement. My contention is that the actualization of a virtuous life is signaled by the extent to which the substantivization of the first-person perspective is minimized, the end-point of that process being a complete ego-neutralization or annihilation of *Ahaṁkāra*.

The burden of substantivization is therefore what negatively lends momentum to the struggle for a virtuous life. It is a struggle of human consciousness against the seemingly insurmountable force of *Avidyā* that gives birth to a *first person* of substantive individuality. Granted that the "first person" in every ordinary person is a diehard, a virtuous life would depend upon a painstaking effort on the part of the person to live a life from the third-person perspective. And this possibility would make the best sense provided the adoption of the third-person point of view is interpreted as part of a continuous process towards the ultimate actualization of entirely nominal individuality, which is illustrated by *Ātman*-consciousness.

(b) The Deflationary Facet

So much for Vedāntic consciousness and the virtue theory underwritten by the Vedāntic view. What about the Buddhist picture of consciousness and its relation to the substantively first-personal point of view? It ought to be eminently clear that, given the idea of consciousness as discrete and ephemeral, the formation of the first-person point of view is certainly not intrinsic to Buddhist consciousness. Being essentially differentiated into fleeting moments, consciousness cannot actually constitute a self, not even an amorphous universal self. And without the presence of a self or any anchorage for ego-specificity, consciousness has absolutely no room for a "first person," let alone a first-personal point of view.

What explains the *sense* of being a self-same person is a self-induced fiction of a continuous and unified consciousness as against what really is a discontinuous chain of ever-perishing conscious moments. A phenomenal self is fictionally created, along with a substantively first-personal perspective that accompanies all along the development of the phenomenal life. Attachment, typical of *Ahaṁkāra*, becomes part and parcel of that life.

Buddhist soteriology, as it is defined in terms of the metaphysics of enlightenment encapsulated in the idea of *Nirvāṇa*, propagates the possibility of total deconstruction of the fictional integration of the series of discrete instants of consciousness. The idea is that it is this fictitious integration of conscious states that underlies the mistaken impression of "oneself" being a permanent and enduring self. The true nature of reality—that is the reality of impermanence—is thereby lost sight of, and the false sense of permanent self-endurance begets desire and other ego-specific cravings, which in turn are bound to bring suffering. Hence the "disintegration" of the phenomenally permanent and integrated self is conceived as the decisive explanation of the possibility of radical self-liberation. The liberated condition would be an order of consciousness of sheer fluidity. It would consist of conscious moments absolutely unattached to one another in any sense, which would therefore be a condition of consciousness that leaves no room for the possibility of a "first person." *Nirvāṇa* would thus depend on the total extinction of the first-person perspective.

Buddhist ethics, to the extent that ethics relate to the maintenance of a virtuous order of phenomenal existence, would, I think, consist in a relatively austere effort to resist the instinct of fictive integration of discontinuous consciousness, and to remind oneself of the ultimate fictionality of an enduring self as the agent that fosters ego-specific desires of various kinds. One might say that it is a virtuous resistance to the instinct of self-formation, and a virtuous reminder of the fact that the first-person perspective is parasitic on that delusive instinct. Ethically relevant virtuous existence would thus be subject to a persistent struggle against the recalcitrance of what might be characterized as phenomenal first-personality.

That desire is the cause of suffering is central to Buddhism. As such, Buddhist virtue-ethics would consist in the development of a character or personality that conduces to maximal moderation of desire, whether it is self-regarding or other-regarding desire. The substantive first-personal perspective that underlies, and gives an egoist thrust to, any desire, would have to be diffused, so that *Karuṇā* (compassion) replaces the life of desire. And a character of compassion truly takes its shape only when consciousness attempts to regain its original fluidity and impermanence, i.e., only when phenomenal consciousness is shaken off its ego-formative inclination.

Universal compassion or *Karuṇā* is itself a cardinal virtue, and a full possibility of universal compassion would necessitate a total dissolution of phenomenal consciousness that expresses itself in the form of a "first person" having an ego-specific point of view on the world. To the extent that phenomenal human existence is hardly ever characterized by a complete dissolution of the first-person point of view, the evaluative criteria for virtue-ethical characterization of phenomenal existence would naturally have to be less stringent. The depth of a phenomenally virtuous life would therefore have to be measured by a progressive weakening of the stronghold of the first-person point of view. And this surely is a matter of transformation of consciousness, in as much as the stronghold of the first-person perspective is ultimately owed to the fact that transitory and insubstantial consciousness suffers the delusion of enduringness and substantiality.

VIRTUE-CONSCIOUSNESS WITHOUT A FIRST PERSON

Throughout the discussion in this paper, I have tried to engage in a virtue-metaphysical enquiry into the nature of consciousness, and argued that the classical Indian conception of consciousness is essentially devoid of any room for the genesis of a first-person perspective. (In this regard it may be noted that the classical Indian conception of consciousness stands in sharp contrast to the Cartesian conception, according to which the first-person perspective is intrinsic to consciousness.) I have also tried to articulate the notion of "nominal" individuality as a crucial mediating link between universal consciousness and phenomenally subjective consciousness. This "link" notion is crucial because it allows one to work out a viable virtue-ethical theory for phenomenally real human existence, while drawing all the resources of ultimate virtue from the classical idea of universal consciousness.

In developing the above position I have adverted to the disunity of views on the nature of consciousness in the classical Indian tradition, highlighting the disunity by reference to Buddhism and Vedānta. But I have argued that, despite metaphysically non-trivial difference between these two classical views, consciousness in either theory is susceptible of a unitary virtue-ethical theory. This is mainly because, as I argued, the nature of consciousness in either view is essentially *non*-first-personal. In either conception, consciousness has no potentiality that would provide ultimate anchorage to substantive individuality. It ought to be noted therefore that the much talked about metaphysical difference between Buddhism and Vedānta also conceals an equally significant metaphysical affinity—an affinity that lends itself to the articulation of a unitary virtue-ethical theory fully grounded in the classical Indian philosophical tradition.

The virtue-theoretic picture painted above deserves a thought-provoking title. For the message of the picture is that, although such a theory is meant to be relevant to the phenomenal order of reality that incorporates human existence, the standards of virtue are set within a timeless order of reality. Such a "set up" underwrites the gravity of the notion of virtue and its uncompromising demand. The practical import of the gravity of this demand is that, even though we humans are bound to fail in meeting this demand, the failure would not settle for a compromise.

NOTES

1 Thomas Nagel, *The View from Nowhere* (New York: Oxford University Press, 1986).

2 Ramchandra Gandhi, *The Availability of Religious Ideas* (London: Macmillan, 1976), Chapter 2.

3 For a recent discussion on the different views of consciousness in both classical and contemporary Indian philosophy, see Bina Gupta, Cit: *Consciousness* (Delhi: Oxford University Press, 2003).

CHAPTER 9

"Purity" in Confucian Thought: Zhu Xi on *Xu*, *Jing* and *Wu*

KWONG-LOI SHUN

I. THE PHENOMENON OF "PURITY"

In the history of Chinese thought, a number of key terms are used to describe an ideal state of existence involving the absence of certain deviant elements that can adversely affect one's response to the world. For convenience, we may refer to such a state of existence as a state of "purity." The phenomenon of "purity" is captured by certain terms that describe what the heart/mind (*xin*), the site of both cognitive and affective activities, should ideally be like. These include *xu* (vacuous, empty), *jing* (still, inactive), and *wu* (not have, nothing), a term that is used to refer to the absence of something, whether it is human activity (*wei*), self (*wo*), emotions (*qing*), desires (*yu*), or thoughts and deliberation.

The idea of absence of deviant influences comes hand in hand with a conception of how one should ideally relate to things. The latter is embodied in terms that have to do with how things operate, such as *zi ran* (self-so) and *li* (principle, pattern), and terms that describe how the self should relate to things, such as *yin* (use as a basis, follow, adapt to). In addition, there are terms that have to do with imageries used to describe the ideal state of the heart/mind and its relation to things. These include terms referring to a mirror, water, fire, sun and moon, as well as terms such as *ming* (bright, clear), *qing** (clear) and *ju* (light up) that describe the ideal state of these things. For example, a mirror should ideally be bright and clear (*ming*), water should be clear (*qing**), and fire (or the sun and moon) should serve to light up (*ju*) what is around it.

The above ideas assume a contrast between how one should ideally respond to things and the factors that can lead one astray. One pair of terms describing the contrast is *tian* (Heaven, Nature) and *ren* (humans);

we should ideally model ourselves on *tian* in our operations and it is human influences of certain kinds that prevent us from doing so. Another pair is *gong* (impartial, public) and *si* (partial, private), or *gong* and *pian* (one-sided); *gong* should characterize the state of one's heart/mind and *si* or *pian* is what could lead one astray.

Throughout the history of Chinese thought, different thinkers and texts place different emphases on these terms and interpret them differently. In this paper, my focus is on how these terms and the related concepts come together in the thinking of Zhu Xi (1130–1200). I will begin by considering the history of evolvement of these terms, paying special attention to Zhuangzi (fourth century B.C.E.), Xunzi (third century B.C.E.), and Guo Xiang (d. 312), whose understanding of these terms has been particularly influential on Zhu Xi's thinking.

II. ZHUANGZI

A prominent concept in the *Zhuangzi* is *xu*, which is used in a well-known passage that discusses what constitutes "fasting of the heart/mind." Before discussing this passage, let us first consider the connotations of the term in texts up to early Han.

In early texts, *xu* is often contrasted with *shi* (real, truly so, with substance) (e.g., *Xunzi* 13/11a), just as *wu* (not have, nothing) is contrasted with *you* (have, exist) (*Lunyu* 8:5). It is also contrasted with two terms meaning "being full" or "filled up": *ying* (e.g., *Lunyu* 7:26, *Zhuangzi* 6/7b) and *man* (e.g., *Xunzi* 6/11a, *Zhuangzi* 7/18a). Thus, *xu* has the connotation of being empty, unfilled, and is often paired with *kong* (empty) in the combination *kong xu* (e.g., *Guoyu* 19/10a, *Mengzi* 7B:12, *Hanfeizi* 1/1a, *Lushichunqiu* 18/22a). In addition, it can be used verbally in the sense of making empty (e.g., *Mozi* 5/5/24, 37/25/20).

Xu, being contrasted with *shi*, can also mean not real, deceptive, or without substance. It is used in conjunction with *jia* (deceptive, false) (e.g., *Mozi* 2/2/7, 2/2/11) and *wei** (human construct, false) (e.g., *Zhuangzi* 9/21b) to mean what is not true and deceptive. It can be used to describe names (e.g., *Hanfeizi* 14/7b, 20/3a), reputation (e.g., *Liezi* 7/2b), words (e.g., *Xunzi* 12/9a), speech (e.g., *Hanfeizi* 2/16a), proverbs (e.g., *Hanfeizi* 4/17b), or modesty (e.g., *Zhuangzi* 9/24b) without substance. It is used verbally to mean "not make real" or "not give substance to"—one can *xu* someone's request in the sense of not granting it and thereby not making it real (e.g., *Zuozhuan* 13/23b).

Although *xu* is often contrasted with *shi*, the two are also related in interesting ways. Certain texts idealize individuals who, while *shi*, appears as if *xu* (e.g., *Lunyu* 8:5, *Huainanzi* 7/5a), while others refer to those who are also *shi* despite being apparently *xu* (e.g., *Lushichunqiu* 26/1a). The *Zhuangzi* talks about how one might opt for *xu* over *shi* and have excess simply because one does not store (10/19a), while the *Liji* talks about how one holds on to *xu* as if one were holding on to what is full (10/16b). There is even reference to how, starting with *xu*, one ends up with *shi* (e.g., *Zhuangzi* 2/16a, *Huainanzi* 2/5a), or how *shi* comes from *xu* (e.g., *Huananzi* 1/11a).

That *xu* is idealized in this way has to do with its connotation of receptivity and responsiveness. If one is *xu* in the sense of being vacuous or unfilled, then one is also open to receiving what is *shi*, namely what is real and substantive. Thus, a number of texts refer to how one uses *xu* to receive what comes in (e.g., *Yijing* 4/1a) and to await it (e.g., *Hanfeizi* 2/8b); there is even specific reference to using *xu* to receive *shi* (e.g., *Huainanzi* 7/5a). Furthermore, one whose heart/mind is *xu* will not have preconceptions and so will not have one's thoughts constrained (*Hanfeizi* 6/1a). This receptivity and the lack of prior constraints allow one to have a proper understanding of things—the *Hanfeizi* talks about how one who is *xu* will understand the *qing* (what is genuinely so, fact) of *shi* (1/10a). These connotations of *xu* are reflected in the idiomatic expression *xu xin* (e.g., *Hanfeizi* 2/3a, 2/11a), which refers to a state of the heart/mind that is able to receive without preconceptions. And because one is receptive and can grasp things accurately, one can also respond appropriately to situations (e.g., *Huainanzi* 1/8a).

So, *xu* carries the multiple connotations of being unfilled and without substance, and being receptive, unconstrained, and responsive in appropriate ways. Let us now return to the passage in the *Zhuangzi* in which we find a hypothetical dialogue between Confucius and Yan Hui about fasting of the heart/mind (2/7a–7b). The passage discusses how one should empty the heart/mind and instead await things and respond with *qi* (vital energies). This is presented in the context of a progression that appears like a reversal of a maxim of Gaozi's found in *Mengzi* 2A:2: "Do not listen with the ear; listen with the heart/mind. Do not listen with the heart/mind; listen with *qi*." *Xu* characterizes this state of the person and *xu* is that in which *dao* (Way) resides. Such a state of the heart/mind is described by Yan Hui as "not having" himself, a state endorsed by the hypothetical Confucius who goes on to talk about how one should reside in and flow along with what is unavoidable (*bu de yi*).

The emphasis of the passage is on the absence of guidance by the heart/mind, contrary to both Mencius and Gaozi's positions as presented in *Mengzi* 2A:2. Mencius and Gaozi agree that the heart/mind should provide guidance to *qi*, while disagreeing on the source of such guidance—whether one derives it form ethical doctrines and place it in the heart/mind (Gaozi) or derives it directly from the heart/mind (Mencius). For Zhuangzi, the heart/mind should not provide such guidance, and instead one should respond with *qi* without direction from the heart/mind. Thus, *xu*'s connotation of being empty and being responsive is emphasized over that of being receptive. This emphasis on *xu* as emptiness is reflected in Yan Hui's remark about "not having" himself—one's heart/mind does not give any direction, and so there is no "self" at work in one's response. The reference to the unavoidable reflects the idea of one's flowing along with things, an idea that we will consider later.

Another important concept in the *Zhuangzi* is *jing*. *Jing* is often contrasted with *dong*, a contrast between not moving and moving, or between inactivity and activity (e.g., *Lunyu* 6:23). It is sometimes used to describe the inactive state of human beings when they are first born and before they interact with things (e.g., *Liji* 11/8b, *Huainanzi* 1/4a). In this context, *jing* is not viewed as a state preferred to *dong*; the two terms just describe whether one is, or is not, interacting with and responding to things.

Jing also characterizes the state of water when it is still and free from disturbance, and it is related to *ding*, a state when water is settled (e.g., *Guanzi* 16/2b, *Daxue* main text). When water is still, sediments will settle and water is clear (*qing**); it is when disturbed that water loses this clarity (e.g., *Lushichunqiu* 1/6b). Hence, *jing* is also related to *qing** (clear) and they occur in the combination *qing* jing* (e.g., *Laozi* no. 45, *Huainanzi* 9/7a). And when water is clear, it acts like a mirror and can accurately reflect what is brought in front of it (e.g., *Zhuangzi* 2/17a, 10/18b–19a). In this context, *jing* is a desirable state of existence, by contrast to a state in which one is subject to disturbances that distort one's response to things. This idea of disturbance is found in the observation in the *Huainanzi* about how cravings and desires can disturb the nature of human beings which is originally *jing* (1/4a). In this sense, *jing* is contrasted with *dong* in the sense of disturbance (e.g., *Mengzi* 2A:2) but not with *dong* in the sense of activity, since one can be active (*dong*) while one's heart/mind is still (*jing*) and free from disturbance (e.g., *Xunzi* 15/4b). Indeed, being *jing* in this sense is a preparation for *dong* (activity), just as *xu* in the sense of receptivity and responsiveness is a preparation for *shi* (e.g., *Zhuangzi* 5/12a, *Hanfeizi* 1/10a).

Jing in the sense of being free from disturbance is often paired with *xu* in the combination *xu jing* (e.g., *Hanfeizi* 1/10a, 1/11a). The *Liezi* contrasts *xu* and *jing* with "taking in" and "projecting onto" (1/13a), and the *Hanfeizi* contrasts them with "using the self" (2/11a). The *Lushichunqiu* describes the person who has attained *dao* (Way) as *jing*, and the person who is *jing* as without knowledge (*zhi*) (17/6b). Thus, *jing*, like *xu*, has to do with the absence of preconceptions that comes from the self and that can adversely affect one's response to things.

The *Zhuangzi* still uses *jing* in the sense of inactivity, by contrast to *dong* in the sense of activity (e.g., 10/18a). Often, it uses *jing* in the sense of being undisturbed, again pairing it with *xu* (5/12a). Interestingly, it relates *jing* to *xu* in apparently opposite directions. On one occasion, *xu* is supposed to lead to *jing* (5/12a); on another occasion, *jing* is supposed to lead to *ming* (brightness, clarity) and *ming* to *xu* (8/9a; cf. *Lushichunqiu* 25/7b). These two statements of the relationship can be reconciled by noting the different connotations of *xu*. *Xu*, in the sense of absence of factors that can potentially disturb the heart/mind, leads to *jing*, the still and undisturbed state of the heart/mind. This in turn enables the heart/mind to be clear, thereby leading to *xu* in the sense of proper responsiveness.

We saw how, in the passage about fasting of the heart/mind, Yan Hui talks about "not having" himself. Other parts of the *Zhuangzi* also refer to losing (1/10a), not having (1/5a), or forgetting (5/20a) the self. Another passage refers to how Yan Hui forgets various things (3/14a–b) and still another passage brings up the idea of not having thoughts and deliberation (7/22a–b). One passage records a dialogue between Zhuangzi and Hui Shi, and Zhuangzi talks about how one should be without *qing* (*wu qing*) (2/22b–23b). This idea he explains in terms of the absence of likes and dislikes that can harm the body; instead, one should *yin zi ran*, or follow what is self-so. So, along with the emphasis on *xu* and *jing*, the *Zhuangzi* also advocates *wu* in the sense of not having, or eliminating, certain kinds of thoughts and deliberation, or likes and dislikes, an idea sometimes put in terms of not having or losing the self.

The expression "*yin zi ran*" takes us from a description of the ideal state of the heart/mind to a description of one's ideal relation to things. *Yin* has the meaning of "using as a basis"; in using something as a basis in the way one operates, one is also "following" or "adapting" to that thing in one's operation. Aside from the use of *yin* in relation to *zi ran*, the *Zhuangzi* also uses it to describe how "this" and "that," "it is so" and "it is not so," mutually generate each other (1/14b–15a). The term is used in other texts to describe how one relates to things (*Lushichunqiu* 24/13b) and to people; the *Shenzi* talks about, presumably in relation to a ruler, how one uses the way people work for themselves as a way to relate to people, rather than making them work for oneself (1/4b–5a). The *Lushichunqiu* (17/13b, 17/21b) and *Shen Buhai* fragments (p. 376) explicitly describe *yin* as the way of the ruler, enabling the ruler to be still (*jing*), by contrast to the activity of officials. This probably refers to how the ruler makes use of the talents and abilities of officials without himself being actively involved in government.

The term *zi ran* refers to how things operate on their own; it is a prominent concept in the *Laozi* (e.g., *Laozi* nos. 25, 64), and other early texts also refer to the idea of following *zi ran* (e.g., *Hanfeizi* 8/12b, 8/14a, *Lushichunqiu* 3/13a–b). Besides speaking of *yin zi ran*, the *Zhuangzi* also speaks of following (*shun*) the *zi ran* of things (3/16b) and of responding with *zi ran* (5/20b). The idea is to not interfere with the way things operate on their own, and instead to flow along with it. The *Zhuangzi* regards *zi ran* as something unalterable (10/5b), and often highlights the notion of *bu de yi*, the unavoidable. Aside from using *bu de yi* in relation to one's place in the political order (2/9a–9b, 2/10b; cf. 2/18a), the text also regards following *bu de yi* as close to the way of the sage (8/10b).

Three other terms are used in connection with the way one should interact with things: *shi** (what is timely), *xing ming** (nature and destiny), and *li* (principle, pattern). The *Zhuangzi* observes that one should match (6/10a) or be at ease in (2/3b) *shi**; similar ideas are found in the *Lushichunqiu* (17/13b) and the *Liezi*, which also pairs *shi** with *ming** (6/11a). According to the *Zhuangzi*, one should give free rein to (4/5b) and be at ease in (4/15b) the *qing* (reality, fact) of *xing ming**. And one should follow *li* (9/23a) or the *li* of *tian* (2/2a, 5/20b, 6/2a). The term *li* is particularly important for our later discussion of Zhu Xi.

Li is used verbally in early texts in the sense of "give order to" (e.g., *Guanzi* 10/3b, *Huainanzi* 21/8a). It is often used in relation to another term *zhi**, meaning "bring order to" or "be in order" (e.g., *Guanzi* 16/3a, *Hanfeizi* 6/6b, *Xiaojing* 7/1b), and is sometimes contrasted with *luan*, or disorder (e.g., *Mozi* 36/25/14). The *Zhuangzi* is probably using *li* in the sense of "bring order to" when it refers to how one *li* one's heart/mind

(8/27b) or one's likes and dislikes (10/5b). *Li* pertains to things (*wu**) (e.g., *Huainanzi* 21/3a, *Liji* 11/15a–b, *Zhuangzi* 10/14a), and the 10,000 things differ in *li* (*Hanfeizi* 6/8a–b, *Zhuangzi* 8/30a–b). Sometimes, early texts regard *li* as pertaining not just to things (*wu**) but also to affairs such as *zhi** *luan* (e.g., *Hanfeizi* 20/7b). *Li* is something to be conformed to (e.g., *Mozi* 3/3/15–17) or followed (e.g., *Guanzi* 13/8b, *Hanfeizi* 20/8a, *Zhuangzi* 10/18a). As such, it is often paired with *dao* (Way) (e.g., *Hanfeizi* 6/3b, *Zhuangzi* 6/3b, 10/17b) and *yi** (propriety) (e.g., *Mengzi* 6A:7, *Lushichunqiu* 18/19b, *Guanzi* 13/4a, *Mozi* 63/39/33). So, *li* resides in things and affairs, is the way things operate, and one's response to things should involve following *li*.

Since one should flow along with things without interference from any pre-conception coming from the self, one's relation to things is like that of accurately reflecting the way things are. This idea is found in a passage in the *Zhuangzi* that comments on the stillness (*jing*) of the sage (5/12a–b). Just as still water can clearly reflect even one's beard and brow, the sage's heart/mind is still and can be the mirror of the 10,000 things. The superior person's heart/mind is also compared to a mirror that is *xu*—it does not store and yet is responsive to things (3/19a). The ideas of still water (2/17a) and of clear mirror that is free from dust (2/18a) are found elsewhere in the text. The idea of *ming* (brightness, clarity) also occurs frequently, at times compared to the brightness or clarity of the sun and moon (5/21a). The imageries of water and mirror also occur frequently in other early texts, and are sometimes mentioned in conjunction (e.g., *Mozi* 30/18/39, *Huainanzi* 1/3b).

What might prevent one's appropriate response to things are certain problematic influences coming from the self, and this idea the *Zhuangzi* presents through two related contrasts. One is that between *tian* (Heaven, Nature) and humans (*ren*). The way things operate on their own is *tian*, and to impose anything from one's heart/mind on one's response is for what is human to intrude into *tian*. Thus, the text idealizes not using the heart/mind to detract from *dao* (Way) and not using what is human to assist *tian* (3/2b; cf. 3/4a). As an example, that oxen and horses have four legs is due to *tian*, and to put a halter on a horse's head and pierce an ox's nose is due to humans (6/11b). Another contrast the *Zhuangzi* uses is that between *gong* (impartial, public) and *si* (partial, private). Flowing along with the *zi ran* of things and not allowing room for *si* will bring order to the world (3/16b), and *dao* is often related to the absence of *si* (8/30a–b; cf. 7/6a–b).

Si, when used to refer to what has to do with oneself, does not by itself carry any negative connotation. The *Lunyu* speaks of examining Yan Hui's *si* in the sense of examining his "private" life (2:9), and the *Mengzi* talks about attending to one's own (*si*) affairs after having attended to public (*gong*) affairs (3A:3). However, *si* does often carry a negative connotation when contrasted with *gong*. *Gong* is opposed to another term *pian* (e.g., *Hanfeizi* 6/4a, *Xunzi* 2/6a, 7/9b), where *pian* has the connotation of being one-sided or focusing on one part to the exclusion of others (*Xunzi* 2/6a). *Si* is a kind of *pian* that is focused on oneself; it is to focus on what is related to oneself in a way that prevents a balanced perspective. Thus, *gong yi**, or propriety that is "public" or "objective," is contrasted with resentment that is self-centered (*si*) (*Mozi* 9/8/20), with private (*si*) affairs (*Xunzi* 8/5a), or with selfish (*si*) desires (*Xunzi* 1/13a). The *Hanfeizi* contrasts *si* with *gong* (5/11b) and sometimes with *gong fa*, or public norms (2/1b). The contrast between *gong* and *si* and that between *tian* and humans are related in early texts, which describe the operation of *tian* as being without *si* (e.g., *Shen Buhai* fragments p. 358, *Liji* 15/12b–13a).

III. XUNZI

These ideas from the *Zhuangzi* are found in other early texts, though with different emphases and interpretations. For example, the *Laozi* highlights the notion of *zi ran*, using it not just to describe how one should flow along with the *zi ran* of things, but to characterize the sage himself (no. 17). Also, not only is the sage himself characterized by *xu*, but the sage also seeks to render *xu* the heart/mind of the people (no. 3). As another example, the "Xin Shu Shang" chapter of the *Guanzi* is notable for its explication of some of the key terms. *Xu* is characterized as not storing and as a result not having pre-conceptions (13/3b), and *yin* as not adding to or detracting from, and as letting go of oneself to follow things (13/4b–5a). *Yin* describes how the ruler makes use of the talents of the worthy (13/5b); those above should not take over the activities of those below, and should instead let them fully exercise their talents and abilities (13/1a, 13/2b–3a). More interestingly, these ideas are set in a Confucian context, with references to the Confucian ideas of *li** (rites) and *yi** (propriety) (13/3b–4a).

Of particular relevance to our later discussion of Zhu Xi is the way Xunzi deploys these terms. In the "Jie Bi" chapter of the *Xunzi*, both *xu* and *jing* are used to characterize the ideal state of the heart/mind (15/4b). The notion of *ming* (bright, clear) is also highlighted; the heart/mind is described as *qing** (clear) and is supposed to be *ming* just like the sun and moon (15/5b). The *qing** and *ming* of the heart/mind is illustrated by the imagery of water that is undisturbed (15/7a) and is compared to *tian* (14/2b). While deploying these ideas and imageries, which are similar to those found in the *Zhuangzi*, the "Jie Bi" chapter sets this discussion in a different context. It emphasizes how the clarity (*qing**) and brightness (*ming*) of the heart/mind is supposed to enable the heart/mind to discern *li* (15/7a).

As in other early texts, the *Xunzi* relates *li* to *zhi** (order) (1/8b, 7/12a, 16/6b, 17/4a–b), and talks about how education can *li* (bring order to) the nature of the common people (19/7a) and how the superior person *li* (bring order to) Heaven and Earth (5/7a). *Li* can pertain to things (*wu**) (15/9b) and affairs such as going against or going along with (12/9a). *Li* is something to be followed and accorded with (4/4a) and is related to *yi** (propriety) (10/8b, 19/3b). Given Xunzi's view on how social distinctions are grounded in their ability to give order thereby enabling satisfaction of human desires, he also relates *li* to *fen*, or social distinctions (12/12b, 17/1a).

In addition, he views *li* as something underlying *dao* (Way) (1/6a, 16/6b) and *li** (rites) (13/5a). It runs through the whole social order (11/14a, 15/9b) and is something that can be known or understood (*zhi*) (15/9b, 17/6a). The ideal state of the heart/mind enables it to grasp *li* (15/7a; cf. 16/8a–9a). It enables the heart/mind to understand (*zhi*) *dao* (Way), thereby enabling one to approve of (*ke*) *dao* and abide by it (15/4a–4b). The connection between understanding and following *dao* is so tight that Xunzi finds it inconceivable that one can truly understand *dao* without following it (16/9b).

This view of Xunzi's sets him apart from Zhuangzi. Zhuangzi emphasizes the connotation of emptiness in the term *xu*, seeing *xu* as a state in which one is free from guidance by the heart/mind. Xunzi, on the other hand, emphasizes the connotation of receptivity, seeing *xu* as a state in which the heart/mind is receptive to *li*, enabling it to discern *li*. The goal is not to eliminate guidance from the heart/mind, but to have its proper understanding guide one's behavior. Unlike Zhuangzi who sees the contribution of human beings as interfering with the operation of *tian*, Xunzi sees the former as distinct from and yet complementing the latter (11/9b). Xunzi's understanding of *ming* (brightness, clarity) is also different. For him, *ming* describes the clarity of one's understanding (*zhi*); study makes possible the *ming* of one's understanding and thereby ensures proper conduct (1/1a). Xunzi often emphasizes the *ming* of understanding (11/11b, 12/12a) or of the heart/mind (15/7a), comparing it to the *ming* of fire or of the sun and moon.

IV. GUO XIANG

A number of the above themes continue to evolve in the Han and Wei-Jin period. The idealization of *xu* in the context of Confucian morality that we have seen both in the "Xin Shu Shang" chapter of the *Guanzi* and in the *Xunzi* continues in Han Confucian thought. For example, Jia Yi regards *xu* as the foundation and *shu* (method) as the branch of *dao* (8/3a–b). *Xu* is illustrated with the imagery of mirror and characterized in terms of the absence of preconceptions, while *shu* is characterized in terms of such Confucian qualities as *ren** (humanity), *yi** (propriety), and *li** (rites). Xunzi's emphasis on understanding (*zhi*) and his view of it as a kind of brightness can also be found among thinkers of this period. Yang Xiong (53 B.C.E.–18 C.E.) regards understanding (*zhi*) as something that can light things up (3/2a–b), and Liu Xiang (77–6 B.C.E.) compares the way of the sage kings to the brightness of the sun or fire (3/6b). Liu Shao (third century) also compares wisdom to the brightness of the sun lighting up the day or of the candle lighting up the night (B/13a–b). Brightness enables one to grasp *li*, and the greater the brightness the further one sees. Another evolvement in the Wei-Jin period is the identification of *zi ran* (self-so) with *xing* (nature). Wang Bi (226–249) regards the 10,000 things as having *zi ran* as their *xing* (A/16b), and speaks of following the *zi ran* of things in parallel with following the *xing* of things (A/15a–b).

During this period, Guo Xiang develops certain ideas that are particularly relevant to our later discussion of Zhu Xi. According to Guo Xiang, everything has its *xing* (nature), *neng* (ability) and *fen* (appropriate position), and one should follow one's *xing*, engage in affairs in a way that is appropriate to one's *neng*, and live in accordance with one's *fen* (1/1a). Different things have different *neng*; those suited to rule have the *neng* to employ officials, while those suited for a certain official position have the *neng* to carry out the responsibility of the office (5/13b–14a). *Fen* is used in the *Xunzi* to refer to distinguishing between different social roles (*Xunzi* 5/2b) as well as to the social distinctions that result (*Xunzi* 5/7b–8a, 6/1b, 6/3b). For Guo Xiang, *fen* refers to one's proper place in the social set up (1/13a); everything, however small or large, has its own *fen* (1/3b). *Fen* is often paired with *xing* in the expression *xing fen* (1/1a, 3/16a), and it is also related to *li* (1/2a), which pertains to everything (1/19a). *Fen* is also related to *zi ran* (1/24b), which is explained in terms of what is so by itself without one's activity (1/5a). Probably, the difference between these concepts is that *li* emphasizes that which resides in a thing and which governs its operation, *xing* emphasizes the thing's possession of *li*, *zi ran* emphasizes the fact that the thing can operate on its own given the *li* it has, and *fen* emphasizes the proper place of the thing given its *li*.

What is particularly noteworthy is Guo Xiang's repeated emphasis on the difference among things, especially the different abilities of people, an idea also found among other thinkers of the period such as Liu Shao (B/1b). In connection with the depiction in the *Zhuangzi* of the behavior of small and large birds, Guo notes that, whether small or large, each lives in accordance with its *xing* (1/2a) and in so doing, neither is to be admired or valued over the other (1/2b, 1/18a–b). This observation is extended to the social realm. Everything has its proper place (*fen*) in the social world, whether high or low, and the important thing is to live in accordance with one's proper place (1/13a). Someone suited to rule should employ able officials and not actively engage in the business of government, while someone suited to a certain kind of office should conduct the affairs assigned to that office. Everything proceeds in accordance with *li* and *zi ran*, and this is what constitutes *wu wei* (5/13b–14a). *Wu wei* is not a matter of inactivity, but a matter of following one's *xing* and as a result being at ease (3/11b, 4/15b). In doing so, though one is socially engaged, one's heart/mind is at ease and engages in the free roaming that is idealized in the *Zhuangzi* (1/6b, 3/10b, 3/12a).

This view results in an understanding of the contrast between *tian* and humans different from that in the *Zhuangzi*. Guo Xiang does advocate ideas similar to the *Zhuangzi*, such as not having the self (*wu ji*) (1/5a) or heart/mind (*wu xin*) (3/14a). Like the *Zhuangzi*, Guo takes this to mean not having preconceptions that interfere with one's flowing along with the way things are (1/5a, 3/10b). However, for Guo, this in turn involves one's fulfilling one's proper place in the social order, and so implies social engagement of a kind appropriate to one's place (1/7b; cf. 3/15a). Like the *Zhuangzi*, Guo relates the operation of *tian* to *zi ran* (3/1a). However, since what is *zi ran* can include one's active social involvement, human activities of this kind are not opposed to *tian*. In connection with the example of oxen and horses in the *Zhuangzi*, Guo notes, contrary to the *Zhuangzi*, that it is the place of humans to ride horses and use oxen to plow, and so it is appropriate for humans to put a halter on a horse's head and pierce an ox's nose. Although such activities are due to humans, it has its foundation in *tian* and is not opposed to it. What is opposed to *tian* are only human activities of the kind that is excessive, not rooted in the proper place of human beings, such as overexerting horses and oxen in these activities (6/11b). Extending this to the social order, Guo sees active human participation in the social order as itself based on, rather than opposed to *tian*.

V. ZHU XI

We have seen how the range of ideas considered in relation to the *Zhuangzi* evolved over time, with new and interesting contributions by thinkers such as Xunzi and Guo Xiang. Xunzi's emphasis on the understanding of *li* and on how this understanding guides human conduct, and Guo Xiang's view that social engagement is compatible with the kind of free roaming of the heart/mind idealized in the *Zhuangzi*, are both shared by Zhu Xi. Other interesting developments can be found in the late Tang and early Song period. For example, Li Ao, who sees *xing* (nature) as originally good and *qing* (emotions) as potentially obscuring *xing*, highlights the imagery of water being made impure by sediments and fire being made dim by smoke (2/1a–b). The task of self-cultivation is to restore the original *xing*; through *xu*, one attains *ming* which will light up everything without omission (2/3a–3b; cf. 2/2a). Shao Yong emphasizes the idea of responding to things in accordance with its *li*, putting this in terms of viewing (*guan*) things with things (6/26b) or with the *li* in things (6/26a). Doing so and thereby going along with things is *xing*, while viewing things with the self, namely, with self pre-conceptions, is *qing* (8b/16a; cf. 8b/27b). By making the heart/mind like still water, the heart/mind will be *jing* and thereby *ming* (8b/25a). Li Ao's conception of self-cultivation as restoring the original *xing*, and Shao Yong's idea of responding to things in accordance with their *li*, are again shared by Zhu Xi.

Zhu Xi continues to emphasize the notion of *li* and relates it to *zi ran*. For example, *ren** (humanity) and *yi** (propriety) (*Mengzi Huowen* 26/3a), and *li** (rites) and *yue* (music) (*Yulei* p. 2253), are all viewed as the *zi ran* of *tian li*. *Li* is also the way things should be (*dang ran*) (*Yulei* p. 863, *Lunyu Jizhu* 2/11a, *Lunyu Huowen* 9/14b); furthermore, what is *zi ran* is also what cannot be otherwise (*Mengzi Huowen* 26/3a; cf. *Yulei* p. 414). In addition, *li* accounts for the way things are (*suo yi ran*) (*Yulei* p. 414, *Mengzi Jizhu* 2/6a). Everything has its *li* (*Yulei* p. 2892) and the difference between *li* and *dao* is that *dao* refers to the general and emphasizes the path that all should follow, while *li* refers to the specific and emphasizes the details (*Yulei* p. 99; cf. *Yulei* p. 840). *Li* is differentiated. The relation between ruler and officials has its *li*, which differs from the *li* pertaining to the relation between father and son; such differentiation of *li* is referred to as *fen* (*Yulei* p. 99). Thus, while *li* is one in that it runs through everything, its differentiations (*fen*) are varied (Commentary on Zhang Zai's *Ximing* 1/7a–7b, *Yulei* pp. 108–9).

Like Guo Xiang, Zhu sees human engagement in the social order as not opposed to *tian*. For him, to put a halter on a horse's head and pierce an ox's nose is itself to follow the *xing* of oxen and horses (*Yulei* pp. 1492, 1494–5) and is in accordance with *tian li* (*Yulei* p. 156). Guo Xiang grounds the social order in the different *li* pertaining to different human beings, making them suited to different social positions. While Zhu Xi does talk about human beings having different talents (*cai*), this has to do with their different ethical qualities rather than their different suitability to different social positions. Unlike Guo Xiang, the differentiation (*fen*) of *li* that Zhu focuses on has to do with the different *li* that pertains to different relations between different social positions, such as that between ruler and official or that between father and son. And it is in terms of this differentiation (*fen*) of *li* that he grounds the social order. It is appropriate for people to stand in different social relations to each other because there are different *li* pertaining to different social relations, not because there are different *li* pertaining to different individual human beings. According to Zhu Xi, without differentiation of *li* in this sense, there will be no social distinction thereby resulting in the Moist idea of indiscriminate concern for all (*Yulei* p. 2521).

Like Xunzi, Zhu emphasizes how understanding (*zhi*) should guide action. Understanding guides action in the way that, in walking, one's eyes guide one's legs (*Yulei* p. 148). Understanding for Zhu Xi is a relation between the heart/mind and *li*, a relation put in a number of ways. The heart/mind can see (*guan*) *li* (*Yulei* p. 1983), and can light up (*ju*) *li* (*Lunyu Jizhu* 5/8a, *Daquan* 67/18a–b). In addition to the imageries of still water and clear mirror (e.g., *Yulei* p. 177), he also uses the imageries of fire (*Yulei* pp. 206, 265) and the sun and moon (*Yulei* p. 205), whose brightness lights up *li*. The difference from Xunzi is that, unlike Xunzi who regards *li* as something learnt, Zhu thinks the heart/mind already has *li* though it can be obscured. Thus, the heart/mind is originally a clear mirror (*Daquan* 67/3b–4a) though it can be obscured by dust (*Yulei* p. 267). Like Li Ao, he regards self-cultivation as a restorative process, comparable to the process of clearing the mirror to recover its original brightness (*Yulei* pp. 92–93).

Both Mencius and Xunzi assign a governing role to the heart/mind over the senses (*Mengzi* 6A:15, *Xunzi* 11/10a), and Mencius regards ethical failure as due to the senses being drawn unthinkingly by external objects (*Mengzi* 6A;15). This view of the relation between the heart/mind and the senses can be found in the *Guanzi*, which also assigns a governing role to the heart/mind (13/1a) and sees external objects as potentially leading the senses, and consequently the heart/mind, astray (13/6a; 16/3a). Zhu Xi, drawing on the "Yue Ji" chapter of the *Liji*, also regards ethical failure as due to external things leading human beings astray. The "Yue Ji" chapter describes how, upon contact with things, likes and dislikes arise; these can lead to problems if they are not regulated. Such likes and dislikes are referred to as "human desires" (*ren yu*), which is contrasted with *tian li* (11/8b–9a). Zhu likewise traces the source of ethical failure to human desires (*ren yu*) (*Yulei* p. 224) or material desires (*wu* yu*) (*Mengzi Jizhu* 2/13b, 2/14b). While sometimes presenting human desires as consisting of such things as desire for food when hungry and for clothing when cold, which are not in themselves problematic (*Yulei* p. 2009), he more often refers to human desires as problematic as such, contrasting the *gong* of *tian li* to the *si* of human desires (*Zhongyong Zhangju* Preface/1a–2a, *Yulei* p. 225). In such contexts, he would describe eating and drinking as *tian li*, and the desire for delicious food as human desire (*Yulei* p. 224). In any instance, what he is opposed to is not desires as such, but desires coming from the self that goes beyond the basic desires that all human beings share.

His view on the emotions is similar. Commenting on *Lunyu* 6:3, which describes how Yan Hui does not transfer his anger nor repeat his errors, Zhu, following the Cheng brothers (*Cuiyan* 2/34b–35a, *Yishu* 18/22a), acknowledges that even the sage will be angry when appropriate (*Yulei* p. 2445). However, this anger is a response to the situation and does not come from the sage, and in that sense the sage has no anger (*Yulei* p. 776). Furthermore, after the incident is over, the anger that was initially an appropriate response goes away and is not stored in the sage (*Yulei* p. 2445). So, what Zhu is opposed to is not emotions as such, but emotions that are not called for by the circumstances and instead originate from the self.

The above account provides the background for understanding Zhu Xi's views on *wu*, *jing* and *xu*. Zhu's advocacy of *wu* is directed to the problematic elements, whether desires or emotions, that come from the self and are a form of *si*. The term *si* can be used in a neutral sense—it can refer simply to what pertains to oneself, such as one's senses and one's desire to meet basic needs such as food and warmth (*Yulei* p. 1486). More often, though, Zhu uses it to refer to something coming from the self that goes beyond these basics—selfish thoughts (*si yi***) are pre-conceptions that one has when approaching things (*Yulei* p. 185), and examples of selfish desires (*si yu*) include the form of problematic desires described earlier. In this sense, *si* is opposed to *gong* and obstructs the manifestation of *ren** (humanity) (*Yulei* pp. 117, 2455). *Ren** can be compared to the original brightness and clarity of a mirror, *si* to dust on the mirror, and *gong* to the absence of dust from the mirror (*Yulei* p. 2454).

As for *jing* , Zhu sometimes uses *jing* by contrast to *dong* to refer to one's state prior to interacting with things. *Xing* (nature) is *jing*, and *qing* (emotions), the activation of *xing*, is *dong*. This contrasts with what he takes to be the point of the observation in the "Yue Ji" chapter of the *Liji* about how *xing* refers to stillness (*jing*) at birth, and how the desire (*yu*) of *xing* refers to activation upon contact with things (*Daquan* 67/8a–8b). Often, he uses the contrast between *jing* and *dong* to refer to the contrast between the unperturbed state of the heart/mind and a state of the heart/mind that is unsettled. In this sense, if the heart/mind is not *jing*, it would be fluctuating between different directions and would not be at ease (*Yulei* p. 278). *Jing* refers to a state when the heart/mind is not so torn, and is not vulnerable to uncertainty (*Yulei* p. 275, *Daxue Zhangju* 1b). And one can achieve this by holding on to *li* (*Daxue Huowen* 1/9a–10a).

Zhu Xi also uses *xu* in two related senses. The heart/mind is *xu* in the sense of being capable of storing; it is because the heart/mind is *xu* that it can store the many *li* (*Yulei* pp. 88, 2514); in that sense, there is *shi* within *xu* (*Yulei* p. 232). Since *li* for Zhu is already in the heart/mind, *xu* for him is not a matter of receptivity to *li* that one learns but a matter of capability of storing the multitude of *li* in the heart/mind. Zhu also uses *xu* in the sense of being free from what is *si* and what is *wei** (false, fake) (*Yulei* p. 1575). By being *xu* in this sense, one is able to observe *li* (*Yulei* p. 155) and follow *li* (*Yulei* p. 145). This is the original state of the heart/mind prior to the influence of selfish desires (*Yulei* p. 94). Drawing on the idea of the "air in the early morning" in *Mengzi* 6A:8, Zhu thinks that this is the state of the heart/mind in the early morning when one just awakens from restful sleep, though that state is soon lost after one starts interacting with things (*Yulei* pp. 349, 1393, 2875).

Returning to the phenomenon of "purity," this was introduced earlier as an ideal state of existence involving the absence of deviant elements that can adversely affect one's response to the world. What we have seen in this paper is that the phenomenon can be differently construed, depending on how one draws the line between proper responsiveness and what can detract from such responsiveness. For Zhuangzi, proper responsiveness involves allowing things to operate on their own without guidance from the heart/mind. Any intervention in the way things operate is seen as human intrusion, and even ordinary human activities like riding horses and using oxen to plow are seen as inappropriate human intrusion into the work of *tian*.

For Xunzi, proper responsiveness involves properly understanding the *li* that underlies the social order and responding to the world under such guidance. Human activities can complete the work of *tian*, and are not problematic as such; it is only disturbances of the heart/mind that prevent proper understanding that constitute inappropriate intrusion. For Guo Xiang, proper responsiveness involves allowing each thing to follow its own *xing* and exercise its own *neng*, thereby occupying its proper place (*fen*) in the world. Human social engagement is compatible with the work of *tian*, as such engagement enables humans to take their proper place in the social order.

Like Xunzi, Zhu Xi sees proper responsiveness to the world as involving proper understanding of *li* and responding under its guidance. Like Guo Xiang, he sees social engagement as something that enables humans to truly partake in the operation of *tian*. He differs from Xunzi in regarding *li* as already in every human being though the understanding of *li* can be obscured. And he differs from Guo Xiang in grounding the social order not in the different *li* in different human beings, but in the different *li* that pertains to different social relations. "Purity" for him involves the absence not of human thoughts, desires or emotions as such, but the absence of human thoughts, desires or emotions that are *si*, understood in terms of an unbalanced perspective due to certain self preoccupations or projections. *Wu* refers to the absence of these factors, while *xu* and *jing* characterize the state of the heart/mind that is free from disturbance by such factors.*

NOTE

* Materials in this paper are based on research related to a book in progress, *The Development of Confucian-Mencian Thought: Zhu Xi, Wang Yangming and Dai Zhen*, sequel to *Mencius and Early Chinese Thought* (Stanford University Press, 1997).

GLOSSARY OF CHINESE WORDS

Bu de yi	不 得 已	*Cai*	才
Dang ran	當 然	*Dao*	道
Ding	定	*Dong*	動
Fa	法	*Fen*	分
Gong	公	*Gong fa*	公 法
*Gong yi**	公義	*Guan*	觀
Jia	假	*Jing*	靜
Ju	炬	*Ke*	可
Kong	空	*Kong xu*	空 虛
Le	樂	*Li*	理
*Li**	禮	*Luan*	亂
Man	滿	*Ming*	明
*Ming**	命	*Neng*	能
Pian	偏	*Qi*	气
Qing	情	*Qing**	清
Qing jing*	清 靜	*Ran*	然
Ren	人	*Ren yu*	人 欲
*Ren**	仁	*Shi*	實
*Shi**	時	*Shu*	術
Shun	順	*Si*	私
*Si yi***	私 意	*Si yu*	私 欲
Suo yi ran	所 以 然	*Tian*	天
Tian li	天 理	*Wei*	為
*Wei**	偽	*Wo*	我
Wu	無	*Wu ji*	無己
Wu qing	無 情	*Wu wei*	無為
Wu xin	無心	*Wu**	物
Wu yu*	物 欲	*Xin*	心
Xing	性	*Xing fen*	性 分
*Xing ming**	性 命	*Xu*	虛
Xu jing	虛靜	*Xu xin*	虛心
Yi	以	*Yi**	義
*Yi***	意	*Yin*	因
Yin zi ran	因 自 然	*Ying*	盈
You	有	*Yu*	欲
Yue	樂	*Zhi*	知
*Zhi**	治	*Zhi* luan*	治 亂
Zi	自	*Zi ran*	自然

PART III

Virtue, Self, and Gender

CHAPTER 10

The Unity of Rule and Virtue in Confucianism

YULI LIU

In the past few decades, philosophical and theological writing reveals a marked revival of interest in virtue ethics. Against the background of the revival of virtue ethics in the West, some philosophers argue that throughout its long history, Confucian ethics has stressed character formation or personal cultivation of virtues. Thus it seems appropriate to characterize Confucian ethics as an ethics of virtue. I will argue that although Confucian ethics puts an emphasis on character cultivation and the importance of personhood, or in short, shares some great similarities with contemporary Western virtue ethics, it is not a virtue ethics in a strict sense. Taking Confucian ethics as a virtue ethics will not reveal its distinctive features. Instead, taking Confucian ethics as a unique ethics, in which rule and virtue are united, will help us not only to understand its distinctive way of understanding morality, but also to understand its contribution to the debate between virtue ethics and rule ethics. More importantly, it will help us show the contribution that this distinctive way of understanding morality might make to contemporary moral philosophy in reconstructing a highly developed moral theory.

VIRTUE ETHICS VERSUS RULE ETHICS

Philosophical interest in virtue and virtues has had a long history, which can be traced back to Aristotle in ancient Greece. But after ancient Rome, a more legalistic way of thinking about morality became dominant, and accordingly, rule-based moral theories have been mainstream moral thought since then. The interest of modern ethicists has largely shifted toward questions of right and wrong, and towards the formulation of principles of duty and obligation. Since the eighteenth century, moral philosophy has been dominated by two basic theories in the West,

Kantianism on the one hand, and utilitarianism on the other. But in the past two decades, philosophical writings reveal a marked revival of interest in virtue ethics and the revival of virtue theory has become one of the most promising recent developments in philosophical ethics. As a result, there has been a rivalry between virtue ethics and rule ethics in the development of contemporary moral philosophy.

The growing attraction of virtue ethics is not only due to the positive features of virtue theory, but also due to growing dissatisfaction with some central features of modern ethical theories. One of the main charges against modern moral philosophy is based on the two general points: first, an adequate theory of ethics must provide an understanding of moral character; and second, modern moral philosophers have failed to do this. Not only have they neglected the topic; their neglect has led them sometimes to embrace doctrines that distort the nature of moral character (see Rachel 1999: 189). In order to remedy this neglect, some have judged it necessary to advocate a revival of virtue ethics, the essence of which is "a focus on character, and on seeing a human life as a whole" (Almond 1998: 110). But as to the issue of the position of virtue ethics and how far we should take the claim about the dominance of the notion of virtue, virtue ethicists have quite different opinions.

A first view which emphasizes the importance of virtue can be called the moderate version of virtue ethics. The moderate version contends that though judgements of character are independent of judgements of actions, at least some judgements of acts are similarly independent of judgements of character. Some actions are wrong, indeed abhorrent, irrespective of who carries them out and what his or her motivation is. According to such moderate versions, ethical theory has (at least) two parts which are irreducible to each other, one dealing with the morality of acts, the other dealing with the morality of character (Statman 1997: 8). Although some actions can be evaluated independently of questions of virtue, morality is mostly connected with character.

The second view that I should mention can be called the radical version of virtue ethics. According to the radical version, the lesson to be learnt from Aristotle's virtue ethics is that virtue concepts are the central concepts in ethical theory and hence ethics is best understood in terms of the virtues. Normative theory must have a structure such that assessment of human character is more fundamental than either the assessment of the rightness of an action or the assessment of the value of the consequence of the action. There are no judgements of acts which are independent of virtue, since right action is defined in terms of virtue. Contrary to deontological ethics, in which virtue is defined as a disposition to do what is right, virtue ethics defines what is right in terms of virtue. According to radical virtue ethicists, both utilitarianism and Kantianism have got the fundamentals of ethics wrong. So instead of taking virtue ethics as a supplement to an overall theory of ethics, these moral philosophers regard virtue ethics as a fully developed, alternative ethical theory. They argue that the ethics of virtue should be considered as an alternative to the other sorts of theories—as an independent theory of ethics that is complete in itself.

Within this view of virtue and its position in ethics, as Phillip Montague shows, we can once more distinguish between two versions. One contends that "act appraisals are explicable in terms of more basic person appraisals"(Montague 1997: 194); that is to say, we can and we should use deontic concepts such as rightness and obligation, as long as we remember that they are derivative from aretaic concepts. This version is also called "the reductionist view." The second version, which represents the most extreme interpretation of virtue ethics, contends that we should get rid of the deontic notions altogether; "the rightness, wrongness, obligatoriness, etc., of acts are either incoherent or pernicious, and should be ignored entirely by ethical theory." (Ibid.) This view is also called "the replacement thesis," and is held by such philosophers as Charles Taylor and Anscombe (Statman 1997: 8).

It is in this sense that David Solomon argues that "the most striking feature of virtue ethics is the near universality of its rejection in contemporary ethical theory and in modern ethics generally."(Solomon 1997: 167) It is this radical view of virtue ethics that has challenged or tried to challenge both traditional deontology and utilitarianism and has become or tried to become a rival to both. But the replacement view of virtue ethics seems to make too extreme a claim for me to consider here. So I will mainly take account of the reductionist view of virtue ethics in the following.[1] A further reason for this limitation is that when philosophers argue that Confucian ethics is a virtue ethics, they are not referring to the replacement view of virtue ethics but, for the most part, to the reductionist view of virtue ethics.

CONFUCIAN MORALITY: THE UNITY OF *DAO* AND *DE*

Against the background of the revival of virtue ethics in the West, some philosophers[2] argue that throughout its long history, Confucian ethics has stressed character formation or personal cultivation of virtues (*de*). Thus it seems appropriate to characterize Confucian ethics as an ethics of virtue.

According to my understanding, although Confucian ethics shares some similarities with virtue ethics, it is not adequate to regard Confucian ethics as a virtue ethics based on these similarities. This is in the same way that we cannot say that a Chinese restaurant can be seen as a Western restaurant of a certain kind because it has the materials for a hamburger. In my opinion, the general overemphasis on surface similarities between these two ethics has shadowed philosophically more important differences between them. The value of Confucian ethics to the development of contemporary ethics does not consist in its being a virtue ethics, as some scholars have argued, but in its distinctive way of understanding morality. With this distinctive understanding of morality, Confucian ethics is better conceived of as a unique kind of ethics, in which rule and virtue are united.

Then what is the Confucian understanding of morality?

The Chinese word for morality is *daode*, which is composed by two characters: *dao* 道 and *de* 德. The original meaning of *dao* is a road or a path. In Confucianism, *dao* is enriched to mean the universal Way or cosmic order applicable and existent in every corner of the universe. *De* 德, which has been translated as "virtue," had been traditionally used of the power to move others without exerting physical force. Sometimes *de* is functionally equivalent to "power," "force," or "potency." More commonly, *de* is rendered as "virtue" in the distinctively ethical sense, as pertaining to excellence of a character trait or disposition.

As the word (*daode* 道德) is an old word and has been used to interpret the Western word "morality," this implies that in traditional Chinese ethics, morality includes two aspects, which are *dao* (the objective way) and *de* (the subjective virtue). It is said that it is since Confucius that *de* is paired with *dao* and obtained a moral meaning (see Graham 1989: 188). As A. C. Graham argues: in Confucianism, the two concepts are interdependent, … a person's *De* is his potentiality to act according to the *Dao* (see Graham

1989: 13). This means that Confucian understanding of *de* has never been separated from the understanding of *dao* (the Way).

The relation between *de* and *dao* has been noticed by some philosophers who take Confucian ethics as a virtue ethics. Basing on their understanding of Confucian *dao* and its relation to *de*, they try to reconstruct Confucian ethics in terms of virtue ethics. For example, in his article "Basic Concepts of Confucian Ethics," the principle aim of which is to present Confucian ethics as an ethics of virtue, A. S. Cua argues:

> *Tao* is an evaluative term. Its focal point of interest lies in the Confucian vision of the good human life as a whole or the ideal of human excellence. Commonly rendered as "the way," *tao* is functionally equivalent to the ideal "way of life." ... Recall that *te* is an individual achievement through personal cultivation. When a person succeeds in realizing *tao*, he or she has attained such basic *te* as *jen*, *li*, and *i* (humanity, righteousness and propriety). ... In this sense, *te* is an abstract noun like *tao*, but it depends on *tao* for its distinctive character. *Te* is thus functionally equivalent to ethical virtue ... With its emphasis in *tao* and *te*, Confucian ethics is properly characterized as an ethics of virtue. (Cua 1998: 273–4)

What Cua has given us seems an Aristotelian way of understanding *dao* and its relation to *de* in Confucian ethics. By taking *dao* as the ideal way of life and the *de* as ethical virtue, Cua seems to have successfully constructed Confucian ethics as an ethics of virtue. But this is based on an inadequate understanding of *dao* and its relation to *de*.

It is well-known that Confucius used the term *dao* in two senses in the *Analects*: one specific, the way of someone or something; and the other, universal. As a specific term, *dao* usually has a modifier. When Cua argues that *dao* is an evaluative term and is functionally equivalent to the ideal "way of life," he seems to use and understand Confucian *dao* only in this sense. According to Cua, it is these specific Ways that were admired and followed by Confucius or his followers and functionally equivalent as an ideal way of life. Although on many occasions Confucius uses *dao* in the specific sense, in his thinking the greatness and nobility of *dao* can be seen only in the other sense, that is, the Way of the universe and the Principle of the Heaven and Earth. Used in this way, the Confucian *dao* has at least the following meanings.

Firstly, *dao* is the Way of universe.

In Confucianism, the original meaning of *dao* as a road or a path is enriched to mean the universal Way applicable and existent in every corner of the universe. The universal Way is understood to originate from Heaven and Earth and therefore to be the source of the meaning and value of human life. It is believed to have been manifest in the wisdom of the ancient sage-kings, in the doctrine of Confucius, and in the ways of life of good people. Understood as such, the Way is the foundation of a harmonious universe, a peaceful society and a good life, and without it the transformation of the universe would break down, human society would fall into chaos, and the state would weaken and collapse (Yao 2000: 139–40). It is described as the following in *Zhongyong*:

> The Way of the superior man functions everywhere and yet is hidden. Men and women of simple intelligence can share its knowledge; and yet in its utmost reaches, there is something, which even the sage does not know. Men and women of simple intelligence can put it into practice; and yet in its utmost reaches there is something even the sage is not able to put into practice. Great as Heaven and Earth are, men still find something in them with which to be dissatisfied. Thus with [the Way of] the superior man, if one speaks of its greatness, nothing in the world can contain it, and if one speaks of its smallness, nothing in the world can split it. (*Zhongyong*, Ch.12)

Dao in Confucianism is not, first of all, an evaluative term as Cua argues, but, as D. C. Lau comments, "very close to the term 'Truth' as found in philosophical and religious writings in the West." It "seems to cover the sum total of truths about the universe and man."(Lau 1982: ix)

In her article "Confucius and Kant: The Ethics of Respect," Sandra A. Wawrytko offers a metaphysical conception of *dao*, explaining it in terms of the Kantian Moral Law (Wawrytko 1982: 237–57). According to her, there is a similarity between *dao* and the Moral Law that is based on the idea that both refer to a universal and unwavering standard. This comparison sheds light on the objective character of *dao* by taking it as a universal principle. We say *dao* is objective in the sense that it has the characteristics of universality and inevitability. From this point of view, *dao* is an objective existence independent of the contingent particulars which it informs.

So we can see that *dao* in Confucianism has been used, in its fundamental sense, as the way of the universe, the Principle of Heaven and Earth in the world. Unlike what Cua has argued, "the pragmatic import of which (*dao*) might be different to the members of community due to their own conceptions of the human excellence (*shan*)" (Cua 1998: 275), *dao* is an objective reality with ontological character rather than only an "ideal way of life."

Secondly, the *dao* has its source in Heaven.

Heaven is the source of Confucian spirituality and is identified as its transcendental power. The character for Heaven (*tian* 天) is traditionally defined as the "Supreme Ultimate (*zhigao wushang* 至高无上)."[3] As the Ultimate Reality, Heaven (*tian*) is the origin of all things in the world. All things generated from Heaven therefore have maintained a certain relation to Heaven and an interrelation with other things. Heaven is not only the initial source for all things but also the ground and justification for the continuous existence of all things. In short, Heaven is immanent in all things and constitutes the very nature of things. This is also true of human existence. The Way of man must follow the way of Heaven.

There is obviously good reason to believe that Confucius treated the spiritual and transcendental belief in Heaven as an ultimate source of support and justification, and also as a supreme model of the power and the virtue of creativity. Confucius appealed to the *tian* for his own *de*-endowment and the value of the *Zhouwen* (周文: the Culture of *Zhou*) (*Analects*, 7:23 and 9:5).[4] It is also clear that he distinguished spirits and ghosts (*guishen* 鬼神) from *tian* and indicated that he acted as if he prayed to *tian* for a long time (ibid., 7:20 and 7:34).[5] He never claimed any positive knowledge of spiritual matters and yet he implied that he had acquired a tacit understanding of Heaven. This was why he lamented, in extreme adversity, that only Heaven knew him (ibid., 2:4). Apparently, for Confucius, the Way of Heaven provides a basis and background for the realization of the way of humanity, and Heaven has embodied all the virtuous qualities that a human person can desire and must emulate. In this sense, the Way of Heaven is not remote but very close to man, indeed (Cheng 2000: 38).

Thirdly, *dao* is not remote from man.

Although the Way has its source in Heaven, it is not something mysterious that cannot be known by humans. As a matter of fact, it is not distinct from human beings and cannot be separated from human life, since it exists in daily life, in ordinary behavior and in mundane matters.

According to Confucianism, although the Way of Heaven predetermines the Way of Humans, the Way of Heaven cannot be fulfilled unless it has been understood as the human way and consciously carried out by individuals in everyday life. To know the Way is, first of all, to know the Way of Humans—to find the Way in themselves. According to Confucian cosmology, man is a product and a form of the Way (*dao*), whose life manifestations are a conscious presentation of the creative energy and power of Heaven and whose organism is a sample microorganism of a whole macrocosm. For Confucians, as the highest living creatures of the *Yin-Yang* dialectic, it is the duty of humans to fully practice the Way of man in order to qualify to coexist with Heaven and Earth. It is up to humans to enlarge or belittle it, to manifest it or to obscure it. So Confucius said, "The Way is not far from man. When a man pursues the Way and yet remains away from man, his course cannot be considered the Way."(*Zhongyong*, Ch.13)

Finally, *dao* and *de* are united in sages' hearts.

De, as we have argued, has been regarded as the inherent power or tendency of a given thing and in particular its natural effect on other people and things. According to *Shuowen Jiezi*, a classical Chinese dictionary, *de* is defined as "to obtain, externally it is obtained from others; internally, from oneself." The reason why it can be obtained from others is that the person of *de*—the person who has understood and practised the *dao* in his everyday life—thus will obtain support from the people. The reason why it can be obtained from oneself is because according to Confucianism, the *dao* is an objective existence, but the *dao* does not become real until it is found by men in themselves. So Confucius said, "it is man that can make the Way great, and it is not the Way that can make man great" (*Analects* 15:28).

Then how can a person make the Way great?

In order to make the Way great, man must first of all, have the capacity or ability to do so. The reason why men are able to find the Way in themselves is because, for many Confucians, the self is endowed with a transcendental "spirit," which if fully developed would enable one to be a co-ordinator of the world, a guardian of natural and social processes, and a partner in the creative transformation of Heaven and Earth. According to Mencius, every man has the presence of *dao* of Heaven in his *xin* 心 (heart/mind),[6] which always reveals correct guidance for action. Therefore if a man fully realized his heart/mind, he will understand his nature; and if he knows his nature, he will know Heaven. Meanwhile, the proper way to serve Heaven is for a man to retain his good heart/mind and nurture his nature.[7] In this way, Mencius talked about nature through heart/mind. Far from being a mere hypothesis, Heaven is thought to manifest itself in the functioning of the heart/mind. The heart/mind as the microcosm of

Heaven represents transcendence in the realm of immanence. So Mencius said, "All things are already complete in oneself. There is no greater joy than to examine oneself and be sincere (*cheng* 诚)."(*The Book of Mencius* 7A:4)

So the Confucians stressed the importance of sincerity (*cheng* 诚)[8] in self-examination. Since human nature is imparted by Heaven and thus originally good, then in order to find out whether we still preserve the good human nature is to look within ourselves and see if it is there. Through being sincere, being true to his own nature, one is able to gain an understanding of the Way of Heaven. As *Zhongyong* argues, "He who is sincere is one who hits upon what is right without effort and apprehends without thinking. He is naturally and easily in harmony with the Way. Such a man is a sage. He who tries to be sincere is one who chooses the good and holds fast to it."(*Zhongyong*, Ch. 20) That is, by being sincere, one obtains an understanding of *dao*. And when one obtains the understanding of the *dao*, one becomes a sage. So the claim was made that "the sage knows the Way of Heaven"(*Guodian Chumu Zhujian* 郭店楚墓竹简, strip 26). This is also the *de* of a sage, the power or the capacity to be in harmony with the Way naturally. So *dao* and *de* are unified in the heart of a sage. This means, human heart/mind in Confucian philosophy is an infinite heart/mind. It is through the infinite heart/mind that the subject can be in a position to be one with Heaven and Earth.

Based on this understanding of *dao* and *de*, we can see the dynamic relationship between *dao* and *de* as such: although the *dao* is an objective existence, it will not become real without being understood and realized by man. Since human nature is imparted and confirmed by Heaven and is an embodiment of the *dao*, to understand and to realize the *dao* is first of all to find *dao* in oneself by being sincere. A person who has found the *dao* in himself is a person of *de*, or a sage. And since a person of *de* is a person who has obtained the understanding of *dao*, the *dao* and *de* are unified in the heart of a sage. When the *dao* and *de* are united in a sage's heart/mind, what his heart/mind desires is just what the *dao* requires. To follow the *dao* is to do both what one desires and what is virtuously required. This is a state which Confucius reached when he was 70 years old: "At 70 I could follow my heart's desire without transgressing the principle." (*Analects*, 2:4) As a consequence, the subjective virtue and objective *dao* becomes one and the same and happiness belongs to the domain of *dao*. In this perfect state, virtue and happiness coincide: virtue is happiness and happiness is virtue.

Confirming that human heart/mind is an infinite heart and thus has the capacity to understand the Way of Heaven is a special characteristic of Confucian moral philosophy. Because they have the infinite heart/mind, humans can obtain the state of *tianrenheyi* (天人合一): the harmonious oneness of Heaven and humanity, in which the objective Way of Universe (*dao*) and subjective personal virtue (*de*) cannot be separated—this is what *daode*, or morality, means in Confucianism. So in Confucian moral philosophy, subjective *de* (virtue) has never been separated from objective *dao*—the Way of Universe and the Principle of Heaven and Earth. The *dao* and *de* are united in a sage's heart/mind. This is the metaphysical basis of the unity of rule and virtue in Confucian ethics.

THE UNITY OF RULE AND VIRTUE IN CONFUCIAN ETHICS

The unity of *dao* and *de* in the sages' heart is the metaphysical basis on which the Confucian rule and virtue—*li* and *ren* are united. In Confucian ethics, both *ren* and *li* are the products of the sages' hearts, that is, both of them are derivative from *dao* (or *de*).

Li is a concept pregnant with ethico-religious connotations. The earliest available dictionary meaning of *li* is "treading" or "following." The understanding of the character was later extended and developed, and consequently the character became a complex term covering a range of rules of individual and social conduct of the nobility who were beyond the reach of *fa*, or law.[9] Later, when the feudal system broke down, the scope of *li* was first expanded to cover the life of common people and then almost the totality of social life, including rules of propriety and the authentic traditions and conventions of society.[10]

The meaning of *li* in Confucian ethics extends from ritual to propriety, from civil laws to codified customs, and from moral rules for behavior to ethical senses for thinking, feeling and acting. In its ethical dimension, *li* "is the principle by which the ancient kings embodied the laws of Heaven and regulated the expressions of human nature. Therefore, he who has attained *li* [ritual] lives, and he who has lost it, dies." (Lin 1994: 229–30) This implies that *li* as moral principles were productions of ancient sages. As we have argued, sages are those who have obtained the *dao* so they are capable of making moral principles for the common people to follow.

As a production of ancient sage-kings, *li* is emphasized by the Confucians. As a result, in the past 2,000 years *li* has executed its functions as moral rules in Chinese society.

Li, then, was an important element in Confucian ethics. As a matter of fact, it is so important that the Confucian positive attitude toward *li* is one of the main differences between Confucianism and other main schools at the time. But the Confucian emphasis on *li* did not lead Confucian ethics to a rule ethics because the Confucians have a different understanding of moral rules from that of Western rule-based moral theories. The emphasis on *li* in Confucian ethics was based on *ren*—it was the introduction of the concept of *ren* that gave life to *li*.

Ren is a prominent word in Confucian Classics. More than 10 per cent of the *Analects* is devoted to the discussion of *ren*. What is more important, Confucius looked at *ren* in a new light. According to Wing-tsit Chan, it is true that in a number of cases Confucius still treated *ren* as a particular virtue. For example, in *Analects* 4:2; 6:12; 9:28; 14:5; 17:8, *ren* is in contrast to other qualities such as wisdom, truthfulness, courage, tolerance, keenness, reverence and generosity, etc., and is usually translated as "benevolence." It includes all the above moral qualities and others as well, and determines their goodness. This shows the "inclusive" character of *ren*. If one achieves *ren*, one at the same time masters other virtues. Thus in its more important uses, *ren* is the general virtue which is basic, universal, and the source of all other specific virtues and connotes the general meaning of moral life at its best. With the general virtue established, Chinese ethics entered upon a higher stage, for virtue as a whole can now be understood and particular virtues can now have a foundation (Chan, 1955: 297–8).

Wing-tsit Chan's distinction between *ren* in its general meaning as moral excellence and *ren* as a particular virtue is insightful. It is almost common knowledge now to regard Confucian *ren* as the virtue of virtues.

Since *ren* is the general virtue and *li* functions as moral rule, the relationship between virtue and rule in Confucian ethics can be concretized as and understood through the relationship between *ren* and *li*.

During the Spring and Autumn period, the *li* were increasingly seen as superficial and ineffective. Nevertheless, for the Confucians, the rules of propriety are indispensable. But the Confucian emphasis on the importance of the *li* does not lead to a kind of formalism. Confucians have realized that a system of perfectly designed moral rules cannot be enforced by people without any virtue. The conventional ethical life must be based on the new foundation of an inner morality. Thus, by introducing the new concept *ren*, the Confucians give *li* a new life. *Ren* becomes the essence and inner strength of *li*.

In the *Analects*, two remarks characterizing *ren* have been thought to be fundamental: "to love men" and "to return to *li* (propriety)" (12:22 and 12:1).

Ren as love and *ren* as return to *li* seem two different aspects of *ren*: one refers to inner feeling—the feeling of love of men, the other refers to its outer expressions—sticking to ritual rules. It seems that the emphasis on the former—seeking human-heartedness within—leads Confucian ethics to an ethics of virtue, whereas the emphasis on the latter—the ritual rules—leads Confucian ethics to an ethics of rule. What, then, is the relation between *ren* as love and *ren* as returning to *li*? In Confucian ethics, returning to *li* is a process of showing and cultivating the feeling of love to those in certain social relations. Because of its distinctive understanding of *li*, Confucian ethics harmonizes virtue and rule in one ethical theory—like two sides of the same coin.

According to the Confucians, *ren* is the essence and content of *li*. Practicing *li* requires more than just the application of established rules or performance of rites. In performing the *li*, what must be emphasized is that one has to perform *li* with the correct attitude. For example, when performing a sacrifice, one has to feel reverence for the spirits; when carrying out the rites of mourning, one has to feel grief for the deceased. So when his disciple Lin Fang asked about the foundation of ceremonies (*li*). Confucius said, "An important question indeed. In rituals or ceremonies, be thrifty rather than extravagant, and in funerals, be deeply sorrowful rather than shallow in sentiment."(*Analects*, 3:4) Without this emotional component, ritual becomes a hollow performance (ibid., 3:3). This means that performing *li* must be based on *ren*. Acting in conformity with the rules of proper conduct requires an inner dimension for its foundation. Otherwise, ritual will only be the mechanism of regulating people's behavior. In this respect, Confucianism contrasts with Legalism which advocated bringing the masses into line by a severe system of penal law. One of the most important differences of the rules of propriety from the rules of law is its emphasizing *ren* as the essence (substance) and inner spirit of *li*. What is important is to perform *li* with *ren* feelings.

Although Confucius is against *li* without *ren*, he values *li* in the real sense because *li* is the concrete manifestation of *ren* and performing *li* helps one to embody *ren*, to find and cultivate *ren* virtue in oneself. Confucius does not advocate acting according to ritual rules without *ren* feelings, thus making *li* a hollow performance, but he values *li* and performs *li* seriously. This is because *ren* needs *li* to express itself. As Tu Wei-ming argues, *li* can be conceived as an externalization of *ren* in a specific social context. No matter how abstract it appears, *ren* almost by definition requires concrete manifestation. To use the remark made by Mou Zongsan, *ren* needs "windows" to expose itself to the outside world, otherwise it will become suffocated (Tu 1968: 29–39). As Xunzi clearly argued, *li* is the road to *ren* and righteousness (*yi*) (in Watson 1963: 21). The ritual rules "present us with models, but no explanations."(ibid.: 20) From this we can see that *li* is concrete expression and manifestation of *ren*. *Ren*-feeling is expressed and fulfilled in actions in accordance with *li*.

Moreover, since in Confucian ethics, performing *li* is not a process of following ritual rules mechanically, but a process that shows and embodies one's feelings, will and emotions, consciously performing *li* leads one to find and nourish *ren* feeling in oneself and thus has a specific function in the cultivation of personal character. It is remarked in the *Analects* that when Confucius offered sacrifice to his ancestors, he felt as if his ancestral spirits were actually present. When he offered sacrifice to other spiritual beings, he felt as if they were actually present (3:12). What Confucius values in ancestor worship is not any formal accordance with ritual rules but the unifying effects it has on the living to cultivate or find the feeling of love and reverence, or in short, *ren*-feeling in oneself. The principles of *li* or rituals are there to express and strengthen this natural human inclination. This is why Confucius on the one hand, warned his disciple Zizhang that *li* did not consist in playing about with sacrificial vessels, just as music did not consist in the mere beating of bells and drums; on the other hand, he thought that that both ritual and music emanated from, and created, a state of mind, a state of respect in the performance of ritual and a state of happiness and harmony in the performance of music (in Lin 1994: 206–7). Therefore, *li* operates not only upon the outward action of man, but also upon human nature, human feelings, and the operation of the human heart. So performing *li* properly has a specific function in the cultivation of character.

So one of the meanings of "To master oneself and return to *li* is *ren*" is that performing *li* is one of the most important means to find or sense the *ren* feeling in oneself. It is possible that one can follow formal prescriptions without any idea of their underlying import, and this is well acknowledged by the Confucian writers. For example, in the chapter on broader sacrifices, the writer of *Liji* states that "what is esteemed in the *li*-performance is its [underlying] significance. When this is missed, the number of things and observances may [still] be exhibited."(in Legge 1968: 439). But it seems that the Confucians also realised that even without an understanding of the underlying import of these rules of propriety, by continuing to perform actions according to rules of propriety that sages have set for us with feeling of love and reverence, we will strengthen our will to act in accordance with the ritual rules. The important point is that if we keep acting this way, it is natural for us to gradually understand the underlying import of *li* and to guide or restrain our feelings and desires in accordance with it. It is important, therefore, to conduct ourselves according to *li* even when *li* appears to be external to us, for it is in this very process that we will gradually start to understand it. As soon as we get the understanding, *li* will no longer appear to be external to us, and we can act according to *li* spontaneously without even noticing it. In the light of the intrinsic connection between *li* and moral virtues, Cua is correct to argue that *li* has a specific function in the cultivation of personal character. In a fundamental way the cultivation consists in the direction or guidance of personal wills, and this in turn involves a discipline of our basic motivational structure of feelings and desires (Cua 1983: 7). So acting in accordance with propriety is one of the most important means to cultivate and obtain the virtue of *ren*. This is one of the meanings of "To master oneself and return to propriety is humanity."

Furthermore, acting according to *li* is not only an instrumental tool to cultivate *ren* feeling, but is itself also an integral part of general virtue *ren*. According to Confucius, performing actions according to *li* is not only one of the most important means to cultivate the virtue of *ren*, but itself also a part of *ren* virtue. In one sense, the observance of *li* is the criterion for the possession of *ren*. For example, according to Confucius, *ren* as love is based on the feeling one has toward one's own parents and brothers. "Filial piety and brotherly love are the roots of *ren*" (1:2). So accordingly, the return to funeral and mourning rituals after a parent dies are fundamental ways for an individual to show gratitude and affection toward the parent. So by one's attitude to the mourning ritual, we can tell whether he is a person of *ren* or not. As the *Analects* (17:21) recorded that Confucius marked Zai Yu as a man who lacked *ren* because he intended to change the three year's mourning, which was one of the most important *li* for parents. This means, for Confucius, the attitude toward performing *li* shows whether one has *ren* virtue. The observance of the *li* practices of his time can be a criterion for distinguishing between possessing or lacking *ren*. So performing in accordance with *li* is an integral part of *ren*. This can be seen as the other meaning of "To master oneself and return to *li* is humanity (*ren*)." An enlightened man follows the rules of propriety because of his intrinsic demands, not because of a desire to copy the behavioral patterns sanctioned by social conventions. Once the intrinsic value of life is realized, one would naturally feel a deep sense of piety toward the sources of life, that is, ancestors, the givers of the life of the family and the self, and Heaven, the ultimate metaphysical principle that give rise to all things in the universe (see *Analects* 9: 16). Sacrificial rites provide an occasion for man to express this deep-seated feeling within himself as well as an occasion to educate the masses. It was in this way that Confucius instilled new life into the practice of traditional ritual ceremonies and thus performing according to *li* becomes an integral part of *ren*.

From the relation between *ren* and *li*, we can see that the content of "*ren* as love" and "*ren* as to master oneself and to return to *li*" is one and the same thing. By emphasizing the emotional elements in performing *li* and taking *ren* as the essence of *li* on the one hand, and emphasizing *li* as the concrete manifested form of *ren* and taking *li* as one of the most important means of obtaining *ren* feelings and also an integral part of general virtue of *ren* on the other hand, Confucian ethics emphasizes both the importance of *li* to *ren* and of *ren* to *li* without assuming the primacy of either concept. The mutually dependent relation between *ren* and *li* neither leads Confucian ethics to virtue ethics nor to rule ethics, but to the unity of virtue and rule in the same ethical theory. As a result, the conflict between virtue ethics and rule ethics in Western ethics never becomes real in Confucian ethics. For them, it is unimaginable that moral act and character cultivation can be understood separately. Or at least, they would agree with those Western moral philosophers who see the ethics of virtue and the ethics of rule as adding up, rather than as cancelling each other out (Louden 1997: 191).

CONFUCIAN ETHICS, RULE ETHICS AND VIRTUE ETHICS

As we have mentioned previously, the contrast between rule ethics and virtue ethics lies in their different views on the position of virtue in ethics. While virtue ethics argues that there are no judgements of acts which are independent of virtue and right action is defined in terms of virtue, rule ethics insists that the virtues are sentiments or desires to act from corresponding moral principles. Due to its distinctive understanding of *li* and its relation with *ren*, it seems that Confucian ethics leads to neither rule ethics nor virtue ethics, but the unity of the two in one and the same ethical theory.

Confucian ethics is not a rule ethics which is commonly criticized in contemporary Western philosophy. In rule ethics, moral rules or principles are taken as impersonal and universal, which should be applied to anyone on relevant occasions. For example, in Kant's moral philosophy, the moral law, since it binds unconditionally, irrespective of the individual's wishes and inclinations, takes the form of a categorical imperative. The test of acceptability for a moral maxim—i.e., a subjective principle governing behavior—is thus placed in its universalisability. The test is whether one could consistently will that everyone should always act on it (or could will, in a different formulation, that it be a universal law of nature) (Crittenden 1990: 176–7).

The difference between Confucian ethics and rule ethics, or particularly, Kant's moral philosophy, does not exist in the universality of the moral law, but in the way that the universal moral law applies to the moral practices. *Dao* in Confucianism is the universal way of Heaven and earth, as well as of human beings'. It is a constant way (*changdao*, 道德) which will not change with the passage of time or the change of subject. It is a *dao* with the characteristics of universality and objectivity. Only when we obtain and act on *dao*, does it become also subjective, but it continues to be objective whether we act on it or not. But the *dao*, as a universal principle, is not the same as the moral rules which can be formulated as "Don't lie," "Keep your promises" and so on. Confucius chooses *ren* as a substitute of *dao*. Even so, he never attempted to give a formal definition of *ren*. Some of his disciples asked him about *ren*, but his answers were different in accordance with the different characters of the disciples and the changing concrete situations. It is *ren* to do one thing in one situation, but another thing in a different situation. So there is no way to give a formal definition of *ren*, because there is no definition which can include every situation in our social practices without any mistakes due to the complication and variety of daily life.

It seems that for the Confucians there is no way to obtain the understanding of *dao* through conceptual reasoning, but through a course of the cultivation of *de* in daily life. The Confucians insist that we can obtain the understanding of *dao* by the cultivation of *de*, or by moral intuition. The reason for the cultivation of *de* is not that we should act in accordance with moral rules rigidly and regardless of the concrete situations. On the contrary, we cultivate *de* to obtain *dao* so that we would know whether we should act in accordance with the moral rules in specific concrete situations or not and why, or why not.

Confucian ethics is not an ethics of moral rules or principles in the sense in which this is usually understood and it does not take the Kantian view that moral rules should be applied universally and impersonally to anybody in relevant situations. Kant's moral philosophy arises out of pure reason. The free moral subject is placed in the *noumenal* world, beyond space and time, while moral education and moral practice take place mostly in the phenomenal world. In an unexplained way, the *noumenal* order gives rise to the phenomenal order and is expressed in it while remaining untouched and untouchable. There is no transition from the phenomenal to the *noumenal*, the emphasis is put on the formal universality of moral rules and the process of moral formation must appear ineffectual. By contrast, the Confucians focus on the moral practice of this world, and the emphasis is put on the universality of the inner spirit of moral rules, that is, *ren*, which can be obtained by everyone who has fully developed his nature. It is through moral cultivation and moral practice of this world that one can obtain the understanding of *dao*, which belongs to the *noumenal* world. Moreover, instead of taking moral virtues as no more than an acquired habit or disposition to act in accordance with moral rules, the Confucians thought we require *de* (virtue) to vouchsafe correct performance of a *dao*, which includes not only acting in accordance with *li*, but also violating certain ritual rules necessarily under certain circumstances. Confucius is respected by Mencius as the "timely sage"(*sheng zhi shi zhe*, 圣之时者) (*The Book of Mencius* 5B: 39), which means that he acted according to the circumstance of the time. He is timely both in what he contributes to the situation and what he appropriates from his context. Confucius also comments himself that he has no absolute *yes* or absolute *no* (*wu ke wu bu ke*, 无可无不可), which means he does not consider himself absolutely attached to a rigid principle for action. He recognizes the variety of actual life situations and recognizes furthermore that good must intrinsically grow out of a concrete situation. Thus he says, "As to how the superior man behaves with regard to others and in view of a situation, he has no particular preference, nor particular prohibition, but only has *yi* as its standard of evaluation."(*Analects* 4:10) This is why the Confucians put an emphasis on the virtue of *yi*, which means what is appropriate (appropriate to *li*, appropriate to the situation-at-hand), and take it as an essential requirement of performing *li*.

However, it is also not possible to interpret Confucian ethics as an ethics of virtue in its usual sense. As we have argued, there are different views on virtues, their functions and position within ethical theory. According to the replacement view of virtue ethics, the deontic notions such as the rightness, wrongness, obligatoriness, etc., of acts are either incoherent or pernicious, and should be ignored entirely by ethical theory. The reductionist view of virtue ethics holds that we can and should use deontic concepts such as rightness and obligations, as long as we remember that they are derivative from aretaic concepts.

Neither of the above theories of virtue ethics can explain very well the difference between the evaluation of moral character and the evaluation of moral action, especially how to evaluate a person's accidental action. For example, a cruel person who murders for money may save a child from a fire. It is hard to say that the murderer is a benevolent person for his accidental action, and it is equally hard to say that this action is not benevolent because it was performed by a cruel murderer. The question may be handled by distinguishing evaluating an action from evaluating an agent. The possibility of deriving act evaluation from some prior evaluation of character has been doubted by many philosophers. For example, Robert B. Louden argues that, according to virtue ethics, being a virtuous person is a sufficient (as well as a necessary) condition for doing the right thing. But this ignores, or rather denies, the possibility of moral tragedy, that is, of situations in which people of excellent character nevertheless do the wrong thing in some situation. Virtue ethics forces us to say that, insofar as the hero has an excellent and stable character, his or her actions cannot be wrong. The reason we find the position of virtue ethics unreasonable is our belief that some actions are not only bad, but intolerable and absolutely forbidden, irrespective of the motive or character of their doers. This belief goes back to Aristotle, who argues that some actions, such as adultery, theft, and murder "are themselves bad," and "simply to do any of them is to do wrong" (see Louden 1997: 180–93). That rightness is independent of persons and that some duties are created irrespective of facts about character is obvious. Such duties bind all moral agents irrespective of their motives or personality.

Confucian ethics is neither a replacement nor a reductionist view of virtue ethics because it puts an emphasis on the importance of *li* in moral practice. As we have argued, firstly, Confucianism takes *li* as one of the most important standards to judge the rightness of a moral action. Secondly, it insists neither that *li* is derivative from *ren* nor that *ren* is derivative from *li*. Both *ren* and *li* are derivative from a common source—*dao* (or *de* of a sage). In this sense, Confucian ethics is not even a moderate version of virtue ethics. According to such moderate versions, ethical theory has (at least) two parts which are irreducible to each other, one dealing with the morality of acts, the other dealing with the morality of character (Statman 1997: 8). But instead of regarding the account of the virtues as the supplement to the account of the right actions, moderate versions argue that although some actions can be evaluated independently of questions of virtue, most of morality is connected with character. This sounds very similar to Confucian ethics. But the point is, instead of taking the account of virtue and the account of rules as two parts irreducible to each other, Confucian ethics holds that the two parts are interdependent, co-related, and derivative from the same source—*dao*. Due to its emphasis on the mutual dependency and close relationship between *ren* and *li*, it is not difficult to see that the Confucians take the ethics of virtue and the ethics of rule as adding up, rather than as canceling each other out.

Confucian ethics is neither a virtue ethics, in which moral rules are derivative from virtues, nor is it a rule ethics, in which virtues are derivative from moral rules. Instead, Confucian ethics implies a moral theory with a pyramidal structure, in which *ren* and *li* are derivative from one and the same source—the universal *dao* of Heaven. Thus the *dao* of Heaven is the common source for both virtues and rules. Confucian ethics, as a complete ethical theory, is the totality of both in its account of virtues and its account of rules. The account of virtues and the account of rules, as parts of the totality, are related to each other. The relation of the account of virtues and the account of rules in Confucian ethics is one of support and recognition, not one of destroying or dominating. Both the account of virtues and the account of rules contribute to the formation of Confucian ethics in the sense of wholeness.

CONCLUSION

In conclusion, the view that Confucian *dao* is an ideal way of life and *de* an achieved condition of an ethically well-cultivated person, with commendable character traits in accord with the ideal of *dao* and thus functionally equivalent to ethical virtue, has dangerously narrowed the meaning of the *dao* and *de* in Confucianism. Regarding Confucian ethics as a virtue ethics, however, is not enough and cannot bring a complete understanding of the whole project of Confucian ethics. As a result, the dynamic relationship between *dao* and *de* has been ignored and Confucian ethics has been regarded as a virtue ethics.

Although Confucian ethics is rich in its account of virtue and virtues, it is not a virtue ethics. Nor is it a rule ethics. The central debate between virtue ethics and rule ethics focuses on the question whether virtue is a disposition to do what is right or whether rule is defined in terms of virtue. While virtue ethics insists that rule is derivative from virtue, rule ethics argues that virtue is derivative from rule. But there is no such distinction or dichotomy between rule and virtue in Confucian ethics. On the contrary, as a living ethical tradition which has lasted for more than 2,000 years, the theory and moral practice of Confucian ethics provides us with a pattern according to which rule and virtue are integrated in one and the same ethical theory.

The unity of *dao* and *de*, *ren* and *li* in Confucian ethics has a lot to offer to the debate between virtue ethics and rule ethics. In this debate, moral philosophers who are used to thinking through traditional rule ethics are anxious to protect rule ethics against the attacks of virtue ethicists. Virtue ethicists are devoted to establishing a systematic virtue ethics which is complete in itself and can act as an alternative to rule ethics. The possibility of the unity of rule and virtue in one and the same ethical theory has been largely neglected by contemporary moral philosophers. The theory and the moral practice of the unity of *ren* and *li* in Confucian ethics may encourage contemporary Western moral philosophers to pay more attention to this third possibility—a possibility which is necessary for them to explore if they are to construct a highly developed moral theory for the contemporary era.

The Confucian understanding of the relationships between *dao* and *de*, *li* and *ren* suggests that a complete ethical theory should include two parts, or two aspects, which are derivative from one and the same common source. The basis of the mutual dependency of rule and virtue is not only a theoretical product of Confucian ethics, but is also the requirement and the reflection of the relationships between moral action and moral character in moral life. Even without reference to the *dao* of Heaven as the common source of virtues and rules in Confucian ethics, it is not difficult for us to know from the history of moral development that human moral practice is one and the same common source of both moral rules and virtues. Or in other words, the development and the formation of morality or ethics always includes two aspects, that is, the externalized aspect and the internalized aspect. This means, on the one hand, in the course of human development and civilization, human beings have summarized and conceptualized certain concepts of moral value in terms of social culture, and have universalized them in the form of moral principles, moral rules and corresponding systems of moral values. This is embodied in the formation of normative ethics and in the establishment of certain moral principles. On the other hand, in the same course of human development and civilization, human beings (as individuals) have individualized, particularized and internalized the moral principles, moral rules and the corresponding systems of moral values through the continuous self-consciousness of human nature and through self-identification with moral values. This is embodied in the construction of some kind of virtue ethics or the cultivation of a certain moral character.

The internal or internalized and the outer or externalized aspects of morality are two aspects, which can both be derivative from human moral practice. They are mutually dependent like the two wings of a bird, or the two wheels of a carriage; one without the other makes morality incomplete. In other words, the two aspects together constitute the wholeness of morality. If the internalized aspect is absent, morality will become impersonal, agent-irrelevant dogma, or even degenerate into legalistic norms or theological doctrines. If the externalized aspect is absent, morality will be deprived of its universal rationality. A complete, highly developed ethics, then, must be a unity of virtue and rule in one ethical theory.

What we learn from Confucian ethics is, as the Chinese character for morality *daode* suggests, that morality is the unity of two aspects, *dao* and *de*— the externalized aspect and the internalized aspect, or the objective aspect and the subjective aspect. So a complete, highly developed ethics must be a unity of virtue and rule in one and the same ethical theory. Virtue ethics, as well as rule ethics, has grasped only one aspect of the whole complete ethical theory and the unity of the two is both necessary and desirable.

NOTES

1 Confucianism is not a virtue ethics of either version. The way to argue that Confucian ethics is not a moderate virtue ethics would be quite different from the argument that is required to argue that it is not a radical virtue ethics. So in this paper, I will mainly be referring to the radical version of virtue ethics, but I will also mention the moderate version when necessary.

2 For example, see Cua 1998; Nivison 1996: 2; Bretzke, 1995; and Wilson, 1995.

3 *Shuowen Jiezi Zhu* 说文解字注, 1981: I.

4 "Heaven produced the virtue that is on me, what can Huan T'ui do to me?" (*Analects*, 7:22); When Confucius was in personal danger in K'uang, he said, "Since the death of King Wen, is not the course of culture (*wen*) in my keeping? If it had been the will of Heaven to destroy this culture, it would not have been given to a mortal [like me]. But if it is not the will of Heaven that this culture should not perish, what can the people of K'uang do to me?"(*Analects*, 9:5)

5 Confucius never discussed strange phenomena, physical exploits, disorder, or spiritual beings (*Analects*, 7:20). Confucius was very ill. Tzu-lu asked that prayer be offered. Confucius said, "Is there such a thing?" Tzu-lu replied, "There is. A Eulogy says, 'Pray to the spiritual beings above and below.'" Confucius said, "I have been praying for a long time."(*Analects*, 7: 34)

6 The term heart is the translation of the Chinese term *xin* 心, which may also be translated as mind. Sometimes it has been put as heart/mind. In the Chinese tradition the mind and the heart have never been sharply distinguished from each other. Hence the conflict between cognitivism and emotivism has never become a serious issue for the Confucian philosophers.

7 *The Book of Mencius*, 7A: 1. "He who exerts his mind to the utmost knows his nature. He who knows this nature knows Heaven. To preserve one's mind and to nourish one's nature is the way to serve Heaven."

8 The term *cheng* 诚 is often translated as sincerity. According to Tu Wei-ming, the complexities of this key concept, however, may be better appreciated by also translating as "genuineness," "truthfulness," and "reality" as well as the common notion "sincerity" (See Tu 1989: 16).

9 Hence it is said in the *Liji* [Book of Rites]: "*Li* does not go down to the common people, *xing* (punishment) does not reach up to the high officials." *(Liji, Chu Li)*

10 In the *Analects*, *li* prescribes not only what relations between ruler and subject should be (3:18, 3:19) and what one ought to do in supporting one's parents, in holding a funeral, and in paying for a sacrifice (2:5), but also what kind of ceremonial cap one should wear, and even when one should prostrate oneself before ascending steps to see a king (9:3).

CHAPTER 11

The Self and Its Virtues: Is There a Chinese-Western Contrast?

A. T. NUYEN

It is often observed that Chinese philosophy, particularly Confucianism, emphasizes social virtues, or those character traits that enable a person to live well as a member of a larger community. Examples include filial piety, loyalty and social propriety (*li*). As Cheng Chung-ying has observed, in Confucianism, "virtues serve the interests of the social order and community harmony (i.e., the common good) ..."[1] Personal virtues, so goes the common observation, are subordinated to the social ones: they are to be cultivated only because they contribute to a person's thriving in the social context. For instance, one is not to cultivate wisdom (*zhi*) in isolation, but as a means to excel as a member of the community: an isolated sage is an oxymoron. In contrast, it is often said that the West stresses personal virtues as much as, if not more than, the social ones, and takes them to be independent of the latter. Indeed, for Aristotle, the virtue of private contemplation is the most prized. Social virtues are fine as long as they do not compromise personal ones, particularly personal integrity, and better if they contribute to the moral standing of the agent as an independent person. How do we account for this observation of a Chinese-Western contrast? Is it accurate? I will argue in this paper that the observed Chinese-Western contrast in conceptions of virtues grows directly out of a more frequently observed and more established Chinese-Western contrast in conceptions of the self. I will argue further that the latter contrast on the one hand runs the risk of misrepresenting the position of Chinese philosophy, and on the other, certainly misrepresents the position of Western philosophy. We have to rethink the idea that there is a Chinese-Western contrast in conceptions of the self, and if I am right about this, then we will have to rethink also the idea that there is a Chinese-Western contrast in conceptions of virtues.

I. THE SELF AND ITS VIRTUES

What is distinctive about virtue ethics is its insistence on a shift of focus away from actions onto agents. With virtue ethics, the moral spotlight is now on the agent, on his or her character as revealed through his or her deliberations and actions. What motivates the agent's deliberations and the manner in which the agent translates the outcomes of those deliberations into actions are important, not so much the rules and principles that guide the process, if there are any. The notions of virtues and vices are meant to capture the moral significance of the agent's deliberations and actions, and through them the agent's character. This does not mean that notions of virtues and vices are constructed and applied subsequently to deliberations and actions, and do not determine the latter. In many cases, how a person deliberates and acts depends on how he or she understands virtues and vices. For instance, I may decide that I shall act in a certain way because I take it that acting in that way is to be generous and because I take generosity to be a virtue, or instead of the latter, because I want others to see me as generous. Likewise, I may decide that I shall not act in a certain way because I take it that acting in that way is to be vengeful and because I take vengeance to be a vice, or instead of the latter, because I do not want others to see me as vengeful. Only if this were so can virtue ethics be a normative theory, stipulating and explicating the virtues and vices in such a way as to be action-guiding. Thus, conceptions of virtues and vices can feature in the agent's deliberations and actions.

However, ultimately, how an agent deliberates and acts depends on the agent's psychological dispositions as well as on the way the agent understands his or her preferences and priorities, and his or her relationships with others and with the environment, that is, on the agent's psychological and epistemic make-up, or what we generally call the "self." It follows that how a person judges the virtues and vices of others, or the virtues and vices that are action-guiding for him or her, depends on the character of the agent's own self. A self with a certain character, or a certain way of understanding itself, may lead the agent to, for instance, agreeing with David Hume that humility is a "monkish" virtue, which in turn leads to a refusal to act "monkishly." It takes a certain kind of person to see that, again for instance, loyalty to the family is more important than civic responsibility, and to deliberate and act accordingly. It is a common complaint by law enforcement agencies that people from certain ethnic groups, such as those from rural areas of Europe, tend to place loyalty to the family and to the clan above their responsibility to co-operate with the authorities. According to Carol Gilligan, women see themselves differently from the way men see themselves, and as a result, they tend to see certain virtues, those under the general heading of care, as more important than other virtues, those under the heading of justice.[2]

From both the normative and the evaluative perspectives, the bearer of virtues and vices is the agent's self. For this reason, virtue ethics typically has something to say about the self, or at least assumes a certain conception of the self. For instance, a Macintyre-inspired virtue theory would assume that the agent has a multi-layered self, engaged in many different "practices." A Confucian virtue theory would build on a Confucian conception of the self. Indeed, the latter is endorsed by Cheng Chung-ying, who has this to say about Confucianism:

> ... we must recognize that virtues are the products of efforts issuing out of the internal abilities and propensities of a person in response to external stimuli, especially the needs and feelings of other people in the community. In Confucianism this presupposed a theory of human nature, which it went on further to articulate. Virtues in this sense have always been community-oriented and community-based.[3]

If I am right, then it is the conception of the self that determines, or at least forms the basis for, the conception of the virtues, and differences about the latter can be attributed to differences about the former. In the passage above, Cheng Chung-ying effective argues that it is the Confucian understanding of the self, which is embedded in its theory of human nature, that produces the Confucian conception of virtues. Add to this the premise that Confucianism understands the self as a being embedded in a community, we get the conclusion that, in Confucianism, virtues are "community-oriented and community-based." By contrast, a conception of the self that understands the self as an entity independent of its community will not understand virtues as "community-oriented and community-based."

I have argued that since the conception of the self determines the conception of virtues, different conceptions of the self lead to different conceptions of virtues. If this is so then we would expect that the contrast between the Chinese and Western conceptions of virtues to be backed by a similar contrast between the Chinese and Western conceptions of the self. As it turns out, those who believe in the former can take comfort in the fact that many commentators endorse the latter. Of course, a consistent observer believes in both contrasts. However, given the causal link between conceptions of the self and conceptions of virtues, we have reasons to question one contrast if we have reasons to question the other. In what follows, I will argue that we do have reasons to question the view that there is a contrast in the Chinese and Western conceptions of the self. On this view, the Chinese, or at least the Confucians, take the self to be a being embedded in the society, or in a network of social relationships. By contrast, again on this view, the West takes the self to be an independent being, standing over and against the society, who may, perhaps typically does, choose to form relationships with others in the society. I will show that this view is mistaken, not so much because of what it says about Confucianism, although there is certainly a risk of misrepresentation here, but largely because it misconstrues the position of the West. More specifically, this view mistakes one particular strand in Western thinking to be the position of the West, or at least representative of the West.

II. A CHINESE-WESTERN CONTRAST ON THE SELF

As mentioned above, we commonly find the contention that in Chinese philosophy in general, and in Confucianism in particular, the self is understood and constituted as an entity embedded in a network of social relationships. For instance, Julia Ching asserts that "the Chinese view of the human being tends to see the person in the context of a social network rather than as an individual."[4] The Chinese view of the self is supposed to stand in contrast with the Western view according to which the self is an individual person independent of others, who chooses to associate with others in various ways. This contrast can be examined in terms of what it says about the Confucian view and what it says about the Western position.

On the Chinese, or Confucian side, there are certainly views that support the notion of a Chinese-Western contrast. For instance, Donald J. Munro believes that there is no self as such in the Chinese understanding of a person. On his reading, the Confucian self is a "selfless person [who] is always willing to subordinate his own interests, or that of some small group (like a village) to which he belongs, to the interest of a larger group."[5] In what follows, I will simply take it that this rather extreme "selfless person" reading of the Confucian conception of the self is mistaken. Indeed, taken literally, Munro's view is incoherent: to be willing to subordinate one's own interests to the interest of a larger group, one must be aware of one's own interests, understand the interest of the larger group, and come to the conclusion that one's own interests must be subordinated to the group's interest, all of which requires a strong sense of the self, not a selfless view of one's self. Somewhat less extreme is Julia Ching's characterization mentioned above: "… the Chinese view of the human being tends to see the person in the context of a social network *rather than* as an individual" (emphasis added). Nevertheless, this characterization still implies that the Chinese do not see the self as an individual at all.

On views such as the above, the contrast between Confucianism and the West is clear enough, almost on any account of the Western position. However, there is enough textual evidence in the Confucian classics to show that Confucianism does see the self as an individual, or an entity, distinct from others in the society, albeit an individual constituted by social relationships. Closer to the mark is the suggestion made by David Hall and Roger Ames. Hall and Ames have employed the focus-field metaphor to characterize the Confucian conception of the self, according to which the "self is a focal in that it both constitutes and is constituted by the field in which it resides," the "field of social activity and relations."[6] In Ching's and Munro's characterizations of the Chinese view, the self's identity is lost in the social field; it lacks a focus. Another characterization that preserves self identity is Chenyang Li's. Li contends that in "the Confucian view, [the] self is not an independent agent who happens to be in certain social relationships."[7] Rather, the self "is constituted of, and situated in social relationships" (ibid.). I read Li's claim to imply that the Confucian view allows for a self with an individual identity even though it is an identity defined in terms of the social relationships.

Although Li, Hall and Ames have preserved self identity in their characterizations of the Confucian view of the self, they still believe that there is a sharp contrast between it and the Western view. Indeed, Li emphatically asserts that the Confucian view of the self is "very different from the traditional Western view …" (p. 95) We can clearly infer from this and the remark above that for Li, the "traditional Western view" takes the self to be "an independent agent who happens to be in certain social relationships." Li's argument for his claim is as follows. Given the Confucian conception of the self (as Li understands it), "self-knowledge can only be reflective [and] can only be gained through knowing people with whom we are in relationships" (pp. 94–5), and this is "very different" from the Western view according to which self-knowledge can be gained without reference to others. As proof, Li cites Chisholm's view that "an individual has 'direct knowledge of himself'" and Russell's contention that a "man may be said to be 'directly acquainted with himself'" (ibid.).

On the Eastern side of the contrast, we might strengthen Li's argument for his East-West contrast by examining the Confucian view of self-cultivation. Thus, as a relational self, the self cultivates itself by cultivating relational virtues. As Tu Wei-ming puts it, "(s)elf-cultivation can very well be understood as the broadening of the self to embody an ever-expanding circle of human relatedness."[8] For Shun Kwong-loi, the Confucian self-cultivation is the cultivation of humaneness and righteousness, the former stressing a "proper affective concern for other living things," and the latter the fulfillment of "obligations one has in virtue of the social positions one occupies, such as being a parent or an official, as well as following certain ceremonial rules of conduct governing the interaction between people in various social contexts."[9] On the Eastern side of the contrast, then, Li seems to be right. However, as we shall see, the problem with Li's East-West contrast lies on the Western side of the contrast, with the claim that the West sees the self as an entity independent of social relationships (and by implication, treats independent study and learning as primary, and regards the learning about "affective concern" for others and about social obligations as "added-on" "ethical" and "social" studies to round out one's education).

Roger Ames, too, sees an East-West contrast on the question of the self:

> It is frequently observed that the Confucian notion of personal realization is irreducibly social. A human being is a social product, defined not as some essential locus of potential or rights claims but in the pattern and roles of social discourse. This stands in contrast to the *liberal democratic* conception of "individual" most familiar to us in our present historical moment.[10]

Ames goes on to add that in the "liberal democratic" tradition, "what is most significant and defining of person is acultural and ahistorical ..." (ibid.) Together with David Hall in the work cited earlier, Ames asserts that in "tracing the complexities of the modern development of the self, one normally begins with Descartes' diremption of mind and body ..." (p. 11). It would appear, then, that Ames supports the view that, metaphysically, the liberal, or "liberal democratic," conception of the self is based on the Cartesian view of the self as a *res cogitans*, whose first and most certain knowledge is the knowledge of itself. Indeed, self-knowledge is thought to be incorrigible. This is consistent with the view of self-knowledge that Li attributes to Chisholm and Russell, as we have seen (which is not to imply that Chisholm and Russell are "liberal" thinkers). In the Cartesian view, the self consists in its own thoughts, not in its relationship with others, not even its relationship with the body in which it resides. The Cartesian self sets up a dualistic relationship with others and with the body, a relationship in which its own identity does not depend on the other term of the dualism. By contrast, Ames takes the Confucian self to be one that stands in a polar relationship with others and with the body. Borrowing the dualism-polarism distinction made by David Hall, Roger Ames claims that classical Chinese metaphysics is characterized by polarism, or the principle of symbiotic existence of polar opposites, "which require each other as a necessary condition for being what they are."[11] In the polar relationship, "each 'pole' can only be explained by reference to the other" (pp. 159–60), precisely because each pole is constitutive of the other. In the Chinese conception, the self-others relationship is a polar relationship and as such, "the 'other' particulars which make up existence are, in fact, constitutive of 'self'" (p. 159). In such relationship, "'self' requires 'other'" (p. 160). In terms of Ames' (and Hall's) focus-field metaphor above, presumably, the "focal self" stands in a polar relationship with the "fielded self" in as much as a focus stands in a polar relationship with a field ("since the field is always entertained from a particular perspective," or the focal point, and since a focal point is always a point in a field). Ames goes on to argue that the Confucian self stands in a polar relationship with the body, not a dualistic relationship as in the Cartesian view of the self. Hall and Ames point out that the Confucian body is a "lived body (*shen*)" (p. 34), which cannot be neglected in the understanding of the self, as it often is in the philosophy of liberalism.

It is clear, then that despite the fact that there are different characterizations of the Confucian view of the self, one thing remains constant, and that is the perception that there is an East-West divide on the self, a contrast between the Western view and the Confucian view. It is this perception that I want to question. In questioning whether there is really an East-West divide on the question of the self, I want to shift the focus away from the East toward the West. I do not want to challenge Li's, Hall's and Ames' characterizations of the Confucian conception of the self, which are now fairly widely accepted. Rather, I want to question their views of the other term of the supposed contrast. Thus, is what Li takes to be the "traditional Western view" of the self really "traditional"? Is the West really sold on the view that the self is an independent, self-sufficient individual who can know himself or herself completely, can cultivate himself or herself without reference to others, and chooses to stand in certain relationships with others? Is the Western self a self prior to the ends it chooses, as Michael Sandel has put it?[12] Likewise, just because the "liberal democratic" worldview is perhaps the dominant view currently, must we take it to be the "traditional view" that typifies the West? To be sure, it is not clear whether Ames would go as far as Li in saying that the "liberal democratic" conception of the self is the "traditional Western view," but given the current dominance of the "liberal democratic" worldview, it is easy enough to equate the two. Indeed, if we believe, as Francis Fukuyama does, that "if we looked beyond liberal democracy and markets, there was nothing else towards which we could expect to evolve," then it is hard not to take the "liberal democratic" conception of the self—of anything for that matter—as the "traditional Western view."[13]

Having identified a "liberal democratic" view of the self that contrasts with the Confucian self, Ames, in a later work (with David Hall) argues that there are in fact many different elements that shape the Western conception of the self. Indeed, Ames and Hall identify "four principal models" that have guided the construction of the self in the West: (1) the "physiological" model in which the self "is ... a physiological mechanism swirling in social space," a model shaped by the writings of Hobbes, Freud and the modern sociobiologists, (2) the Cartesian dualistic model in which the self is a "mind or consciousness detachable from its bodily housing," (3) the Aristotelian model of organic naturalism (reinforced by the pragmatism of Mead and Dewey) in which the self is "an organic, socially interactive, goal-achieving organism" and (4) the existentialist model in which the self is a "willing, deciding, potentially self-creating agent whose meaning is determined by persuasive agency."[14] From this rich brew, it is no wonder that many views can emerge. The liberal, or "liberal democratic," conception of the self emerges from a blend of (1) and (2) above. But elsewhere in the intellectual landscape of the West, where (3) and (4) above dominate, some other conception has grown. In what follows, I will put together a view of the self that has a rightful claim to being "Western," that is, not to be excluded by some other "traditional Western" view. It is a view based largely on the last of the above four models identified by Hall and Ames.

Against the "liberal democratic" view of the self, which, in Ames' words, takes what is "most significant and defining" of self to be "acultural and ahistorical," Heidegger takes the self, or the being that exists there in the world, *Dasein*, as fundamentally social and historical: The I is "situational"; it is "primordially historical."[15] Indeed, this conception of the self remains unchanged between the earlier Heidegger of *Being and Time* and the later Heidegger. Socially and historically constituted, the self understands itself through its understanding of its social relationships and of its history. There is no self before, or independent of, this understanding. The contrast, drawn by Li above, between the Confucian idea of self-understanding and what Li takes to be the Western idea can be seen here as well. Thus, the Heideggerian self also does not have "direct knowledge of himself," and also is not "directly acquainted with himself," contrary to what Russell and Chisholm have claimed. Indeed, Heidegger criticizes the Western presumption that the self is the most obvious and most easily understood We may add that given the claim that "the I is situational [and] historical," self-cultivation is not possible without cultivating one's social and historical relationships, and without cultivating a sense of sociality and historicality.

On the surface at least, the account of the self in *Being and Time* embeds the self in a social context in terms that are remarkably similar to the Confucian view. There, Heidegger argues that the self is only a self insofar as it is a being-in-the-world. This existential "category" encompasses many sub-categories, including being-with-others. As a being-in-the-world, the mode of existence for the self is *care* (*Sorge*). The world here is a social world, the one that we share with others.[16] It is the sharing that constitutes the world. Thus, it is not a world in which I just happen to find myself, nor one in which there happen to be others, with whom I have no choice but to share the world. If it were so, *care* would just be the result of an ethical decision; it would not be primordial as Heidegger claims.

In the world that we share, the self, or the one (*das Man*), constitutes the others, and conversely, in something like a polar relationship that Hall and Ames speak of in their reference to the Confucian self. It is not the case that "I am ... present-at-hand alone, and ... Others of my kind occur" (BT120). Rather, as Heidegger puts it in a 1924 lecture, "The Concept of Time," "Dasein, [the] entity that I am ... is simultaneously determined as being-with-one-another[;] it is not I myself who for the most part and on average am my Dasein, but the others."[17] I am who I am insofar as "I am with the others," and the others are who they are insofar as they are "likewise with ... others" (ibid.) Indeed, the social network that defines the self extends to the self's environment as well. The self understands everything in its environment in terms of social relationships, or "concerned dealings" as Heidegger puts it. Thus, a ladder is a ladder only in terms of the carpenter's relationship with it, a relationship in which it is a "ready-to-hand" to the carpenter, that is, something ready to be used as an instrument. All things possess "instrumentality," which is a social relationship. Something is not an instrument to me, a "present-at-hand" rather than a "ready-to-hand," nevertheless is understood as an instrument for someone with whom I have an actual or possible social relationship. In the essay "The Thing," Heidegger extends his account to the natural environment as well. Thus, the river is first and foremost understood as a source of water, which flows down from the mountain where I may obtain timber, and so on with all things in nature, which are "things" as opposed to being meaningless objects only because I have "concerned dealings" with them. These "concerned dealings" in turn signal and presuppose the self's relationships with others.

It would seem then, that, for Heidegger too, the self is seen in "the context of a social network," to use Julia Ching's words, or "constituted of and situated in social relationships," in Li's account. However, there appears to be an important dissimilarity between Heidegger's account and the Confucian view, and that is Heidegger's emphasis on the historicality of the self. Indeed, the social relationships that define the self are themselves historical. Even in *Being and Time*, where Heidegger is most concerned with sociality, he speaks of the "historicizing of the community, of a people" (BT384). Does the emphasis on the historical in Heidegger constitute another kind of East-West contrast? To see that we can answer this question in the negative, notice, first of all, that the idea of tradition has a crucial importance in Confucianism, and is captured in the Confucian notion of *li*, which refers to rites, rituals and propriety. In *li*, the Confucian sociality takes on a historical dimension. *Li* is the sediment of traditional wisdom. Great examples of *li* are all drawn from historical records. Indeed, we may borrow the words from Heidegger to characterize *li* as the "historicizing of the community, of a people." Secondly, it is worth pointing out that Heidegger does not subordinate sociality to historicality. Rather, he speaks of both as interchangeable. The social is not synchronic but diachronic; social relationships are not ahistorical but relationships formed through time and tradition. Conversely, history is not a collection of past events, but a lived history that exhibits itself in the very social world that the self discovers itself: "… what is historical is the entity that exists as Being-in-the-world."[18] This is why the historicality of the self cannot be uncovered by the science of history any more than sociality can be uncovered by the science of sociology.

From a different angle, Jean-Paul Sartre has come to a conclusion about the self similar to Heidegger's. For Sartre, the self is a for-itself (*pour-soi*), in contrast to an in-itself (*en-soi*). What distinguishes a for-itself from an in-itself is the fact that the former makes choices that are determined solely by its freedom. Instead of being a self prior to the ends it chooses, in Michael Sandel's characterization of the liberal self mentioned earlier, the Sartrean self *is* the totality of the ends chosen. Further, in choosing ends, the Sartrean self is conscious of others who also make choices for themselves. Indeed, the self-consciousness of the self is constituted by the consciousness of an other as a *for-itself*. Without this other, without being subject to *the look* (*le regard*) of the self-conscious other, there would not be self-consciousness, hence no self. Once again, self and others stand in a polar relationship. While the others are apt to generate the feeling of *angst* in the self, a feeling captured in Sartre's well known remark "Hell is the others," there would be no self without the others. Intentionally constituted, the self cannot know itself independently of others. Whatever it knows about itself is mediated by the others. There is no self-transparency. Thus, complete self-certainty and self-knowledge, the primary states of the self in the "liberal, democratic" tradition, which are made possible by the Cartesian assumption of self-transparency, are for Sartre impossible. To be sure, Sartre maintains that the self's choices are made in *angst* and are conditioned by absurdity. These characterizations of choices are very un-Confucian. However, in invoking Sartre, I am not suggesting that his account of the self makes sense only if we follow him all the way down the existentialist route. In particular, we need not follow his metaphysical path outlined in *Being and Nothingness*. The path that runs much closer to the Confucian account of the self is described in his *Critique of Dialectical Reason*.[19] A brief excursion along this path will be useful.

It is in *Critique of Dialectical Reason* that the social dimension of the self is clearly articulated. Here, the various layers of sociality are revealed, and the self is shown clearly as being constituted by and in turn constituting a complex social network. The society is not a group of individuals nor is it a collective whole over and above the individuals. An individual self, in turn, is not an isolated being. For this self to exist in the world is for it not only to encounter others at every turn, it is also to find itself engaged in complex relationships with them. Moreover, "[It is through] confronting others ... that I come to conceive myself; and in making myself ... I discover [others] as they make themselves" (CDR 101). The self does not apprehend itself as the master of its own situation, the author of events and the consequences that arise out of the actions that it has undertaken. It apprehends itself in terms of the work relationships, or the praxis, that it has with others in the society. This is so because the self apprehends itself in terms of its own needs and desires and then realizes that those needs and desires can only be satisfied through praxis, through a network of social relationships. ("Everything is to be explained through need (*besoin*); need is the first totalizing relation between the material being, man and the material ensemble of which he is part"—CDR 80.)

Even in its most passive mode of existence, the self still stands in a network of relationships with others, one that Sartre calls "seriality." In one of Sartre's well-known examples, the person standing in a queue waiting for a bus understands himself or herself as a *me* waiting for a bus only in the context of a seriality, that is, only insofar as there are others waiting in the same queue for the same bus. The seriality of the queue eliminates the isolation of the self: I am sixth in the queue not because of my qualities as an individual, but rather because of the serial relationships in which I find myself. But I also contribute to the seriality. Because of me, the person in front of me is fifth in the waiting queue, and the one behind seventh. I am who I am at that moment, and all others in the queue are who they are, by virtue of a "principle of unity and of determining everyone's fate as Other *by every Other as Other*" (CDR 261), not by virtue of anything I or they decide to do on my or their own. Seriality is "*a mode of being for individuals both in relation to one another and in relation to their common being* and this mode of being transforms all their structures" (CDR 266). Seriality affects the being of the self in a much more fundamental way than being in a queue and in similar situations. As Sartre points out, there are not just serial behaviors but also serial feelings and serial thoughts. How are we, for instance, to understand self-descriptions such as shy and reserved, or extrovert and exuberant, without being a person standing in the kind of serial sociality that Sartre speaks of?

In addition to the passive structure of seriality, the self also finds itself in structures in which its being is conditioned by, as well as contributes to, the social relationships. There is first of all the structure of a "fused group" which determines what I do and what everyone else does in terms of what we all do together as a group. There is no storming of the Bastille without the social relationships and interactions of a fused group. To be a revolutionary in the French revolution is to stand in a social relationship determined by a fused group, but there would be no French revolution without individual revolutionaries. Likewise, no individual can be a football player without a fused group, and there can be no football without individual players. Secondly, there is what Sartre calls an "organization." A group becomes an organization when members give a "pledge" to it. Through the pledge, an organization has a greater permanence than a fused group. The French resistance movement, as an organization, had a greater continuity than any fused group. A football team is more enduring than a spontaneously fused group playing a football game on a Sunday afternoon. Organization "refers to the internal action by which a group defines its structures and to the group itself as a structured activity in the practical field, either on worked matter or on other groups" (CDR 466). In an organization, what one is and does depends on what others are and do. This does not mean that the self in an organization has no freedom, or individuality. Indeed, there is enough freedom and individuality for each person to take destructive actions, leading to the downfall of an organization. Football clubs are not the only things that come and go; Confucius is fond of reminding us how empires can self-destruct because of individuals acting without propriety, going against the *li* that governs the being of the self in the society. For Sartre, an organization can also ossify into an "institution" in which relationships are determined by an authoritarian figure, who destroys reciprocities. The equivalent in Confucian writings is an empire ruled by a tyrant, who destroys the social relationships, the reciprocities, determined by *li*.

Heidegger and Sartre are just two in a long line of philosophers who reject the conception of the self that has been typically contrasted with the Confucian self. Most notable among those who came before them is Hegel. For Hegel, self-knowledge and self-certainty come only to the self at the end of its metaphysical journey, before which point the self constitutes itself dialectically through others and thus knows itself only through others. The Hegelian legacy can be seen in the writings of many thinkers after Heidegger and Sartre. For instance, Jacques Lacan argues that the self goes through the crucial stage that he calls the "mirror stage" during which the self constitutes itself through others, who act as mirrors in which the self can see its own reflection. What the self sees in the mirror that is the others is often opaque. Many German thinkers, such as Hans-Georg Gadamer, think of it as a hermeneutical process in which the self interprets itself through the clues provided by others. Any resulting interpretation is always provisional and uncertain, just as a self reflected in the mirror of the others, which can only be as clear as the mirror permits. To be sure, this self is not fragile, unstable and prone to disintegration as the postmodernists are apt to claim. At the same time, it is not the liberal-democratic self that has been contrasted with the Confucian self. There is thus a venerable tradition in Western thinking that rejects the idea of a Cartesian self that stands over and against others, seeing itself clearly through the mirror of its own mind and utterly certain of itself, a self that liberal democratic thinkers take ourselves to be. For thinkers in this tradition, there is no self that is first a self and then chooses to relate to others, no self that is prior to all its ends and to all social relationships; for them, no self is a self without first choosing its ends in a social context.

To strengthen the point that the conception of self discussed above receives sufficient support to make it a rival to the "liberal-democratic" conception, mention can be made of Wittgenstein, at least the Wittgenstein of the *Philosophical Investigations*. It is not unreasonable to interpret Wittgenstein as saying that the human self is essentially a language user. Adding to this claim Wittgenstein's account of language will yield a self that is socially constituted through language. For Wittgenstein, the meaning of language lies in its use, and the context of language use is social. This is the effect of Wittgenstein's well-known argument against the idea of a private language. It is not unreasonable to suggest that the private language argument is directed at a larger target, namely the Cartesian self who can communicate to itself in its own language. The case of the Chinese language provides a solid support for Wittgenstein's argument. Based on ideograms, the Chinese language cannot be mastered independently of the social context which underlines the meaning of nearly every word. It follows that if language plays a part in the constitution of the self then social relationships are responsible to the same extent for the constitution of the self. If Wittgenstein is right, there is indeed a contrast between the Cartesian self and the self as a language-user, which must be a social self. Likewise, there is indeed a contrast between the Cartesian self and the Confucian self, but none between the latter and the self as language-user. It follows that there is an East-West contrast only if the West is represented by one particular position.

III. CHINESE AND WESTERN CONCEPTIONS OF VIRTUES REVISITED

If I am right, it is at least highly misleading to say that there is an East-West contrast in the understanding of the self, or to say that the East sees the self in terms of a network of social relationships to the point of sacrificing self-identity, while the West sees the self as an independent individual who chooses to associate with others in certain ways in its promotion of self interests. There is certainly a Western conception of the self that supports this view, what Roger Ames calls the "liberal democratic" conception, a conception in which the self is prior to the ends it chooses, including ends concerning how it should relate to others. However, there is also another Western conception that sees the self in a way very similar to what we find in Confucianism. At the same time, the Confucian notion of the self indeed presupposes self identity. If all this is right then we have to rethink the idea that there is a contrast in the Chinese and Western conceptions of virtues.

On the Chinese side of the contrast, we have seen that there is enough textual evidence to show that individual identity is by no means obliterated in Confucianism. As pointed out above, this is acknowledged by commentators such as Chenyang Li, Roger Ames and David Hall. Given the link between the self and its virtues, if there is an individual identity, there have to be virtues pertaining to the individual self, virtues that are not subordinated to social considerations. Are there such virtues in Confucianism? The answer is clearly yes, and the prime example is the virtue of sincerity (*cheng*). In the *Great Learning*, sincerity is explicated in terms of "allowing no self deception." The sincere person is true to his or her own self, which is the natural self, and being so true, he or she will hate what is bad and love what is good, just as it is natural to "hate a bad smell or love a beautiful color." Thus, the sincere person will naturally act morally. Insofar as morality lies in one's behavior towards others, sincerity is the moral basis of social relationships. Not surprisingly, one Confucian declares that "(s)incerity is the foundation of the sage." Given the centrality of sincerity, it is not true that Confucianism speaks only of social virtues and leaves no room for virtues pertaining to the self. Indeed, for one Confucian, social virtues such as humanity (*ren*) and propriety (*li*) are based on sincerity, as are other virtues, and without sincerity "the Five Constant Virtues and all activities will be wrong."[20] Cheng Chung-ying was cited earlier as someone who has drawn our attention to the prominence of social virtues in Confucianism, but it is important to note that Cheng in fact believes that the self-related virtues are also important and that they and the social virtues are complementary: "… virtues represent the individual creative inputs into the community serving the needs of both the community and the individual selves. They are composed of both self and community and serve the two together."[21]

Turning to the West, it is true that individualism is celebrated in the "liberal democratic" tradition, and with it the self-related virtues. However, liberalism is primarily a defense of the individual against the *state*; it is not a doctrine about the primacy of the individual over his or her community. The celebration of social virtues is not inconsistent with liberalism. It does not take much effort to discover that the liberal West has not entirely forgotten social virtues, nor has it entirely subordinated the latter to the cultivation of the individual. Furthermore, a great deal of social thought in the West has been constructed on the basis of the third of the four models of thought identified by Hall and Ames mentioned above, namely the Aristotelian model of organic naturalism (reinforced by the pragmatism of Mead and Dewey) in which the self is "an organic, socially interactive, goal-achieving organism." Influenced by such models, socialism and much of communitarianism stress the primacy of social virtues. We may add to this the Judeo-Christian model, which also contributed to a strong sense of the importance of social virtues in the West. Significantly, in the area where individualism is expected to reign supreme, namely Western commerce, good teamwork has long been recognized as a key ingredient in commercial success, and as a result, a successful person in this area tends to be someone with a strong sense of other-related virtues and vices.

Since much has been made of the conception of the self in Western thinkers such as Sartre and Heidegger, we need to ask what view of virtues and vices such conception would endorse. Here, it may be said that since the Sartre-Heidegger ontology puts a stress on individuality, the conception of virtues and vices that it would endorse would be one that stresses individual virtues and vices. It might be said, for instance, that authenticity would be one such individual virtue, and bad-faith one such individual vice. However, insofar as an ethical theory can be constructed on the basis of the existentialist ontology, such theory typically turns out to be one that either blends individual virtues and vices with the social ones, or indeed puts the primary stress on the latter. For instance, Cooper has argued that a plausible basis for an existential ethics is the idea of reciprocal freedom, which is entailed by the kind of radical freedom that existentialists subscribe to.[22] Reciprocal freedom, in turn, can be best promoted in a framework of reciprocal sociality built on ideas of social virtues and vices. In such an ethics, authenticity can be interpreted as a virtuous tendency to see oneself as embedded in a social reciprocity, and bad faith as the vice of pursuing freedom outside of it.

It may still be insisted that, ultimately, the West values individuality and the pursuits of individual interests, and this is what puts it in a contrast with the Confucian East. However, there is in this objection a confusion between individuality and individualism. To value individuality, the perception of the self as a unique entity with its own virtues and vices, is not the same thing as to value individualism, the view that stresses the primacy of individual interests. There is no reason why social relationships cannot serve as the prism through which individuality, or self identity, is perceived. It is true that the Confucian East on the whole rejects individualism, but it does not follow that it rejects individuality and the cultivation of individual virtues. On the other hand, it is true that the West has strongly defended individuality, as is evidenced in influential writings such as J. S. Mill's *On Liberty*, but it does not follow that the West is thoroughly committed to individualism, thus ignoring or subordinating social virtues. If there is a difference on the conception of the self and the conception of virtues between the West, liberal or otherwise, and the Confucian East, the difference is merely one of emphasis, not a gap so large as to be called a "contrast."

NOTES

1 Cheng Chung-ying, "Transforming Confucian Virtues Into Human Rights," in *Confucianism and Human Rights*, ed. by W. Theodore de Bary and Tu Weiming (New York: Columbia University Press, 1998), pp. 142–53, at p. 148.

2 See her *In A Different Voice* (Cambridge, MA: Harvard University Press, 1982).

3 Cheng Chung-ying, "Transforming Confucian Virtues Into Human Rights," in *Confucianism and Human Rights*, ed. by W. Theodore de Bary and Tu Weiming (New York: Columbia University Press, 1998), p. 148.

4 Julia Ching, "Human Rights: A Valid Chinese Concept?" in *Confucianism and Human Rights*, ed. by W. Theodore de Bary and Tu Weiming (New York: Columbia University Press, 1998), pp. 67–82, at p. 72.

5 Donald Munro, *The Concept of Man in Contemporary China* (Ann Arbor: University of Michigan Press, 1797), p. 40. See also Donald J. Munro, *Individualism and Holism: Studies in Confucian and Taoist Values* (Ann Arbor: University of Michigan Press, 1985).

6 David Hall and Roger Ames, *Thinking from the Han: Self, Truth and Transcendence in Chinese and Western Cultures* (Albany: SUNY Press, 1998), p. 43.

7 Chenyang Li, *The Tao Encounters the West* (Albany: SUNY Press, 1999), p. 94.

8 Tu Wei-ming, *Confucian Thought: Self as Creative Transformation* (Albany: SUNY Press, 1985), pp. 57–8.

9 Shun Kwong-loi, "Self and Self-cultivation in Early Confucian Thought," in *Two Roads to Wisdom?* ed. by Bo Mou (Chicago and La Salle, Illinois: Open Court, 2001), pp. 229–44, at pp. 232–33.

10 Roger T. Ames, "On Body as Ritual Practice," in *Self as Body in Asian Theory and Practice*, ed. by Thomas P. Kasulis (with Roger T. Ames and Wimal Dissanayake), (Albany: SUNY Press, 1993), pp. 149–56, at p. 151 (emphasis added).

11 Roger T. Ames, "The Meaning of Body in Classical Chinese Philosophy," in *Self as Body in Asian Theory and Practice*, ed. by Thomas P. Kasulis (with Roger T. Ames and Wimal Dissanayake), (Albany: SUNY Press, 1993), pp. 157–77, at p. 159.

12 Michael Sandel, *Liberalism and the Limits of Justice* (Cambridge: Cambridge University Press, 1982), p. 19.

13 Francis Fukuyama, "History is Still Going Our Way," *Wall Street Journal*, 21 October 2001 (http://www.opinionjournal.com/editorial/feature.html/?id=95001277).

14 David Hall and Roger Ames, *Thinking from the Han: Self, Truth and Transcendence in Chinese and Western Cultures* (Albany: SUNY Press, 1998), p. 6.

15 Martin Heidegger, *Being and Time*, trans. by John Macquarie and Edward Robinson (New York: Harper and Row, 1962), ss. 66 & 76. See also David Weberman, "Heidegger's Relationalism," *British Journal for the History of Philosophy*, Vol. 9 (2001), pp. 109–22.

16 *Being and Time*, s. 43(a).

17 Heidegger, "The Concept of Time," trans. by William McNeill (Oxford: Blackwell, 1992), p. 8E.

18 *Being and Time*, English version, p. 440.

19 Jean-Paul Sartre, *Critique of Dialectical Reason*, trans. by Alan Sheridan-Smith (London: Verso, 1976).

20 The Confucian in question is Chou Tun-I. See *A Source Book in Chinese Philosophy*, ed. by Wing Tsit Chan (New Jersey: Princeton University Press, 1963), p. 466.

21 Cheng Chung-ying, "Transforming Confucian Virtues Into Human Rights," in *Confucianism and Human Rights*, ed. by W. Theodore de Bary and Tu Weiming (New York: Columbia University Press, 1998), p. 148.

22 David Cooper, *Existentialism: A Reconstruction* (Malden, MA: Blackwell, 1999).

CHAPTER 12

Women's Virtues and the *Analects*

SOR-HOON TAN

A 1997 country profile on women in China, commissioned by the United Nations, informs readers that "according to the feudalistic Confucian dogma of the past, women were regarded and treated as inferior creatures who had to obey their fathers until marriage, their husbands after marriage, and their sons after the death of their spouses. Women were also obliged to practice four virtues: morality (*de*), proper speech (*yan*), modest manners (*rong*), and diligent work (*gong*)."[1] The progress women in China have made, which is also an important indicator of its modernization, is measured by women's emancipation from this "feudalistic Confucian dogma of the past."

Recently, a growing scholarship challenges the view that women have been universally oppressed throughout China's history by showing that the oppression varies in nature and degree in different historical periods and in different regions and strata of society; at times, women have been important agents in China's history.[2] But these studies often present women's achievements against the framework of a Confucian ideology justifying patriarchal social structures. Wing-tsit Chan once remarked, "from Confucius down, Confucianists have always considered women inferior."[3] Margery Wolf argues that the diametrically different experiences of men and women in Chinese society render the overwhelmingly male Confucian philosophy, even a contemporary "humanistic" Confucianism such as Tu Wei-ming's, irrelevant to Chinese women.[4]

The culpability of Confucianism for Chinese sexism has become a matter of debate. Some scholars deny that Confucianism itself is patriarchal. Heiner Roetz argues that "the patriarchalism of the conventional morality, however, contrasts with the fact that none of the essential post-conventional achievements of the classical (Confucian) ethics—the Golden Rule, the egalitarian anthropology, and even less the idea of compassion—can earnestly be considered as an expression of "male" ideals. It is rather in the name of those achievements that the injustice which the officially Confucian Chinese society allowed to happen to women should be criticized."[5] Chenyang Li believes that sexist views are mostly later "add-ons," which are not characteristic of early Confucians.[6] It could be argued that rather than Confucianism making Chinese society sexist, Confucianism itself was made more sexist by various developments in Chinese society.[7] Recent explorations of common ground between Confucianism and feminism reveal various resources in Confucianism for what might be called a modern feminist-Confucian ethics. Sandra Wawrytko argues that "feminist sentiments are inherent in Confucian philosophical principle in their original form, in the sense of maximizing the potential of individual human being. Hence, were Kongzi (Confucius) to visit contemporary society, he can rightly be considered as among the strongest advocates of the feminist agenda."[8]

Confucianism may be understood as a "comprehensive doctrine," comprising metaphysical and cosmological world views, including beliefs about the place of human beings in the cosmos, an ethical discourse about how human beings should live, what kind of knowledge they could and should pursue, a whole way of life for individuals in community. It does not only exist in the texts identified with the tradition; it also subsists in the actual practices that are identified as Confucian by those who contribute to the definition of the tradition. Confucianism therefore is not a consistent monolithic system of thought. Rather than a static closed order with some essence or absolute truths to be possessed and revealed by the initiated, it is a multi-dimensional, dynamic, open-ended, historical phenomenon that is constantly being constructed and reconstructed, transformed by internal tensions and contradictions as well as external pressures. Rejection of sexism requires us to condemn sexist practices of past Confucian societies and sexist views of Confucians, but we need not consign Confucian texts to the dustbin of history unless they explicitly advocate sexism or contain teachings that will inevitably lead to sexism. Even when they do contain sexist content, it may still be possible to salvage the texts and learn valuable lessons from them after exorcising the sexist parts—there is no need to accept or reject a text in *toto* as if everything in it is inextricably enmeshed with one another.

This paper aims to engage the *Analects* afresh and establish a reading of the text that resists sexism and render it useful for modern society. The history of Confucian scholarship is littered with attempts to "redefine" the tradition by reinterpreting the core texts. My project may be located within this context. It is part of an attempt to resist any "Confucian revival" that aims to strengthen or revive authoritarian patriarchy, and solve the dilemma of those who see in Confucian philosophy much that is valuable and could still be relevant to contemporary experience but nevertheless consider some views that have been presented as Confucian, including sexist views on women and gender relations, ethically and politically unacceptable.

GENDERING OF VIRTUES

One aspect of sexism is double standards in morality that reinforce a stereotype of women as weak and passive, by nature formed to please and serve men, to be subject to them. Jean Jacques Rousseau, who proclaimed that "man is born free," considered women by nature inclined to excesses and not suited to liberty. What are faults in men are "virtues" in women. According to Rousseau, "the man should be strong and active; the woman should be weak and passive."[9] If "men and women are and ought to be unlike in constitution and temperament, it follows that their education must be different."[10]

> What is most wanted in a woman is gentleness; formed to obey a creature so imperfect as man, a creature often vicious and always faulty, she should early learn to submit to injustice and to suffer the wrongs inflicted on her by her husband without complaint; she must be gentle for her own sake not for his.[11]

In *A Vindication of the Rights of Women*, Mary Wollestonecraft attacked Rousseau's view of different virtues being suited to man and woman. She insisted that

> not only the virtue but the *knowledge* of the two sexes should be the same in nature, if not in degree, and that women, considered not only as moral but rational creatures, ought to endeavor to acquire human virtues (or perfections) by the *same* means as men instead of being educated like a fanciful kind of half being—one of Rousseau's wild chimeras.[12]

Underlying the gendering of virtue is the belief that men and women are different in nature and "naturally" occupy different positions in the social hierarchy with different roles and responsibilities. Given that gender differences historically have been so mired in inequalities synonymous with the subjugation of women, it is not surprising that the import of the gendering of virtue has been "to degrade one half of the human species, and render women pleasing at the expense of every solid virtue."[13]

In Chinese society, we also find a gendering of virtues based on an argument that men and women are different in the earliest extant educational text for women, *Lessons for Women* (*Nü Jie* 女誡, ca. 106 A.D.):

> As *yin* and *yang* are not of the same natures (*xing* 性, tendencies), so man and woman have different characteristics (*xing* 行, conduct). The distinctive quality of the *yang* is rigidity; the function of the *yin* is yielding. Man is honored for their strength; a woman is beautiful on account of her gentleness.[14]

The author, Ban Zhao 班昭 (c. 48–c.117 C.E.), mentioned four areas of normative requirements for women: virtue (*de* 德), speech (*yan* 言), bearing (*rong* 容), work (*gong* 功). The *Book of Rites* (*Li Ji* 禮記) also mentions these as areas in which a bride-to-be should be educated.[15] Excellence in these four areas became the "four virtues" in the "three obediences and four virtues (*san cong si de* 三從四德)" Chinese women were taught to observe, which symbolize the sexism of Chinese society for many critics.[16]

Natural differences are reinforced by gender segregation and division of labor. The *Lessons for Women* operates within the framework of placing women as daughters, wives and mothers in a society centered on the family. The ethical development of women occurs within these familial positions. This alone is not discriminatory in itself, since for Confucians, at least from Mencius down, the formation of families is an imperative both natural and ethical.[17] The discrimination lies in limiting women to these positions *only* and strict prescription of how they should function within them. Susan Mann observes that, in eighteenth-century China, "There was no comfortable, legitimate place in the upper-class Chinese family for a daughter who had passed marriageable age. Not only was an unwed daughter a social anomaly; she was a ritual anomaly as well. Her tablet could not reside on her natal family's ancestral altar when she died; it could be installed only in the ancestral shrine of another descent line, following betrothal and marriage."[18]

In the *Book of Rites*, males and females chart specific paths to social and ethical development, following the biological markers of each phase in the life course. According to its ritual prescriptions, distinction between men and women begins at birth.[19] Within the household, physical segregation and injunction against casual contact are strictly observed from seven to 70.[20] The inner-outer separation of women and men regulates the rituals of everyday living. "Men do not speak of the inner, women do not speak of the outer.... Words of the inner quarters do not go out; words from outside do not enter."[21] Within the family-centered ethics of Confucianism, the *inner-outer* polarity nevertheless indicates a gender difference in the meaning and importance of the family. Richard Guisso considers the *Book of Rites* as the most influential among the *Five Classics* in restricting Chinese women to home and hearth.[22] In late imperial times, this polarity degenerates into a rigid divide that seeks to confine women to their households, to exclude them from public life and politics completely.

The early classics such as the *Book of Poetry* (*Shi Jing* 詩經) lend support to the exclusion of women from politics.

> (Disorder) does not come down from Heaven;
>
> It is produced by the woman.
>
> Those from whom come no lessons, no instruction,
>
> Are women and eunuchs.
>
> ...
>
> So a woman who has nothing to do with public affairs
>
> Leaves her silkworms and weaving.[23]

Commentators speculate that this is a criticism of King You of Zhou 周幽王 (r. 781–771 B.C.E.) and his concubine Bao Si 褒姒.[24] Later, Song neo-Confucian Zhu Xi 朱熹 (1130–1200 C.E.) also stressed the dangers of women's participation in political life, recommending that women should remain indoors and never take independent action or initiate activities outside the home.[25] Patricia Ebrey finds that women's virtues during Song dynasty cast upper-class women as "inner helpers (*nei zhu* 內助)," dutiful wives and daughters-in-law, competent household managers and teachers of young children.[26] This was not always the case. According to Lisa Raphals, under the influence of Song and Ming neo-Confucianism, earlier flexible formulations of separate spheres were reinterpreted and reinforced to a hitherto unknown degree, emphasizing physical, social and intellectual separation; submission of wife to husband within the family;

requirements for women's chastity and prohibition against remarriage of widows; and the exclusion of women either from direct or indirect political activity.[27]

Ban Zhao's *Lessons for Women*, which maintains that "womanly virtue need not be brilliant ability, exceptionally different from others," became in later dynasties a prohibition of women improving themselves and achieving anything other than the most mundane of existence within the confines of their households.[28] A well-known Ming dynasty saying proclaims that "Lack of talent is a virtue in a woman." Raphals argues that such reading is however incompatible with the second chapter of *Lessons for Women*, which argues that girls as well as boys should begin education at eight.[29]

> Yet only to teach men and not to teach women—is that not ignoring the essential relation between them? According to *The Record of Rites*, it is the rule to begin to teach children to read at the age of eight years, and by the age of 15 years they ought then to be ready for cultural training. Only why should it not be (that girls' education as well as boys' be) according to this principle?[30]

Ban Zhao's authority is also cited in the *Classic of Filial Piety for Women* (*Nü Xiao Jing* 女孝經), written during the Tang dynasty, to argue for both intellectual and ethical virtues, even to advocate female independence. This text, modeled on the *Classic for Filial Piety*, compares the wives of the discerning kings of the Three Dynasties with their worthy ministers, and argues that instead of merely following her husband's commands, a woman should remonstrate and admonish her husband if she wishes to become worthy (*xian* 賢).[31]

Raphals's nuanced study of representations of women and virtue in early China highlights the differences between the narratives of virtuous women from the eighth to first centuries B.C.E. and those of later dynasties. The *Biographies of Women* (*Lie Nü Zhuan* 列女傳) by Liu Xiang 劉向 (79–8 B.C.E.) set a trend of identifying female exemplars in every dynasty to promote women's virtues. The *Biographies of Women* identifies six categories of virtues in women: maternal rectitude (*mu yi* 母儀); sage intelligence (*xian ming* 賢明); benevolent wisdom (*ren zhi* 仁智); purity and obedience (*zhen shun* 貞順); chastity and righteousness (*jie yi* 節義) argumentative skill (*bian tong* 辯通). Together with other pre-Han and Han narratives, Liu Xiang's *Biographies* shows virtuous women as exemplary in their sagacity, prescience, expertise, political acumen, and rhetorical skill—virtues that corresponded closely to those of their male counterparts. In contrast, later instruction texts for women and the selection of women's biographies in Song and Ming dynastic and local histories categorize virtues in terms of women's roles as daughters, wives, and mothers, focusing narrowly on family and propriety—reflecting the normative concerns of neo-Confucian orthodoxy, notably its concern for training women to be mothers and its obsession with chastity.[32]

The Chinese tradition is not monolithically sexist. However, in Raphals's view, the gender-neutral epistemology and ethics evident in the early Chinese narratives cannot be extended to Confucianism. "Specifically Confucian ideologies and social practices from the Later Han through Song and Ming Neo-Confucianism overwhelmed the earlier pattern of an ungendered approach to wisdom and the capacity for moral judgment."[33] But what about early Confucian teachings that also "predate the establishment of Confucianism, either as hegemonic ideology or as prevailing social practice"? Although some Song and Ming dynasty Confucians were among advocates of sexist womanly virtues, especially chastity, this is also a late development since the early Confucian texts of the Warring States period do not have clear views about women's virtues—I shall show this to be the case with the *Analects*. The *Analects* need not be read through the tinted glasses of later dynasties; to be relevant to contemporary life it needs to be reinterpreted.

To what extent can we find support for sexist gendering of virtues in the *Analects*? Some scholars have read *Analects* passages that appear sexist as a product of its time. Joel Kupperman suggests that "Confucianism in its initial phase simply took over (without any reconsideration) attitudes toward gender, family life and also social hierarchy that had been deeply entrenched in the culture by the time of Confucius."[34] The implication is that such sexism reflecting specific historical conditions could be left out in the application or revival of Confucianism in different historical circumstances. But Raphals argues that Warring States and Han historical narratives represent women as possessing the same virtues valued in men; they do not imply any gendered virtue theory.[35] I would argue that there is no theory of gendered virtue in the *Analects* either. If Chinese thinking during the Warring States and early Han was indeed less sexist than subsequent dynasties, I would argue that rather than reading the *Analects* solely through the interpretations of later dynasties, we should re-contextualize it within the historical period of its formation. This does not mean we dismiss the latter readings. Rather we should recognize that commentators of different dynasties interpreted the text within their respective historical periods, just as it is up to today's readers to reinterpret the *Analects* for the present and near future.

WOMEN AND VIRTUES IN THE ANALECTS

The *Analects* does not mention the four women's virtues that dominated women's education in China for centuries, nor is there any discussion about women's chastity. However, this silence does not necessarily mean that Confucius or his students believe that virtues are gender-neutral. It may be a reflection of the neglect of women's education before the Han dynasty—which gives credence to those who see Ban Zhao's *Lessons for Women* as an argument for educating women. The *Analects* has a couple of passages about Confucius teaching his son, but no mention of his teaching his daughter and niece. The only favor he had done them, which was considered worthy of comment, was finding them good husbands (*Analects* 5.1, 5.2, 11.6).

Women rarely appear in the *Analects*. The few passages that mention women are all too easily given sexist readings. The most notorious of these is *Analects* 17.25:

> The Master said, "In one's household, it is the women (*nü zi* 女子) and the small men (*xiao ren* 小人) that are difficult to deal with (*nan yang* 難養). If you let them get too close, they become insolent. If you keep them at a distance, they complain."[36]

In the *Analects*, *xiao ren* 小人 (small man, petty man) often appears as the antithesis of the *jun zi* 君子 (gentleman, noble man) who is a moral exemplar. Hence, a statement to the effect that women are similar to small men amounts to asserting the general inferiority of women. Some recent editions of the *Analects* still read this passage as simply reflecting Confucius' sexist belief that women are inferior while others try to downplay the sexist implications.[37]

One way to rescue this *Analects* passage from sexism is to limit the comparison and maintain that rather than stating an important universal truth, Confucius was making an observation based on his experience and its significance should not be exaggerated. Some considered the passage a later interpolation rather than Confucius' own view.[38] Without dismissing the passage or suppressing its significance, one could argue that women and small men are similar not in all ways but only in the specified aspect, becoming insolent when you get close to them and complaining when you keep them at a distance. Taking this further, one could argue that women behaved thus because they had been denied the opportunity of education and moral cultivation, and their social position of dependence rendered them insecure. Some see the significance of this passage as cautioning men in superior positions not to take their subordinates and women who are dependent on them for granted, emphasizing the ethical importance of treating these groups well and behaving properly towards them.[39] From a contemporary perspective, one would conclude that this passage, thus interpreted, reflects the undesirable consequences of discrimination against women, especially in denying them education and independence—something to be avoided or changed rather than accepted or defended.

Other interpretations of the passage contextualize the sexism so that it may be rejected as a sign of the prevailing state of society at the time that need not be defended in a more enlightened age. Arthur Waley notes that "standard interpreters soften the saying by making it apply to "maids and valets." Although he clarifies that he takes *nü zi* in its ordinary sense of "women" as opposed to "men" and *xiao ren* in its ordinary sense of "cads" as opposed to "gentlemen," he nevertheless gives some weight to those standard interpretations by translating "*nü zi yu xiao ren*" as "women and people of low birth."[40] James Legge translates the phrase as "girls and servants," adding in the notes that *nü zi* "does not mean *women* generally, but girls, i.e., concubines."[41] These common interpretations of *nü zi* as concubines and *xiao ren* as servants can be traced to Song dynasty Zhu Xi's commentaries.[42]

However, this reading is not supported by other texts from the Warring States period, which more often use *nü zi* in the sense of "woman" or "female child/daughter" rather than concubine or handmaiden. For example, the *Book of Poetry* uses the term to refer to young women (*nü zi*) leaving their homes: two of the poems (*Mao Shi* 毛詩 39, 59) are about a daughter of the house of Wei behaving appropriately, a third poem (*Mao Shi* 51) questions an unidentified woman's virtue.[43] In the *Zuo Commentary on the Spring and Autumn Annals*, *nü zi* means "daughter" in one commentary.[44] The term is also applied to "a woman," whose ritual propriety during a battle so impressed the Marquis of Qi that the latter gifted her husband, a superintendent of the entrenchments, with a city.[45] Commenting on the death of Duke Xi's 僖公 mother (*Jiang shi* 姜氏), Zuo remarked that "*nü zi* is one who follows (the man of the family)"—Legge explains this as meaning that "a woman follows—has her obediences to be rendered to—the determinate male relatives," which in the case of a married woman are those of the family she marries into.[46] We find the term in the argument by a sister of the king that she must marry the man who has carried her on his back and none other, because "a young lady (*nü zi*) shows what she is by keeping far from all men."[47] Going by the common usage of the term during the period the text was formed, there seems little reason to read *nü zi* in *Analects* 17.25 as "concubines" or "handmaidens."

If women and small men are "difficult to deal with," could the problem be solved by educating them? This is challenged by a different reading of *nan yang* 難養 that locates the problem in educating these two groups rather than their lack of education. Paul Goldin translates *nan yang* as "difficult to nourish," a charge which according to Goldin is more severe than commonly recognized. Goldin argues that, since "nourishing" frequently has a philosophical or pedagogical component in Confucian parlance, this passage may be questioning women's ability to learn and improve themselves and perhaps excluding them from the Confucian project of self-cultivation.[48] Goldin cites phrases from the *Mencius* that indicates the philosophical and pedagogical connotations of *yang*. In the *Analects*, besides 17.25, *yang* 養 occurs in two other passages. In relation to a son's treatment of parents, *yang* is translated as "providing with food"—Confucius dismisses *yang* as an inadequate understanding of filial piety even though the two notions are apparently often associated (*Analects* 2.7).[49] This use of *yang* does not have pedagogical connotations. In the case of *Analects* 5.18, Confucius described Zi Chan 子產, a prominent official of the state of Zheng, as being generous in "caring for the people (*yang min* 養民)"—this could have pedagogical connotations since Confucius believed that a government's responsibility towards the people includes their education as well as their material welfare (*Analects* 13.9).

If *yang* indeed means nurturing in a sense that includes educating and improving another, then *Analects* 17.25 asserts that women are difficult to educate. This is not as extreme as claiming that women *cannot* be educated.[50] And at least one commentary suggests that this passage is intended to draw attention to the difficulty and importance of education, not only for great men and *jun zi*, but also for women and small men.[51] Why would "women and small men" be difficult to educate? Nature seems to be the obvious answer. Indeed, some commentators interpret the passage as referring to women's and small men's "lack of proper nature (*zheng xing* 正性)."[52] This would parallel arguments in Western thought that women are *by nature* incapable of the morality expected of men. An example may be found in Aristotle's virtue ethics, with which Confucian ethics has been compared.[53]

For Aristotle, the "human good turns out to be activity of the soul in conformity with excellence [*arête*, also translated as virtue], and if there are more than one excellence, in conformity with the best and most complete" (1098a16–17).[54] These virtues are not gender-neutral *human* virtues because Aristotle maintained that though the parts of the soul are present in both men and women, they are present in different degrees: the woman has deliberative faculty, "but it is without authority" (1260a14). It is no secret that Aristotle considers women inferior to men.[55] A woman's character "being a sort of natural deficiency" (775a15), there is no chance that she could ever attain "the best and most complete" virtue and enjoy contemplation, the highest form of human flourishing (*eudaimonia*). Though man and woman belong to the same species (1058a29–b25), virtues are gendered because "functions are divided, and those of man and woman are different" (1162a22–23).

Is *Analects* 17.25 proclaiming the *natural* inferiority of women? If so, it must also assert that *xiao ren* are naturally inferior to other men, especially the *jun zi*. The contrast of *jun zi* and *xiao ren* in Confucian texts exhorts its readers to emulate the former and avoid *becoming* the latter. If "small men" are born rather than made, there would be no point in such exhortation. The Mencian strand of Confucianism which dominated Song and Ming neo-Confucianism insists that human nature (*xing* 性) is good and unethical behavior and characters result from neglect of the "four sprouts (*si duan* 四端)" of human goodness.[56] It is more difficult to know what Confucius himself thought of human nature; his student Zi Gong claims that "one cannot get to hear his views on human nature and the Way of Heaven" (*Analects* 5.13). Nevertheless, there is one *Analects* passage in which the Master spoke of human nature: "Men are close to one another by nature, they diverge as a result of repeated practice" (*Analects* 17.2).[57] Men become differentiated into *jun zi* and *xiao ren* through repeated practice rather than by nature. If women behave similarly to small men, it is through repeated practice rather than because of their nature.

The subject "men," though implied by the text which was addressing men primarily if not exclusively, does not translate a specific Chinese character but has to be added to the English translation of the pithy passage (17.2). One could argue that, reading the text in the twenty-first century, it makes better sense to add "men and women," "human beings," or "people" as the subject of the passage.[58] However, one cannot employ

Wollestonecraft's enlightenment argument for gender equality or gender neutral virtues based on the assumption of universal human nature. Even among men, the *same* nature does not apply to all, they are only *close* not *equal* in nature. What needs emphasizing is the recognition that ethical character and behavior is an *achievement* that comes about through practice. This is recognized even in the *Mencius*—the "four sprouts" has to be cultivated to become the fully flourishing virtues of *ren* 仁 (benevolence, authoritative humanity), *yi* 義 (rightness), *li* 禮 (ritual propriety), and *zhi* 智 (wisdom).

According to Richard Guisso, the *Five Classics* (the core Confucian canon), which enshrines the equation of male and female with *yang* 陽 and *yin* 陰, all insist "that there is a natural and immutable difference between male and female."[59] Wendy Larson claims that an "essentializing practice of gendering" is "present in the application of *yin-yang* theories to the social world and in the long textual tradition that associates women with a set and ritualized behavior, language and social context." In her view, *nü zi* in *Analects* 17.25 "is neither a biological construction nor a familial or kin category, but rather was a term for essential femaleness."[60] However, *yin-yang* terminology is absent from the *Analects* (and the *Mencius*). In the Xunzi, *yin-yang* appears only as a dynamic polarity constituting processes of change.[61] While that is not sufficient to prove that Confucius and early Confucians therefore did not equate gender differences with *yin-yang* differences, it at least shows that such an equation is not *central* to the core teachings. Moreover, *yin* and *yang* in pre-Han Chinese thought is better understood as a language of contrasting and interdependent relationships between things rather than one of essential dualism.[62] Even if Confucianism from the Han dynasty onwards subscribes to an essentialist gender distinction based on *yin-yang* metaphysics, we need not retrospectively impose it onto the *Analects* for a twenty-first century reading of the text.

If we read Confucius' comparison of women with "small men" as implying that women are also lacking in the *jun zi*'s virtues, it is not primarily due to a difference in the natures they are born with. The "small man's" ethical inferiority results primarily from his failure to cultivate himself, not because he is by nature a "small man." The most common obstacle to virtuous behavior mentioned is insufficient effort. This focus on nurture makes the rendering of "*nan yang*" as "difficult to nourish," implying that women are difficult to educate, less likely than the more popular "difficult to deal with." The small man's ethical failure does not result from any inherent difficulty in educating him but from a lack of education, or of efforts at self-cultivation. If we insist on the translation that questions both women and small men's ability to be educated, we could still locate the source of the difficulty in the social environment rather than essentially differentiated nature. If women Confucius encountered were difficult to deal with, it was due to lack of opportunities for personal cultivation; if they were difficult to educate, it was probably because of their position in the social hierarchy.

Virtues, whether Confucian or Aristotelian, are acquired through repeated practice. Such practices are embedded in the prevailing social structure. Unless you occupy a social position that presents the occasions for exercising a certain virtue, you will not be able to acquire that virtue. Virtues are acquired through repeating the respective actions associated with them. As Aristotle points out, "we become just by doing just acts, temperate by doing temperate acts, brave by doing brave acts" (1103b1). Women's ethical inferiority in Aristotle's philosophy has as much to do with their limited social roles as their "deficient" natures—the former also being justified by the latter.

Virtue (*de* 德) in the *Analects* is often associated with political leadership.[63] This is elaborated in *The Great Learning*,

> The ancients who wished to illustrate illustrious virtue throughout the kingdom, first ordered well their own States. Wishing to order well their States, they first regulated their families. Wishing to regulate their families, they first cultivated their persons.[64]

Zi Lu, presumably with Confucius' support, asserted that

> Not to enter public life is to ignore one's duty (*yi* 義). Even the proper regulation of old and young cannot be set aside. How, then, can the duty between ruler and subject be set aside? ... The gentleman takes office in order to do his duty. (*Analects* 18.7).

In Confucianism, limited political involvement will limit ethical achievement. If a sage is one who "gives extensively to the people and brings help to the multitude" (*Analects* 6.30), those who are excluded from positions of power with command over considerable resources will also be excluded from sagehood. Women in China, being confined to the inner quarters, could have at best achieved part of "illustrious virtue." Women's exclusion from political participation has also limited their ethical achievement.

Some might argue that such exclusion does not really deprive women of much in the context of Confucius' belief that "Simply by being a good son and friendly to his brothers a man can exert an influence upon the government" (*Analects* 2.21). One should not underestimate the interdependence of the inner and outer realms. Like Aristotle (1269b13–19), Liu Xiang in compiling the *Biographies of Women*, recognized the importance of women's virtues to social order. According to his biography in the *Han History*, Liu wanted to persuade Emperor Cheng to recognize the influence of women on the state at all levels of society, but especially at the level of statecraft.[65] Unfortunately, the argument about the relation between women's virtues and statecraft disappeared from later biographies of women and the focus became more and more confined to the family. Mencius (6B6) also recognized that, even from the inner quarters, women could influence the fate of a country: "the wives of Hua Zhou and Qi Liang, being supreme in the way they wept for their husbands, transformed the practice of a whole state. What one has within, it necessarily shows itself without." However, one must keep in mind Confucius' strenuous efforts to find political employment so that he could realize his politico-ethical vision. To that end, he was even prepared to offer his counsel to rebels and one whose character was questionable (*Analects* 17.5, 17.7). From that perspective, women's confinement to the inner quarters was a handicap in the acquisition of Confucian virtues.

To what extent does the *Analects* support the exclusion of women from politics? *Analects* 6.28 refers to Confucius' visit to the wife of Duke Ling of Wei, Nan Zi, who was notorious for her incestuous relationship, but wielded great political influence in Wei.[66] Though Confucius swore that he did nothing improper when his student Zi Lu was openly disapproving, the passage did not elaborate on his reason for the visit. We could speculate he hoped to influence (educate?) the lady so that she would exercise her power over Duke Ling to help bring about good government.[67] We cannot be certain whether Confucius considered women's political power and participation one of those cases where "the way did not prevail in the world" but was prepared to make do with available even if questionable means (of using women's influence over rulers) to bring about good government, or whether he saw nothing reprehensible in women having political power, or even saw it as something praiseworthy if they used that power ethically.

This ambiguity is reinforced in *Analects* 8.20, where Confucius corrected a reported claim by King Wu, the founder of Zhou dynasty, that he had "10 capable officials," with the remark that there was really only nine because a woman was among the 10 mentioned. It is not altogether clear whether Confucius separated out the woman from the men because he considered her not capable or he objected to calling her an official. There is some disagreement about the woman's identity. If the passage is referring to the mother of King Wen, Tai Ren, as most commentators believe, then the objection is probably against calling her an official rather than questioning her capability, as King Wu should not make his grandmother an official, a position subordinate to him. While some commentators argue that "woman (*fu ren* 婦人)" should have been "the man from *yin* (*yin ren* 殷人) as it was unacceptable to attribute Zhou's success even partly to a woman, Huang Kan 皇侃 (488–545 C.E.) maintained that Confucius was emphasizing that the success of Zhou was due not only to the men, but also to women. Others who accept that the passage attributes Zhou's success partly to a capable woman qualify this by limiting her contribution to "ordering the inner quarters."[68]

One way of resolving the ambiguity is to consider the general attitude to gender segregation and the exclusion of women from politics during the period of the composition of *The Analects*. Goldin has shown that in the early texts, the *nei-wai* distinctions, which became the basis of gender segregation in later Confucian thought, "are blurry at best, and often thoroughly irrelevant."[69] Given that there is no shortage of references to women who gave wise political counsel, or influenced the government positively through their virtuous behavior in the early texts, the condemnation of women who "destroyed" entire states must be read, not as advocating a blanket prohibition of women's involvement in politics, but emphasizing the importance of women being virtuous rather than vicious, not only for the good of the individual or family, but sometimes also for the state. Against this background, and given its emphasis on nurture rather than nature in the ethical quest as well as the ambiguity of the passages hitherto taken to be sexist pronouncements, there is sufficient flexibility for us to construct a reading of the *Analects* that would not exclude women from attaining the central Confucian virtues.

A PERSON'S VIRTUE AND PLACE IN SOCIETY

Could we reject whatever remains sexist in the few passages mentioning women in the *Analects* and construe the rest so that Confucian ethics offers a gender neutral account of virtues and the good life, notwithstanding the intention of the authors? Could women today acquire the key Confucian virtues such as *ren* 仁 (benevolence, authoritative humanity), *yi* 義 (rightness), *li* 禮 (ritual propriety), *zhi* 智 (wisdom), *xiao* 孝 (filial piety), *xin* 信 (trustworthiness), *zhong* 忠 (loyalty), *yong* 勇 (courage)? There is little reason today to think women are not as able as men when it comes to acquiring a virtue such as *ren*, understood as "loving others," (*Analects* 12.22) or "Do not impose on others what you yourself do not desire" (*Analects* 12.2). We may compare this with the revival of Aristotelian virtue ethics; its present advocates understand Aristotle's account of virtue as gender neutral, as universal, despite his specific descriptions of virtues in the context of Greek men in certain social positions and his views about the inferior nature of women.[70] A revival of the ethics of the *Analects* does not have to contend with an explicitly erroneous sexist biology or any essentialist theory about women's nature; but is Confucianism committed to a social hierarchy that subordinates women, even if it may not insist that women are by nature inferior?

When asked what he would do first if given the administration of the government in the state of Wei, Confucius replied that he would first "rectify names (*zheng ming*, 正名)" (*Analects* 13.3). Together with *Analects* 12.11, "Let the ruler be a ruler, the subject a subject, the father a father, the son a son," this is understood as advocating that in a well-governed society everyone should behave as their respective social role/position demands of them. Li Zehou and others believe that these social roles and positions are defined by the clan-based social organization and government of the Zhou dynasty, a hierarchical order based on ritual deference. They view Confucius as an ultra conservative trying to reinstate an obsolete patriarchal social hierarchy that is undoubtedly sexist.[71] The term for the Confucian ethical exemplar, *jun zi* 君子, in early China referred only to men—rulers, lords or the lord's sons. Even *ren* 人, the term we now translate as "human," or when translated as "man" is taken to refer to the entire human species, specifically referred to the male (probably of a certain class rather than all) of the species to the exclusion of the female in both *Analects* 8.20 and 17.25.

Confucius is not totally against change; he was willing to adopt novel practices which are better in some way (*Analects* 9.3). While he claimed to "transmit but not create" (*Analects* 7.1), what he transmitted was not a mummified past. After all, a worthy teacher needs to "revitalize the past in order to realize the new" (*Analects* 2.11). Confucius set an example by transforming *jun zi* from a term denoting nobility of rank and birth to one denoting ethical character—against this background, translating *jun zi* today as "exemplary person" rather than "gentleman," *ren* as "human/people" rather than "man/men" does not do violence to the text.[72] The "rectification of names" need not mean an absolute top-down prescription of social roles and responsibilities defined by an archaic patriarchal hierarchy. It can and should be understood to mean that the political leadership, given its prominent social position, has a responsibility to make clear through exemplification the actions and virtues appropriate to various social roles during any period. The social roles should be understood as flexible and changing with the times, and hence the "rectification" cannot be done once and for all, each age requiring its own "rectification." In different circumstances, the responsibility may not be limited to the political leadership, as others may also occupy prominent positions in their society and hence be in a position to discharge this responsibility.

Social order as depicted in the *Analects* is constituted by everyone having his or her rightful place, which circumscribes what each should do.[73] Confucius advised, "Do not concern yourself with matters of government unless they are the responsibility of your office (*wei* 位)" (*Analects* 8.14). Zeng Zi added that "the gentleman does not allow his thoughts to go beyond his office" (*Analects* 14.26). The term *wei* is often translated as "office" or official position in the *Analects*. This character is composed of the radical for "human" (*ren* 人) and *li* 立, the character for "stand," and in *Analects* 10.4 describes the actual position where someone is standing. While Confucius may have strict ideas about keeping to one's position in a community and following its ritual dictates, it must be emphasized that *wei* is not one's "station in life." One is not born into a position; the legitimacy of any occupation of a position depends on abilities and virtues.

In Confucian ethics, one's virtue and one's legitimate position in one's community mutually define each other.[74] It is virtue which enables one to occupy a position legitimately, to take a stand that contributes to social order. Confucius says to his son, "If you do not study the *Rites*, you will be ill-equipped to take your stand" (*Analects* 16.13, 20.3). The ethical importance of being able to "take a stand" is evident in the *Analects*' description of Confucius "taking his stand," from 30 years old, as part of the process of his self-cultivation (*Analects* 2.4). Confucius describes the benevolent man as one who "helps others to take their stands in so far as he himself wishes to get there" (*Analects* 6.30).[75] A position is where a person may stand; a person in taking a stand could also create a position for himself or herself. Whether one looks for an existing position to stand, or one creates a position, what matters is the appropriateness of one's arriving and of being there. "Do not worry because you have no official position. Worry about your qualifications" (*Analects* 4.14). What is translated as "qualifications" in this passage, *suo yi li* 所以立, is literally "the means by which you take your stand." It is better not to have any official position than to occupy one without the requisite virtues. Confucius frowned upon one who occupied a position when he was not the best man for the job.

> The Master said, "Has Tsang Wen-chung not occupied a position that he is not entitled to (*qie wei* 竊位)? He knew of the excellence of Liu Hsia Hui and yet would not yield to him his position. (*Analects* 15.14)

Even if the *Analects* does not explicitly authorize social changes, the text could only be useful today if it does not ignore the changes that have already taken place and adapts itself accordingly. Given that restructuring of gender relations is a fundamental characteristic of modernity, Confucian meritocracy should be extended to both genders, whatever might be the intention of Confucius himself.[76] If positions are not assigned by birth but to be gained through qualifications, especially virtues, then one could argue that women are as entitled to any position as men, competing on the same terms. A modern society is one wherein women are liberated from patriarchal control, released from the confinement of the family, to take their rightful place together with the rest of humanity in a society built on the assumption that all human beings, regardless of gender, are entitled to live a good life, to improve themselves and contribute to their communities. This does not mean that women should take over wholesale a virtue ethics that has been articulated in almost exclusively male context. Even asserting that there are human similarities underlying gender differences, it must be explicitly recognized that the inclusion will change our understanding of virtues such as *ren*, *yi*, *li*, *zhi*, as we acknowledge and explore women's practices that embody them.

Emancipation of women from patriarchal domination is not a simple matter of walking out of the home to take up a career. That may be as much a move controlled by others as being confined to the home. A woman is empowered when she is able to *make* her own position in her community and actually does so. She may have a career or not, she may marry or not, if married she may devote all her time to her husband and children or not. She may try to succeed at both career and home-making, or to walk a never-traveled path. In other words, a modern woman's position in her community is not a given, certainly not determined by others. Even in occupying a pre-existing position, a modern woman makes it her own by "recreating" it through an investment of personal meaning, and her "taking a stand" could also contribute to the remaking of society.

Confucian personal cultivation (self-making) is inextricably bound up with making a position for oneself within a community. This should not be understood as fitting individuals into pre-given slots in a fixed social structure. Making a position for oneself in a community could also (re)-make the community itself, for better or for worse. In an ideal Confucian society, which would be a harmonious community, or more likely, a cluster of overlapping, interrelated communities, a person's position should depend on that person's virtues. But a person's virtues also depend on his/her position. This means we should not be carried away by any optimistic expectation that reading the Confucian virtues in a gender neutral way and adapting Confucian views about social order and community making to a context that reject gender discrimination will immediately eliminate sexism from Confucian societies. We would do well to pay attention to some feminist criticisms of contemporary virtue ethicists, even when they explicitly reject the overt sexism of Aristotle, for failing to go far enough, as they take for granted the naturalness of prevailing social hierarchies, sexist divisions of labor, and exclusion from ethical discourse of practices that are predominantly women's domain.[77] As long as the prevailing social structure still discriminates against women, then women and men do not have the equal chances of living a good life and having their ethical achievements recognized.[78] However, recognizing that the *Analects* could be reinterpreted and Confucian virtue ethics expanded so that it could apply to women as well as men will provide a Confucian argument for eliminating gender discrimination, since such discrimination obstructs women's self-cultivation and the realization of a truly harmonious community wherein every member fulfils his or her ethical potential.

NOTES

1 Economic and Social Commission for Asia and the Pacific, *Women in China: A Country Profile* (New York: United Nations, 1997).

2 Dorothy Ko, *Teachers of the Inner Chambers*; Patricia Ebrey, *The Inner Quarters* (Berkeley: University of California Press, 1993); Susan Mann, *Precious Records: Women in China's Long Eighteenth Century* (Stanford: Stanford

University Press, 1997); Lisa Raphals, *Sharing the Light* (Albany: State University of New York Press, 1998); Maria Jaschok and Suzanne Miers, *Women and Chinese Patriarchy: Submission, Servitude and Escape* (London: Zed Books, 1994); Kathryn Bernhardt, "Chinese Women's History," in *Re-mapping China: Fissures in Historical Terrain*, G. Hershatter, E. Honig, J. Lipman and R. Stross, eds. (Stanford: Stanford University Press, 1996); Li Yu-ning, *Chinese Women through Chinese Eyes* (Armonk: M. E. Sharpe, 1992).

3 Wing-tsit Chan, *A Source Book in Chinese Philosophy* (Princeton: Princeton University Press, 1963), p. 47.

4 Margery Wolf, "Beyond the Patrilineal Self: Constructing Gender in China," in *Self as Person*, Roger Ames, W. Dissanayake and T. P.Kasulis, eds. (Albany: State University of New York Press, 1994).

5 Heiner Roetz, *Confucian Ethics of the Axial Age* (Albany: State University of New York Press, 1993), p. 126.

6 Chenyang Li, "Confucianism and Feminist Concerns: Overcoming the Confucian 'Gender Complex,'" *Journal of Chinese Philosophy* 27:2 (2000), pp. 192–3. Lin Yutang took the same line earlier, Lin Yutang, "Feminist Thought in Ancient China," in Li, *Chinese Women through Chinese Eyes*.

7 There are some interesting speculations about what these causes might include, in Sandra Wawrytko, "Prudery and Prurience: Historical Roots of the Confucian Conundrum Concerning Women, Sexuality and Power," in *The Sage and the Second Sex*, Chenyang Li, ed. (La Salle: Open Court, 2000); see also K. C. Wu, *The Chinese Heritage* (New York: Crown Publishers, 1982), p. 23.

8 Sandra Wawrytko, "Kongzi as Feminist: Confucian Self-Cultivation in a Contemporary Context," *Journal of Chinese Philosophy* 27:2 (2000), p. 177. Among various other less extreme arguments about the feminist potential of Confucianism are Joel Kupperman, "Feminism as Radical Confucianism," Philip Ivanhoe, "Mengzi, Xunzi and Modern Feminist Ethics," and Ingrid Shafer, "From Confucius through Ecofeminism to Partnership Ethics," in Li, *The Sage and the Second Sex*. In his chapter in the same book, "The Confucian Concept of *Jen* and the Feminist Ethics of Care: a Comparative Study," Chenyang Li notes that there are significant similarities between the Confucian ethics of *ren* and feminist ethics of care. In contrast, Julia Tao emphasizes differences between the two ethics and Raphals criticizes the attempt to align Confucianism with a "female ethic." Julia Tao, "Two Perspectives of Care: Confucian *Ren* and Feminist Care," *Journal of Chinese Philosophy* 27:2 (2000), pp. 215–40; Lisa Raphals, "Gendered Virtues Reconsidered: Notes from the Warring States and Han," in Li, *Sage and the Second Sex*, pp. 235–38.

9 Jean Jacques Rousseau, *Emile*, first published in 1780 (London: J. M. Dent & Sons, 1911), p. 326. Book V of the work is about Emile's "promised helpmeet": "Sophy, or Woman" represents the ideal woman, someone who is "as truly a woman as Emile is a man" (ibid., p. 321).

10 Ibid., p. 322.

11 Ibid., p. 333.

12 Mary Wollestonecraft, *A Vindication of the Rights of Women*, first published 1792 (New York: Prometheus Books, 1989), p. 48 (italics in original).

13 Ibid., p. 32.

14 References for the Chinese text is from Fan Ye 範曄, *Later Han History* 後漢書, vol. 54–5, *Sibubeiyao* (Shanghai: Zhonghua shuju, 1935), *juan* 104: 1048–1050. I have followed Nancy Lee Swann's translation for the title, while others have also translated it as *Admonitions for Women*, *Instructions for Women* or *Women's Precepts*. Swann's translation of the work is collected in Robin Wang, *Images of Women in Chinese Thought and Culture* (Indianapolis: Hackett, 2003), chapter 25, p. 181. I have quoted this translation, with alternative translation of some key terms in brackets.

15 Fan Ye, *Later Han History*, p. 86; Wang, *Images of Women*, p. 184; *Book of Rites* 45.7/168/8, in D. C. Lau and Cheng Fong Ching (eds.), *A Concordance to the Li Ji*, (Hong Kong: Commercial Press, 1992). According to Ban Zhao, "To guard carefully her chastity; to control circumspectly her behavior; in every motion to exhibit modesty; and to model each act on the best usage, this is womanly virtue." Her authority is among those cited in later dynasty, when emphasizing chastity as the key womanly virtue.

16 See UN report. The "three obediences" (obeying her father and brother before marriage, obeying her husband upon marriage, and obeying her son upon her husband's death) are mentioned in the *Book of Rites* 11.25/72/12, but not in *Lessons for Women*.

17 *Mencius* 4A26, 5A2, in D. C. Lau, *Mencius* (Hong Kong: Chinese University Press, 1984).

18 Mann, *Precious Records*, pp. 47, 54.

19 *Book of Rites* 12.42/78/12. Also *Book of Poetry*, *Mao Shi* 189, in James Legge, *Chinese Classics* (Hong Kong: Hong Kong University Press, 1960), vol. 4, pp. 303–7.

20 *Book of Rites* 12.52/79/20; 12.41/78/7.

21 *Book of Rites* 12.12/74/13–16.

22 Richard Guisso, "Thunder Over the Lake: The Five Classics and the Perception of Woman in Early China," in *Women in China: Current Directions in Historical Scholarship*, R. W. Guisso and S. Johannesen, eds. (Youngs Town: Philo Press, 1981) pp. 57–9.

23 Legge, *Chinese Classics*, vol. 4, pp. 560–4.

24 The latter appeared in the "Vicious and Depraved Women" chapter of Liu Xiang's *Biographies of Women*. Liu Xiang 劉向, *Lie Nü Zhuan* 列女傳, *Sibucongkan* (Shanghai: Commercial Press, 1936), p. 91. See also Goldin, "The View of Women in Early Confucianism," pp. 133–7; Guisso, "Thunder Over the Lake"; Raphals, *Sharing the Light*, chap. 3.

25 Zhu Xi 朱僖, *Xia Xue Ji Zhu* 小學集注, *Sibubeiyao* 168 (Shanghai: Zhonghua, 1935), pp. 11–12. Scholars have noted that Zhu Xi did say some positive things about women. Lisa Raphals, *Sharing the Light*, pp. 255–6; Bettine Birge, "Chu Hsi and Women's Education," in *Neo-Confucian Education: The Formative Stage*, W. T. de Bary and J. W. Chaffee, eds. (Berkeley: University of California Press, 1989).

26 Ebrey, *Inner Quarters*, pp. 114–30.

27 Raphals, *Sharing the Light*, p. 254.

28 Wang, *Images of Women*, p. 184.

29 Raphals, *Sharing the Light*, pp. 242–6.

30 Wang, *Images of Women*, p. 181.

31 *Classic of Filial Piety for Women* 女孝經, in *Congshu Jicheng Xinbian* 33 (Taipei: Xinwenfeng, 1985), p. 473a; Wang, *Images of Women*, p. 388. See also Raphals discussion in *Sharing the Light*, pp. 252–4.

32 Raphals, *Sharing the Light*, chapters 2 and 5. During the Song and Ming Dynasties, a veritable cult of female purity developed. When asked "If a widow is alone and poor with no one to depend on, is it all right for her to remarry?" Song-dynasty neo-Confucian Cheng Yi replied, "Starving to death is a small matter; losing one's chastity is a matter of the highest importance." Cheng Hao 程顥 and Cheng Yi 程頤, *Er Cheng Yi Shu* 二程全書, *Sibu Beiyao* 161 (Shanghai: Zhonghuashuju, 1935), pp. 22B: 3a; also in Wing-tsit Chan (trans.), *Reflections on Things at Hand: the Neo-Confucian Anthology compiled by Chu Hsi and Lü Tsu-ch'ien* (New York: Columbia University Press, 1967), p. 177. Birge points out that this statement is extreme, even for Song neo-Confucianism, and did not reflect actual practice, even within the Cheng family. Birge, "Chu Hsi and Women's Education," pp. 339–40. Confucian philosophy alone cannot explain the rise and nature of the chastity cult during the Ming and Qing dynasties. See Fangqin Du and Susan Mann, "Competing Claims on Womanly Virtue in Late Imperial China," in *Women and Confucian Cultures*, Dorothy Ko, Jahyun Kim Haboush and Joan Piggott, eds. (Berkeley: University of California Press, 2003), pp. 219–47.

33 Raphals, *Sharing the Light*, p. 237.

34 Kupperman, "Feminism as Radical Confucianism," p. 48; see also Wawrytko, "Prudery and Prurience," p. 165.

35 Raphals, "Gendered Virtue Reconsidered," and *Sharing the Light*; cf. Richard Guisso, "Thunder Over the Lake."

36 Unless otherwise stated, translation cited is from D. C. Lau, *Confucius: the Analects* (Hammondsworth: Penguin, 1979).

37 Chen Guoqing 陳國慶, *Lun Yu* 論語 (Shanxi renmin chubanshe, 1999), p. 318.

38 Bruce Brooks and Taeko Brooks, *The Original Analects* (New York: Columbia University Press, 1998), p. 240. Brooks and Brooks date book 17 to around 270 B.C.E.

39 Cheng Shude 程樹德 (ed.), *Lun Yu Ji Shi* 論語集釋, Min Guo Cong Shu 5:2–3 (Beijing: Huabei bianyi guan, 1943), p. 1078; Deng Qiubo 鄧球柏, *Lun Yu Tong Shuo* 論語通說 (Changsha: Hunan renming chubanshe, 2000), vol. 2, p. 401; Lai Kehong 來可泓, *Lun Yu Zhi Jie* 論語直解 (Shanghai: Fudan daxue chubanshe, 1996), p. 501.

40 Arthur Waley (trans.), *Confucius: the Analects* (Ware: Wordsworth, 1996), p. 121.

41 Legge. *Chinese Classics*, vol. 1, p. 330. Many modern Chinese editions of the *Analects* (*Lun Yu*) adopts this reading, including Qian Mu 錢穆, *Lun Yu Xin Jie* 論語新解 (Beijing: Sanlian shudian, 2002), p. 464.

42 Zhu Xi 朱熹, *Si Shu Ji Zhu* 四書集注, *Sibu beiyao* 8 (Shanghai: Zhonghua shuju, 1935), p. 86a.

43 Legge, *Chinese Classics*, vol. 4, pp. 63, 83, 101. See also *Mao Shi* 54 and 189, Legge, pp. 88, 306–7.

44 Twenty-sixth year of Duke Xiang 襄公, in Legge, *The Chinese Classics*, vol. 5, pp. 520, 525.

45 Second year of Duke Cheng 成公, ibid., pp. 340, 346.

46 First year of Duke Xi 僖公, ibid., pp. 133, 135.

47 Fifth year of Duke Ding 定公, ibid., pp. 759, 760.

48 Goldin, "View of Women in Early Confucianism," p. 139.

49 For a study of the relation of *yang* and *xiao* in the early medieval period (100–600 C.E.), see Keith Knapp, "Reverent Caring: the Parent-Son Relationship in early Medieval Tales of Filial Offsprings," in *Filial Piety in Chinese Thought and History*, Alan K. L. Chan and Sor-hoon Tan, eds. (London: RoutledgeCurzon, 2004).

50 Goldin points out that difficulty is different from impossibility and it is not easy to educate men either ("View of Women in Early Confucianism," pp. 139–40).

51 Cheng, *Lun Yu Ji Shi*, p. 1078.

52 Deng, *Lun Yu Tong Shuo*, vol. 2, p. 400.

53 For comparisons of Confucian ethics with Greek virtue ethics, see Yu Jiyuan, "Virtue: Confucius and Aristotle," *Philosophy East and West* 48 (1998); Sor-hoon Tan, "Mentors or Friends: Aristotle and Confucius on Equality and Ethical Development in Friendship," *International Studies in Philosophy* 33:4 (2001), pp. 99–121. Cf. a skeptical view about the viability of such comparisons, in Alasdair MacIntyre, "Incommensurability, Truth, and the Conversation between Confucians and Aristotelians About Virtues," in *Culture and Modernity*, E. Deutsch, ed. (Honolulu: University Of Hawaii Press, 1991). I believe that Confucian ethics can be described as a form of virtue ethics since it provides an account of the excellences of human activity and achievement, and is concerned with what kinds of character we should admire, and how one should live to shape one's character.

54 All citations from Aristotle's translated works from Jonathan Barnes (ed.), *The Complete Works of Aristotle* (Princeton: Princeton University Press, 1984).

55 For other mentions of woman's inferiority in Aristotle's works, see 648a14, 727a22, 728a18 ("the woman is as it were an impotent male"), 737a27–28 ("the female is, as it were, a mutilated male"), 766a30–31, 775a5–b24, 1171b11, 1254b13–14.

56 There has been some debate over the suitability of translating *xing* as "human nature," and whether there is an implied idea of universal human nature in Confucianism, especially in Mencius' philosophy. Roger Ames, "The Mencian Conception of Renxing: Does it mean 'Human Nature'?" in *Chinese Texts and Philosophical Contexts*, Henry Rosemont, ed. (La Salle: Open Court, 1991); Irene Bloom, "Mencian Arguments on Human nature (Jen-hsing)," *Philosophy East and West* 44 (1994); also articles in the special issue on "Human 'Nature' in Chinese Philosophy," *Philosophy East and West*

47:1 (1997).

57 In their classification of the passages in book 17, Brooks and Brooks present 17.25 as a return to the opening topic of human nature in 17.2 (*The Original Analects*, pp. 161, 166).

58 Waley's translation (p. 115) does not specify the subject; for a translation using "human beings," see Roger Ames and Henry Rosemont, Jr. (trans.), *The Analects of Confucius: a Philosophical Translation* (New York: Ballantine, 1998), p. 203.

59 Guisso "Thunder Over the Lake," p. 48.

60 Wendy Larson, *Women and Writing in Modern China* (Stanford: Stanford University Press, 1998), p. 37.

61 The notion occurs in both "Discourse on Heaven" and "Discourse on Ritual." Burton Watson (trans.), *Hsün Tzu: Basic Writings* (New York: Columbia University Press, 1963), pp. 80–84, 103.

62 Roger Ames, "Yin and Yang," in *Encyclopedia of Chinese Philosophy*, A. S. Cua (New York: Routledge, 2003), pp. 846–7. See also Angus Graham, *Yin Yang and the Nature of Correlative Thinking* (Singapore: Institute of East Asian Philosophies, 1986).

63 *Analects* 2.1, 2.3, 8.1, 8.20, 16.1. For more detailed discussion of the relationship between politics and ethics, see Sor–hoon Tan, *Confucian Democracy: A Deweyan Reconstruction* (Albany: State University of New York Press, 2004), pp. 127–32.

64 Legge, *Chinese Classics*, vol. 1, p. 357.

65 Ban Gu 班固, *Han Shu* 漢書 (Beijing; Zhonghua shuju, 1975), vol. 36, pp. 1957–8.

66 Some consider this the most incomprehensible passage in the *Analects*. Commentaries range from disclaiming that the visit ever took place, explaining that Confucius did not willingly meet Nan Zi but was forced by circumstances to do so, to justifying the visit on the grounds that nothing is absolutely impermissible to a sage who would be able find an acceptable way of meeting people with questionable characters. Cheng, *Lun Yu Ji Shi*, pp. 365–70.

67 He Yan 何晏 et al., *Lun Yu Ji Jie* 論語集解, *Sibub eiyao* 8 (Shanghai: Zhonghua shuju, 1935), p. 30a.

68 Cheng, *Lun Yu Ji Shi*, pp. 479–83. Hu Shih and Goldin took the same line. Hu Shih, "Women's Place in Chinese History," in Li, *Chinese Women through Chinese Eyes*, p. 4; Goldin, "The View of Women in Early Confucianism," p. 140. Cf. Liu Yongcong 劉詠聰 sees *Analects* 8.20 as rejection of women's political role, in *Women and History*女性與歷史 (Hong Kong: Commercial Press, 1993), p. 63.

69 Goldin, "The View of Women in Early Confucianism," p. 149.

70 Some goes so far as to argue that Aristotle's philosophy has much to offer to feminism. Cynthia Freeland (ed.), *Feminist Interpretations of Aristotle* (University Park: Pennsylvania State University Press, 1998). Cf. Li, "Confucian Concept of *Jen* and Feminist Ethics of Care."

71 Li Zehou 李澤後, *Zhong Guo Gu Dai Si Xiang Shi* 中國古代思想史 (Taipei:

Sanmin shuju, 1996), p. 7. Cf. scholars who believe that Confucius is more revolutionary than conservative, Herlee Creel, *Confucius: the Man and the Myth* (New York: John Day, 1949), pp. 143–4; Herbert Fingarette, *Confucius: The Secular as Sacred* (New York: Harper & Row, 1972), 57–70; Julia Ching, *Mysticism and Kingship in China* (New York: Cambridge University Press, 1997), pp. 69–74.

72 For such non-sexist translations of *jun zi* and *ren*, see Ames and Rosemont, *The Analects of Confucius*. This paper has not adopted this translation so that it would not assume what it is trying to prove, that a non-sexist reading of the *Analects* is not only hermeneutically possible, but also more rather than less enlightening.

73 I leave open the question of how hierarchical a Confucian society has to be. Most scholars believe hierarchy to be central to Confucian conception of the good society; I believe otherwise and argue against that view in my book, Tan *Confucian Democracy*, chap. 3.

74 Cf. Kupperman's different treatment of rituals and differentiated roles showing that, in Confucianism, "both ritual and the fundamental sense of what it is to be a 'good' person will involve, from the start, a strong and inescapable sense of one's place in a family and a social order." Kupperman, "Feminism as Radical Confucianism," p. 47.

75 For other instances of relation of "taking a stand" to ethical conduct or personal cultivation, see *Analects* 9.11, 9.30, 19.25.

76 On restructuring gender as central to modernity, see Barbara Marshall, *Engendering Modernity* (Cambridge, UK: Polity, 1994), p. 2.

77 An example of such criticisms is Susan Moller Okin, "Feminism, Moral Development, and the Virtues," in *How Should One Live?* Roger Crisp, ed. (Oxford: Oxford University Press, 1996); see also John Exdell, "Ethics, Ideology, and Feminine Virtue," in *Science, Morality and Feminist Theory*, Marsha Hanen and Kai Nielsen, eds., *Canadian Journal of Philosophy* 13 (1987).

78 By "equal" I do not mean "the same," but giving to each what will be best for him or her as a unique individual. For an account of equality based on individuality, and therefore respects differences, see Tan, *Confucian Democracy*, p. 104.

References

Ackrill, J. L. 1981. *Aristotle the Philosopher*. Oxford: Oxford University Press.

Adams, Robert M. 1976. Motive-Utilitarianism. *Journal of Philosophy*, 73: 467–81.

Adams, Robert M. 2000. *Finite and Infinite Goods*. Oxford: Oxford University Press.

Allan, Sarah. 1997. *The Way of Water and Sprouts of Virtue*. New York: State University of New York Press.

Almond, Brenda. 1998. *Exploring Ethics: A Traveller's Tale*. Oxford: Blackwell.

Ames, Roger. 1991. The Mencian Conception of *Renxing*: Does it mean "Human Nature"? In *Chinese Texts and Philosophical Contexts*. Edited by Henry Rosemont. La Salle: Open Court.

Ames, Roger. 1993a. On Body as Ritual Practice. In *Self as Body in Asian Theory and Practice*. Edited by Thomas P. Kasulis, Roger T. Ames, & Wimal Dissanayake. Albany: SUNY Press.

Ames, Roger. 1993b. The Meaning of Body in Classical Chinese Philosophy. In *Self as Body in Asian Theory and Practice*. Edited by Thomas P. Kasulis, Roger T. Ames, & Wimal Dissanayake. Albany: SUNY Press.

Ames, Roger. 2003. Yin and Yang. In *Encyclopedia of Chinese Philosophy*. Edited by A. S. Cua. New York: Routledge.

Ames, Roger, & Henry Rosemont, Jr., trans. 1998. *The Analects of Confucius: A Philosophical Translation*. New York: Ballantine.

Annas, Julia. 1993. *The Morality of Happiness*. New York: Oxford University Press.

Anscombe, G. E. M. 1958. Modern Moral Philosophy. *Philosophy* 33: 1–19.

Apte, V. S. 1998. *The Practical Sanskrit-English Dictionary* (revised and enlarged ed.) Kyoto: Rinsen Book Co.

Aquinas, Thomas. *Summa Theologiae*, various editions.

Aristotle. *Magna Moralia*, various editions.

Aristotle. *Nicomachean Ethics*, various editions.

Bacon, Francis. 1897. *Essayes or Councels, Civill and Morall*. London: J. M. Dent & Co.

Badhwar, Neera K. 1996. The Limited Unity of Virtue. *Nous*, 30(3): 306–29.

Ban, Gu [班固]. 1975. *Han History* [漢書]. Beijing: Zhonghua shuju.

Barnes, Jonathan, ed. 1984 *The Complete Works of Aristotle*. Princeton: Princeton University Press.

Baron, Marcia. 1997. Kantian Ethics. In *Three Methods of Ethics*. Edited by Marcia W. Baron, Philip Pettit, & Michael Slote. Oxford: Blackwell.

Berkeley, George. 1710. *A Treatise Concerning the Principles of Human Knowledge*, various editions.

Bernhardt, Kathryn. 1996. Chinese Women's History. In *Re-mapping China: Fissures in Historical Terrain*. Edited by G. Hershatter, E. Honig, J. Lipman, & R. Stross. Stanford: Stanford University Press.

Birge, Bettine. 1989. Chu Hsi and Women's Education. In *Neo-Confucian Education: The Formative Stage*. Edited by William T. de Bary & John W. Chaffee. Berkeley: University of California Press.

Bloom, Irene. 1994. Mencian Arguments on Human nature (Jen-hsing). *Philosophy East and West*, 44.

Blum, Lawrence. 1980. *Friendship, Altruism, and Morality*. London: Routledge and Kegan Paul.

Blum, Lawrence. 2000. Against Deriving Particularism. In *Moral Particularism*. Edited by Brad Hooker. Oxford: Oxford University Press.

Brandt, Richard B. 1969. A Utilitarian Theory of Excuses. *Philosophical Review*, 78: 337–61.

Brandt, Richard B. 1970. Traits of Character: A Conceptual Analysis. *American Philosophical Quarterly*, 7: 23–37.

Bretzke, James T., S. J. 1995. The Tao of Confucian Virtue Ethics. *International Philosophy Quarterly* 35(1): 25–41.

Broadie, Sarah. 1991. *Ethics with Aristotle*. Oxford: Oxford University Press.

Brodbeck, Simon. 2004. Calling Kṛṣṇa's Bluff. *Journal of Indian Philosophy*, 32(81-1-3).

Brooks, Bruce, & Taeko Brooks. 1998. *The Original Analects*. New York: Columbia University Press.

Chan, Wing-tsit. 1955. The Evolution of the Confucian Concept Jen. Philosophy East & West 4: 297–8.

Chan, Wing-tsit, trans. 1963. *A Source Book in Chinese Philosophy*. New Jersey: Princeton University Press.

Charkrabarti, Arindam. 1988. The End of Life: An Nyāya-Kantian Approach to the *Bhagavadgītā*. *Journal of Indian Philosophy*, 16(4): 327–34.

Chen, Guoqing [陳國慶]. 1999. *Lun Yu* [論語]. China: Shanxi renmin chubanshe.

Cheng, Chung-ying. 1998. Transforming Confucian Virtues into Human Rights. In *Confucianism and Human Rights*. Edited by W. Theodore de Bary & Tu Weiming. New York: Columbia University Press.

Cheng, Chung-ying. 2000. Confucian Onto-Hermeneutics. *Journal of Chinese Philosophy* 27(1): 33–68.

Cheng, Hao [程顥], and Cheng Yi [程頤]. 1935a. *Complete Works of the Cheng Brothers* [二程全書], Sibubeiyao 161. Shanghai: Zhonghua shuju.

Cheng, Hao, and Cheng Yi. 1935b. *Cuiyan*. In *Complete Works of the Cheng Brothers*], Sibubeiyao 161. Shanghai: Zhonghua shuju.

Cheng, Hao, and Cheng Yi. 1935c. *Henan Chengshi Yishu* (*Yishu*). In *Complete Works of the Cheng Brothers*, Sibubeiyao 161. Shanghai: Zhonghua shuju.

Cheng, Shude [程樹德], ed. 1943. *Lun Yu Ji Shi* [論語集釋]. Min Guo Cong Shu 5. Beijing: Huabei bianyi guan.

Ching, Julia. 1997. *Mysticism and Kingship in China: The Heart of Chinese Wisdom.* New York: Cambridge University Press.

Ching, Julia. 1998. Human Rights: A Valid Chinese Concept? In *Confucianism and Human Rights.* Edited by W. Theodore de Bary & Tu Weiming. New York: Columbia University Press.

Chong, Kim-chong. 1996. *Moral Agoraphobia: The Challenge of Egoism.* New York: Peter Lang.

Chong, Kim-chong. 1998a. The Aesthetic Moral Personality: *Li*, *Yi*, *Wen* and *Chih* in the *Analects*. *Monumenta Serica*, 46.

Chong, Kim-chong. 1998b. Confucius' Virtue Ethics: *Li*, *Yi*, *Wen* and *Chih* in the *Analects*. *Journal of Chinese Philosophy*, 25.

Cicero. 44 B.C.E. *de Officiis*. Translated by Walter Miller, Latin text edited by Jeffery Henderson for the Loeb Classical Library 30. 1913. Cambridge, MA: Harvard University Press.

Clark, A. 1997. *Being There: Putting Brain, Body and World Together Again.* Cambridge, MA: MIT Press.

Classic of Filial Piety for Women [女孝經]. 1985. Congshu jicheng xinbian 33. Taipei: Xinwenfeng.

Cooper, David. 1999. *Existentialism: A Reconstruction.* Malden, MA: Blackwell.

Cooper, John M. 1975. *Reason and Human Good in Aristotle*. Cambridge, MA: Harvard University Press.

Creel, Herlee. 1949. *Confucius: The Man and the Myth.* New York: John Day.

Crittenden, Paul. 1990. *Learning to be Moral: Philosophical Thoughts about Moral Development*. New Jersey & London: Humanities Press.

Cua, A. S. 1983. *Li* and Moral Justification: A Study in the *Li Chi*. *Philosophy East & West*, 33(1): 1–16.

Cua, A. S. 1998a. Basic Concepts of Confucian Ethics. In *Moral Vision and Tradition: Essays in Chinese Ethics.* Edited by A. S. Cua. Washington, D.C.: Catholic University of American Press.

Cua, A. S. 1998b. Confucian Vision and Experience of the World. In *Moral Vision and Tradition: Essays in Chinese Ethics.* Edited by A. S. Cua. Washington, D.C.: The Catholic University of American Press.

Daxue Zhangju (Sikuquanshu edition).

Deng, Qiubo [鄧球柏]. 2000. *Lun Yu Tong Shuo* [論語通説]. Changsha, China: Hunan renming chubanshe.

Dent, N. J. H. 1984. *The Moral Psychology of the Virtues*. Cambridge: Cambridge University Press.

Du, Fangqin, & Susan Mann. 2003. Competing Claims on Womanly Virtue in Late Imperial China. In *Women and Confucian Cultures*. Edited by Dorothy Ko, Jahyun Kim Haboush, and Joan Piggott. Berkeley: University of California Press.

Ebrey, Patricia. 1993. *The Inner Quarters*. Berkeley: University of California Press.

Economic and Social Commission for Asia and the Pacific. 1997. *Women in China: A Country Profile*. New York: United Nations.

Eliot, George. 1976. *Middlemarch*. Harmondsworth: Penguin.

Exdell, John. 1987. Ethics, Ideology, and Feminine Virtue. In *Science, Morality and Feminist Theory*. Edited by Marsha Hanen and Kai Nielsen, *Canadian Journal of Philosophy*, 13.

Fan Ye [範曄]. 1935. *Later Han History* [後漢書], Sibubeiyao. Shanghai: Zhonghua shuju.

Fingarette, Herbert. 1972. *Confucius: The Secular as Sacred*. New York: Harper & Row.

Flanagan, Owen. 1991. *Varieties of Moral Personality*. Cambridge, MA: Harvard University Press.

Foot, Philippa. 1978. *Virtues and Vices*. Oxford: Basil Blackwell.

Foot, Philippa. 1983. Moral Realism and Moral Dilemma. *Journal of Philosophy*, 80 (July): 379–98.

Frankena, William K. 1973. The Ethics of Love Conceived as an Ethics of Virtue. *Journal of Religious Ethics*, 1: 21–36.

Frankena, William K. 1988. *Ethics*. New Jersey: Prentice Hall.

Freeland, Cynthia, ed. 1998. *Feminist Interpretations of Aristotle*. University Park: Pennsylvania State University Press.

Foot, Philippa. 1978. *Virtues and Vices*. Berkeley: University of California Press.

Fried, C. 1976. The Lawyer as Friend: The Moral Foundations of the Lawyer-Client Relation. *Yale Law Journal*, 85: 1060–89.

Fukuyama, Francis. 2001. History is Still Going Our Way. *Wall Street Journal*, 21 October.

Gandhi, Ramchandra. 1976. *The Availability of Religious Ideas*. London: Macmillan Press.

Geach, Peter. 1969. *God and the Soul*. London: Routledge and Kegan Paul.

Geach, Peter. 1977. *The Virtues*. Cambridge: Cambridge University Press.

Gewirth, Alan. 1988. Ethical Universalism and Particularity. *Journal of Philosophy*, 85: 283–302.

Gill, Christopher. 1988. Personhood and Personality: The Four-*Personae* Theory in Cicero *de Officiis* I. *Oxford Studies in Ancient Philosophy*, 6: 169–99.

Gilligan, Carol. 1982. *In A Different Voice*. Cambridge, MA: Harvard University Press.

Goldie, Peter. 2000. *The Emotions*. Oxford: Clarendon Press.

Goldin, Paul. 2000. The View of Women in Early Confucianism. In *The Sage and the Second Sex*. Edited by Chenyang Li. La Salle, IL: Open Court.

Graham, A. C. 1989. *Disputers of the Tao*. La Salle, IL: Open Court.

Graham, Angus. 1986. *Yin Yang and the Nature of Correlative Thinking*. Singapore: Institute of East Asian Philosophies.

Graham, Angus. 1990. *Studies in Chinese Philosophy and Philosophical Literature*. Albany: State University of New York Press.

Guanzi (Sibubeiyao edition).

Guisso, Richard. 1981. Thunder Over the Lake: The Five Classics and the Perception of Woman in Early China. In *Women in China: Current Directions in Historical Scholarship*. Edited by R. W. Guisso and S. Johannesen. Youngs Town: Philo Press.

Guo Xiang. *Zhuangzi Zhu* in *Zhuangzi* (Sibubeiyao edition).

Guodian Chumu Zhujian [郭店楚墓竹簡]. 1998. Beijing: Wenwu Chubanshe.

Guoyu (Sibubeiyao edition).

Gupta, Bina. 2003. *Cit: Consciousness*. Delhi: Oxford University Press.

Hall, David, and Roger Ames. 1998. *Thinking from the Han: Self, Truth and Transcendence in Chinese and Western Cultures*. Albany: SUNY Press.

Hanfeizi (Sibubeiyao edition).

He, Yan [何晏], et al. 1935. *Lun Yu Ji Jie* [論語集解], Sibubeiyao 8. Shanghai: Zhonghua shuju.

Heidegger, Martin. 1962. *Being and Time*. Translated by John Macquarie and Edward Robinson. New York: Harper and Row.

Heidegger, Martin. 1992. *The Concept of Time*. Translated by William McNeill. Oxford: Blackwell.

Hu, Shih. 1992. Women's Place in Chinese History. In *Chinese Women through Chinese Eyes*. Edited by Yu-ning Li. Armonk: M. E. Sharpe.

Huainanzi (Sibubeiyao edition).

Hursthouse, Rosalind. 1999. *On Virtue Ethics*. New York: Oxford University Press.

Im, Manyul. 1999. Emotional Control and Virtue in the *Mencius*. *Philosophy East and West*, 49: 1.

Im, Manyul. 2004. Moral Knowledge and Self Control in *Mengzi*: Rectitude, Courage, and *Qi*. *Asian Philosophy*, 14: 1.

Inwood, Brad. 1999. Rules and Reasoning in Stoic Ethics. In *Topics in Stoic Philosophy*. Edited by Katerina Ierodiakonou. Oxford: Oxford University Press, 95–127.

Irwin, T. H. 1988a. Disunity in the Aristotelian Virtues. *Oxford Studies in Ancient Philosophy*. Supp. vol.

Irwin, T. H. 1988b. Disunity in the Aristotelian Virtues: A Reply to Richard Kraut. *Oxford Studies in Ancient Philosophy*. Supp. vol.

Ivanhoe, P. J. 1990. *Ethics in the Confucian Tradition*. Atlanta: Scholars Press.

Ivanhoe, P. J. 2000. Mengzi, Xunzi and Modern Feminist Ethics. In *The Sage and the Second Sex*. Edited by Chenyang Li. La Salle, IL: Open Court.

Jaschok, Maria, and Suzanne Miers. 1994. *Women and Chinese Patriarchy: Submission,*

Servitude and Escape. London: Zed Books.

Jia, Yi. *Xinshu* (Sibubeiyao edition).

Kant, Immanuel. 1797. *Metaphysics of Morals.* Translated and edited by Mary Gregor. 1996. Cambridge: Cambridge University Press.

Knapp, Keith. 2004. Reverent Caring: The Parent-Son Relationship in Early Medieval Tales of Filial Offsprings. In *Filial Piety in Chinese Thought and History.* Edited by Alan K. L. Chan and Sor-hoon Tan. London: RoutledgeCurzon.

Knoblock, John. 1994. *Xunzi: A Translation and Study of the Complete Works.* Stanford: Stanford University Press.

Ko, Dorothy. 1994. *Teachers of the Inner Chambers*. Stanford: Stanford University Press.

Korsgaard, Christine. 1983. Two Distinctions in Goodness. *Philosophical Review.* 92(2): 169–95.

Kraut, Richard. 1988. Comments on "Disunity in the Aristotelian Virtues" by T. H. Irwin. *Oxford Studies in Ancient Philosophy*, Supp. vol.

Kupperman, Joel. 2000. Feminism as Radical Confucianism. In *The Sage and the Second Sex*. Edited by Chenyang Li. La Salle IL: Open Court.

Lai, Kehong [來可弘]. 1996. *Lun Yu Zhi Jie* [論語直解]. Shanghai: Fudan daxue chubanshe.

Laozi (Sibubeiyao edition).

Larson, Wendy. 1998. *Women and Writing in Modern China*. Stanford: Stanford University Press.

Lau, D. C., trans. 1979. *Confucius: The Analects*. Harmondsworth: Penguin.

Lau, D. C., trans. 1984. *Mencius.* Hong Kong: Chinese University Press.

Lau, D. C., and Fong-ching Cheng, eds. 1992. *A Concordance to the* Li Ji. Hong Kong: Commercial Press.

Legge, James. 1960. *Chinese Classics.* Hong Kong: Hong Kong University Press.

Legge, James, trans. 1968. The *Li Ki* or the Collection of Treatises on the Rules of Propriety or Ceremonial Usages. In *The Sacred Books of the East.* Edited by F. Max Muller. Vols. 27–8. Oxford: Clarendon Press (1885), reprinted by Motilal Banarsidass (1968).

Li, Ao. *Liwengong Ji* (Sikuquanshu edition).

Li, Chenyang. 1999. *The Tao Encounters the West.* Albany: SUNY Press.

Li, Chenyang. 2000a. The Confucian Concept of Jen and the Feminist Ethics of Care: A Comparative Study. In *The Sage and the Second Sex*. Edited by Chenyang Li. La Salle, IL: Open Court.

Li, Chenyang. 2000b. Confucianism and Feminist Concerns: Overcoming the Confucian "Gender Complex." *Journal of Chinese Philosophy*, 27: 2.

Li, Chenyang, ed. 2000c. *The Sage and the Second Sex*. La Salle, IL: Open Court.

Li, Yu-ning, ed. 1992. *Chinese Women through Chinese Eyes*. Armonk: M. E.

Sharpe.

Li, Zehou [李澤後]. 1996. *History of Ancient Chinese Thought* [中國古代思想史]. Taipei: Sanmin shuju.

Liezi (Sibubeiyao edition).

Liji (Sibubeiyao edition).

Lin, Yu-tang. 1992. Feminist Thought in Ancient China. In *Chinese Women through Chinese Eyes*. Edited by Yu-ning Li. Armonk: M. E. Sharpe.

Lin, Yu-tang, ed. and trans. 1994. *The Wisdom of Confucius*. New York: The Modern Library.

Liu, Shao. *Renwuzhi* (Sibubeiyao edition).

Liu, Xiang [劉向]. 1936. *Biographies of Women* [列女傳], Sibucongkan. Shanghai: Commercial Press.

Liu, Xiang [劉向]. *Shuoyuan* (Sibubeiyao edition).

Liu, Yongcong [劉詠聰]. 1993. *Women and History* [女性與歷史]. Hong Kong: Commercial Press.

Liu, Yuli. *The Unity of Rule and Virtue: A Critique of a Supposed Parallel between Confucian Ethics and Virtue Ethics*. Singapore: Eastern Universities Press.

Louden, Robert B. 1997. On Some Vices of Virtue Ethics. In *Virtue Ethics*. Edited by Daniel Statman. Edinburgh: Edinburgh University Press.

Lunyu. 1980. Yang Bojun, *Lunyu Yizhu*, 2nd ed. China: Zhonghua shuju.

Lushichunqiu. 1988. In *Lushichunqiu Jishi*. Edited by Weiyu Xu, 4th ed. Taipei: Shijie shuju.

MacIntyre, Alasdair. 1981. *After Virtue*. Notre Dame: University of Notre Dame Press.

MacIntyre, Alasdair. 1991. Incommensurability, Truth, and the Conversation between Confucians and Aristotelians about Virtues. In *Culture and Modernity*. Edited by Eliot Deutsch. Honolulu: University of Hawaii Press.

MacIntyre, Alasdair. 1998. *A Short History of Ethics* (2nd edition). London: Routledge.

Mahābhārata. 1950. Critically edited by Vishnu S. Sukthankar and S. K. Belvalkar. *Droṇaparvan*, pt. 3B, 1958, vol. 9 (fasc. 29B). Pune, India: Bhandarkar Oriental Research Institute.

Mahābhārata. 1950. Critically edited by Vishnu S. Sukthankar and S. K. Belvalkar. *Śāntiparvan: apaddharma*, 1950, vols. 12–13 (fasc. 20–1). Pune, India: Bhandarkar Oriental Research Institute.

Mahābhārata. 1950. Critically edited by Raghunath Damodar Karmarkar. *Āśvamedhikaparvan*. 1960, vol. 18. Pune, India: Bhandarkar Oriental Research Institute.

Mann, Susan. 1997. *Precious Records: Women in China's Long Eighteenth Century*. Stanford: Stanford University Press.

Maritain, Jacques. 1964. *Moral Philosophy: An Historical and Critical Survey of the Great Systems*. London: Geoffrey Bles.

Marshall, Barbara. 1994. *Engendering Modernity*. Cambridge: Polity.

Matilal, Bimal K. 2002a. Elusiveness and Ambiguity in Dharma-ethics. In *Epics and Ethics*. Edited by Jonardon Ganeri. Delhi: Oxford University Press, 91-108

Matilal, Bimal K. 2002b. In Defence of Devious Divinity. In *Epics and Ethics*. Edited by Jonardon Ganeri. Delhi: Oxford University Press, 89–107.

McDowell, John. 1979. Virtue and Reason, *The Monist*, 62(3): 331–50.

Mellema, Gregory. 1991. *Beyond the Call of Duty: Supererogation, Obligation, and Offence*. Albany: State University of New York Press.

Milgram, S. 1974. *Obedience to Authority: An Experimental View*. New York: Harper and Row.

Montague, Phillip. 1997. Virtue Ethics: A Qualified Success Story. In Virtue Ethics. Edited by Daniel Statman. Edinburgh: Edinburgh University Press.

Moore, G. E. 1968. *Principia Ethica*. Cambridge: Cambridge University Press.

Mou, Zongsan [牟宗三]. 1997. *Fourteen Lectures on the Route Connecting Chinese and Western Philosophy* [中西哲學之會通十四講]. Shanghai: Guji chubanshe.

Mozi. A Concordance to Mo Tzu, in Harvard-Yenching Institute Sinological Index Series, 1961, 2nd ed.

Munro, Donald. 1797. *The Concept of Man in Contemporary China*. Ann Arbor: University of Michigan Press.

Munro, Donald. 1985. *Individualism and Holism: Studies in Confucian and Taoist Values*. Ann Arbor: University of Michigan Press.

Nagel, Thomas. 1986. *The View from Nowhere*. New York: Oxford University Press.

Nivison, David S. 1996. *The Ways of Confucianism: Investigations in Chinese Philosophy*. Edited by Bryan W. Van Norden. Chicago and La Salle, IL: Open Court.

Odo, Gerard of (Geraldus Odonis). *Expositio in Aristotelis Ethicam*, various editions.

Okin, Susan Moller. 1996. Feminism, Moral Development, and the Virtues. In *How Should One Live?* Edited by Roger Crisp. Oxford: Oxford University Press.

Olivelle, Patrick, trans. 2000. *Dharmasūtras: The Law Codes of Āpastamba, Gautama, Baudhāyana, and Vaśiṣṭha*. 2000. Annotated text by Patrick Olivelle. Delhi: Motilal Banarsidass.

O'Neill, Onora. 1983. Kant after Virtue. *Inquiry*, 26: 387–405.

Paton, H. J., ed. 1948. *The Moral Law: Kant's Groundwork of the Metaphysic of Morals*. London: Hutchinson Library.

Pence, Greg. 1991. Virtue Theory. In *A Companion to Ethics*. Edited by Peter Singer. Oxford: Blackwell.

Penner, T. M. I. 1973. The Unity of Virtue. *Philosophical Review*, 82: 35–68.

Perry, R. B. 1954. *Realms of Value*. Cambridge: Harvard University Press.

Prichard, H. A. 1968. Does Moral Philosophy Rest on a Mistake? In *Moral Obligation*. Oxford: Oxford University Press.

Plato. *Euthyphro*. Oxford Classical Texts: *Platonis Opera* I. 1995. Oxford: Oxford University Press.

Plato. *Laches*, various editions.

Plato. *Meno*, various editions.

Plato. *Protagoras*, various editions.

Plato. *Theaetetus*. Oxford Classical Texts: *Platonis Opera* I. 1995. Oxford: Oxford University Press.

Qian, Mu [錢穆]. 2002. *Lun Yu Xin Jie* [論語新解]. Beijing: Sanlian shudian.

Rachels, James. 1999. *The Elements of Moral Philosophy*. Singapore: McGraw-Hill.

Raphals, Lisa. 1998. *Sharing the Light*. Albany: State University of New York Press.

Raphals, Lisa. 2000. Gendered Virtues Reconsidered: Notes from the Warring States and Han. In *The Sage and the Second Sex*. Edited by Chenyang Li. La Salle, IL: Open Court.

Rawls, John. 1971. *A Theory of Justice*. Cambridge, MA: Belknap Press.

Riegel, Jeffrey. 1979. Reflections on an Unmoved Mind. *Journal of the American Academy of Religion*, Thematic issue 47(3).

Robinson, V. M. J. 1993. *Problem Based Methodology: Research for the Improvement of Practice.* Oxford: Pergamon Press.

Roetz, Heiner. 1993. *Confucian Ethics of the Axial Age*. Albany: State University of New York Press.

Rooney, Paul. 1996. *Divine Command Morality*. Alershot: Avebury, Ashgate Publishing.

Ross, W. D. 1930. *The Right and the Good*. Oxford: Clarendon Press.

Roth, Harold D. 1999. *Original Tao*. New York: Columbia University Press.

Rousseau, Jean Jacques. 1911. *Emile*, first published 1780. London: J. M. Dent & Sons.

Sabini, John, and Maury Silver. 1990. *Moralities of Everyday Life*. Oxford: Oxford University Press.

Sandel, Michael. 1982. *Liberalism and the Limits of Justice*. Cambridge: Cambridge University Press.

Sartre, Jean-Paul. 1946. *L'existentialisme est un humanisme*. Paris: Nagel. Translated by Philip Mairet. 1948. *Existentialism and Humanism*. London: Methuen.

Sartre, Jean-Paul. 1976. *Critique of Dialectical Reason*. Translated by Alan Sheridan-Smith. London: Verso.

Sen, Amartya. 2000. Conwequential Evaluation and Political Resason. *Journal of Philospohy*, 97:2

Shafer, Ingrid. 2000. From Confucius through Ecofeminism to Partnership Ethics. In *The Sage and the Second Sex*. Edited by Chenyang Li. La Salle, IL: Open Court.

Shao, Yong. *Huangji Jingshishu* (Sibubeiyao edition).

Shen Buhai fragments. In Herrlee G. Creel, 1974, *Shen Pu-Hai: A Chinese Political Philosopher of the Fourth Century B.C.* Chicago: University of Chicago Press.

Shenzi (Sibubeiyao edition).

Shun, Kwong-loi. 1997. *Mencius and Early Chinese Thought.* Stanford: Stanford University Press.

Shun, Kwong-loi. 2001. Self and Self-Cultivation in Early Confucian Thought. In *Two Roads to Wisdom? Chinese and Analytic Philosophical Traditions.* Edited by Bo Mou. Chicago and La Salle, IL: Open Court.

Shuowen Jiezi Zhu [說文解字注]. 1981. Shanghai: Shanghai guji chubanshe.

Sidgwick, Henry. 1960. *Outlines of the History of Ethics*, 6th ed. Boston: Beacon Press.

Sidgwick, Henry. 1966. *Methods of Ethics*, 7th ed. New York: Dover Press.

Slote, Michael. 1995. *From Morality to Virtue*. Oxford: Oxford University Press.

Slote, Michael. 1997. Agent-based Virtue Ethics. In *Virtue Ethics*. Edited by Roger Crisp and Michael Slote. Oxford: Oxford University Press.

Slote, Michael. 1997. Virtue Ethics. In *Three Methods of Ethics*. Edited by Marcia W. Baron, Philip Pettit, and Michael Slote. Oxford: Blackwell.

Slote, Michael. 2001. *Morals from Motives*. Oxford: Oxford University Press.

Smith, B. K. 1989. *Reflections on Resemblance, Ritual and Religion*. New York: Oxford University Press.

Solomon, David. 1997. Internal Objections to Virtue Ethics. In *Virtue Ethics*. Edited by Daniel Statman. Edinburgh: Edinburgh University Press.

Sorabji, Richard. 2000. *Emotion and Peace of Mind*. Oxford: Oxford University Press

Statman, Daniel, ed. 1997. *Virtue Ethics*. Edinburgh: Edinburgh University Press.

Styron, W. 1979. *Sophie's Choice*. New York: Random House.

Swann, Nancy Lee. 2003. Lessons for Women. In *Images of Women in Chinese Thought and Culture*. Edited by Robin Wang. Indianapolis: Hackett.

Swanton, Christine. 1995. Profiles of the Virtues. *Pacific Philosophical Quarterly*, 76.

Swanton, Christine. 2001. A Virtue Ethical Account of Right Action. *Ethics*, 112(1): 32–52.

Swanton, Christine. 2003. *Virtue Ethics: A Pluralistic View*. Oxford: Oxford

University Press.

Swanton, Christine. Forthcoming. Virtue Ethics, Role Ethics, and Business Ethics. In *Working Virtue: Virtue Ethics and Contemporary Moral Problems*. Edited by R. Walker and P. J. Ivanhoe. Oxford: Oxford University Press.

Swinburne, R. G. 1993. *The Coherence of Theism*. Oxford: Clarendon.

Tan, Sor-hoon. 2001. Mentors or Friends: Aristotle and Confucius on Equality and Ethical Development in Friendship. *International Studies in Philosophy*, 33: 4.

Tan, Sor-hoon. 2004. *Confucian Democracy: A Deweyan Reconstruction*. Albany: State University of New York Press.

Tao, Julia. 2000. Two Perspectives of Care: Confucian Ren and Feminist Care. *Journal of Chinese Philosophy*, 27: 2.

Telfer, Elizabeth. 1989. The Unity of the Moral Virtues in Aristotle's Nicomachean Ethics. *Proceedings of the Aristotelian Society*, 90: 35–48.

Tu, Weiming. 1979. *Humanity and Self-Cultivation: Essays in Confucian Thought*. Berkeley: Asian Humanities Press.

Tu, Weiming. 1985. *Confucian Thought: Self as Creative Transformation* Albany: SUNY Press.

Tu, Weiming. 1989. *Centrality and Commonality: An Essay on Confucian Religiousness*. Albany: State University of New York Press.

van Buitenen, J. A. B., trans. 1981. *The Bhagavadgītā in the Mahābhārata: Text and Translation*. Chicago: University of Chicago Press.

van Norden, Bryan W. 1992. Mengzi and Xunzi: Two Views of Human Agency. *International Philosophical Quarterly*, 32(2).

Velazco y Trianosky, Gregory. 1990. What Is Virtue Ethics All About? Recent Work on the Virtues. *American Philosophical Quarterly*, 27: 335–44.

Velazco y Trianosky, Gregory. 1991. Natural Affections and Responsibility for Character: A Critique of Kantian Views of the Virtues. In *Identity, Character, and Morality: Essays in Moral Psychology*. Edited by Owen Flanagan and Amélie Rorty. Cambridge, MA: MIT Press.

Velazco y Trianosky, Gregory. 1999. Supererogation. *Concise Routledge Encyclopedia of Philosophy*. London and New York: Routledge Press.

Velazco y Trianosky, Gregory. 2004. *The Power of Love: The Altruistic Virtues Conceived as Powers*. Unpublished manuscript.

Waley, Arthur, trans. 1996. *Confucius: The Analects*. Ware: Wordsworth.

Walker, A. D. M. 1989. Virtue and Character. *Philosophy*, 64: 349–62.

Wallace, J. D. 1978. *Virtues and Vices*. Ithaca: Cornell University Press.

Walsh, J. J. 1986. Buridan on the Connection of the Virtues. *Journal of the History of Philosophy*, 24: 453–82.

Wang, Bi. *Laozi Zhu*. In *Laozi* (Sibubeiyao edition).

Watson, Burton, trans. 1963. *Hsün Tzu: Basic Writings*. New York: Columbia

University Press.

Watson, Gary. 1984. Virtues in Excess. *Philosophical Studies*, 46: 57–74.

Wawrytko, Sandra A. 1982. Confucius and Kant: The Ethics of Respect. *Philosophy East & West* 32(3): 237–57.

Wawrytko, Sandra. 2000a. Kongzi as Feminist: Confucian Self-Cultivation in a Contemporary Context. *Journal of Chinese Philosophy*, 27: 2.

Wawrytko, Sandra. 2000b. Prudery and Prurience: Historical Roots of the Confucian Conundrum Concerning Women, Sexuality and Power. In *The Sage and the Second Sex*. Edited by Chenyang Li. La Salle, IL: Open Court.

Weberman, David. 2001. Heidegger's Relationalism. *British Journal for the History of Philosophy*, 9: 109–22.

Wellman, Carl. 1962. Wittgenstein's Conception of a Criterion. *The Philosophical Review*, 71(4): 433–47.

Williams, B. A. O. 1981. *Persons, Character, and Morality. Tn Moral Luck: Philosophical Papers* 1973-1980. Cambridge: Cambridge University Press.

Williams, B. A. O. 1985. *Ethics and the Limits of Philosophy*. London: Fontana.

Williams, Bernard. 1973. A Critique of Utilitarianism. In *Utilitarianism: For and Against*. Edited by J. J. C. Smart & Bernard Williams. Cambridge: Cambridge University Press.

Williams, Bernard. 2002. *Truth & Truthfulness*. Princeton, NJ: Princeton University Press.

Wilson, Stephen A. 1995. Conformity, Individuality, and the Nature of Virtue. *Journal of Religious Ethics* 23(2): 263–87.

Winch, Peter. 1972. Moral Integrity. In *Ethics and Action*. New York: Routledge & Kegan Paul.

Wolf, Margery. 1994. Beyond the Patrilineal Self: Constructing Gender in China. In *Self as Person*. Edited by Roger Ames, W. Dissanayake, and T. P. Kasulis. Albany: State University of New York Press.

Wollestonecraft, Mary. 1989. *A Vindication of the Rights of Women*, first published 1792. New York: Prometheus Books.

Wu, K. C. 1982. *The Chinese Heritage*. New York: Crown Publishers Inc.

Xiaojing. In *Xiaojing Zhushu* (Sibubeiyao edition).

Xunzi (Sibubeiyao edition).

Yang Bojun, 1984. *Mengzi Yizhu*, 2nd ed. China: Zhonghua shuju.

Yang, Xiong. *Fayan* (Sibubeiyao edition).

Yao, Xinzhong. 1996. *Confucianism and Christianity: A Comparative Study of Jen and Agape*. Brighton, UK: Sussex Academic Press.

Yao, Xinzhong 2000. *An Introduction to Confucianism*. Cambridge: Cambridge University Press.

Yearley, Lee H. 1990. *Mencius and Aquinas*. Albany: State University of New York

Press.

Yijing. In *Zhouyi Wang-Han Zhu* (Sibubeiyao edition).

Yu, Jiyuan. 1998. Virtue: Confucius and Aristotle. *Philosophy East and West*, 48.

Zaehner, C., trans. 1973. *Bhagavadgītā*. Oxford: Oxford University Press.

Zhu, Xi [朱熹]. Commentary on Zhang Zai's *Ximing* in *Zhangzi Quanshu* (Sibubeiyao edition).

Zhu, Xi. *Daxue Huowen* (Sikuquanshu edition).

Zhu, Xi. *Daxue Zhangju* (Sikuquanshu edition).

Zhu, Xi. *Lunyu Huowen* (Sikuquanshu edition).

Zhu, Xi. *Lunyu Jizhu* (Sikuquanshu edition).

Zhu, Xi. *Mengzi Huowen* (Sikuquanshu edition).

Zhu, Xi. *Mengzi Jizhu* (Sikuquanshu edition).

Zhu, Xi. *Zhongyong Zhangju* (Sikuquanshu edition).

Zhu, Xi. *Zhuzi Daquan* (Daquan) (Sibubeiyao edition).

Zhu, Xi. 1935a. *Si Shu Ji Zhu* [四書集注], Sibubeiyao 8. Shanghai: Zhonghua shuju.

Zhu, Xi. 1935b. *Xia Xue Ji Zhu* [小學集注], Sibubeiyao 168. Shanghai: Zhonghua shuju.

Zhu, Xi. 1986. *Zhuzi Yulei (*Yulei*)*. Shanghai: Zhonghua shuju.

Zhu, Xi and Lü Tsu-ch'ien. 1967. *Reflections on Things at Hand: The Neo-Confucian Anthology*. Translated by Wing-tsit Chan. New York: Columbia University Press.

Zhuangzi (Sibubeiyao edition).

Zuozhuan. In *Chunqiu Zuoshizhuan Dushijijie* (Sibubeiyao edition).

Contributors

Bijoy H. Boruah is Professor of Philosophy in the Department of Humanities and Social Sciences at the Indian Institute of Technology, Kanpur, India. His area of specialization includes Philosophy of Mind and Philosophical Aesthetics. He has authored *Fiction and Emotion: A Study in Aesthetics and the Philosophy of Mind* (Oxford: Clarendon Press, 1988). His current research interest is in the metaphysics of the self from a virtue-theoretic perspective.

Amber Danielle Carpenter is Assistant Professor of Philosophy at Franklin & Marshall College. Her research interests are Plato's ethics and the connections generally between idealistic ethics and the metaphysics, epistemology and psychology that support them. Her publications include "Phileban Gods" (*Ancient Philosophy* 23, 2003) and "Hedonistic Persons" (*British Journal of the History of Philosophy*, forthcoming). She is currently working on essays on Plato's *Philebus*.

Kim-chong Chong is Associate Professor in the Division of Humanities, The Hong Kong University of Science and Technology. His research interests are in Ethics, Chinese Philosophy and Comparative Philosophy. Some publications include "Egoism, Desires, and Friendship" (*American Philosophical Quarterly*, 1984), "Xunzi's Systematic Critique of Mencius" (*Philosophy East and West*, 2003), and the co-edited *The Moral Circle and the Self* (Open Court 2003). His book on *Early Confucian Ethics* (Open Court) is forthcoming.

Jonardon Ganeri is a Reader in Philosophy at the University of Liverpool. He read mathematics at the University of Cambridge, and philosophy at the Universities of London and Oxford, and has held visiting positions at the Universities of Chicago and Pennsylvania. His work has been in the treatment of Indian philosophical theory from the perspective of contemporary analytical philosophy. His first book was on Indian philosophy of language from the seventeenth century (*Semantic Powers*, Oxford University Press 1999), and his second on Indian accounts of rationality (*Philosophy in Classical India: The Proper Work of Reason*, Routledge 2001). He has published widely on topics in Indian logical theory, Indian epistemology and philosophy of mind, and more recently, Indian ethics. He is now working on a book on the themes of truth and concealment.

Manyul Im is Associate Professor in the Department of Philosophy at the California State University, Los Angeles. His research interests are early Chinese philosophy, primarily in the Warring States Period. His publications include: "Moral Knowledge and Self Control In Mengzi: Rectitude, Courage, and Qi" (*Asian Philosophy* 14:1, 2004); "Action, Emotion, and Inference in Mencius" (*Journal of Chinese Philosophy* 29:2, 2002); "Emotional Control and Virtue in the Mencius" (*Philosophy East and West* 49:1, 1999). He is currently working on logic, ontology, and the idea of moral physiology in Warring States philosophy.

Yuli Liu received her Ph.D. (2003) from the University of Hull, UK. She was a Postdoctoral Research Fellow of the Department of Philosophy, National

University of Singapore in 2003. She is currently a senior lecturer at the Department of Philosophy, the Party School of the Central Committee (CCPS) of the CPC, Beijing. Her published books includes *The Unity of Rule and Virtue: A critique of a supposed parallel between Confucian ethics and virtue ethics*, (Singapore: Eastern Universities Press, 2004); *Mencius: The Second Sage of Confucianism* (in Chinese, co-authored with T. Zhang), (Beijing: Overseas Chinese Press, 1996). Her main research is in Early Confucianism and Buddhism.

A. T. Nuyen received his Ph.D. from the University of Queensland, Australia. He is now Associate Professor in the Department of Philosophy at the National University of Singapore. His research interests include the philosophy of Hume and Kant, contemporary Continental philosophy, ethics and applied ethics and comparative Chinese-Western philosophy. He has published in many international journals, including *Hume Studies*, *Kant-Studien*, *History of Philosophy Quarterly*, *American Philosophical Quarterly*, *Journal of Chinese Philosophy* and *Asian Philosophy*. He is currently editing a volume on *Self and Others: Some Chinese and Comparative Perspectives.*

Kwong-loi Shun is Vice President and Professor of Philosophy and East Asian Studies at the University of Toronto, and Principal of University of Toronto at Scarborough. Prior to joining the University of Toronto, he was Dean of Undergraduate Division and Professor of Philosophy at the University of California at Berkeley. He holds degrees from the University of Hong Kong, London University, Oxford University, and Stanford University. His main research is in Confucian thought and moral philosophy, and has published several articles in these areas. He is the author of *Mencius and Early Chinese Thought* (Stanford 1997), the first volume of a three-volume project, and is currently working on the second volume, *The Development of Confucian-Mencian Thought: Zhu Xi, Wang Yangming and Dai Zhen.*

Christine Swanton is at the philosophy department, University of Auckland. Her field is virtue ethics and her book *Virtue Ethics: A Pluralistic View* was published by Oxford in 2003.

Sor-hoon Tan teaches philosophy at the National University of Singapore. She is the author of *Confucian Democracy: A Deweyan Reconstruction* and editor of *Challenging Citizenship: Cultural Identity and Group Membership in a Global Age.* She also co-edited *The Moral Circle and the Self* and *Filial Piety in Chinese Thought History*. Besides articles in journals and chapters in various collections on Chinese Philosophy, Pragmatism and Comparative Philosophy, she also contributed to the *Encyclopedia of Confucianism.*

Gregory Velazco y Trianosky is Professor and Chair of the Department of Philosophy at California State University, Northridge. For the past 10 years his research has focused primarily on issues about race, ethnicity, and identity. He also maintains his strong interest in virtue ethics. His most recent publication, "Beyond *Mestizaje*: The Future of Race in America", is being reprinted in the third edition of *Contemporary Moral Issues: Diversity and Consensus*, edited by Lawrence Hinman. His work in progress includes: "Radical Race: Reconceiving Our Idea of

Blackness"; "Judging The Past: Prophetic Challenge and Moral Responsibility," and "The Power Of Love: The Altruistic Virtues as Powers."

A. D. M. Walker was a member of the Philosophy Department at the University of Hull, England for more than 30 years before retiring in 1998, and he still continues to teach in the Department on a part-time basis. His publications include *The Definition of Morality* (co-edited with G. Wallace, Methuen 1970), "The Ideal of Sincerity" (*Mind* 1978), "Political Obligation and the Argument from Gratitude" (*Philosophy and Public Affairs* 1988), and "Virtue and Character" (*Philosophy* 1989). His current interests lie in Aristotelian moral philosophy and in philosophical psychology.

Index

International Board of Advisors

Titles on Philosophy

Elements of Sentence Logic (2nd ed.)
by Wayne A. Patterson
ISBN 981-210-305-8

Conceptions of Virtue: East and West
edited by Kim-chong Chong and Yuli Liu
ISBN 981-210-303-1

The Unity of Rule and Virtue: A Critique of a Supposed Parallel between Confucian Ethics and Virtue Ethics
by Liu Yuli
ISBN 981-210-350-3

Casteism and Human Rights: Toward an Ontology of the Social Order
by Sebastian Velassery
ISBN 981-210-428-3